D
IS FOR DEATH

ALSO BY SOPHIE DUFFY

The Generation Game

This Holey Life

Bright Stars

Betsy and Lilibet

D
IS FOR DEATH

An Alphabetical Journey through Life's Ultimate Enigma

Sophie Duffy

HERO, AN IMPRINT OF LEGEND TIMES GROUP LTD
51 Gower Street
London WC1E 6HJ
United Kingdom
www.hero-press.com

D Is for Death is based on an article with the same title published by the RLF (www.rlf.org.uk/posts/d-is-for-death)

This book first published in English by Hero in 2024

© Sophie Duffy, 2024

The right of Sophie Duffy to be identified as the author of this work has been asserted in accordance with the Copyright, Designs and Patents Act 1988. British Library Cataloguing in Publication Data available.

Front cover design and illustration by Laura Brett

ISBN: 978-1-91564-325-4

Printed by Akcent Media, 5 The Quay, St Ives, Cambs, PE27 5AR

All the pictures in this volume are reprinted with permission or presumed to be in the public domain. Every effort has been made to ascertain and acknowledge their copyright status, but any error or oversight will be rectified in subsequent printings.

All rights reserved. No part of this publication may be reproduced, stored in or introduced into a retrieval system, or transmitted, in any form or by any means (electronic, mechanical, photocopying, recording or otherwise), without the prior written permission of the publisher. This book is sold subject to the condition that it shall not be resold, lent, hired out or otherwise circulated without the express prior consent of the publisher.

CONTENTS

Introduction — vii

A IS FOR ACCIDENTS — 3
B IS FOR BONES — 29
C IS FOR CONTAGION — 47
D IS FOR DISPOSAL — 68
E IS FOR ELEGY — 88
F IS FOR FUNERAL — 107
G IS FOR GHOSTS — 127
H IS FOR HEALTH; **I** IS FOR ILLNESS — 142
J IS FOR JET; **K** IS FOR KEENING; **L** IS FOR LAMENT — 164
M IS FOR MYTHS — 179
N IS FOR NEXT OF KIN — 199
O IS FOR OPERATION LONDON BRIDGE — 211
P IS FOR POTTERS FIELD — 227
Q IS FOR QUILT; **R** IS FOR RAINBOW; **S** IS FOR SCARVES AND SHOES — 243
T IS FOR TERROR — 265
U IS FOR UNFINISHED — 287
V IS FOR VALHALLA — 302
W IS FOR WELLINGTON — 320
X IS FOR X-FILES — 339
Y IS FOR YEW — 343
Z IS FOR ZADUSZKI — 358

Endings — 370
Acknowledgements — 373
Endnotes — 375
Bibliography and Useful Books — 395
About the Author — 399

Introduction

We are such stuff
As dreams are made on, and our little life
Is rounded with a sleep.
THE TEMPEST

I saw my first dead body when I was two years old. I hold no fixed memory of that day in 1970, only snapshots developed over time from my mother's recollections. We had recently moved to Teignmouth in Devon, into a detached interwar house on the edge of town with a view over Labrador Bay. Our neighbours on one side were two elderly ladies who shared a house, Mrs Gracie and Miss Bowles. The day in question began as usual, but soon after my father had left for work, dropping my two brothers at school, there was a desperate knock at the door. Mrs Gracie.

'Please can you come?' she urged my mother. 'I think Miss Bowles is dead.'

'Of course.' My mother is calm in a tricky situation. 'But I'll have to bring Sophie.'

At this point I was attached to her hip, eyes wide. So, we trooped next door to the accompaniment of Mrs Gracie chanting: *I-think-Miss-Bowles-is-dead*. Once inside their hall, we looked ahead, up the stairs. And there she lay, Miss Bowles, as if climbing a mountain. Only quite, quite still.

A moment of silence.

I pointed at Miss Bowles.

'Don't point,' my mother said. 'It's rude.'

More silence. Just the tick from the sunburst clock on the wall.

Then, after ringing 999, we waited with Mrs Gracie until help arrived. Finally, it was all over.

Except that it wasn't. On our way back next door, I took up my own chant: *Poor-Miss-Bowles-is-dead*. This carried on and off for days – *Poor-Miss-Bowles-is-dead* – until, with time, poor Miss Bowles was no longer my own memory but my mother's hand-me-down one, still vivid fifty years on. I had no inkling then of what had become of Miss Bowles. I didn't know what 'dead' was. Or grief. Or anything much outside my small world: cat, guinea pigs, stick insects, garden, swing, brothers, Andy Pandy. But I must have grasped something of the gravity of the situation; although I had only just met her, I knew that I would never see Miss Bowles again.

This was perhaps the beginning of my interest in death, but by no means the only contributory event. I can pinpoint a more definite, explicit engagement to 1972, a couple of years after the demise of Miss Bowles when my parents bought a newsagent's in Torquay. The cat came with us, downgrading from garden to urban backyard. As for the guinea pigs, they were dead. All that remained of them was left behind – a row of lollypop-stick crosses in an herbaceous border.

Living above a sweet shop (this was so much more than a newsagent's) made up for this current lack of outside space. And, anyway, my brothers and I had a new playground – the churchyard up the road, which we nicknamed the Boneyard. Having no grasp of graveyard etiquette, we played hide-and-seek amongst the tombs and sat around eating Spangles, listening to Slade et al. on a transistor radio. Perhaps it was here, hopping over the bones of the dead, that I made the connection between Miss Bowles and the guinea pigs. That one day you are here, the next… not.

This disappearing act has been the backdrop to my life. A sleight of hand, some misdirection and *ta-dah*! Loved ones vanish into thin air. During my turn on this earth, I have gathered an impressive cast of deaths, including my father's when I was ten. He really was there one day, gone the next. *Poof!* With a knowledge beyond my years, I learned by heart that death is only one step ahead.

And death has recently tried to trip me up. During the first lockdown, while a clever virus was having a field day all over the world, I was diagnosed with cancer. Early but aggressive and difficult to treat, my prognosis to survive beyond five years a 'moderate' seventy per cent. I am doing my level best to challenge these odds, but death might have other ideas.

Over the last eighteen months, I have spent much time pondering how we live with death-anxiety. My conclusion: address it. Deal with it. After all, everyone dies, so why do we resist the very idea of death? The simple facts are these: we don't want to lose the people we love because living without them is hard, all day, every day, hard. And nor do we want to leave our loved ones behind because how can they possibly live without us? We believe it easier to push aside such thoughts. But that's a limited view which only adds to the fear and anxiety. We need to counteract this with the knowledge that these questions of death are actually questions of life.

Therefore, to live a full life, one without death-anxiety, we must face up to death. We must rationalise it. There are already enough gut-wrenching thoughts to wrestle with – the planet, the cost of living, war – so let's take death off the worry-list. Change our thinking. When a loved one is not where they are supposed to be at the time agreed, we must not assume they were

INTRODUCTION

involved in a fatal accident. Maybe they decided to buy a soya flat white or bumped into a chatty neighbour. And, as for yourself? What can you do to ease your own death-anxiety? You can dig deep into faith – light a candle, do yoga, go on a pilgrimage. You can bump up the endorphins – buy a bike, complete a marathon, backpack across South East Asia. You can talk – go to therapy, volunteer, attend a death café. Or you can write.

That is the path I have chosen. At a time of mass grief and personal trauma, I have researched and written a book about death and dying. Why? To contribute something death-positive to the growing conversation. To help prepare us for our own death and for the death of others. To discuss the options for funerals, memorials, legacies. To explore the effects of grief, celebrity death, mourning rituals. To consider war, murder, suicide, unexpected death, expected death, assisted death. To examine our physical body and what happens to it at the point of death and post-mortem, including its place in the afterlife, in myths and legends. Most of all, I want to remind the reader, you, and myself, me, that life – and love – win.

During my research, I read a lot, but have yet to find a comprehensive book that covers all aspects from anatomy to zombies. I want to fill this gap with an accessible read that both challenges and comforts whilst being informative and entertaining, using an A-to-Z structure and the power of stories that focus on the human element – stories of those I've read about, stories from those I know, and stories from my own life, starting with the death of poor Miss Bowles.

I am not a death expert. I am not an undertaker, an archaeologist, a surgeon, or an end-of-life doula. However, I am a writer whose five-decades-and-a-bit on this earth has included a litany of loss, not least a lime-sized aggressive bastard of a tumour in my right breast which will potentially cut a life short. Every day I remind myself that, amongst all this uncertainty, there is one surety: we should strive to live our best life, to do our best work, to use our talent for good, because tomorrow, or next year, or in five decades, the curtains will close on our time here on this earth and we will all follow in the footsteps of poor Miss Bowles.

Poof!

We will leave loved ones behind – people such as poor Miss Gracie, who, like Chekhov's gun, appeared at the start of this introduction. I'd like this book to be for all the Miss Gracies of this world. So let me be your curator of death.

Finally, if nothing else, remember this: it's not all doom and gloom; by dragging death into the open, we can live life more fully. And that's something to celebrate.

D
IS FOR DEATH

A
IS FOR ACCIDENTS

Modern Life in Britain

accident *noun*
1. an unexpected event which causes damage or harm.
2. something which happens without planning or intention.
3. chance • *managed it by accident.*
ETYMOLOGY: 14c: from Latin *accidere* to happen.

Tis a vile thing to die, my gracious lord,
When men are unprepared and look not for it.
RICHARD *III*

☠☠☠

Here doth lye the bodie
Of John Flye, who did die
By a stroke from a sky-rocket
Which hit him on the eye-socket.
DURNESS CHURCHYARD, SUTHERLAND

Accidents Will Happen

Accidents happen. People get hurt. People die. This is the nature of accidents and has been since time began. A caveman's head is ripped off by a hungry, sabretoothed tiger. A Roman slave is crushed by a falling boulder. A Celtic child falls in a fire. You can think up any number of wild scenarios that might lead to death by accident and they'll have happened at some point. Have you ever watched 'Stupid Death' in *Horrible Histories*? Here, we learn about Edmund II, who was allegedly stabbed in the bottom by a Viking hiding in the privy; Aeschylus, the ancient Greek playwright, killed by a tortoise dropped on his head by an eagle; Jean Baptiste Lully, a seventeenth-century composer, who died from gangrene after stubbing his toe with his baton. Stupid, perhaps. Unexpected, definitely.

It's not only the past that is littered with fatal comedy banana skins; the present has its fair share, highlighted by the Darwin Awards, whose *modus operandi* is to 'salute the improvement of the human genome by honoring those who accidentally remove themselves from it in a spectacular manner!'[1] Their website describes outlandish deaths, including the rhino-hunter who was killed by an elephant, then eaten by a lion, and the man (they're usually men) who crawled under the guardrail of a roller coaster to retrieve his hat, only to lose his head.

Most fatal accidents are not so bizarre, but they do happen unexpectedly, otherwise they're not accidents. And, after they've happened, the victims' loved ones will not only need answers but will also be driven to prevent similar tragedies from happening to anyone else.

Despite our best efforts, accidents happen because they are beyond our control.

Or are they?

That's what interests me: how far can tragedies be avoided?

In the past, a bad accident almost inevitably led to death; there were no first responders, no trained surgeons, no infection control, no knowledge of medicine or anatomy beyond what the local wise woman or quack could offer. Should you need an operation or amputation, the local butcher or barber[2] would step up. Without anaesthetic. Or sterilisation. And you'd probably die anyway.

Things heated up with the Industrial Revolution. By 1914, the British Empire stretched round the world, leaving destruction in its wake, thanks to factories, mills, ironworks, railways, canals, bridges, shipping and, of course, slavery. (*Rule, Britannia!*) 'Progress' was accompanied by mass migration from countryside to town and an exponential expansion of the population, resulting in cheap labour working long hours in hazardous conditions.

More accidents, more death.

In this chapter, I will tell the stories of some well-known and some not-so-well-known disasters – referred to in the emergency management sphere as 'mass fatality incidents' – in the workplace, in the leisure industry, on transport and, in that deadliest place of all, the home.

But why this fascination? (I'm not the only one – why are *Titanic* and *Casualty* so popular?) Kari Fay, creator of the *Great Disasters* podcast, sums it up:

> Disasters come with victims, witnesses, and in some cases survivors... These are ordinary people, just like you and me, suddenly thrown into extraordinary situations, forced to make split-second decisions that could literally make the difference between life and death. Confronting these stories often makes us look a little harder at ourselves. What would we do, if we were in that situation?... It's hard to know. But the more we know, the better prepared we can be, so understanding past disasters can lead to prevention or mitigation of future ones.[3]

WORK

☠☠☠

Black Gold

Work is dangerous. Take the miner. Coal powered the Empire but, in the twentieth century alone, there were fourteen mining disasters in the UK, including one near the village of Gresford, which I bypass en route to my Shropshire caravan. Gresford lies in the North Wales Coalfield, where mining was a way of life for centuries, but industrial relations had always been poor. By the 1920s, due to high unemployment and defeat in the general strike, they were fraught. Stanley Williamson argues that miners bore the brunt of the cost of mechanisation, seeing their wages cut, 'in much the same way as the advent of power-looms had affected handloom weavers a century earlier'.[4]

By 1934, 2,200 men were working at Gresford with a three-shift system. On the night of Friday, 21 September, many of them were 'doubling'[5] so they could watch the football, Wrexham against Tranmere, on Saturday afternoon. Although illegal, management turned a blind eye; the mine was running at a loss, the owners breathing down their necks; they'd do anything to keep up productivity. But more dangerous than this was the poor ventilation. The Coal Mines Act of 1911 legislated that new mines should have two ventilation shafts, rather than the standard one, to provide air for the miners and to help disperse the firedamp (methane). This would cost; safety always does. Williamson suggests there was a push to open the colliery before this Act came into force, thus 'avoiding the obligation to provide a second airway and unwittingly sowing more seeds for the tragedy which overwhelmed them twenty years later'.[6]

In the early hours of Saturday, due to a build-up of firedamp, an explosion in the deep Dennis section kills 266 men, including some of the rescue team. Only six survive. Two hundred widows, 800 fatherless children, 1,600 without jobs. The owners dock the wages of over a thousand miners for failing to finish their shift. And, because the dead miners had 'risen their pay' before their shift, the money is buried with them. No compensation, no benefits. Nothing.

There follows a national outpouring of sympathy. Answers are demanded. Closer to home, there is high emotion. The grieving families demand their men's bodies be exhumed from the pit but, instead, the section is sealed by the management, outwardly cautious of further deaths. But is this a cover-up?

Despite a long, bitter inquiry which highlights management failures, lack of safety and poor ventilation, it is unclear who is to blame. But one thing is certain: the appalling working conditions. David Grenfell (remember that name), Welsh MP and former miner, opens the parliamentary debate in 1938 with this description:

> There were men working almost stark naked, clogs with holes bored through the bottom to let the sweat run out … the air thick with fumes and dust from blasting, the banjack hissing to waft the gas out of the face into the unpacked waste, a space 200 yards long and 100 yards wide above the wind road full of inflammable gas and impenetrable.[7]

Eventually, nationalisation brings more safety, but it also buries the full story of Gresford; as part of the negotiations, all records are destroyed. To this day, those men lie entombed in the Dennis section. Williamson makes a poignant observation, echoing a recent tragedy with the same surname as the Welsh MP:

> Irrational as it might seem, when the men already lay deep in the earth to which a funeral service could only commit them again, a fierce emotional need, older and more deep-rooted than mining itself, required that the due forms and ceremonies be observed. Without them it was as though the dead could never be at rest.[8]

The colliery closed in 1973. In 1982, the Prince and Princess of Wales opened a memorial in the grounds of the Colliery Club, a pithead wheel supported by pillars of Welsh slate. Howard Williams describes it as 'a sad and evocative cenotaph that has had a lasting impact on the landscape and identities of those living in Wrexham and its environs', the word 'cenotaph' echoing war memorials which 'presence absent bodies which cannot be recovered'.[9] Indeed, the parallels between pit and trench were pointed out in the *Sunday Times* in 1934: 'the men at the coal face are on constant active service, as soldiers are in time of war… To the miners who daily risk their lives to provide us with this precious "black gold" the whole community owes a profound debt of gratitude.'[10]

At a recent visit, the comparison was apparent. I walked around the pithead wheel, sat on one of the benches looking over at another, dedicated to the war dead. I took in the fresh flowers, candles and Buddha statues placed around the site, a visible reminder that the events of that tragic day still echo down the years.

Gresford Memorial

This isn't the end of the story. In 2014, to the horror of the locals, the long-closed colliery was the subject of a fracking proposal. Though Wrexham Council refused planning permission, this was overturned by the Welsh government. Steve Bellis, whose grandfather worked in a neighbouring mine, said fracking would 'inject a toxic cocktail of chemicals into the ground in order to extract the very gas that killed the miners. The gas will be extracted from the lungs of dead miners for profit… The Welsh government have overturned the wishes of the local people and have shown no regard for the memory of the miners.'[11]

Despite nationalisation, there were further disasters, with one etched in our public consciousness. In 1966, in Aberfan, a waste tip from Merthyr Vale colliery slid down a mountainside, engulfing the primary school, killing 116 children and twenty-eight adults. My mother, whose father was from South Wales, had spent the war evacuated in Carmarthen, about sixty miles away from Aberfan. She now had two young boys and the tragedy touched her, as it did everyone. Those children should never have been killed. And, just recently, I met a fellow caravanner who told me he was from Aberfan. When I looked surprised, he asked me if I'd heard of it and I said, yes, of course. A young man in 1966, he was away at the time of the landslide, racing back as soon as news reached him, believing both his younger brother and sister to be dead. His little sister had indeed been killed that day. But not his brother. There he was, waiting for him at home. But, sadly, the repercussions were tragic, with his mother taking her own life two years later. She is buried next to her daughter in the cemetery, in the rows of white graves shining out over the hillside. In the footprint of the old school, there is a memorial garden, next to a playground.

The last mining disaster in Britain was in 1978, when eighteen men were killed in Markham colliery, Derbyshire. The following year, Thatcher became prime minister. She shut the mines, decimated communities and wiped out a traditional way of life. But this did at least end the mass fatalities.

And a footnote. In December 1952, due to very cold weather, an anticyclone and windless conditions, airborne pollutants from coal dust formed into a smog. The Great Smog was so thick that for four days it hung like a pall over London, bringing the city to a standstill and killing as many as 12,000 Londoners with hypoxia and respiratory infections. The one good outcome was the Clean Air Act of 1956.

☠☠☠

All at Sea

The sea is a dangerous place to work. According to the Fishermen's Mission, fishing is the UK's most dangerous peacetime occupation, with fishermen 115 times more likely to suffer a fatal accident than the rest of the workforce.[12] I could write a lot about this, as my brother Peter was a trawlerman in his youth. I witnessed how my mum worried when he was at sea for days at a time. But here I'm remembering the crew of a much larger ship with a name to match. In 1912, the White Star Line's *Titanic* hit an iceberg on her maiden voyage and went down, with 1,500 people dying in the freezing waters off Newfoundland. Nearly 700 were crew, almost three quarters of the staff, a higher death rate than even the third-class passengers.

There are many memorials to the dead on both sides of the Atlantic, including a grand one in Liverpool across the Mersey from where I live, initially built to remember the engineers of the *Titanic*'s engine room. Their bravery kept the power going to maintain the wireless telegraph until ten minutes before the ship sank and the lights until two minutes before, making it possible to summon help and to lower the lifeboats. None of the engineers survived. By the time the memorial was unveiled, many more ships had gone down in the

Great War, so its inscription bears no reference to the *Titanic* but is broad enough to include all those lost in engine rooms. If you look closely, you can see pockmarks made by German bombers in the following war.[13]

☠☠☠

More recently, a year after the *Herald of Free Enterprise* capsized outside Zeebrugge, killing 193 passengers and crew, there was an industrial accident 120 miles north-east of Aberdeen in the North Sea. On 6 July 1988, an explosion on an ageing oil platform called Piper Alpha killed 165 workers and two rescuers. Only sixty-one men survived, many of whom went on to suffer from PTSD, finding it difficult to gain further employment as they were considered Jonahs. The worst offshore disaster in British history could have been avoided. There had already been a fire on the platform four years earlier, but there were no unions, whistle-blowers were blacklisted and health and safety measures did not apply offshore, so its operator, Occidental Petroleum, kept drilling. Production took precedence. The inquiry blamed not only Occidental but also the government, fatal decisions, mistakes and human error. And the legacy: a chapel in St Nicholas in Aberdeen; a sculpture in Hazelhead Park; a wreck buoy at the remains of the platform; the establishment of the Offshore Industry Liaison Committee. The Piper Alpha Families and Survivor's Association continues to campaign for North Sea safety.

☠☠☠

One year on, almost to the day, I graduated from Lancaster University, then moved with my fiancé to south London. To save up ahead of our September wedding, I got a summer job at Greenwich dole office, not far from the Thames, a bus ride from our flat. In the early hours of 20 August, while I was at home, dreaming of table settings and catering, there was a party on board one of the river's pleasure steamers. But the celebration came to a disastrous end when a dredger hit and went right over *The Marchioness*, sinking her in less than thirty seconds, drowning fifty-one including four crew members. The partygoers were young, our age; while we were making plans for our future, their lives ended.

However, they are not forgotten and their legacy is far-reaching: a Thames search and rescue service and four new RNLI stations; the Civil Contingencies Act 2004, which provides a framework for emergency planning and response; and Lord Justice Clarke's report of 2001, which overhauled the coroner system, resulting in the Coroners and Justice Act 2009. Disaster specialist Professor Lucy Easthope says that following the tragedy 'the work of caring for the dead of disaster in the UK was transformed. We became world-leading in disaster victim identification (DVI).' In her work, she strives to keep respect at the centre, for both the deceased and the bereaved.[14]

Over the years, on visits to Southwark Cathedral, I spend a moment at the memorial, whispering the names of the dead written there in stone, a few hundred metres from where they lost their lives. And I remember that I have grown older, as they did not.

☠☠☠

Look for the Helpers

Wherever accidents happen, there are helpers. Fred Rogers famously advised children to 'look for the helpers' but, as adults, we can be those helpers. We have wonderful paid emergency workers in this country, even though sometimes the institutions in which they serve are flawed. But let's not forget those unpaid helpers, volunteers who sacrifice their time and sometimes their lives for charities such as the RNLI.

On 13 December 1981, St Peter Port lifeboat crew in Guernsey responded to a mayday: the crew of the Ecuadorian cargo ship *Bonita* was floundering in a hurricane in the Channel. With immense bravery, twenty-nine were saved. But just six days later, in similarly atrocious weather, whilst on a shout to rescue the crew and passengers of the *Union Star*, the crew of the Penlee lifeboat *Solomon Browne* was not so lucky. The coaster was being swept towards the rocky Cornish coast. After several efforts to get alongside her, the lifeboat crew rescued four of the eight people onboard. But, during a final heroic rescue attempt, all radio contact was lost. Ten minutes later, the lights of the *Solomon Browne* disappeared. No one survived.

Every year on 19 December, the Christmas lights at Mousehole are dimmed between 8 and 9 p.m. in memory, leaving just the Cross and Angels shining out to sea.

In the north-west, the Morecambe Lifeboat crew say the search for Chinese cockle pickers on the evening of 5 February 2004 was the 'most distressing and demanding' mission in their history.

I know Morecambe. I lived there during my second year from 1987 to 1988, sharing a Victorian terrace with my best friend and six male rugby players, just one shower and loo between us. Since we were a street back from the seafront, we got off lightly compared to those on the front itself who had to scrape ice from the inside of the toilet bowl on a winter's morning.

When it was nice, I'd stroll along the prom but, having grown up by the sea, I knew ignorance is dangerous and never ventured onto the mudflats. In fact, the Bay is so treacherous that, for centuries, the Crown has appointed a Guide to the Sands to help travellers cross it. But I had no need to go out there. A privileged undergraduate on a full grant, the only danger I ever encountered was student night at the (splendidly dingy and now defunct) Carleton. What if I'd been born in a different time and place and been forced to work the cockle beds, with no knowledge of tides, and no English?

A IS FOR ACCIDENTS

One winter's day, the festival day Yuan Xiao, groups of trafficked Chinese labourers were driven from cramped housing in Liverpool, up the Lancashire coast to Morecambe, to do back-breaking cockling. All for a pittance. Mr Wen, one of the workers, was reluctant, because 'you're not supposed to work on Yuan Xiao.' Looking back, he says the journey on the motorway that day 'seemed particularly long and bleak. Some of us were taking a nap in the van. I just felt exhausted at the thought of raking cockles.' Mr Wen had a 'lucky' escape; the van broke down and they returned to Liverpool.[15]

But what of the others who went out onto the sands, facing foul weather and unknown dangers, with only flimsy waterproofs and wellies for protection? Cedric Robinson, Queen's Guide from 1963 to 2019, compared the rushing tide to 'a galloping horse',[16] a tide that can't be heard when a wind's blowing. As evening approached, the cocklers were encircled by the sea. Later, Robinson said the decision taken in 2003 to grant cockle licences to inexperienced people was 'a disaster waiting to happen'.[17]

Back on that awful night, Li Hua realised the danger when water covered the wheels of the vehicle that had taken them onto the sands. It couldn't move. 'Everyone was panicking. They got out of the vehicle and tried to swim, but the water was flowing so quickly some were dragged under it straight away … I thought, am I going to die tonight?' He somehow made it onto a sand bank and hung on, against all odds, until he was eventually spotted by the emergency helicopter's thermal imaging camera and rescued. Although fourteen men and women swam to safety, the lifeboat crew, some of whom had never seen a corpse, were confronted with 'a sea of bodies'. Nineteen were found by the following afternoon, then a further two. One body was washed up in 2012. It is believed that one is still to be found. Imagine the impact of that.[18]

Easthope was called in to advise the Home Office Mass Fatalities Team. Not only does she plan for emergencies but, when invited, she will also assist in both the immediate response and the long-term recovery. Easthope is a helper. She followed the RNLI, recovering personal effects from the sands for days afterwards. The force of the sea had torn the clothes from the victims. 'Disaster death is never gentle or peaceful. The bodies are rarely unharmed and they are usually hard to identify,' she says. 'So one of the most important parts of the disaster plan is how to give them back their name.'[19] Michael Guy, lifeboat operations manager that night, also acknowledges how important it was to retrieve the bodies. It gave some closure. A body to bury rather than being 'lost at sea'.[20]

It was a long, expensive, dangerous journey from rural China to Morecambe and, when the workers finally reached Britain, they were at the mercy of gangmasters; if they failed to repay their debts, their families would be in danger. As a 'Lancashire lad', Mick Gradwell, detective-in-charge, wasn't used to dealing with international organised crime. 'I didn't know a cockle from a mussel. I didn't know about safety issues within the industry, or Snakehead gangs.'[21] Not only did silence hamper the inquiry – the language barrier, the gang threats, the illegal status of the workers – but also the investigators faced something which reached far beyond Lancashire.

Eventually, there was a trial. Li Hua, in witness protection, gave evidence from behind a screen. Jurors were taken out onto the sands in a hovercraft.[22] Criminal gangmaster Lin Liang Ren was convicted of twenty-one counts of manslaughter, facilitating illegal immigration and perverting the course of justice. Although he was sentenced to fourteen years, he was released and deported in 2012, having served just four months for each victim.[23]

A decade later, Gradwell, now retired from Lancashire Police, said that they dealt with the people responsible for the deaths that night but 'did not make any dent into these wider criminal gangs who traffic people around the world…'[24] Despite the establishment of the Gangmasters Licensing Authority (GLA) in 2005, with a remit to protect workers in agriculture, horticulture, shellfish gathering, food processing and packaging (now the Gangmasters and Labour Abuse Authority (GLAA)),[25] the fight against modern slavery is hampered by a lack of resources.[26]

Back in Morecambe, close to the lifeboat station, there is a memorial garden dedicated to the cockle pickers. The plaque there, overlooking the Bay, has their names, a poem and an etching of China's national bird, the red-crowned crane. As for Li Hua, he still lives somewhere in the UK under his assumed identity, in his own home with his family, running a restaurant. He finally paid off the gangs in 2012 and still has panic attacks and night sweats. Despite this, his life is good, though he often thinks about other enslaved workers. Jason Cowley interviewed him for his book *Who Are We Now*. He writes that Li Hua 'mourns the dead whose stories briefly become news whenever their bodies are discovered in lorry parks or in sealed containers, or when they fall from the undercarriage of an aircraft, or when they drown while trying, in small boats, to cross the English Channel'.[27]

☠☠☠

Crowning Glory

No one can count the number of workplace deaths since the Industrial Revolution. In previous centuries, due to poor literacy, poor management and a dispensable workforce, deaths simply weren't recorded. Today every work fatality should be recorded by the Health and Safety Executive, with each person remembered annually on 28 April, International Workers' Memorial Day (IWMD). But what of those non-accidental workplace deaths? The miners who died from lung diseases and cancer, for instance.[28] Deaths from epidemics due to overpopulation and poor sanitation during the Industrial

A IS FOR ACCIDENTS

Revolution. Deaths from stress and depression. And what about the victims of colonialism and slavery?

Causes might not always be obvious, but many strive to prevent accidents: trade unions, charities, think tanks, politicians, charities and families work tirelessly to improve working conditions. But, in 1974, an industrial accident in North Lincolnshire was a watershed moment.

Saturday, 1st June 1974. Elaine White is fourteen years old, living at the village shop that her parents run in Burton-Upon-Stather. It is an important day in the local calendar – the annual Appleby-Frodingham steelworks gala in nearby Scunthorpe. But no one knows quite how memorable this day will turn out to be.

Elaine's ten-year-old sister, Julie, is already in Scunthorpe with an auntie and cousin and, while her mum and dad are still busy in the shop next door, Elaine is getting ready with her friend Wendy. While Wendy has popped into the shop, Elaine turns her attention to her hair. She plugs in her Carmen rollers but, at the very moment she switches them on, at around 16.50, all the electrics suddenly go off. Wendy, between two glass doors at the time – one leading into the shop and the other to the hallway – comes back to Elaine, wondering what is going on. The floor shakes beneath their feet. The windows rattle. A moment's pause and then a loud, terrifying blast and everything caves in around them. Elaine stares in disbelief at the glasses and bottles of alcohol on her parents' drinks trolley, which have all shattered. But worse. The windows have blown in. What on earth has happened?

Then her dad appears. 'What have you done, Elaine?'

'I just plugged in my curlers!'

Alec is in shock. Everyone is in shock. He had been standing by the shop doorway when it exploded inwards missing him by inches while a large glass window fell on Flo's head. Miraculously they are both uninjured. But there is commotion. Amidst the chaos, someone mentions a bomb. Bombs are always in the news. Maybe one has gone off in the village. Wendy runs back home and Elaine is asked to check on an elderly lady up the road. She is ok but people in the street are saying the explosion must have something to do with the Nypro chemical plant in Flixborough, a mile away as the crow flies. It must be. There is a huge mushroom of smoke in the sky. And panic now. There could be toxic fumes.

Soon after, the emergency services order everyone to immediately evacuate the village. In the hurry, Flo forgets her handbag and purse but scoops up a cooked chicken (the butt of family jokes for years to come). Then they realise they don't have the car because Elaine's older sister, Maureen, who lives in Scunthorpe, has borrowed it. Flo and Alec manage to flag down a car, which takes the three of them, plus the chicken, to her auntie's house. Julie is there, in tears, worried sick because they heard and felt the blast, then saw the mushroom cloud. Along with everyone else at the busy gala, they had rushed home, hoping to find loved ones safe, followed by the terrifying wait until they were reunited, only to realise that, in all the haste, the dog has been left behind. Julie cries again. Alec drives back to the village and persuades a reluctant police officer to let him rescue the dog, who is thankfully unscathed.

In time, they discover what happened – though, as is the way when disaster strikes, it can take a long time to unearth the truth. One thing is for sure, it wasn't Elaine's Carmen rollers that caused the power outage; that was due to an initial minor explosion at the plant. But the following much larger blast killed twenty-eight people working at the plant that day, seriously injuring thirty-six others.

Looking back, Elaine can remember one of the workers, 'a lovely young chap who lived in the village. Dad was very upset because earlier that afternoon, he'd come into the shop for supplies to take to work. They'd chatted and laughed before he left to start his shift. We never saw him again.'

The number of fatalities and casualties would have been in the hundreds if the explosion had occurred on a weekday. Elaine's sister Maureen worked at the Nypro site, in the office block, which was reduced to rubble with the first, minor explosion. For a long time, the family could not stop thinking about how lucky Maureen and her colleagues were.

As well as the death toll and fallout on families and the community, there were other repercussions. About a thousand buildings were damaged in the area and a further 800 or so in Scunthorpe. Elaine says the damage to their home was 'unbelievable'. Most of the windows had blown in and the roof was damaged. The property had to be surveyed and it was some time before they could return home to live. For months, Elaine and Julie's school bus had to take a detour, and when they finally returned to their normal route, they had to pass the devastated Nypro site, a large, black, mangled mass of metal. Even today, Elaine can still picture the haunting image. She believes the whole experience and its aftermath was one of the deciding factors which led to the family moving down to Devon to start a new chapter in their lives, though Maureen continued to work for Nypro, living in temporary accommodation, until she and her family also relocated to Devon.

Looking back at this traumatic time, Elaine says there were positive stories that she remembers. Stories of close escapes such as the man who was in his greenhouse when the explosion tore down the whole structure around him, leaving him unharmed, like something out of a Harold Lloyd film. As for Elaine herself, she was about to go up and have a bath while her rollers heated up when the electricity went off. If she had been in the bath, she might not have survived the large shards of glass from the window which blew in with such force that they were impaled in the wall above the bathtub. And, if Wendy had not moved away from those two glass doors, she too would have been injured.

As for the chemical plant, Maureen recalled that there had been warning signs around the site regarding leaks leading up to that day and the following inquiry finds that – just as with all previous workplace accidents – what happened that June Saturday could have been avoided. But now there was momentum to prevent such disasters from happening in the future. According to Jenson et al, 'In 1974, UK legislation relating to industrial sites was still based on industrial revolution style factories of the early 1900s, such as steam powered textile mills.'[29] Change was needed. After the explosion, the government set up an Advisory Committee on Major Hazards. Their recommendations led to the milestone Health and Safety at Work Act 1974, which, in turn, created the Health and Safety Executive to regulate and reinforce it. Jenson et al go as far as to say: 'Flixborough led to a cultural revolution in the way people viewed safety.' Not just in Britain, but in the EU and across the developed world. 'One of the most important lessons taken from Flixborough is for the need of procedures and protocols to match the development of new equipment and processes... It is vital here that we remember the past failings which led to accidents.'[30] Following the Act, there was a massive 73 per cent reduction in workplace fatalities between 1974 and 2007.[31]

Every five years, a service is held at All Saint's Church, Flixborough, where a memorial lists the dead. What I find particularly poignant is that Flixborough is one of only fifty-three civil parishes in England and Wales to be a 'thankful village', thankful because all serving personnel returned after WW1. But the village did not escape its share of tragedy.

LEISURE

☠☠☠

A Matter of Life and Death

Accidents in leisure activities can involve significant numbers of casualties. Take football, a national pastime, which has seen several stadium disasters over the last century or so. Ibrox in Glasgow, Rangers' ground, has suffered more than its fair share, with three separate incidents where fans died and a further two where they were injured, the worst in 1971, at an Old Firm game involving, not for the first time, notorious Stairway 13. As fans tried to leave after the match, sixty-six supporters, including children and teenagers, were crushed to death. Finally, the stadium was redeveloped.

It's not always crushes that kill at matches. Saturday, 11 May 1985, was supposed to be a celebration at Valley Parade, with Bradford City promoted to the Second Division. But it turned into tragedy when a discarded cigarette set fire to rubbish accumulated beneath the old wooden Main Stand. Within four minutes, the stand was ablaze, killing fifty-four Bradford fans and two

D IS FOR DEATH

Lincoln City supporters and injuring 265 others. I'd just turned seventeen and remember seeing it on the news, horrified that teens like me were now dead.

☠☠☠

Back to 1946, to Burnden Park. 85,000 people crowded into the home of Bolton Wanderers to watch the FA Cup match against Stoke, desperate to return after the war, especially as Sir Stanley Matthews would be playing. The stadium, previously requisitioned by the army, was in disrepair and not all parts were open. This created a bottleneck. The Embankment terrace was well over capacity and, when the crowd pressed forward, two metal crush bars broke, killing thirty-three and injuring another 400.[32] A foreshadow of events to come forty-three years later.

In 1989, during an FA Cup semi-final between Liverpool and Nottingham Forest at Hillsborough Stadium, overcrowding in the away stand led to a mass crush. In all, ninety-seven Liverpool fans died – the highest death toll in British sport. This shocking event was played out before us, but in the days, weeks, months, years that followed, there was more horror to come: drawn-out inquiries, false newspaper stories,[33] skewed court processes, faulty inquests, blame-throwing, cover-ups, failures of accountability. Finally, in 2016, the Hillsborough Independent Panel concluded that fans were unlawfully killed due to police failures, stadium design faults and a delayed response by the ambulance service. Upon receiving the verdict, Hillsborough Family Support Group chair Margaret Aspinall – whose eighteen-year-old son James was killed in the disaster – said: 'Our city always gets brought down, but yet again it's the tough people of Liverpool who have had to fight a cause that was so unjust.'[34]

Despite prosecutions, no individuals were convicted. Andy Burnham, advocate for the families of his home city, came to a far-reaching conclusion:

> Back in 2009, on the evening of the 20th anniversary, I made a promise to the Hillsborough families at Liverpool town hall that I would do everything I could to support them. Twelve years on, we have arrived at the end of the legal line. But there is one more battle left and the biggest of them all: the root-and-branch reform of English justice.[35]

Easthope was at school in Liverpool when the tragedy happened. She knew people who were killed. She knew first-hand the long-term effects on the community. She would come to know first-hand that 'disaster exposes us, our society, and our leaders, to our core'.[36]

☠☠☠

That's Entertainment

In Sunderland, there was once a large Gothic-style building called the Victoria Hall and Temperance Institute, used for social, political and religious meetings and performances, with star appearances from Elgar in 1910 and Emmeline Pankhurst in 1912.[37] It was also the scene of a tragedy.

On 16 July 1883, 2,000 eager children are crowded inside for a show which promises to be 'the greatest treat for children ever given', with every child offered the chance of a prize.[38] Part of the entertainment is a conjuring act, with a hat trick as its finale. This is the moment the children have been waiting for.

The magician produces toys from his hat.

He throws them into the stalls. To calm the ensuing pandemonium, he tells the gallery they'll get their presents as they leave. This excites them even more. They race to the staircase. To the exit door. A mass of children. But the door is wedged partially open, inwards. Only one at a time can get out.

There is a crush.

183 children are killed.

Some families lose all their children.

A Sunday school class loses all thirty members.

Body after body is carried outside, laid on the pavement. Later, they are brought back inside the hall, to be identified. All have been asphyxiated.

This tragedy did lead to national safety legislation for entertainment venues, later recognised as one of the first examples of health and safety legislation. But there was another interesting development. Robert Alexander Briggs, a young man living in Sunderland at the time of the disaster, later invented a type of bolt which was patented in 1892. This panic bolt is now compulsory on fire exit doors in all public venues.

As for Victoria Hall itself, it was destroyed by the Luftwaffe in 1941.

A restored memorial, a statue of mother and child, now stands in Mowbray Park, a heart-breaking reminder of those lost children.[39]

A tragic postscript. Thirty-seven years after Victoria Hall, Robert Briggs's bolt was yet to be compulsory, so that, on the afternoon of 31 December 1929, one of the worst disasters in Scotland took place. Hundreds of children were packed into Glen Cinema in Paisley, watching a cowboy film, when smoke came out of the spool room and filled the auditorium. In the panic, the children swarmed downstairs, aiming for the exit, but the door would not open. In the stampede, seventy-one children were killed. The Cinematograph Act of 1909 was finally amended to ensure all cinemas had a capacity limit, a ratio of adults to children and exit doors with push bars. Too late for these children, but, every Hogmanay, they are remembered at Paisley's Cenotaph.[40]

I can't finish this section without mentioning the fire that swept through Summerland in Douglas on the Isle of Man, which, according to Dr Ian Phillips, is 'one of the most forgotten news stories in the post-war history of the British Isles'.[41] Although I was only five at the time, I had no recollection of it until researching for this chapter.

Opened in 1971, Summerland was a vast state-of-the-art indoor leisure complex, designed for a capacity of 10,000, consisting of dance hall, roller-skating rink, restaurants and bars. But its glory days were short-lived. On the evening of 2 August, a smouldering cigarette butt caught fire in an outside kiosk. Flames spread to the main building and, because of its poor fire retardancy and open-plan design, there was soon an inferno. Fifty people died. At the public inquiry, the deaths were attributed to misadventure, but a delay in evacuation and the flammable building materials were condemned. In addition to the fatalities, there were many badly injured, both physically and psychologically. I've barely touched on this aspect but, in the aftermath of a disaster, so many are left with life-changing injuries.

Scars run deep.

TRANSPORT

The Age of the Train

A 70s child, I was brought up on a diet of public information films which I'm still digesting. Thanks to Tufty the Squirrel and the Green Cross Code Man, I won't cross the road without looking left-right-and-left-again and I always drive extra slowly past an ice cream van. Nor will I venture into dangerous waters in an unseaworthy boat or accept sweets off a stranger. But it's those scary films that haunt me, the ones often narrated in the deceptively soothing tones of Bernard Cribbins.[42] They told us to play safe. They warned us of death traps. It says something about a 70s childhood that we had the freedom to stumble upon these death traps. My 90s children never went out unsupervised. They never flew a kite near an overhead power line. Never broke into an electric substation. Not with this Gen-Xer helicopter parent, frightened of every unforeseen circumstance. (Though one did get rescued by the lifeboat – thank you, RNLI, thank you, coastguards – when he ventured into Lyme Bay in an unseaworthy boat.)

I blame my railway phobia on these films, particularly *The Finishing Line* (1977), a British Transport film directed by John Krish.[43] It opens with a boy sitting on a railway bridge, dangling his flared-trousered legs over the tracks. Cue voiceover of doom-laden headmaster: 'It has been brought to my notice that some of you have been playing on the railway again... the railway is not the game field.' Cut to boy, daydreaming: a brass band, preparations for what appears to be an ordinary sports day, ordinary except that it will take place on railway cuttings. A creeping unease: why are paramedics lining up stretchers? Then, announcements. A loudspeaker organising teams for gruesome events. The 'Nine and Under Fence Breaking'. The 'Twelve and Under Stone Throwing'. After each event, we watch casualties lined up on those stretchers, little bodies stained with blood, just enough so you know these children are dying, if not actually dead. Then the finale: the Great Tunnel Walk. Children disappear into this tunnel. Cut to the other end, where blood-streaked children are carried out to the finishing line, laid on the tracks, the brass band playing sombre music reminiscent of the Last Post. Cut back to headmaster: 'If any of you think that playing on the railway is a good idea, perhaps he or she would care to stand up...' Boy looks ruefully at track. Ends.

I inadvertently watched this as a nine-year-old. More terrifying than any episode of *Doctor Who*. These children were my age. Imagine a sports day like that? The three-legged race was perilous enough. But it did the trick. I have never been near a railway track. I always stand way behind the yellow line on the station platform. And don't even mention level crossings.

We're right to be afraid. From the first outing of a locomotive in 1830, there have been fatalities. At the opening of the Liverpool and Manchester railway, William Huskisson MP travelled with dignitaries on the Duke of Wellington's special train, pulled by the *Northumbrian* and driven by George Stephenson himself. When it stopped to take on fuel, about fifty passengers disembarked, including Huskisson, who approached the Iron Duke, in the hope of shaking his hand.[44] Following a series of unfortunate events, Huskisson ended up in the path of the *Rocket* and was struck, his leg mangled. He died later that night.

Despite this inauspicious start, the railway would be a vast improvement on the unreliable canals and horse-driven roads, strengthening the Liverpool-Manchester route, which was crucial to the expansion of British manufacturing; raw cotton from the slave plantations of America crossed the Atlantic into Liverpool and could now be transported at speed to the mills of Manchester to be made into finished cloth. It would then be returned to the Liverpool docks for export to the empire.

These new power-horses ran on coal. They powered the Industrial Revolution. In addition to transporting goods and people, the railways connected cities with post, newspapers, fresh milk, fruit, flowers, fish, bringing new opportunities to Britain's growing population. But not everyone was a fan. Dickens viewed progress as relentless, streets demolished to make room for new railways with no compensation for the dispossessed. What use was connectivity if at the cost of human life? But surely even the great man himself did not foresee the Tay Bridge disaster.

1879. One December evening, a force 10 gale smashes chimney pots and tears off roof tiles in nearby towns, rushing down the swelling estuary at right angles to the bridge. In the midst of this storm, a train leaves Edinburgh Waverley on its journey to Dundee, north over the Firth of Tay across the newly opened two-mile-long Tay Bridge, the longest in the world. It never reaches its destination. As it chugs out of Wormit station, a suburb of Fife on the south side of the Tay, it disappears into the darkness. The bridge collapses and the train plunges into the freezing river below.

Rescue boats are sent out. No survivors are found.

The official inquiry found the bridge had been 'badly designed, badly constructed and badly maintained', putting most of the blame onto its designer, Sir Thomas Bouch, who died aged fifty-eight just three months later. Even today, though, it is unclear if the train caused the bridge to collapse or the bridge caused the train to collapse. Either way, the same outcome.[45]

The death toll also remains uncertain. Fifty-nine death certificates were issued as bodies were recovered, but seventy-five is often quoted, if you account for crew and tickets. Over the years, new evidence suggests there could be a further ten victims, bringing the total to eighty-five; though their bodies were never found, neither children under five nor railway workers needed tickets. When a memorial was eventually put near the site with just fifty-nine names, there was understandably some controversy.[46]

Today, you can still see the stone piers of the old bridge. Some of the undamaged girders were reused in the building of the new steel bridge – a deathly construction process where a further fourteen men died, mostly from drowning.[47]

☠ ☠ ☠

Fast forward to south-east London, 1989. Our first flat in Grove Park. At night, while I'm trying to sleep on our new futon, bright lights keep me awake, coming from the continental freight depot between Grove Park and neighbouring Hither Green. I have no idea that this was the scene of a tragedy some twenty-two years previously on Bonfire Night 1967, when the 19.43 Hastings to Charing Cross derailed, killing forty-nine people.[48] Awful, especially when you consider this happened just a decade after ninety people died in nearby Lewisham when two trains crashed in fog in December 1957.

The futon has long gone, and so has my marriage. But there is a plaque in Hither Green station commemorating the victims where wreaths and flowers are laid every year on the anniversary. I've passed through this station countless times but never thought about it until now.

The shunt of impact.

The pause. The quiet.

Panic. Screams. Cries for help.

Creaking metal. Shards of glass.

The stink. Darkness.
    Fear. Confusion.
        A scramble.
A reaching hand.
Flashing lights.
Hospital.
Aftermath.

1957, 1967 and then, that 'Year of Disaster', 1987. Another railway catastrophe, this time underground. On 10 November, a match falls through a gap in the wooden Piccadilly line escalator at King's Cross Tube station, igniting the grease and litter beneath, starting the worst fire in the history of the London Underground. Several fires have previously been extinguished here, the big one just waiting. Until now. Thirty-one people die, including the officer-in-charge of Red Watch, Soho Fire Station. Overcome by smoke in his attempt to save lives, he is posthumously awarded the George Medal.

Looking back, it's hard to believe you could smoke hundreds of feet below London's streets, with highly calorific, combustible wood beneath your feet. The public inquiry will end that.

Meanwhile, at Soho Fire Station, a peg in the locker room remains empty next to Station Officer Colin Townsley's name.[49]

The importance of a name.

☠☠☠

Since WW2, the railways have been in decline, hastened by John Major's privatisation in the 1990s. One sunny October morning in 1999, soon after it leaves Paddington, a Thames train runs through the red signal at Portobello Junction, the infamous signal SN109, which, due to poor visibility, has been passed at danger[50] several times before, and was the cause of seven fatalities in the Southall crash two years previously. As the train approaches Ladbroke Grove, it collides with a Great Western train, killing both drivers and twenty-nine passengers. 417 are injured, many with horrific burns. Greg Treverton-Jones, junior counsel for Great Western in the Southall inquiry, is actually on the Great Western train at Ladbroke Grove. In the following inquiry,[51] which is fused with Southall's to consider railway safety, he agrees both to represent Great Western and to be a witness. Driver training is found to be inadequate and Railtrack, the private company responsible for track and signals, points the finger at the newly qualified Thames driver. However, the inquiry concludes that disaster struck not only because the low, bright autumn sun gave the red light a different aspect, but also because years of underinvestment resulted in failure to fix the problem.[52] 'It was a lamentable story,' Greg says, remembering. A story which 'revealed inertia and incompetence on a worrying scale'.[53]

D IS FOR DEATH

☠☠☠

On the Road

Back to 1987. *Fatal Attraction* is a box office hit, Rick Astley is number one, *Spycatcher* is published (and then banned), the Church of England votes for the ordination of women (and no one is struck down), Terry Waite is captured in Lebanon and one person a day is dying of AIDS.

1987: 'Year of Disasters'. An *annus horribilis* for all of us on these isles, due to a sorry catalogue of mainly preventable man-made disasters. King's Cross, Zeebrugge, Hungerford, Heart of Wales line, Enniskillen, M6. This doesn't even include the Great Storm – a natural disaster. Nor the less quantifiable stock market crash. Or Thatcher winning her third term.

But then, just after Christmas, disaster struck at the heart of my own family.

I am spending Christmas at my stepsister's house in Wandsworth. A big family gathering. It's nice to be treated as I'm an impoverished student (despite that full grant) and I'm also the youngest. On Boxing Day, I make my excuses and stay at my fiancé's family home in Hither Green. I go from a middle-class fun-and-games extravaganza in Yuppyville to a more modest family get-together overshadowed by his parents' divorce shenanigans. It's all a bit Den and Ang at the Queen Vic.

The next day, the house is woken early by a phone call. It's my brother, Peter. I know it is bad news. And it really is. My Auntie Helen and my eight-year-old cousin, Siobhan, have both died in a motorway collision, along with another of Siobhan's cousins, just a few years older.

I go back to bed. I lie there, wide awake, in shock. Has this actually happened?

The funeral is arranged quickly and, a few days later, I make the train trip alone to Oxford, where Peter picks me up from the station. I have found a black skirt and jumper and I sit in these unfamiliar clothes in an unfamiliar pub eating a cheese-and-pickle sandwich before we travel on to the church.

My first funeral is the most difficult. My uncle's only child and her mother, gone. We sing 'Silent Night'. A carol for a child's nativity play, not for their funeral. The words 'mother and child' hit home, and I crumble into my sister-in-law's arms.

☠☠☠

During this 70s childhood of mine, it wasn't uncommon for drivers to imbibe more than their fair share. Country pubs, one for the road. But, in 1967, transport minister Barbara Castle introduced the breathalyser, and the following Road Safety Act meant drink-driving was becoming a stigma and incidents were reduced. But there's always more to do. Cue horrifying television adverts such as 1992's *Don't Drink and Drive in the Summertime*, which shows a lovely summer's day at the pub turning sour. Despite the shamefully outdated words of the Mungo Jerry song, the hard-hitting advert did its job.

Somehow, I survived summers with my cousins, bouncing around Bristol in the back of Nan's van, sprawled on a mattress. Seatbelts would have removed the jeopardy but, even though car manufacturers had to install them in 1965, it wasn't until 1983 that drivers and passengers had to wear them.[54] They have saved countless lives, and yet, according to road safety charity Brake, despite every road death being preventable, five people still die every day on the road in the UK, with many more seriously injured.[55]

In my first term as a nursery teacher in Camberwell, in the early 90s, a little girl in my class was knocked down on her way home. She didn't survive. This was my second funeral, and I hope never again to witness a coffin so small. The following campaign resulted in safety bumps being installed in the road, but, sadly and all too often, it takes a death before action is taken on a hazardous street.

☠☠☠

Then there's Princess Diana. We've already seen her at Gresford, opening the miners' memorial, but who there could have predicted her untimely death? Every year, on 31 August, the anniversary of that fatal car crash, a service is held in Liverpool Cathedral for the princess and all road crash victims, organised by RoadPeace, who campaign for victims and bereaved families. One of their core beliefs is that, for a family, 'a road death has the same effect as a murder, and its investigation should be no less thorough'.[56]

Roadpeace also has the most insightful words about roadside memorials:

A roadside memorial indicates where an unnatural, violent, premature and unnecessary death has taken place... families who need them are driven by grief, loss and trauma. Bereaved families do not want their loved one's death to go unnoticed and they need a connection with the last place that they were alive...[57]

☠☠☠

Fly Away

A hot summer's day in 1971. A village somewhere in the Midlands. A wedding breakfast in a marquee. Auntie Liz, pregnant with her first child, and Uncle Dick are seated at a table, celebrating the marriage of two of their friends. It's a beautiful day, though sweltering inside the glorified tent. Speeches have been spoken. Champagne glasses chinked. Stomachs filled. Outside, across the fields, up in the heat-hazy sky, an aeroplane is buzzing. A perfect summer's afternoon.

And then it's not.

A guest points to the small aircraft.

Something's wrong.

It's falling.

My aunt and uncle leap up and, with another couple, rush to Dick's Rover and drive away from the wedding party, down the country lane, heading to where the plane has dipped, two fields away.

When they reach the first field, they come across what looks like a ragdoll. It is a dead man. Without trousers. Dick takes off his jacket, lays it over his dignity. They stand there, the two couples, stunned. Unsure what to do.

Here's a handbag, someone says. There must be another passenger. A woman. They start searching for her.

A few yards away, they find three more bodies, lying one in front of the other as if queuing up, even in death.

A policeman appears. For some reason, he removes my uncle's jacket from the dead man. This upsets my aunt so much that her quiet shock turns to noisy tears. She's supposed to be celebrating, it's supposed to be a joyful occasion and yet here she is, in a field, a baby tucked inside her, witnessing four dead people.

She tells me this story when I am quite small. Probably six or seven. I ask for all the details and they have lodged, vividly, in my mind all these years.

Imagine that happening on a quiet afternoon at a wedding.

Imagine.

HOME

☠☠☠

There's No Place Like Home

You'd think it best to stay at home. Think again.

According to the Royal Society for the Prevention of Accidents (ROSPA), the home is the most likely place for an accident. The home is littered with hazards: hot water, matches, gas boilers, medicines, cleaning products, ponds, barbecues, windows, cookers, candles, log burners, electric blankets, knives, power tools, plants, trampolines, rugs, ladders, peanuts. Dr Cliff Mann, late president of the College of Emergency Medicine, said in 2014 that improvements in road safety and workplaces mean that homes and leisure pursuits now cause far more injuries and deaths. 'The reality is that you are more likely to die sorting out the Christmas lights by taking them out of the loft, or trying to fix the faulty plug or flex, than an electrician is on a building site.'[58]

I, for one, am grateful for improvements such as oven chips, fire-regulated furniture and integral plugs on electrical appliances, but many more accidents could be avoided with precautions and education. (Bring back public information films!)

Whatever our circumstances, we can all tell stories of accidents in the home.

☠☠☠

We were staying in a holiday cottage, when our daughter, then a toddler, had an accident. Her two older brothers were messing around and 'somehow' the coffee table was tipped up and sliced through her big toe. There was a lot of blood. A trip to A&E. A holiday cut short. Daily follow-ups with the district nurse. A consultation with a plastic surgeon. And, thankfully, due to the marvellous ability of a toddler's digits to regenerate, and the fact her nail bed was intact, most of the toe grew back. And the result of this? Gratitude to the NHS, relief it wasn't more serious, a wariness of coffee tables. And my daughter won't wear open-toed shoes. It's also a dinner-party story which will admittedly put some off their food, especially the detail of the slice of toe left in the foot of her Babygro.

☠☠☠

There was a far worse accident in the Carmarthen childhood home of my grandfather. There were three boys and three girls in the Morris family in St David's Road. When the youngest brother, Rhys, was just two years old, he fell out of a downstairs window and died a few days later from his injuries. An accident like this has an impact on the immediate family, but its aftershocks filter down the generations. As I've already said, I am risk-averse. I have passed this trait to my kids, one I inherited from my forebears. One of my earliest memories is of my grandmother crawling across the Clifton Suspension Bridge, so terrified was she of heights. Why she agreed to take us is beyond me, but she did love that iconic bridge, a fan of Isambard Kingdom Brunel. And she loved to tell the story of twenty-two-year-old Sarah Henley, who in 1885, having been spurned by her fiancé, jumped off the bridge, hoping to end her life. She was unsuccessful; her crinoline became a parachute and she drifted down into the mud, where she was rescued. Not a bone in her body was broken and she lived another sixty-three years.

There is an argument that one should take some risks – not as drastic as Sarah Henley's – because risk-taking allows personal growth, preventing you from a life of fear, enabling you to try new things. A small example. When I was four, Mum, being a good parent, told me not to touch the hob. 'It's hot,' she said. But what did I do? I touched the hob. A silly risk because it was very hot. I escaped with a mild scald, but never did it again.

☠☠☠

Finally, we return to money and accountability. To poorly maintained private rentals and unethical landlords. According to Shelter, '45% of private renters have been victims of illegal acts by their landlord or letting agent'.[59] Once again, those less privileged are at greatest risk.

And then there's Grenfell.

The importance of a name.

A twenty-four-storey block of flats, Grenfell Tower was part of the Lancaster West Estate in North London, a social housing complex of almost 1,000 homes built in the 1970s and renovated in 2016. In the early hours of 14 June 2017, a fire broke out in the kitchen of a fourth-floor flat. Due to the tower's cladding, the fire spread rapidly up the exterior and soon Grenfell was a towering inferno, which resulted in the deaths of at least seventy-two people.

Whilst the Queen and Duke of Edinburgh visited survivors and families of the victims, the prime minister did not. Ahead of the one-year anniversary, Theresa May apologised. A year later, in her resignation speech, she said: 'the unique privilege of this office is to use this platform to give a voice to the voiceless. To fight the burning injustices that still scar our society… it is why I set up the independent public inquiry into the tragedy at Grenfell Tower, to search for the truth so nothing like it can ever happen again, and so the people who lost their lives that night are never forgotten.'

Not everyone was happy with this. Matt Wrack, Fire Brigades Union general secretary, said: 'Many of the underlying issues at Grenfell were due to unsafe conditions that had been allowed to fester under Tory governments and a council for which Theresa May bears ultimate responsibility. The inquiry she launched has kicked scrutiny of corporate and government interests into the long grass, denying families and survivors justice while allowing business as usual to continue for the wealthy.'[60]

The housing safety saga continues, with dangerous cladding all over the country. As for the families and survivors of Grenfell, they are still waiting for the outcome of the inquiry[61] which began in September 2017 and closed in November 2022. The Phase 1 report, establishing what happened on the night of the fire, was published in October 2019, but we are still awaiting the Phase 2 report, which will focus on the causes of these events. It is due in 2024. Easthope suggests that Grenfell is likely to involve 'some of the most drawn-out corporate litigation and criminal investigation ever seen in the UK'.[62] And, in an interesting twist, the Health and Safety at Work Act 1974 (of Flixborough fame) could be deployed. Designed to stop employers putting the public at risk, not just employees in the workplace, it could be used against the organisations involved, including London Fire Brigade, and could see individuals prosecuted.[63]

On the first anniversary, seventy-two doves were released at the base of the tower in memory of the dead, with an extra dove released 'for the unknown'. And there have been discussions of a fitting memorial, one of the ideas being a 'living tower', a 'vertical forest' with seventy-two species of plants, one for every person who died. But there is another spanner in the works: a distinct possibility that, in the interests of health and safety, the tower will be taken down. Hisam Choucair, who lost six family members, gives us profound words: 'A tragedy has taken place that must never be forgotten at this location. If they take it down, they will obliterate that memory and they would be putting people through another unimaginable trauma. The ashes of our loved ones are in the fabric of that building.'[64]

This begs the question: do the powers-that-be want the tower brought down? After all, this would prevent further investigation and destroy evidence. Cynical, yes, but remember Gresford, the sealed Dennis section, the entombed miners? So too the grieving Grenfell families have no bodies to bury. Easthope, who worked with the community, knows the relationship between tower and people is complicated. She believes that Grenfell is 'a grave, a sacred, hallowed space and a terrible reminder of what was lost'. But it also offers 'the chance to dissent'. While the tower remains, the disaster will be present: 'It is a rebellion against the most common behaviour of all in disaster response – the act of forgetting.'[65]

Then there's another link, to another disaster. Grenfell tower is just over a mile from the scene of the Ladbroke Grove crash. On Saturday, 5 October 2019, thirty-one candles were lit at St Helen's Church, one for each of the rail crash victims. In the same church on 14 June, the second anniversary of Grenfell, seventy-two candles were lit. But, according to the Bennett Institute of Public Policy, that is not the only connection; in both cases 'individuals raising concerns have been portrayed in ways that silence their voice'.

> But the failure to listen to and tap the tacit knowledge of those at the front line is common, it is present in most major accidents including Piper Alpha, Chernobyl and the Challenger Space Shuttle disasters. Whilst many argue the moral case for engaging with residents and front-line workers, it is their tacit knowledge that is so critical to safety. The experience and concerns of those at the sharp edge can help identify deeper issues.[66]

Britsafe concurs:

> We can't do anything to mitigate the impact of the Grenfell Tower fire on those involved, but we have a duty to ensure that lessons are learned and applied to minimise the risk of a similar incident occurring in the future. This needs to be the start of a step change in the way that we approach the safety of residents in multi-occupied buildings.[67]

Hillsborough, Covid, Grenfell. Will their public inquiries deliver the necessary change? Will they make governments, other bodies and the media accountable? We can only hope. And we can push for a Hillsborough Law which will 'criminalise lying to the British public, and support those fighting for the truth'.

As for me, I will remember one victim. Our paths crossed briefly, three times. This young man worked in the building in Soho where I celebrated the launch of my first three novels. He was so kind, letting us overrun so I could catch up with family and friends. I won't forget that kindness.

☠☠☠

Don't Worry, Be Happy

When I began researching death through accidents, I had no agenda. I certainly didn't expect to find so many connections or that they would lead me to the obvious conclusion: the majority of these 'accidents' could have been avoided if not for the relentless pursuit of progress.

You might be asking yourself: why must I read about people dying suddenly and unexpectedly? What am I supposed to do now? I can't even sit at home without worrying.

There are things you can do.

Fight for better safety legislation, for accountability, for social justice.

Remember those who died through little or no fault of their own but through circumstance, neglect, and greed.

Visit a memorial and when you read the names engraved in stone, in slate, in marble, be thankful and hopeful that the lost didn't die in vain. That you have lived longer because of them and because of the determined campaigning of those they left behind.

Read Lucy Easthope's book and remember:

> It is not possible, or healthy, to live every day wondering how effective the control measures are at the nearest nuclear power station. It is completely natural, and psychologically healthy, for the human mind to turn itself away from these risks and not linger upon them. Could we really function day to day – raise babies, teach a class of children, drive a car, fly a plane – if we thought constantly about the risks we have chosen to tolerate?[68]

Yes, take sensible precautions – limit your risks, look after your mental and physical health – but don't live a life of worry. Certainly, don't sweat the small stuff. One day, your time on this earth will end and, while you can't know exactly when that day will be, you owe it to others, in the meantime, to live a full life, one free of fear.

That is the best death you can have – one that follows a life well lived.

Oh, and I almost forgot to say: before you go to sleep tonight, once you've locked your front door (if you're lucky enough to have one), remember that most people are good.

B
IS FOR BONES

What Bodies Tell Us about Life and Death

bone *noun*
1. the hard dense tissue that forms the skeleton of vertebrates, providing structural support for the body and serving as an attachment for muscles.
2. any of the components of the skeleton, made of this material.
3. (bones) the skeleton.
4. (*chiefly* one's bones) the body as the place where feelings or instincts come from • *I feel in my bones something is wrong*.
5. a substance similar to human bone, such as ivory and whalebone, etc.
6. (bones) the basic or essential part.

When that churl Death my bones with dust shall cover
SONNET 32

Here lies interr'd beneath these stones
The beard, the flesh, and eke ye bones
Of Wrexham's clerk, old Daniel Jones
FROM WREXHAM CHURCH

☠☠☠

Poor Miss Bowles

Thirty-seven years after poor Miss Bowles, I came face to face with my second dead body. Once again, I was with my mother, in Teignmouth, only this time it was personal. I'd recently moved with my family from Worthing to support her, caring for my stepfather, Ralph, who had Alzheimer's. When the disease became too advanced, the only remaining option was a nursing home. One evening, Mum rang me. The home had just called her. Ralph was 'very poorly'. I rushed round, picked her up, and we headed there, unsure what to expect when we arrived.

Usually, he would be sitting in an armchair in what used to be a very grand ballroom when the Victorian villa was in its heyday, but now the nursing assistant showed us into his bedroom. She didn't say much. Most importantly, she didn't tell us that Mum's husband and my stepfather of twenty-four years was dead. Which he clearly was. A shock. It wasn't upsetting, the seeing a dead body part. It was upsetting that, whoever he was, the person, was no longer here.

Someone made us a cup of tea and we sat together by his bedside. We might even have had a biscuit. This was what my mother had done with him every day for the previous nine months, downstairs in that ballroom, and for the last quarter of a century in their various homes. This is what we did together now, sharing this last ritual as we said our goodbyes.

They say Alzheimer's is the long goodbye, but this was final now.

He was gone.

And you'd think, because we saw him moments after his death, that would be enough but, a few days later, when the funeral director asked Mum if she'd like a viewing, she said yes, she would. So, I went with her. Ralph was laid out in his coffin in the chapel of rest in the funeral parlour. He was dressed in a sort of night shirt, and we could see his face and hands, which looked remarkably like him, but also very different. It was comforting.

Not everyone has a positive experience. Maybe the body is a little decomposed. The face overly made-up. Maybe it is the shock of seeing a corpse in the place of their father or daughter or dear friend. Maybe it's the first time they've seen a dead body; we're not accustomed to corpses these days. They are not kept at home, until the funeral, as in times gone by. They are removed from the place of death, usually a hospital, quietly, discreetly and, if you're lucky, you might get a good experience in a chapel of rest. Mum and I were glad of the opportunity, thankful for the services of a good funeral director.

In the previous chapter, with reference to Gresford and Grenfell, I touched on the significance of having the body of your loved one to say goodbye to. The body is important in death. At Easter, if you go to church, you will hear how Mary Magdalene goes to the borrowed tomb early in the morning to anoint Jesus's body with specially prepared spices. When she finds it empty, his grave clothes folded neatly, she is distraught. *They have taken my Lord away and I don't know where they have put him.*[1] And on Remembrance Sunday we remember the war dead, at the Cenotaph, at the Tomb of the Unknown Soldier, at war memorials in every village, town, and city in the country. We must remember them communally, here, on these Isles, in their absence, because they died overseas and, in the name of equality, their bodies were never repatriated.

The body is important.

☠☠☠

'We are biology. We are reminded of this at the beginning and the end, at birth and at death. In between we do what we can to forget.' Mary Roach[2]

My body has been strong and resilient. It has also let me down. I was an active child and young person. I did cross-country all through secondary school, often twice a day, running thousands of miles over Devon lanes and moors. I went to swimming club three times a week and was a qualified lifesaver at fourteen. I took up ballet aged five, went on pointe at twelve and danced all through my teenage years. I had two older brothers who played rough with me. I climbed trees, roller-skated and swam in the sea. I played tennis, table tennis and badminton. I even played rugby at university. Despite all this, I have never broken a bone apart from a chip in my big toe when I fell over in high heels after a book event (in a funeral parlour for the launch of *Betsy and Lilibet*, my novel about an undertaker born on the same day as the Queen).

The hardest thing I have ever done is give birth. My first labour was eight hours, with four of those spent in a birthing pool. The second stage was difficult, with Johnny back to front, his spine lying across my spine. Fortunately, he turned before the birth, but I tore badly. I have never known such pain. When I was labouring in the pool, I was only allowed gas and air, but it made me sick, so I made do without. Later, while I was stitched up by the registrar (she took a whole hour), I gulped it in. (It took the edge off.) Turfed out the next day, too sore to sit, I learned to breastfeed lying down. (Thank goodness for Hyacinth, my glorious midwife.) Inevitably, after a third-degree tear, I had an infection right at the time my milk was coming in. Why had the NCT classes not prepared me for this? And, moreover, I had a colicky new-born to look after.

You'd think once would be enough but, guess what, I did it another couple of times. Seventeen months after Johnny, I found myself back in the same delivery room at King's College Hospital, Camberwell, in the same birthing pool. I was petrified of tearing again so, for better control, the midwife helped me clamber out of the pool for the delivery. Another tear, but not so bad. Edward was here, a brother for Johnny. Two babies. And then, twenty-seven months later, I was back at King's, this time in a different room, as the birthing pool was already in use. A fantastic male midwife helped me give birth on the bed on all fours. A small tear. A daughter. Isabel. And then there were three. Under the age of four.

My childbirth experiences were pretty good really. I didn't die. None of my children died. Today, in our affluent nation, childbirth is relatively safe. According to MBRRACE-UK,[3] in 2017–19, '8.8 women per 100,000 died during pregnancy or up to six weeks after childbirth or the end of pregnancy'.[4] But there is always an underlying fear. Birth and death are inextricably linked. And we are not all equal. Age and affluence aside, the most shocking example is that 'women from Black ethnic groups [are] four times more likely to die than women from White groups'.[5]

Watching my children grow up has shown me how the body can both work and fail. When he started on solids at five months, Edward developed severe atopic eczema. I was very careful what I fed him and continued breastfeeding until he was fourteen months, believing I was passing nourishment from my body to his, which no doubt I was. But, within two weeks of complete weaning, and with the aid of a strong steroid cream, his skin cleared up. By this time, he had been diagnosed with asthma and anaphylaxis (to milk and eggs). If he ate the wrong thing, he could literally die. And then, when his sister was born, the same thing. She too had severe allergies which we all had to learn to live with as a family. As for my oldest, he hasn't escaped his health issues, though his have been from having a neuro-diverse brain. While at university, he was diagnosed with ADHD, which hugely impacts his daily life.

As for me, my health struggles include a type of breast cancer for which there is no targeted treatment. In 2020, my doctors threw everything at it. I had specialised surgery, a MICAP flap procedure[6] which took tissue from my chest wall to fill the gap left by the removal of the tumour, followed by sixteen rounds of chemotherapy (including the 'red devil'), topped off with radiotherapy. Every six months, I have an infusion of bisphosphonates to strengthen my bones in the hope of making them a hostile environment for tumours (who love a post-menopausal less-dense bone). I've just had my three-year mammogram with no concerning features. Thank you, NHS.

One day my body will give up. There will be a last breath. A final beat of the heart. It could be sudden. It could be a slow decline. I might be unaware. I might be prepared. The only certainty is that it will happen. This earthly existence will end. My body will have done its job. For me, at any rate.

☠☠☠

'Now I am cast down: and turned into food for worms.'
Archbishop Henry Chichele

So, what happens to our body at the point of death? To answer this, let's time-travel to the Middle Ages for a checklist quoted in *Death in England*:

'When my eye mists / And my hearing fails
And my nose goes cold / And my tongue curls back
And my face falls in / And my lips blacken
And my mouth gapes / And my spittle runs
And my hair stands on end / And my heart trembles
And my hands shake / And my feet go stiff.'[7]

Rosemary Horrox tells us this list also had a moral purpose, in line with Church teaching, 'encouraging the sinner to think on his ultimate fate and to recognise the approach of death in time to make proper spiritual preparation'. It ends with a blatant reminder: 'All too late, all too late / When the bier is at the gate.'

By the sixth century, Christianity was embedded in everyday life and death on the British Isles. Frightening illustrations of Purgatory and Hell adorned church walls, a helpful reminder for worshippers to worry about the afterlife, not what they'd have for dinner. As well as striving to be good in this life, preparations were essential for the soul after death. These bargaining tools included the lighting of candles, giving to the poor and going on pilgrimage, and were not only used in life: after death, others could intercede. In 1496, William Courtney, Archbishop of Canterbury, took this to the extreme, paying up front for 15,000 masses to be said to speed his soul through Purgatory and (hopefully) to Heaven (more than the reigning monarch, Henry VII, who only managed a measly 10,000).[8]

The moment of dying was the moment one's fate and significance were judged. A good death meant that, as the time approached, the family gathered around the deathbed. The priest arrived, ringing a handbell. There was contrition and penance, confession and absolution, the physical anointing of oil with the sacrament of extreme unction (last rites), a crucifix placed before the eyes until the final breath, when doors and windows were opened to free the soul.[9]

Inevitably, there was a fear of unexpected death (*mors improvisa*). Unprepared, you could end up Downstairs. There were constant reminders to think on. The Dance of Death (*Danse Macabre*) was a Christian iconography that personified Death as a decomposing cadaver, dancing among the living. A memento mori that we all must die, so if we 'fess up, and maybe indulge in some self-flagellation, then we might avoid a lifetime trip to Hell. Later the skeleton was simplified to a skull with perhaps an accompanying hourglass or spade;

you can still see these symbols on memorials and tombs, from cathedrals to the humble country churchyard. The kirkyards of Edinburgh have exceptional examples, but wander to your local graveyard and see if you can spot one. (You can even post it on Twitter with the hashtag #MementoMoriMonday.)

We tread a thin line between life and death, especially so in the time of plague, war or famine, rife in the Middle Ages. Horrox says: 'Thinking on death in general, and the bodily dissolution which would accompany one's own death in particular, would inculcate humility and put worldly glory in its proper perspective.'[10] The body was important. Because of the resurrection, Christians believed that you needed an intact body at death so that, at the Last Judgement, you could rise again as you once were in life, warts and all. 'Not only was dying part of life; the dead, especially dead bodies, were part of life as well.'[11]

The Reformation ended Purgatory; the fate of the soul was now sealed at death; you absolutely needed your ducks in a row. With no more chantries to pray for the dead, the living could do no more for their dearly departed.

Scientific and social advances in the second half of the eighteenth century brought more knowledge of the physiology of the body and a change in religious attitude. At the deathbed, the doctor replaced the priest, opium the crucifix. The terror of a bad death was eased because the God of the Enlightenment was 'a rational being, distant, benevolent, tolerant and unmysterious. The image of such a God did not sit happily with the notion of eternal damnation and hellfire.'[12]

But it was still tricky to diagnose death. After all, people have been known to come back from beyond the grave. (Think Lazarus. Think Bella Montoya, the seventy-six-year-old Ecuadorian woman found alive in her coffin at her funeral in 2023.) This anxiety – or taphophobia – was fuelled by the press and literature such as Edgar Allan Poe's short story 'The Premature Burial' (1844) and even Mary Shelley's earlier *Frankenstein* (1818). How could you be certain someone was dead? Inevitably, tests were devised. Some were, quite frankly, macabre. Powner et al. outline these:

> [A]bsent inflammatory response to subcutaneously injected ammonia (Monteverde's sign); no movement of flags attached to needles inserted into the heart (Balfour's test); direct palpation of the heart via an intercostal incision (Foubert's test); failure of a fingertip with a proximal ligature to become congested (Magnus' sign); and persistent eyeball indentation following external pressure (Ripault's sign).

In addition, there were tests of 'sensibility' which included 'smelling salts, mustard up the nose, objects inserted under the fingernails, loud noise such as blowing a trumpet in the ear, scalding, and instilling tobacco smoke per rectum.'[13]

But what if these failed? What if you still ended up buried alive? Not to worry: there were handy gadgets (if you had the money). Why not invest in a rope bell for your coffin? Then if you woke up, entombed, you – or any other rich revenant – could ring it and thus be 'saved by the bell'. (My auntie Liz had her own idea, which she talked about when I was a child: a glass coffin, in the manner of Snow White, but with a telephone.)

Reception houses or 'waiting mortuaries' (or more bluntly the 'dead house') were built in the nineteenth century to store the dead until burial. Bodies could be kept here under lock and key until decomposition was not only evident but also advanced enough so that they were of no use to the body snatchers (more of these in a bit). Also, rather than keeping the body at home until funds were raised for a funeral and burial, dead houses were believed to prevent the spread of disease.

Matthew Wall lived in Braughing, Hertfordshire, in the sixteenth century, before the introduction of these measures. On the way to his grave, his pallbearers slipped on wet leaves and dropped the coffin. He woke up, knocked on the lid and was spared a premature burial. In fact, he lived for another twenty-four years. Every 2 October is celebrated as Old Man's Day.

Detail of a miniature of the *Three Living and the Three Dead*,
from the De Lisle Psalter, East Anglia, c.1308–40

Being buried alive is unthinkable, but a correct diagnosis is important on many levels. As we know from the death of Queen Elizabeth II, when death is pronounced, it 'signals the start of the mourning period; various rights and rituals can proceed; legal affairs may be settled; succession can take place'. For us ordinary mortals, and in certain circumstances, a correct diagnosis also allows 'a person's organs [to] be removed for transplantation; and medical treatment [to] be terminated'.[14]

Fortunately, now, we have the medical know-how to get this right. It's technical, so I'll hand you over to Stephen Jacobe:

> There is arguably a narrow yet profound difference between 'dying' and 'dead'. Doctors must ensure that they do not confuse the two and are clear about how to diagnose death. Death should not be diagnosed until at least 2 min of electrical asystole has been observed or, in the presence of cardiac pulseless electrical activity, 2 min of 'acirculation' confirmed either by echocardiography/cardiac ultrasound or intra-arterial pressure monitoring. If neither is available, careful palpation of a central pulse for at least 60 s is recommended prior to declaring death.[15]

Not so much as a puff of smoke up the bum.

☠☠☠

Invasion of the Body Snatchers

The body is crucial to our beliefs surrounding death and dying. It also teaches us about life. Which brings us to the resurrectionists, more aptly known as the body snatchers (or 'sack 'em up men' or 'corpse kings'). Anatomy is a centuries-old branch of science concerned with the workings of the body – and one wrought with difficulty. According to Mary Roach, '[f]ew sciences are as rooted in shame, infamy, and bad PR as human anatomy'.[16]

Nevertheless, there are some big players in anatomy: Herophilus, Hippocrates, Aristotle, Hildegard, Galen, Da Vinci, Vesalius. And then there's Harvey. Harvey is a legend on my mum's Bristolian side of the family. Not just because of their penchant for a certain brand of cream sherry but also because Mum was told that William Harvey – the sixteenth-century English physician who discovered the circulation of the blood – was an ancestor of ours. As a young girl, she used to visit Elizabeth Harvey and her sister, Jane, cousins of my grandmother, who claimed descent from the great man. (Mum describes Elizabeth and Jane as Victorian spinsters and, in my head, they are much like Hinge and Bracket.) But, from a little research, I understand that Harvey had no children, so I can't find a connection. I do, at least, possess a bowdlerised complete works of Shakespeare once belonging to the sisters.

Ancestor or not, Harvey understood the importance of learning from the body: 'I profess to learn and to teach anatomy not from books but from dissections, not from the tenets of Philosophers but from the fabric of Nature.' (He even dissected his father and sister. Well, their corpses.)[17] But with the growth of anatomy schools in the eighteenth and nineteenth centuries, there was a lack of corpses for students to learn from first-hand, the only legal source being the gallows. (Part of the punishment for the worst crimes was the delivery of the criminal to the surgeons at the scaffolds before public execution, after which there would be a public exhibition of the dissection.) This shortage was worsened by the Judgement of Death Act 1823 which resulted in fewer executions. And, in those days, nobody donated their cadaver to medical science, not when you needed it intact for the resurrection. As Roach points out: 'Who's going to open the gates of heaven to some slob with his entrails all hanging out and dripping on the carpet?'[18]

This sparsity of cadavers led to the illegal trade of body snatching; those without conscience would dig up a recently buried corpse and sell it to anatomy students. If the corpses were too putrid for dissection, they would extract the teeth to sell to dentists. These 'Waterloo teeth' could then be used for dentures for the rich. One such chap was Joseph Naples, a former sailor turned gravedigger at Spa Fields, Clerkenwell. Naples soon became involved in this lucrative side hustle.[19] A ghoulishly fascinating character, he kept a logbook of his 'things', the corpses he exhumed and sold. This *Diary of a Resurrectionist* is kept at the Royal College of Surgeons in London.[20]

By the late eighteenth century, there was such fear of bodysnatchers that watch boxes were erected in graveyards to provide night-time shelter for guards, while elaborate iron cages called mortsafes were placed around tombs or underground around the coffin itself. And, of course, these options were only available to those with money. We might all be equal in death, but our dead bodies are not. In fact, Julie Rugg contends that '[p]erhaps at no time in the modern period has the contrast been so marked between the death of the rich and the death of the poor: as the middle classes purchased often massive memorials to mark the passage of their loved ones, the poor were deprived even of a body over which to mourn.'[21]

And then there's the legendary double-act of 1820s Edinburgh: William Burke and William Hare ratcheted up body snatching to another level. Hare lived with his common-law wife, who ran a boarding house. Burke lived with his mistress in the same road. When an elderly gent died owing rent, the pair seized the opportunity to recoup the money and make a little extra by selling his body to Professor Robert Knox of the medical school at Edinburgh University. Next time, they hastened the death of another ill tenant by drugging him with whisky and then suffocating him. This became their preferred method of murder as it left the corpse unmarked. Once they'd run out of tenants, they lured victims into their homes until eventually they were discovered. Hare did a deal with the police and Burke was sentenced to death by hanging. His execution took place at Lawnmarket to a huge crowd. Afterwards, his body was donated to medical science. (Oh, the irony.) As for Knox, he might have been cleared of the charges, but his reputation was in ruins. No one knows for sure what happened to Hare, but Burke's death mask, with its accompanying noose marks, can be seen in Edinburgh's magnificent and macabre Surgeons' Hall, alongside a book said to be made from his skin.

The Anatomy Act 1832 legally recognised the rights of the corpse. Its intention was to stop the body snatchers by creating a free supply of corpses because now the unclaimed bodies of paupers could also be used. 'Unclaimed' bodies in institutions such as asylums, hospitals, workhouses and prisons, without funeral funds or family, could now legally be taken after forty-eight hours and given to anatomists.

'Dissecting a Human Body', William Hogarth

Gray's Anatomy

In 1858, Sir Henry Gray published his book *Anatomy Descriptive and Surgical*, now commonly known as *Gray's Anatomy* and still the basis for most medical students. A story about this. At some point in the 1980s, my stepfather consulted his GP about the painful ganglion cyst on his wrist. The doctor asked him to wait a moment while he retrieved his copy of this thick, heavy book. Expecting him to refer to its contents, my stepfather was caught unawares when the doctor slammed it against the cyst. 'Ow!' he yelped. But it did the trick, dispersing the fluid. Claudia Hammond[22] says it was common practice to do this using a Bible, hence the nickname for ganglia being 'bible bumps'.

Ralph got off lightly. Hammond cites German anatomist Lorenz Heister who, in 1743, listed treatment options which included wiping the lump with saliva, taking a bullet that had killed a wild animal (ideally a stag) and strapping it to the cyst, and rubbing it with the hand of a dead man. As for my mother, when she also had one, she bought a gold bracelet and after a few weeks of wearing it on the affected wrist, the ganglion disappeared. Make of this what you will, though current medical opinion is to leave alone unless painful – then surgery or aspiration is a safer option. (You could always borrow that hefty Shakespeare that once belonged to the Harvey sisters.)

These days, while some medical students continue to use cadavers for anatomy, such as at the University of Manchester, others learn through state-of-the-art computers. The University of Bradford, for example, opened a multi-disciplinary Integrated Life Sciences Learning Centre in 2016.[23] The centre has a Simulation Suite with a 3D dissection table and human patient simulator. In addition to this, the Anatomy and Pathology Resource Centre has a digital autopsy table and there are osteology laboratories for the analysis of archaeological human remains. What would Knox reckon to that?

The jury is out. Cadaver or computer? It has been claimed that dissections enable medical students to learn about death but Roach questions this. 'If you're going to bring in an outsider to teach students about death, a hospice patient or grief counsellor surely has as much to offer as a dead man does.'[24]

Silent Witness

Corpses are also employed in the arena of forensics. In the chapter 'Life after Death', Roach describes her visit to the University of Tennessee (UT) Anthropological Research Facility, a field research facility like no other, 'the only one in the world dedicated to the study of human decay', where donated cadavers help 'in their mute, fragrant way, to advance the science of criminal forensics'.[25] Here, students study the biological and chemical phases the cadavers go through and how the environment affects these, enabling the police to work out more precisely the time of death. Because there are so many variables which alter decomposition, bodies are buried in shallow graves, entombed in concrete, wrapped in plastic bags. 'Pretty much anything a killer might do to dispose of a dead body the researchers at UT have done also.'[26]

Professor Dame Sue Black, renowned anatomist and forensic anthropologist, works with forensic pathologists on human remains of the recent past[27] to identify the deceased and to discover how they lived and died. She says: 'There is barely a single region of the body that cannot tell a part of our story, and the longer we live, the richer the narrative.'[28]

What would your body say about you and how you have lived your life? Do you have tattoos, scars, arthritis, gout, congenital abnormalities? Have you drunk, smoked, given birth? What was your age, height, ethnicity? Did you have modifications – hip replacement, fillers, implants, pacemaker, amputations, major injuries?

We are all different.

Though perhaps not all like my great-grandmother, Minnie Lovell, proud owner of four kidneys.

☠☠☠

The Heebie-Jeebies

There is a fascination and horror of the cadaver. Some of us might love a zombie film. But the BBC will only broadcast a corpse 'if necessary for the public good'. A scene from Channel 4's *Derry Girls* is a great example of this dichotomy.

It is Auntie Bridie's wake and her open coffin lies in the front room.

'She really suits being dead, doesn't she?' Orla says to Erin as they stand over Auntie Bridie.

Then the English cousin comes in, with the other two girls. He is shocked to see an open coffin where people usually watch the telly.

'It's just Bridie,' Erin tells him.

James replies, 'It's Bridie's corpse. It's Bridie's dead corpse.'

'Haven't you ever seen a dead body before?' Erin asks, facetiously.

'Of course not,' he says, outraged.

'Christ, but the English are weird,' Michelle says, equally appalled at this reaction.

To which Clare adds, 'It's just a dead body, James. We're all going to be one someday.'

By now James is incredulous. 'Thanks, Clare, that's helped.'

What is it we don't like? The corpse itself? Or what the corpse represents? Here, the girls are at ease with death. James, on the other hand, is horrified; not only are his friends happy to commune with the dead, but also they are comfortable with the idea of their own mortality. A big difference in Irish and much of English culture.

Body Worlds addressed this by continuing the work of the anatomists. Gunther von Hagens created a travelling educational exhibition containing real bodies which had undergone a preservation process called 'plastination'. In his words, 'the anatomist alone is assigned a specific role – he is forced in his daily world to reject the taboos and convictions that people have about death and the dead'. The website is well worth a look, with its brief history of anatomy and dissection, including links to art.[29] Since 1995,[30] *Body Worlds* has attracted over fifty million visitors in over 150 cities across the globe. Education aside, there are echoes of La Morgue of Paris, which, in the nineteenth century, was a top visitor attraction, where crowds could go for free to look at anonymous naked corpses, apparently for identification but really for whatever reason you can think of. The corpses were removed after a few days due to decomposition. Not on my bucket list.

Though many try to slow it down, you can't stop decay. In fact, Buddhism embraces this process. The Sutra on Mindfulness, known as the Nine Cemetery Contemplations, is a meditation practice of memento mori which includes thinking about decomposition.

So maybe now is the time to do that.

☠☠☠

Post-Mortem

In hospital, once death has been certified, the body will be removed to a refrigerated mortuary. At home, it is common practice these days in the UK for the body to be removed by a funeral director to their funeral home, which also contains refrigeration (more of this later). Here the body might also be embalmed, a process which slows decay, where natural fluids of the body are replaced via the arterial system with a preservative solution. So, under usual circumstances, the body doesn't decompose too much before burial or cremation. Left to its own devices, it will, though the process varies according to the conditions to which it is exposed.

If a body is discovered after death, there are post-mortem signs which give an indication of time and cause of death and whether the body has been moved. The first is a paleness of the skin, more noticeable in white skin, known as *pallor mortis*. The second sign is the cooling of the body known as *algor mortis*. The third is *rigor mortis*, a stiffening of the limbs due to chemical changes in the muscles. This happens a few hours after death and can last for a few hours to a few days depending on the conditions. The fourth post-mortem sign is *livor mortis*, a gravitational pooling of the blood to the lower areas of the body, resulting in a red-purple colouration.

There are various stages of decay, again dependent on circumstances. The first is autolysis (self-digestion) which begins immediately after death, as soon as blood circulation and breathing stop, when the body can no longer get oxygen or remove waste and cells break down. While autolysis is an entirely cellular process, decomposition involves breakdown by bacteria, insects and microorganisms. In her book *Will My Cat Eat My Eyeballs*, Caitlin Doughty does some straight talking:

After you die, your gut is party central, with billions of bacteria eating away at your intestines before moving on to your liver, your heart, your brain. But, with all that feasting comes waste. Those billions of bacteria produce gases like methane and ammonia, which bloat your stomach.

This is stage two and lasts for about a week. Doughty goes on to say:

> …bloat means internal pressure, and if the pressure builds up enough, your body can purge, releasing vile-smelling liquid or air. When a body purges, it may make a creepy whooshing sound. Worry not, this isn't the horrible ghost wails of the dead, it's … bacteria farts.[31]

Then the final stage: putrefaction and decay. The breaking down and gradual liquefaction of tissue which starts during the bloat stage now becomes obvious. Microorganisms and bacteria produce unpleasant smells called putrefaction. Catlin Doughty describes this in her vivid way: 'Think: your grandma's heavy sweet perfume sprayed over a rotting fish. Put them together in a sealed plastic bag and leave them in the blazing sun for a few days. Then open the bag and put your nose in for a big whiff.'[32] In fact, putrescine is such a strong smell that Roach tells us that human remain dogs can 'detect the lingering scent molecules of a decomposing body up to fourteen months after the killer lugged it away.'[33]

How whiffy those dissecting rooms of the body-snatching era must have been!

Old Bones and Hollow Crowns

Since prehistory, people have tried to slow decomposition, and not all bodies are simply bones. The mummification process of the Egyptians is well known, a process of conservation which consists of the dehydration and exsiccation of tissues, effective in the dry north African climate. But what of the bodies found in the raised peat bogs of northern Europe? We don't know why the corpses known as Lindow Man and Windeby Girl ended up there, but we do know they were naturally preserved in the bogs, where layers of sphagnum moss formed a dome fed by rainwater, which had the effect similar to that of a morgue chiller. But usually, inevitably, the very end result of decomposition is skeletonisation, the removal of all soft tissue from the bone. Bones still have much to tell us about life and death, the 'last sentinels of our mortal life to bear witness to the way we lived it'.[34] In 2011, near Cambridge, the bones and grave goods of a teenage girl were discovered in an extremely rare bed burial some 1,300 years old. While we don't know who she was in life, the position of her skeleton and the accompanying gold and garnet cross (known as the Trumpington Cross) suggest something of her early Christian faith and high status. Dental analysis not only revealed her age but also a childhood illness with iron deficiency, possibly caused by a parasite, or leprosy, or even heavy blood loss. A brilliant example of the crossover of archaeology and forensics.

The following year, during an excavation of a car park in Leicester, once the site of the old Greyfriars church, researchers from the Richard III Society and archaeologists from the University of Leicester found a skeleton with battle scars and a curved spine. They believed it to be the remains of Richard III, killed at Bosworth Field in 1485, the last English king to die in battle. But what had brought them to this point?

It was largely due to a member of the Society from Edinburgh. Phillipa Langley's passion and determination enabled the quest to find the lost grave in the hope of showing that the king had been much maligned:

> The Richard III Society was founded on a simple principle, that truth is more powerful than lies. It also considers that, when investigating someone, if you have two sources, those who knew him and those who didn't, your primary source must always be those who knew him. After Richard's death at Bosworth the men of the north who had known Richard, man and boy, described him thus: The most famous Prince of blessed memory.[35]

After years of research, Philippa was sure she knew where to dig.

> The moment I walked into that car park in Leicester the hairs on the back of my neck stood up, and something told me this was where we must look. A year later I revisited the same place, not believing what I had first felt. And this time I saw a roughly painted letter 'R' on the ground (for 'reserved parking space' obviously!). Believe it or not, it was almost directly under that 'R' that King Richard was found... This was the first area we excavated in fact, and it proved to be the choir of the church, the very place where we knew he was buried. And it was on the very first day, the anniversary of Richard's burial, that we came across his remains.[36]

The skeleton was exhumed. The bones were identified to be of a man in his late twenties/early thirties and carbon dated to 1455–1540. DNA sampling linked the skeleton to descendants of Richard III. The University of Leicester announced in February 2013 that the skeleton was indeed that of King Richard. But, while the curved spine did show he had scoliosis, the Plantagenet king was not the limping hunchback with withered arm that Tudor propagandists would have us believe. Revisionists have gone back and forth over the centuries as to what sort of monarch and man he was, but it is generally accepted now that he wasn't the Richard III that Shakespeare portrayed, with a deformed body reflecting a deformed soul. As Langley says:

> ...it is Richard who has finally been able to reveal himself. When Richard's body was stripped naked at Bosworth his physical condition, his scoliosis, became known, and it was used to insult and degrade him. Today we know that a physical abnormality is not a sign of evil. We find this idea abhorrent. We are no longer in the Tudor-mindset.[37]

Finally, Richard was laid to rest in Leicester Cathedral, in an English oak and yew coffin made by a descendant who happened to be a cabinetmaker.

But what of those lost princes in the Tower? On the death of his brother Edward IV in 1483, Richard, Duke of Gloucester, became the protector of his nephews, Edward V and his younger brother, Richard, Duke of York. He put the boys in the Tower of London, apparently for their protection, while they awaited Edward's coronation. But their claim to the throne was discredited on the grounds of illegitimacy, and Richard, their protector, took the crown. It has always been assumed that the boys were murdered while in the Tower and, though never scientifically identified, two hundred years later, the bones of children were discovered in a chest during building work. Charles II had them interred in Westminster Abbey. But some say the boys escaped. After all, where there is no body, there is no certainty, and this can lead to claims by alleged descendants. 'Medieval Europe was roamed by Perkin Warbeck and Lambert Simnels, imposter kings and princes, whose ghostly resurrections afforded legitimacy to political opposition.'[38]

The body is important. Think of those heads on spikes on London Bridge – belonging to the likes of William Wallace, Thomas More and Oliver Cromwell. They were a warning. They were evidence. So too, Richard's corpse was taken from Bosworth to Leicester, strapped to a horse, and left in public for two days so the people would know he was dead. The victor, Henry Tudor, married the boys' elder sister, Elizabeth of York, sealing his claim to the throne and ending the War of the Roses.

The Two Princes Edward and Richard in the Tower, 1483
by Sir John Everett Millais, 1878

Life after Death

And what of those bodies who linger somewhere between life and death, aka the beating heart cadaver? Brain death might be the legal definition of death, but respirators can beat the heart and pump the blood to keep organs and tissue 'alive' for recovery. The horrors of premature burials aside, this blurring of boundaries, according to Roach, 'reflects centuries of confusion over how, exactly, to define death, to pinpoint the precise moment when the spirit – the soul, the chi, whatever you wish to call it – has ceased to exist and all that remains is a corpse'.[39]

'If only the soul could be seen as it left the body, or somehow measured,' Roach adds. 'That way, determining when death had occurred would be a simple matter of scientific observation.'[40] She recounts an experiment to do exactly this. In 1907, American doctor, Duncan MacDougall, reckoned one of his patients lost twenty-one grams[41] at the point of death, concluding that this was indeed the soul leaving the body. A few years later, he even took photographs of his patients at the moment of death and believed these images captured a light around their skulls.

And where exactly does the soul reside (however much it weighs)? Egyptians believed it was in the *ka* or heart, and therefore it was the only organ left in a mummified corpse. Babylonians believed it was the liver, Descartes the pineal gland, Strato 'behind the eyebrows', Plato the brain, St Augustine the blood.[42] The Greeks called the vital spirit *pneuma*, or breath, therefore the soul could be said to live in the lungs or the respiratory system. Some surgeons have said they feel a presence in the room as the heart is taken out, while it keeps beating on its own, until there's a lack of oxygen. But we now know the heart keeps beating 'not because the soul is in there, but because it contains its own bioelectric power source, independent of the brain'.[43]

Despite this, there are testimonials of people who have received heart transplants who claim to feel they have taken on some attributes of the donor. Wishful thinking, perhaps. But we do know for sure that these donors have saved lives. Roach discusses H, a cadaver: 'She has made three sick people well. She has brought them extra time on earth. To be able, as a dead person, to make a gift of this magnitude is phenomenal. Most people don't manage this sort of thing while they're alive. Cadavers like H are the dead's heroes.'[44]

To go a step further, there is the possibility of donating your body to medical science. This was the fervent wish of my great-uncle, Tom. A scientist through and through, he stipulated in his will that this is what he wanted. But unfortunately, after he died, aged ninety-one, a post-mortem rendered his cadaver unsuitable for donation. He would have been gutted (if you'll pardon the pun).

The body is important in death as well as in life. We know this from the families of Gresford and Grenfell. Later, we will look at the war dead. In the next chapter we will consider those who die from contagion. But, in all respects, it is important how we handle bodies in death. Grief is compounded when we are unable to lay our dead to rest. And this brings us full circle, back to the Middle Ages. Caroline Walker Burnham wrote this: 'For medieval people understood that our death is ours, that we die in our bodies, and they knew – as we all find when our own time comes to sit beside our brothers and sisters – that it is to bodies that we must say "good-bye."'[45]

C
IS FOR CONTAGION

Epidemic Disease

contagion *noun*
1. the transmission of a disease by direct physical contact with an infected person.
2. dated a disease that is transmitted in this way.
3. a harmful influence.
4. the transmission of an emotional state • contagion of excitement.
ETYMOLOGY: 14c: from Latin contagio touching, contact, from con together + *tangere* to touch.

Tis the times' plague,
When madmen lead the blind.
KING LEAR

Here lies I and my two daughters,
Killed by drinking Cheltenham waters;
If we had stuck to Epsom salts,
We shouldn't be lying in these here vaults.
FROM A CHELTENHAM CHURCHYARD

Invisible Killers

We like playing games in my blended, extended family. A favourite during lockdown was Deadly Disease Trumps,[1] thirty cards with different contagious diseases, from Anthrax to Whooping Cough, ranked by Incubation, Deaths, Fatality Rate, Pain Rating and Date of Discovery. While I'm unsure of the accuracy or current relevance of the facts, it was a good starting point for discussion. And macabrely entertaining. My stepdaughter, then aged ten, particularly liked playing it. A product of *Horrible Histories*, she likes gruesome facts, and we found that humour was a way to deal with the horrors of Covid.

Humankind has always lived in the shadow of contagion. Although epidemics play a lesser part in today's Britain – thanks to modern medicine, hygiene and access to healthcare – every now and then, a pandemic will surge like the wave of the Severn Bore. But, like the Bore, surely we should be able to work out when and how it will surge? Shouldn't we hear its rumble from miles away? Shouldn't we have the medical equivalent of a tide table? At the very least, in preparation, we should talk about contagion – with each other, to children – so that we can hope to navigate a way to live without terror of its visitation.

What is an epidemic? Peter Furtado gives this definition:

> [A]n infectious pathogen requires a population sufficiently settled and tightly grouped to allow it to spread from person to person… epidemics occur where enough people move far enough to encounter unfamiliar bacteria, viruses or parasites… a pandemic that causes widespread disease and death, bringing serious disruption to societies and their economies regionally or even globally, is not just a human tragedy or a medical event. It is one of historical importance.[2]

How does an invisible killer wheedle its way into our midst? Why does it strike down some and not others? How does it spread? We can listen to scientists, politicians and quacks for answers, but 'the popular response will reveal much about existing tensions in society'.[3] The Black Death, for example, was explained away as God's punishment on a sinful people. It was also blamed on outsiders, usually lepers or Jews. As for Covid, the finger has been pointed at China, at super-spreaders, at Big Pharma. And we know that some were more vulnerable to its grip. Those in care homes, the Black and Asian communities, the clinically vulnerable. There is no fairness in contagion.

The current threat of coronavirus is lessening. Masks have been tucked into kitchen drawers and hand sanitiser is being sold off cheap, but whether it's grief for loved ones, the persistence of long Covid, battling mental health issues or facing an uncertain future, the presence of contagion is still felt all around us. But we can look back to the beginning of 2020 and realise how far we've come, how much we've learned about ourselves and each other. And, whereas contagion has been a new experience for all of us currently on these isles, the people who went before knew it only too well.

☠☠☠

BUBONIC PLAGUE
Yersinia pestis
INCUBATION (AVG):   3–7 days
DEATHS/YEAR (currently): 125
FATALITY RATE: 30 to 100% if left untreated
PAIN RATING: 9
DISCOVERED: 541 AD

According to WHO,[4] contagion caused over fifty million deaths in Europe during the fourteenth century. In 1348, the bubonic plague, known as the Black Death, returned to Europe for the first time in six centuries, decimating sixty per cent of the population in some areas. Death really did do some serious dancing. Catherine Arnold says: 'Death, once the inevitable conclusion of a good Christian life, now became a terrifying apparition, striking without warning and wiping out an entire generation.'[5] At least a third of its victims died within five days due to 'the toxins that the germs make and huge lumps of germs breaking up vital bits of the body'.[6] Internal bleeding caused black bruises on skin, buboes or tumours on the neck, armpit and groin. Sometimes the infection attacked the brain and blood, sometimes it dissolved the lungs. It spread quickly. Varying theories were put forward, in particular, the 'miasma', a belief that the very air contained the disease – though there was agreement that close contact was a no-no.

It wasn't until 1894 that Alexandre Yersin, a Swiss-French physician and bacteriologist who had worked for Pasteur, isolated the bacterium responsible, a bacterium carried by fleas on the rats that swarmed the cities and made their way out to the countryside, burrowed in cloth and carried by people. It was named *Yersinia pestis* and, from this discovery, an anti-toxin was made. With the advent of antibiotics and good hygiene, the plague could finally be treated successfully. But until then, the plague would be back. As would something rather more mysterious.

☠☠☠

Fast-forward to summer 1485. Richard III has been slaughtered on Bosworth Field and the sweating sickness has killed off 900 poor souls in Shrewsbury within a week.[7] *Sudor anglicus* – the English Sweat – mainly affected well-off, native-born Englishmen aged fifteen to forty-five. It caused death within hours of symptoms first appearing and had a mortality rate of thirty to fifty per cent. Historians have suggested it may even have impacted Richard's defeat, because his powerful ally, Thomas Stanley, Earl of Derby, refused to fight, citing sickness as his excuse. Others suggest it may have arrived with the French mercenary army of Henry Tudor.[8] But there is little doubt that Henry postponed his coronation, as 15,000 Londoners (out of 50,000) had died of contagion within six weeks.

Henry VII was right to be fearful; seventeen years later, his son and heir, Prince Arthur, died of the Sweat in Ludlow Castle[9] as a young, fresh husband of Catherine of Aragon. Little did anyone know this would spark the Reformation. For, when Arthur's younger brother became Henry VIII, he married the widowed Catherine. When she failed to produce a male heir, Henry attempted to have the marriage annulled, claiming incest – that God would not recognise his marriage to his brother's wife. A good try but the Pope wasn't having it. Henry broke away from Rome, setting himself up as the new defender of the faith of the Protestant religion. When really, at the root of all this, was Anne Boleyn, the woman he'd set his sights on. Oh, the horror when Anne too caught the Sweat. Henry sent her far away, to isolate in her family home at Hever Castle, though he did at least have the goodness of heart to send his second-best physician. She pulled through. Only to have her head lobbed off a few years later. Bummer.[10]

In *Wolf Hall*, Hilary Mantel describes how the Sweat cast a large shadow over anti-hero Thomas Cromwell's life: '… gossip in the shops is all about pills and infusions, and friars in the streets are doing a lucrative trade in holy medals. This plague came to us in the year 1485, with the armies that brought us the first Henry Tudor. Now every few years it fills the graveyards. It kills in a day. Merry at breakfast, they say: dead by noon.'

You might think this strange contagion confined to the past but, in 1993, there was an outbreak of a similar disease among the Navajo people in Gallup, New Mexico. Known as the Four Corners infection, it was caused by *Sin Nombre*, hantavirus pulmonary syndrome (HPS).[11]

☠☠☠

'A plague o' both your houses!'

Back to our old enemy, *Yersinia pestis*, this time to Shakespeare, who lived his life under its brooding cloud. Same old buboes, same old skin lesions ('God's tokens'), but with a new grander name: the Great Plague. In 1564, the year of Shakespeare's birth, an outbreak wiped out a quarter of the population of his hometown, Stratford-upon-Avon. Down the line, in 1596, his eleven-year-old son, Hamnet,[12] died and, although there is no cause of death recorded in the parish register, it is assumed the plague was responsible.

Personal tragedy aside, the plague deeply affected Shakespeare's professional life. Theatres closed during peak times of contagion, as they did during Covid. Some even held the playhouses accountable. In 1577, for example, Preacher

Thomas White gave a Mary-Whitehouse-type sermon in the City, stating 'the cause of plagues is sin... and the cause of sin are plays... the cause of plagues are plays'.[13] When an outbreak in 1592–93 closed London's theatres, just as we found alternative creative outlets during lockdown, so too did Shakespeare, turning to poetry. He did alright.

The plague would return time and time again. According to Oliver Ainley, from 1603 to 1613, the Globe and other London theatres closed for seventy-eight months. Shakespeare retreated to Stratford. 'Without the distractions of Netflix or Joe Wicks workouts, historians reckon that during a quarantine period in 1606, Shakespeare used the time to write *King Lear*, *Anthony and Cleopatra* and *Macbeth*. Not a bad effort at all.'[14]

☠☠☠

The Play's the Thing

Shakespeare never explicitly portrays the plague on stage – certainly no one dies of it – but there are allusions to pestilence throughout his plays. According to Austin Tichenor, 'plague and pandemic cause chaos and disruption, pervasive themes throughout Shakespeare's plays, which are filled with reversals of fortune where loved ones die, allies are betrayed, kingdoms are lost, and characters are banished or flee.'[15]

And contagion is threaded through Shakespeare's language. Images and curses abound. Stephen Greenblatt says contagion is 'present for the most part as a steady, low-level undertone, surfacing in his characters' speeches most vividly in metaphorical expressions of rage and disgust.'[16]

> *He will hang upon him like a disease.*
> *He is sooner caught than the pestilence,*
> *and the taker runs presently mad.*
> *All the contagion of the south light on you*

Be as a planetary plague, when Jove
Will o'er some high-viced city hang his poison
In the sick air.

> *You herd of—Boils and plagues*
> *Plaster you o'er, that you may be abhorred*
> *Farther than seen, and one infect another*
> *Against the wind a mile!*

> *plagues that hang in this pendulous air.*

D IS FOR DEATH

> *It is now the very witching time of night*
> *when churchyards yawn and hell itself breathes out*
> *Contagion to this world*

Contagion is perhaps most obvious in *King Lear*. Imagine your father calling you 'a plague sore, an embossed carbuncle in my / Corrupted blood'. This is what Lear aims at his daughter, Goneril. The play's bleak atmosphere reflects the king's state of mind and, says James Shapiro, he is a changed man by the end, acknowledging his failure to ease his people's suffering. Shapiro adds: 'It may be too much to hope that our national leaders and international leaders right now may have a similar response.'[17]

These are difficult times. In October 1606 there are nearly 600 deaths in London. King James demands tougher measures, as tough as in Scotland (sound familiar?). The man of the house must report within two hours any plague symptoms in his home (all this without NHS Track and Trace). The household faces a vicious quarantine, shut up for forty days, their front door marked with a foot-long red cross and the words, 'Lord, have mercy upon us'. And mercy is needed; this is virtually a death sentence imposed on all the occupants. Watchmen are positioned outside, but a lack of resources and manpower means there are still escapes. But, even if you do manage to slip the watchmen, you can still be caught on the streets. If you are, and have no mark of plague, you will be whipped. If you have plague sores, you will be executed. (And we complained of a £100 fine.) Some might escape to the countryside, but cue villagers with pitchforks.

There are other similarities to our very own pandemic. Funeral attendance is limited to six people including the pallbearers and minister, with strict rules for burial. There is also PPE. Plague doctors wear beaked masks filled with herbs, long leather gloves and gowns. But there are no dogs for daily walks: they have been rounded up and killed to prevent transmission. Instead of barking, there is death knell after death knell, church bells often ringing for an hour at a time. This reminder of death is so constant that the authorities stop the ritual for fear of a downward spiral of morale – just as, in 1915, a law was passed to end it and likewise, during WW2, deaths were no longer reported in newspapers. This is echoed in *Macbeth*:

> *The dead man's knell*
> *Is there scarce asked for who, and good men's lives*
> *Expire before the flowers in their caps*
> *Dying or ere they sicken.*

As Shapiro notes: 'Though less than four lines long, there's probably not a better description of the terror and malaise plague carried with it.'[18]

The Diary of Samuel Pepys, Aged 32

Back in London, Samuel Pepys recorded the progress of the Great Plague of 1665 in his diaries. Excellent first-hand anecdotal evidence and surely the inspiration for Charles Pooter, Adrian Mole and Bridget Jones. The diary entries show the daily impact of living in the time of contagion.

> *June 7*, 1665: I did in Drury Lane see two or three houses marked with a red cross upon the doors, and 'Lord have mercy upon us' writ there; which was a sad sight to me, being the first of the kind that, to my remembrance, I ever saw.

Things soon move on apace.

> *July 20*: So walked to Redriffe, where I hear the sickness is, and indeed is scattered almost every where, there dying 1089 of the plague this week. My Lady Carteret did this day give me a bottle of plague-water home with me.[19]

By August, Pepys says the first day of the month is a 'publique fast... for the plague'. A communal ritual, like clapping for the NHS. But, by the 10th, death rates have soared. In London, the Company of Parish Clerks prints bills of mortality, the weekly numbers of burials (the earliest public health records and like the BBC's daily Covid updates). They show how people have died and, centuries later, we can track the huge weekly increases of plague deaths, though it is impossible to ascertain just how many have succumbed to the visitation. This grim job is given to 'sober Ancient Woemen' aka 'searchers of the dead', two in each parish. Summoned by the ringing of a bell, they must examine every corpse for buboes and record the cause of death, data which will be used for the bills of mortality. Not only are they putting their own lives at risk but, as they could be carriers, they must carry a red wand and keep their social distance. Some are considered witches and others are vulnerable to bribery – after all, the consequence of a reported plague death will lead to the shutting up of a house.[20]

> *Aug 12*: The people die so, that now it seems they are fain to carry the dead to be buried by day-light, the nights not sufficing to do it in. And my Lord Mayor commands people to be within at nine at night all, as they say, that the sick may have liberty to go abroad for ayre.

By now Pepys is facing his own mortality:

D IS FOR DEATH

Aug 16: I did deliver to him my last will, one part of it to deliver to my wife when I am dead... But, Lord! how sad a sight it is to see the streets empty of people... and about us two shops in three, if not more, generally shut up.

On 3 September, he writes a more mundane entry:

Up; and put on my coloured silk suit very fine, and my new periwigg, bought a good while since, but durst not wear, because the plague was in Westminster when I bought it; and it is a wonder what will be the fashion after the plague is done, as to periwiggs, for nobody will dare to buy any haire, for fear of the infection, that it had been cut off of the heads of people dead of the plague.

(I get it. A sad matter for me when I lost my hair during lockdown thanks to chemo and couldn't get a wig fitting or a hairdresser to at least give me a buzz cut. My partner made do with his nasal hair trimmers.)

Though this is no Partygate, Pepys does use alcohol as a coping mechanism:

Sept 15: ...thence with Captain Cocke, and there drank a cup of good drink, which I am fain to allow myself during this plague time, by advice of all, and not contrary to my oathe, my physician being dead, and chyrurgeon out of the way...

Then we are back to his hair:

Sept 20: ...the first time I have been touched by a barber these twelve-months... But, Lord! What a sad time it is to see no boats upon the River; and grass grows all up and down White Hall court, and nobody but poor wretches in the streets ... [the death count] is encreased about 600 more than the last... contrary to all our hopes and expectations, from the coldness of the late season...

A week later, things are a little more hopeful:

Sept 27: Here I saw this week's Bill of Mortality, wherein, blessed be God! There is above 1800 decrease, being the first considerable decrease we have had.

And then a Matt Hancock moment:

Nov 5: ...down by water to Deptford and there to my Valentine. Round about and next door on every side is the plague, but I did not value it, but there did what I would 'con elle'.

By now complacency has set in:

> *Nov 7*: Talking with him in the high way, come close by the bearers with a dead corpse of the plague; but, Lord! to see what custom is, that I am come almost to think nothing of it.

But still not good:

> *Nov 16*: Thence I walked to the Tower; but, Lord! how empty the streets are and melancholy, so many poor sick people in the streets full of sores; and so many sad stories overheard.

Six weeks later, by New Year's Eve, he tells us:

> 'the plague is abated almost to nothing… the town fills apace, and shops begin to be open again. Pray God continue the plague's decrease.'

By February 1666, the king and his court have returned to London.

☠☠☠

Daniel Defoe: A Journal of the Plague Year

One could mistake Defoe's book for another diary, but it is actually a work of fiction. After all, he was only five years old in 1665. *A Journal of the Plague Year* was published in 1722, alongside *Moll Flanders* and several other works, which makes Defoe's demise in poverty, less than a decade later, hiding from creditors, such a sad ending. A curious mix of stories, documents, graphs and stats, the book is 'a sort of cross between a novel, a memento mori, and a self-help book, for which Defoe studied the medical treatises, the official broadsides, and the Bills of Mortality of 1665 to ground his stories and London's cultural memories in historical fact'.[21]

The narrator stays in London throughout the epidemic and relies 'upon the Goodness and Protection of the Almighty' and, just as Pepys recorded, the narrator describes public prayers and fasting days which 'implore the Mercy of God, to avert the dreadful Judgment, which hung over their Heads'. He also tells us that playhouses, gaming tables, public dancing rooms, music houses and puppet shows are shut down – 'Death was before their Eyes, and every body began to think of their Graves, not of Mirth and Diversions.'

Defoe wrote *A Journal* during the Age of Enlightenment, with a more reasoned thought process than Pepys, understanding that plague is spread by infection, 'by some certain Steams, or Fumes, which the physicians call Effluvia, by the Breath, or by the Sweat, or by the Stench of the Sores of the sick Persons'. And, although all creation belongs to God, including infection, he believes the science that 'no one in this whole Nation ever receive'd the Sickness or Infection, but who receive'd it in the ordinary Way of Infection from some Body, or the Cloaths, or touch, or stench of some Body that was infected before'. He knew the source of the plague could be traced to a ship coming from Holland, and before that from the Levant, and 'that it proceeded from Person to Person, and from House to House, and no otherwise'.

Furthermore, the narrator understood that contagion was worsened by a lack of preparation, not laying in provisions (oh, the toilet paper!) and by people becoming blasé, mixing with the 'Well' (the asymptomatic) who 'breathed Death in every Place, and upon every body who came near them'. This is why shutting up households would only work if you shut up everybody its members had come into contact with. Far better to have more pest-houses and far more effective to have social distancing and bubbles, 'separating the People into smaller Bodies, and removing them in Time farther from one another'.

However, basically, he knows that 'the best Physick against the Plague is to run away from it'. He has witnessed the horrors, epitomised by his visit one night to a plague pit:

> [T]he Cart had in it sixteen or seventeen bodies, some were wrapt up in Linen Sheets, some in Rugs, some little other than naked, or so loose, that what Covering they had, fell from them, in the shooting out of the Cart, and they fell quite naked among the rest; but the Matter was not much to them, or the Indecency much to anyone else, seeing they were all dead, and were to be huddled together into the Common Grave of Mankind ... for here was no Difference made, but Poor and Rich went together.

He is also aware that contagion highlights disparity. Servants and workers inevitably come off worse, becoming infected while running errands and doing their own chores. The poor have the most dangerous jobs – nursing victims, taking the ill to the pest-house, pushing dead carts, burying corpses. Our modern-day paramedics, nurses, doctors and social care workers.

As for himself, the narrator spends lockdown reading books and writing this account. He also makes his own beer and bread – not sure if it was sourdough – but can't get hold of meat, as the plague 'raged so violently among the Butchers, and Slaughterhouses' (which might be karma according to some militant vegans). He also describes the precautions taken when people must venture out. Just as we became accustomed to contactless payments to limit infection spread, shoppers during the Great Plague put coins into vinegar, using small denominations to avoid handling change and carrying 'Bottles for Scents, and Perfumes in their Hands', as we used hand sanitiser and facemasks.

During the height of our lockdown, when no partners could be present for childbirth in hospital, there was always a midwife. However, during Defoe's plague, women mostly had to make do without a midwife, as most of them were dead. There were many stillbirths and maternal deaths, particularly amongst the poor. He warns that if this happens again, 'all Women that are with Child or that give Suck should be gone; if they have any possible Means out of the Place; because their Misery if infected, will so much exceed all other Peoples'.

As time goes on, in an echo of the great fire that would burn London to the ground the following year, the narrator describes how the plague raged out of control 'with such Violence that the Citizens in Despair, gave over their Endeavours to extinguish it', the people believing 'all regulations and Methods were in vain, and that there was nothing to be hoped for, but an universal Desolation'.

Finally, 'the Malignity of the Disease abated'. People no longer worry (just as with the Omicron variant). Physicians advise people 'to continue reserv'd, and to use still utmost Caution in their ordinary Conduct … not to entertain in their Houses, or converse with any People who they knew came from such infected Places'. Just as we were told to be 'vigilant'.

☠☠☠

While in the world of fiction, I must mention Terry Nation's *Survivors*, a post-apocalyptic 1970s TV drama with tie-in novels. The preface: how do you live, beyond survival, when 95 per cent of the population has died within a very short time? How do you build for the future? I was a child of about seven or eight when I first watched this series, with some scenes so vivid that, when I re-watched it recently on Britbox, after nearly fifty years, I was taken right back to being that child, wondering what would happen if my world turned upside down. It put Covid into a little perspective, but there is a small part of me that thinks this scenario could actually happen. Would I be a survivor? Would you?

Let's keep funding scientists, people!

☠☠☠

True Story

9 May 2023, a birthday treat. A visit to the village of Eyam in Derbyshire, a village with a remarkable past. In 1665, a tailor ordered some cloth from London. Unknowingly, this delivery was flea-infested and brought with it the plague. Before the summer months, when instances of contagion inevitably increase, the vicar and the previous incumbent got together and decided on a course of action. They must close the church and have open-air services in

family groups. The dead must be buried in unconsecrated ground without funerals. But, most drastically, they would persuade the village to quarantine, with no one allowed to enter or leave until the plague has passed. And this the villagers agreed to.

To prevent starvation, people from the neighbouring area left food on the village boundary and, as payment, the inhabitants put coins into the vinegar-filled holes of the boundary stone. But there are some terrible stories, the most heart-breaking that of Elizabeth Hancock of Riley Farm, situated a quarter of a mile outside the village. During eight days in August 1666, poor Elizabeth lost her husband and six children, having to take on the role of sexton and bury them herself on her land. Out of perhaps 350 inhabitants of Eyam, only eighty-four survived.

The museum puts this time of turmoil into context – especially so since the visitation of Covid-19. I walk around the village, to see the homes where households were wiped out and to visit the church, which remembers the self-sacrifice of their parishioners and their pioneering effort of social distancing. I think of these people and marvel.

Elizabeth Hancock

A few decades earlier, there is a similar response to the plague of 1632–33 by the village of Oberammergau in Bavaria. During the church festival in 1632, a man called Kaspar Schisler[22] brings contagion into the village. The leaders come together. They pray and they pledge to hold a Passion play every ten years. From then on, although many catch the plague, it kills no one. The villagers have been answered by God and, keeping their word, they stage the first Passion play during the Whitsun celebrations of 1634, on a stage erected on the cemetery containing the graves of plague victims.

The promise has been kept throughout the following centuries, and every ten years the play is performed. From Ash Wednesday onwards into the end of the play season, the members observe the 'Hair and Beard Decree', which asks that all participants 'let their hair grow out, and the males to also grow a beard' (apart from the Romans!). There have only been a few misses. In 1920, the play was postponed until 1922, following the upheavals of WW1. On the 300th anniversary in 1934, Hitler showed up with some leading Nazis. Impressed, he called Pilate superior in 'race and intelligence… a rock in the midst of the Jewish vermin and swarm'. In 1940, there was no performance for obvious reasons. By 1990, the play had been modernised and its antisemitism revised. In 2020 the Passion play once again had to be postponed, for the same reason it was started in the first place: as a response to contagion. And would you believe it, I had booked tickets! The 42nd Oberammergau Passion Play took place from 14 May to 2 October 2022. Sadly, I was unable to go, my finances stretched with the challenges of Covid. But I am saving up for 2030.[23]

☠☠☠

CHOLERA
Vibrio cholerae
INCUBATION: 12 hours to 5 days
DEATHS:/Year: 142K
FATALITY RATE: 1%
PAIN RATING: 6
DISCOVERED: 1854

Cholera is an acute diarrhoeal infection caused by food or water contaminated with the bacterium *Vibrio cholerae*. It is an easily treatable disease through prompt administration of oral rehydration solutions, but it persists as a problem. According to the WHO:

> Cholera remains a global threat to public health and an indicator of inequity and lack of social development and can kill within hours if left untreated. Cholera might be easy to treat but a multifaceted approach is needed to control it, and to reduce deaths in the developing world: surveillance, water, sanitation and hygiene, social mobilisation, treatment, and oral cholera vaccines.[24]

We might be a developed nation now, but things were grim epidemic-wise here in the nineteenth century, due to the insanitary conditions of crowded cities brought about by the Industrial Revolution, in addition to the movement of large armies and refugees. Cholera struck Britain in the 1830s and, because local boards were established to reform sanitation and provide clean water and safe sewage disposal, it has been linked to the development of public health.[25]

In 1832, there were cholera riots in Liverpool due to fear of the disease and worry that bodies of the poor would be used for dissection (remember those body snatchers?). Kitty Wilkinson took a more practical approach. Living in one of the worst slums in the city, she allowed her neighbours to wash their clothes in her kitchen and to dry them outside, all for a penny to help towards expenses. She did this for over eighty families a week. 'Here then,' says Newland, 'was the germ of public wash-houses, institutions called into existence as a means of palliating a great evil.'[26]

In 1855, an outbreak of cholera killed 3,000 Londoners. Dr John Snow of Soho identified a water pump close to his home as the source of the infection. After its handle was removed, the outbreak ended. It was discovered that the well had been contaminated by a nearby cesspit. Three years later, in the summer of 1858, the height of the Industrial Revolution, raw sewage in the Thames combined with hot weather to result in the Great Stink. This ultimately led to the construction of London's vast sewage system, the brainchild of Joseph Bazalgette, which would end the threat of cholera in this country.[27]

The Silent Highwayman (1858)

TYPHOID FEVER
Salmonella typhi
INCUBATION (AVG): 12 days
DEATHS/YEAR: 160K
FATALITY RATE: 4%
PAIN RATING: 8
DISCOVERED: 1880

Typhoid fever is a highly contagious, life-threatening bacterial infection that can spread into the bloodstream and affect many organs. Without treatment, it can be fatal. The bacterium, *Salmonella typhi*, is related to the bacteria that causes food poisoning, and the disease is transmitted by consuming food or water contaminated with the faeces of an infected person. Therefore, typhoid is associated with poor sanitation and unhygienic preparation of food. According to the WHO, '[u]rbanization and climate change have the potential to increase the global burden of typhoid. In addition, increasing resistance to antibiotic treatment is making it easier for typhoid to spread through overcrowded populations in cities and inadequate and/or flooded water and sanitation systems.'[28] A very good reason to vaccinate.

During a typhoid fever outbreak in New York in the 1900s, George Soper, an expert in sanitation and self-titled 'epidemic fighter', set out to find the source, believing disease could be spread by a single carrier. During his investigation, he discovered the common denominator of each infected household: Mary Mallon. Mary, an Irish immigrant, worked as cook to rich New Yorkers in their summer homes. Her signature dish, served on Sundays, was ice cream with fresh peaches; here the germs were carried, in uncooked food. After refusing to give samples, Mallon was escorted to hospital, where she tested positive as a carrier for *Salmonella typhi*, the first identified asymptomatic carrier.

Mary was quarantined in a house in the grounds of the hospital, located on North Brother Island on the East River outside New York City. Now known as Typhoid Mary, she was eventually released on condition she no longer cook for others. But, having no other skills, and not believing that she was the carrier, she went back to cooking, under various assumed names, in various places including a hotel, a spa, and a restaurant. When there was an outbreak of typhoid in 1915 at a maternity hospital, Soper was called in and discovered – yes, you got it – the cook was Mary, the quintessential superspreader. She was taken back to the island, where she remained for the next twenty-three years until she died of a stroke in 1938. At least fifty-one people caught typhoid from Mary and three of them died.

☠☠☠

And a story from my own family, of my great-uncle, Thomas Gibson Gillespy, a microbiologist who worked in the canning industry at the research station in Chipping Campden. His research took him to the beef canning plants of Argentina, where he discovered that *Salmonella typhi* from the contaminated water of the local river could leak into the can during the cooling process. During the 1960s, back in the UK, there were outbreaks of typhoid, the most infamous in Aberdeen in 1964, where 507 people caught the disease and three died. The source was a can of corned beef from Argentina. Aberdeen found itself at the centre of a political and food policy scandal and the Queen had to visit the city to boost its morale and reputation. To this day, its people are said to wash their hands more than anyone else in Scotland. As for Uncle Tom, he received an OBE for his services to food safety in 1968, which hopefully made up for not being able to donate his body to science.

☠☠☠

TUBERCULOSIS (TB)
Mycobacterium tuberculosis
INCUBATION (AVG):   6 weeks
DEATHS/YEAR: 1.5M
FATALITY RATE: 43%
PAIN RATING: 7
DISCOVERED: 4000 BC

TB is caused by bacteria (*Mycobacterium tuberculosis*) and most often affects the lungs. The disease is spread through the air when people with TB cough, sneeze or spit. A person only needs to inhale a few germs to become infected. According to the WHO, every year, 10 million people fall ill with tuberculosis and, despite being a preventable and curable disease, 1.5 million people die from it, making TB the world's top infectious killer. It is also the leading cause of death of people with HIV and a major contributor to antimicrobial resistance.[29]

Classic symptoms of tuberculosis of the lungs include fevers, night sweats, weight loss, chronic coughing and sputum containing blood. The 'wasting away' led to the nineteenth-century name of 'consumption', as the disease was seen to be consuming the individual. At this time, overcrowding and poor sanitation meant TB thrived, becoming the primary cause of death among the urban working classes.

TB also affected the rich and famous and, despite its horrors, became synonymous with beauty and creativity. John Keats, who had trained in medicine, saw his blood-stained handkerchief after a coughing fit and said: 'I cannot be deceived in that colour; – that drop of blood is my death-warrant; – I must die.' He was seen to be of 'heightened sensibility' and his work was 'elevated because of consumption's effect on the mind'.[30] (More of him later.)

In 1882, Robert Koch proved that *Mycobacterium tuberculosis* caused the disease, establishing its contagious nature. '[T]he disease, once so clouded in romantic imagery and mystery, was revealed to be much more prosaic. Romantic portrayals and perceptions of consumption were gradually replaced with scientific facts, and the once-mysterious disease was transformed into a public health problem.'[31]

Young woman dying of TB, represented by the Grim Reaper

INFLUENZA
Orthomyxoviridae
INCUBATION (AVG): 2 days
DEATHS (/YEAR): 290K to 650K
FATALITY RATE: 0.1%
PAIN RATING: 1 (according to Deadly Diseases. I beg to differ)
DISCOVERED: 2400BC

It is the eve of the new millennium. Midnight. I am standing at the bedroom window of our boys' bedroom in East Dulwich, where we have a view of the City. I am holding our middle child, a proficient non-sleeper, not yet three-and-a-half years old, now with a temperature. It's going to be a long night. But he is alert enough to point at the pretty colours lighting up the night sky over St Paul's, our council taxes literally going up in smoke.

I feel like I have recovered from the brink of death. This is no exaggeration. (Maybe a tad.) A few days before Christmas I was struck down with what is becoming known as millennium flu. What starts with aches and pains late one afternoon, sees me on my hands and knees crawling up to bed a couple of hours later. I do not leave my bed for a week, passing days sleeping fitfully and nights adrift with feverish hallucinations, my head filled with my very own fireworks display. One night, I wouldn't have cared if I died. I would have welcomed it. (If you *think* you've had the flu, you probably haven't. You *know* when you've had it.) Another week and I'm still weak. My chest hurts. I see a doctor, who says there's nothing he can prescribe except rest, hydration, paracetamol. I must wait it out.

Another week and I am a little better, but it is months before I slough off the fatigue. I sometimes wonder if this was the turning point for my health. Did it trigger the fibromyalgia I was finally diagnosed with a decade later?

Influenza or flu is a highly contagious virus that attacks the respiratory system, transmitted when the infected person coughs, sneezes or speaks, spreading droplets that those nearby can inhale. It can also spread through touching something that has been touched by an infected person and then touching your mouth or nose or eyes. I could have caught the flu anywhere, but it was most likely from our older son, who was in reception at primary school. He had a nasty cold which, now I look back, I can see was probably flu. I then passed it onto our two other children and my mother, who came to look after us. None of the others were quite as ill as me. If I had lived a hundred years previously, would I have died in the flu pandemic of 1918 to 1920? After all, the Spanish flu accounted for anything between fifty and a hundred million global deaths, spread by post-war military movement across the world and with no effective drugs. No antibiotics. No vaccines.

This event always seemed far off, but we have all experienced something similar of late. Those staggering numbers are now shot through with more personal significance.

☠☠☠

AIDS/HIV
human immunodeficiency virus
INCUBATION (AVG): 5 years
DEATHS (/YEAR): 1.6M
FATALITY RATE: 90%
PAIN RATING: 2
DISCOVERED: 1983

According to the WHO, human immunodeficiency virus (HIV) is 'an infection that attacks the body's immune system, specifically the white blood cells called CD4 cells ... weakening a person's immunity against opportunistic infections, such as tuberculosis and fungal infections, severe bacterial infections and some cancers'. In 2021, 38.4 million people worldwide were living with HIV, with 75 per cent having access to antiretroviral therapy.[32]

Just over forty years ago, on 4 July 1982, Terry Higgins, aged thirty-seven, was one of the first people to die in the UK of an AIDS-related illness, though it wasn't diagnosed as such then. A month earlier he had collapsed in Heaven, a gay nightclub under the arches of Charing Cross station, a place

I'd visit five years later, on a night out with my boyfriend, his sister and a group of her friends, gay and straight. Back in Lancaster, we students were urged not to die of ignorance, the Tombstone campaign breathing terror through campus.[33]

Terry's partner and friends set up the Terrence Higgins Trust in his memory, using his name to personalise and humanise AIDS, the stigma of which, because it was sexually transmitted, was associated with promiscuity. Their intention was to prevent others from suffering and to raise funds for research and awareness of the illness. They were the first charity in the UK to be set up 'in response to the HIV epidemic and have been at the forefront of the fight against HIV and AIDS ever since'.[34]

Effective treatment now means a diagnosis of HIV is no longer a death sentence. Antiretroviral drugs (ARVs) are so effective that this triple therapy has been known as the Lazarus effect, 'pulling individuals from the jaws of death'.[35] As well as having 'new life', there is also a huge economic benefit, as there is once again the chance to earn a living.

But these treatments have not been easy to come by. Activists have worked hard for them. Sufferers have endured gruesome experimental treatments. But now, it is possible to live a good life with HIV, as long as there is free access to these ARVs.

CORONAVIRUS DISEASE (COVID-19)
severe acute respiratory syndrome coronavirus 2 (SARS-CoV-2)

INCUBATION:	2–10 days
DEATHS (/YEARS):	TBC
FATALITY RATE:	TBC
PAIN RATING:	TBC
DISCOVERED:	2019

According to the WHO, as of 13 July 2023, the pandemic for our times has killed nearly seven million people across the globe.[36] I'm not going to write much here about Covid as we have all just lived through its contagion. We still are. We don't know what the future holds, and we still need time to process events. As for me? I have been lucky. I haven't lost a loved one. Despite receiving a diagnosis of breast cancer during lockdown in 2020, I had prompt surgery and my treatment wasn't impacted, the only difference being that I had to shield and go through the treatment alone. But I thank the NHS from the bottom of my heart. And, thanks to four vaccinations, and sensible precautions, I have yet to catch this disease.

SMALLPOX
variola major and minor
INCUBATION: 12 days
DEATHS (/YEAR): 2M (before eradication)
FATALITY RATE: 30%
PAIN RATING: 7
DISCOVERED: 1500 BC

Smallpox is an acute contagious disease caused by the variola virus, a member of the orthopoxvirus family. Believed to have existed for 3,000 years, it has been one of the most devastating diseases known to humanity, killing millions.

Lady Mary Wortley Montagu is known as the woman who introduced smallpox inoculation into Britain. Born in 1689, she was a remarkable lady of letters, a scientist and a feminist. She married Edward Wortley Montagu and lived briefly in Wortley Hall in South Yorkshire (the 'Workers' Stately Home' associated with the British Labour Movement and well worth a visit). At twenty-six, Mary contracted smallpox, as did her brother. He died and, although she recovered, she was badly marked. The following year, she accompanied her husband to Istanbul when he was appointed ambassador to the Ottoman Empire. Here, Mary visited a bath house where she noticed the women's unblemished skin. She went on to witness the practice of smallpox inoculation, where a child's arm was scratched by a needle dipped in smallpox matter. So impressed was she that, whilst her husband was away, she arranged for her son, Edward, to be inoculated by English surgeon Charles Maitland. Edward had a mild form of the disease, made a quick recovery and gained lifelong immunity.

They returned to England in 1718 and, during a smallpox epidemic of 1721, Mary had her daughter inoculated – the first recorded case of inoculation (variolation) here. Like her brother, little Mary responded well. According to Jennifer Rudd, 'Edward Jenner is rightly remembered as the "father of vaccination", but Mary was the "mother of inoculation", taking the first steps in preventative medicine 75 years before him.'[37]

C IS FOR CONTAGION

Lady Mary Worley Montagu with her son Edward
by Jean Baptiste Vanmour, c.1717

The mantle was taken on by Catherine the Great of Russia, whose country was blighted with the disease. She persuaded an English doctor and expert inoculator, Thomas Dimsdale, to travel in secret to St Petersburg and inoculate her. Backed by her Enlightenment ideals, she fought superstition with science and became a pioneer in vaccine rollout. She wrote to her friend, Voltaire, about the success, calling the sceptics 'truly blockheads, ignorant or just wicked'.[38] You can read all about it in Lucy Ward's novel, *The Empress and the English Doctor: How Catherine the Great Defied a Deadly Virus*.

End note: good news. Following widespread immunisation, in 1980 the WHO declared smallpox eradicated, the only infectious disease to achieve this. It is one of the most profound public health successes in history. And I have the scar to prove it.

☠☠☠

Only now there's monkey pox… Maybe one day that will be added to Deadly Disease Trumps? And who knows what else lies ahead? So, meanwhile, play the game, talk about it, joke, be serious, and try not to live in fear but with sense and science.

D
IS FOR DISPOSAL

Resting Places of the Dead

disposal *verb*
1. the act of disposing of something; the act of throwing something away.
e.g. rubbish, nuclear waste, a human cadaver.

A pick-axe, and a spade, a spade,
For and a shrouding sheet:
O, a pit of clay for to be made
For such a guest is meet.
HAMLET

Even dust as I am now
And thou in time shall be
Such one was I as thou:
Behold thyself by me.
ST STEPHEN'S, IPSWICH

☠☠☠

The disposal of human corpses is the practice and process of dealing with the remains of a deceased human. Some of the more thoughtful and forward-thinking of funeral directors don't like the phrase 'disposal', with its connotations of waste, but I will use it here (for the sake of my alphabet if nothing else).
Disposal methods vary according to circumstance, location, belief system,

the law, the manner of death and the condition of the body. Across the globe, you can be buried six feet under, left on a mountain top for the birds to pick away your flesh, or – if you have the money and inclination – put in a deep freeze in the hope of time travel to a future where you could be thawed, when science and medicine has advanced enough to prolong your life, possibly for eternity. Or you could go for a natural burial, your body returning to the earth, the ultimate in recycling. The alternative is cremation, at a crematorium or on a pyre. Your ashes can then be scattered at a favourite or sacred place or kept on the mantelpiece in the family home, or stored on a shelf in a columbarium or shot into space or made into a piece of memorial jewellery or tattoo. Or there are new, developing ways such as resomation or terramation. Whichever disposal method is chosen, your body should be treated with respect and dignity. And then, hopefully, your name will be recorded somewhere, a marker for your loved ones to visit you in memoriam and for future generations to know who went before them.

Honouring the dead is part of being human. And possibly even Neanderthal. A 50,000-year-old skeleton was discovered in a cave in France early last century, and recent analysis by archaeologists suggests that, because it had been found in a depression fashioned into some sort of grave, it had been intentionally buried. This 'raises the possibility that the evolution of human burial began with the simple modification of natural pits for funerary use'.[1]

A history of the disposal of human remains is the history of our world.

☠☠☠

And All Things Draw towards St Enodoc

When I was two, not long after I saw poor Miss Bowles on her staircase, we went on holiday to Trebetherick on the Camel estuary in Cornwall. My father was a golfer and, looking back, I understand the lure of this place, deeper than its obvious charm; our hotel was practically on the links course. As you crossed the fairway, you could see the top half of the wonky spire of St Enodoc's rising out of the sand dunes. Legend has it that a Victorian vicar and his parishioners had to be lowered once a year through the roof of the half-buried church to allow it to remain open, though, eventually, much of the sand was cleared. Former poet laureate and lover of English churches, John Betjeman, is buried in the churchyard here, his happy place. I don't remember this first visit to Trebetherick, but we returned two years later, to the same hotel, grandparents in tow, and I have vague memories: the smell of crispy bacon and the tang of grapefruit juice for breakfast. Concealing myself in a wardrobe during a game of hide-and-seek with my brothers and being toppled over against the bed, so I was trapped inside. And I remember seeing the church on one of our walks and being mesmerised by the sight of it shimmering in the dunes. A mirage. 'Sometimes dodging golf balls, other times battling Atlantic gales – a visit to St Enodoc's is never straightforward, ever different, and always a delight.'[2]

Seventeen years later, as young honeymooners, we were driving through Trebetherick in my mother-in-law's yellow Triumph Dolomite, a new exhaust just fitted by my uncle, who conveniently lived in Newlyn. Long-hidden memories rushed back. Dad's Rover. The three of us squabbling in the back. 'The Age of Aquarius' playing on Dad's 8-track player. The golf course. The St Moritz Hotel. The church with its wonky spire. We parked up now, pilgrimaged across the fairways, chasing ghosts, hunting for something and, having just graduated with an English degree, I was ecstatic to worship at the literary shrine of Betjeman's grave. Then we had a cream tea on the terrace of the hotel, basking in a late September sun. The start of my married life, and I was looking back over my shoulder. But that is what graveyards do, they connect us to the dead. To those who have gone before.

☠☠☠

Tombstone Tourist

I am a taphophile. A lover of graves. A church crawler. Ever since living in the sweet shop in Torquay, where the boneyard up the road became our back garden, I have been drawn to burial grounds and cemeteries of all sorts and sizes. I have visited Bristol's Arnos Vale and seen the final resting places of a suffragette and an Indian raja; I've endured a ghost tour of Greyfriar's Kirkyard in Edinburgh's Old Town; I've enjoyed the famous splendour of Highgate in north London and, south of the Thames, I've taken my young children to open days at the lesser-known Nunhead. Further afield, I've travelled to Paris's Père Lachaise, inspiration for the Magnificent Seven garden cemeteries of Victorian London. I've climbed up the Mount of Olives in the heat of the day, touched the ancient olive trees in the Garden of Gethsemane and, next to the bus station, ducked into the coolness of the borrowed tomb at Golgotha, the Place of the Skull. Just recently I hustled through the souks of Marrakesh to admire the exquisitely tiled Saadian Tombs of the Moorish sultans in the shadows of the Kasbah Mosque. Still on my list is Glasgow's Necropolis, Belfast's Milltown cemetery, the Isle of the Dead (Oileán na Márbh), where lost babies are buried, the Isle of Iona, resting place for sixty kings (including Macbeth), and Bardsey Island (Ynys Enlli), where 20,000 saints are alleged to be buried (including King Arthur).

In between forays to grand cemeteries and ancient burial sites, I like nothing more than to bob into the country churches of Devon and the Marches. Go to any rural parish and you will discover that these hallowed sites are nearly always open,[3] always free, and they hold a millennium and more of social history, important collections of the nation's art, and are the go-to place for genealogy. Most have a churchyard where parishioners have been buried, body upon body, layer upon layer, century after century, raising the ground so high that the path to the church itself is often sunk well below the level of the graves. And it is in these churchyards, and within the churches themselves, that I have realised my passion for tombs, deepened by the knowledge of experts such as Nikolaus Pevsner and a whole online community.

If you're ever at a loose end, go to your local parish church, where, if you get past the Victorian restoration, you might find a Norman tower, a Romanesque doorway, an Anglo-Saxon font, a Jacobean pulpit. You might spot a faded fresco, a piece of medieval morality whitewashed over during the Reformation and rediscovered centuries later. Look up at the ceiling: this is the universe. Examine the bosses, the wooden carvings and stone sculptures of angels and green men and all manner of fantastical creatures. Sit in the choir stalls and smile at the humour of the misericords or in Georgian boxed pews with names of the gentry who poured money into their parish to secure front-row seats and whose families commissioned the best of wall plaques, for, even though they too could die young, they at least would be remembered, their monuments protected inside from the ravages of nature and time. Read about those knights with feet resting on tiny lions,[4] not necessarily warriors but captured in the prime of life, their armour showing off their status. And their widows, sleeping eternally beside them, hands in prayer – sometimes looking more than a little fed-up. You might be lucky enough to come across a cadaver tomb or cenotaph[5] such as the skeletal effigy of Abbot John Wakeman (designed by himself as a memento mori) in Tewkesbury Abbey. Or follow the path of pilgrims and stay awhile at the shrine of a saint such as St Werburgh in Chester Cathedral.

Look down at the flagstones beneath your feet, worn with the footsteps of worshippers over centuries. Marvel at the medieval tiles with fleurs-de-lys and more tiny lions. Decipher the inscriptions on the ledger stones, the names of the dead engraved in marble, alabaster, slate, brass. And back to the walls where many English parish churches have one or two diamond-shaped funerary hatchments dedicated to local dignitaries with Latin inscriptions related to death or resurrection. *Resurgam. Memento mori. In coelo quies.*

Such history, such art, such memorialisation. Layer upon layer.

Much of the medieval was destroyed in the Reformation. Later the memorials contained more classical imagery such as urns or inverted torches which signified death, angels which represented everlasting life or, if playing trumpets, raising the dead on Judgement Day. In some churches, such as St Giles's in Wrexham, several worshipping angels soar up high playing instruments including the bagpipes, just as in St Giles's in Edinburgh[6] or nearby Rosslyn Chapel.[7]

Dip down to the crypt with its vaulted ceilings. Feel the cold on your skin and hear the whisper of bones as you step back through the centuries. Undercrofts in churches like St Bride's off Fleet Street reveal a microcosm of life. Rebuilt by Sir Christopher Wren after the Great Fire, St Bride's has been a place of worship and burial since Roman times. Although it yet again suffered devastating fire during the Blitz, its wedding-cake spire and outer walls stayed intact. During its restoration, excavations in the crypt revealed six previous churches on the site, the remnants of a Roman pavement and stained glass warped by the Great Fire. More astonishing were the nearly 7,000 human remains unearthed in a medieval charnel[8] (or bone) house, exhumed and relocated from their original burial ground, grouped together by bone type. Femurs, ulnas, skulls. Some of them were victims of the Great Plague and the cholera epidemic of 1854, which claimed 10,000 Londoners, leaving churchyards and crypts dangerously overflowing. When Parliament decreed there should be no more burials in the City, the crypts were sealed.

Known as the journalists' church, St Bride's has long been associated with the press, ever since Wynkyn de Worde, apprentice to Caxton, set up shop in the churchyard in 1500. St Bride's has a fascinating history. During the reign of Queen Mary, for example, one of its priests and two parishioners were burned at the stake for their beliefs, and there are connections to the Pilgrim Fathers, who travelled the Atlantic to find a new life where they could worship freely. And then there's our friend Mr Pepys, born next door and baptised in the church. His mother even had her own pew here.

During September 1665, the height of the Plague, the vicar buried 636 people; 2,111 died in the parish that year. Peirson remained in situ throughout. He survived. But his successor was only in post for two weeks when, after a summer of drought, on the evening of 2 September 1666, fire broke out in a bakery on Pudding Lane. Two days later, St Bride's was engulfed in flames and destroyed.

> Up by five o'clock; and blessed be God! find all well: and by water to Paul's wharf. Walked thence, and saw all the towne burned; and a miserable sight of Paul's church, with all the roof fallen, and the body of the quire fallen into St Fayth's; Paul's school also, Ludgate and Fleet-street, my father's house and the church [St Bride's]... the like.[9]

All this history on one sacred site.

D IS FOR DISPOSAL

St Bride's Church

God's Acre

In parts of the UK, surviving Neolithic tumuli[10] and dolmen[11] reveal our long-standing need to bury and mourn the dead, to send them on their way to the next world with rituals and ceremonies. The most impressive space I have stood in is Maeshowe on Mainland Orkney built around 5,000 years ago in one of the richest Neolithic landscapes in Europe – 'a place of stone circles, villages and burial monuments, where people lived, worshipped, and honoured their dead'.[12] Its grass mound conceals passages and chambers built of flagstone, aligned so the winter sun illuminates the rear wall of the central chamber. During its long history, it was looted by Vikings, who left drunken graffiti, throwaway comments for them but, for us, 'the largest collection of runic inscriptions to survive outside Scandinavia – and a powerful reminder that Orkney was under Norwegian rule until 1469'.

As a means of disposal of human remains, burial was the Christian tradition, reflecting the burial and resurrection of Christ. Over the last 1,500 years of Christianity on these islands, burials have taken place within the church or in the churchyard (a burial site attached to a church as opposed to a graveyard or burial ground without a church). These churches were sometimes built on pagan sites, while others remained where they had been established in Roman times. These hallowed, liminal spaces have provided a place for the dead of a community, pastoral care for the dying and for mourners, and a sense of place and local identity.

The churchyard, known as God's Acre,[13] or kirkyard in Scotland, had purposes other than burial; in medieval times, it was also used for fairs, markets, sports and sheep grazing. Few ancient grave markers remain in situ; some have been brought inside for protection, such as the highly decorated Viking hogback stone in my parish church of St Bridget's in West Kirby. Outside, you will usually find the oldest tombs closest to the church, though no grave may be dug within twelve feet of its wall, with most on the south side so the shadow of the church would not fall across the burial place. The north side was reserved for outsiders or outcasts. Witches. Suicides.

Local stone was used for marker stones – granite in Cornwall, flint in East Anglia, slate in Wales – and stonemasons had their own style. You can wander amongst chest and altar tombs, bolster graves, upright headstones, ledgers, obelisks, angels, Celtic crosses, Calvary crosses, Anglo-Saxon crosses, pedestal tombs, huge mausolea, cast-iron railings separating the well-to-do from the hoi polloi, and mort safes to keep off those body snatchers. You might come across a rare stone sarcophagus, possibly Anglo-Saxon, once used as an actual coffin, such as in the churchyard of St Lawrence's, Church Stretton, or St Thomas's in Box. Or even a pyramid tomb such as Sophie Rutherford's, made of pink granite in Dean Village, Edinburgh, or William Mackenzie's in Liverpool or, back in St Thomas's, Box, built in this shape, it is said, to prevent the occupant's wife from dancing on his grave.[14]

Hunt for those skulls and hourglasses, the winged cherubs, the clasped hands, a broken column to indicate a life cut short, a memento mori sundial, or the early Christian symbol of anchors on the graves of sailors and fishermen. Ponder the epitaphs of lost loves, lost infants, lost mothers. Head for the further parts of the graveyard, perhaps in an adjacent field, and you might see the body mound of a freshly filled grave, with flowers all around. Search out a simple headstone made of gleaming white Portland stone. A Commonwealth war grave.[15] Weaving through the tombstones, pick your way around the hollows brought about by disintegrating coffins beneath. Remember the Christian tradition of burying the body with its head to the west and feet to the east so the resurrected would be facing the right direction on Judgement Day.

Death, memory and the afterlife are all around.

There are thousands of churchyards in England alone, with some containing hundreds of historic memorials, all demanding upkeep, though burial in the churchyard has never been permanent, which is why you might spot grave slabs stacked against church walls or supporting the verges of sunken paths. Once the family's money ran out or there were no more descendants to pay for the upkeep, to make space for newbies, the bones would be dug up and removed to the charnel house until their reassembly on Judgement Day. Until then, the souls in Purgatory could be prayed for by the living in the church above, whilst the bones below would also serve as a memento mori. In the bone crypt of St

Leonard's in Hythe, 1,001 skulls lie directly beneath the altar. On All Souls' Day, following Holy Communion, worshippers descend to the ossuary, light candles and pray for the dead and, while this might be frowned upon by the C of E, the parishioners believe this ritual offsets it being a tourist attraction, money from which is needed for its upkeep.[16]

☠☠☠

More Necropolis than Metropolis

Graveyards show us the history of a place – nowhere as much as in London. The city has disposed of the bodies of rich and poor, plague and cholera victims, dissenters, prostitutes, Catholics, gypsies, Quakers and the dead of any religion you can think of. According to Catharine Arnold, 'London is one giant grave'. In her book *Necropolis*, she examines the capital's history through its disposal of its inhabitants: 'So many generations have lived and died here within such a small span – pagan, Roman, medieval, Victorian – and left intriguing traces of their lives.' She describes the skulls of Romans recovered from the Thames, victims of Boudicca's army, which razed London to the ground, creating a fire so intense that it melted bronze coins, 'scorching the earth so profoundly that archaeologists discovered a seared layer of soil centuries later'.[17]

The Romans disposed of their dead beyond the city walls, frightened of revenants. Long after the Romans had gone, in AD 752, Cuthbert, Archbishop of Canterbury, obtained papal permission to build churchyards in towns,[18] and from then on the Anglo-Saxons[19] lived cheek-by-jowl with the dead until the Black Death, when the first cemeteries since the Romans had to be built. By the time of the Great Plague of 1665, London had again run out of space, and the high cost of securing a grave meant that many victims ended up in unconsecrated mass graves. In May 1666, the Privy Council banned the burial of future plague victims in churches and small churchyards, ordered the use of quicklime (to speed decomposition) and forbade the re-opening of graves within a year, for fear of reinfection, though, due to poor records, and the subsequent Great Fire of 1666, it is hard to know whether these rules were adhered to. Following the fire, St Paul's and many other London churches were rebuilt by Wren, who, believing that corpses contributed to rot and damp, proposed cemeteries on the edge of town, as in Roman times. His pleas were ignored. Churches were rebuilt on old sites and the sites of the churches not rebuilt were used as extra burial grounds. Wren himself was interred at St Paul's in 1723.[20] (Is he still spinning?)

Over time, during construction of the railways and streets, hundreds of thousands of bones have been recovered. Between 1986–88, the Black Death cemetery was unearthed in East Smithfield. 636 burials were excavated, from both mass graves and single inhumations. It is estimated that as many again lie below the courtyard of the Royal Mint.[21] These bodies were carefully placed, head to the west.[22] Later, in 2015, while working on the ticket hall at Liverpool Street Station, Crossrail engineers uncovered a burial site dating from the Great Plague, the first of this period to be conclusively found in London: 3,500 bodies were buried beneath the station, from when the land was part of Bedlam Cemetery. Despite finds such as these, the plague dead's resting places remain unmarked, with no official memorial.

In 1801, London's population was under one million. By 1841 it had doubled. In 1842, in part due to overcrowding and contagion, the life expectancy of a professional man was thirty; for a labourer it was seventeen. Again, burial space was at a premium, worsened by cholera outbreaks in 1831 and 1848 which 'kept the scythe sweeping sharp and swift'.[23] In 1843, a government report stated that there were 50,000 burials each year in 203 acres of ground, with a reckoning of one million burials during that generation. Arnold says, as ever, the poor bore the brunt.

> In shocking reality, London was more necropolis than metropolis, her bustling thoroughfares and sophisticated highways paved with gold for the fortunate few, her side-streets reeking of decay ... the poor lived in such squalid and overcrowded conditions that their grim interments were but an extension of their oppressed and miserable lives.[24]

Burial in shallow graves was common, and sometimes partially decomposed bodies were exhumed to make room for a fresher corpse. More bones for the charnel house. Or, worst-case, chopped up along with the coffins. Sometimes, sextons and gravediggers would move remains from expensive plots to pauper ones, selling the vacated graves to those who could afford it. You never knew if you were mourning the right person.

Not all graveyards were so hideous as those of the Church. In 1659, England's first Jewish burial ground, the Sephardi Velho cemetery, opened in London. A few decades later, in 1697, Alderney Road Jewish Cemetery was established for the Ashkenazi community of Stepney. Under Jewish law, bodies had to be buried in single graves, six feet deep, within twenty-four hours and never overcrowded. By the mid-nineteenth century, Jewish cemeteries were in much better order than their C of E counterparts.

Post-Reformation, Nonconformists also required their own burial grounds, as they did not want to be buried in consecrated ground. In 1665, Bunhill Fields (Bone Hill) was opened for these dissenters. A former Saxon burial ground and the final resting place of the bones from the charnel house of St Paul's Cathedral and thousands of plague victims, famous residents include

William Blake, John Bunyan, Daniel Defoe, Isaac Watts and Susannah Wesley. Bunhill closed in 1832 and re-opened as a 'public walk' in 1869. Now it is a public space in the heart of London.

Quakers also took care of their own burial grounds, not allowing them to be commercial concerns. The dead would be buried seven feet deep and, if they had tombstones at all, they would be plain and small. Before I moved up north, I spent many a Saturday afternoon in Exeter's Meeting House, where Exeter Writers still gather for their weekly session. During our tea break in a room overlooking the graveyard, I'd wonder at its simplicity. Not an angel or obelisk in sight.

But what about those Baptists? Well, one in particular...

☠☠☠

Gatherings from Graveyards

In 1839, surgeon, apothecary and sanitation fanatic, George Alfred Walker (aka Graveyard Walker) wrote *Gatherings from Graveyards* on his specialist subject. Here, he gave graphic accounts of poor practice, none as disturbing as that of Enon Chapel off the Strand, founded by a Baptist minister. Rev W. Howse thought it a good idea to have worship upstairs and burial in the vault below, the living and the dead separated by floorboards alone. At first coffins were buried, but once the ground was full they were piled up to the ceiling, with only a few inches of soil scattered over them. Sometimes Howse cleared the vault and dumped the remains into the Thames or landfill, but terrible smells and flies known as 'body bugs' pervaded the chapel until the scandal was uncovered in 1839, when a sewer was run under the building. Walker was called in. He estimated that, over a sixteen-year period, 12,000 bodies had been squeezed into a space of sixty feet by thirty feet. He had some sympathy for the Baptists. If they were unable to secure graves in dissenter cemeteries, then they would take their chances here rather than burial in the common grave. Plus, they'd be safe from those body snatchers. Maybe these were good enough reasons, but the fact the minister charged a little less than other burial grounds meant it was very popular. Too popular.

Enon Chapel was closed down and the bodies left to rot. In time, it became a dance hall, known locally as 'dances on the dead', until Walker took possession of it in 1847 and had the remains exhumed, exposing a pyramid of bones and piles of coffin wood. About 6,000 people visited the site before the bones were interred – at Walker's own expense – in a pit in the recently opened Norwood Cemetery. Known as 'Millionaires Cemetery' as so many wealthy bodies reside there, Peter Ross says: 'It is pleasant to think that the poor, jumbled mass of Enon Chapel came to reside, at last, at a respectable address.'[25]

As for the chapel, it was demolished and the site now lies beneath the LSE.

Walker went on to establish the Society for the Abolition of Burials in Towns, demanding the closure of city churchyards, arguing for Londoners to be buried in new large cemeteries such as Kensal Green, safely away from the population. With support from campaigning journalist Chadwick, 'The Health of Towns and the Sanitary Condition of the Labouring Classes' was produced in 1842. Burials Act, 15 and 16 Victoria, was passed in 1851 (and three years later Scotland passed something similar). Londoners would now bury their dead beyond the city walls in cemeteries, just as the Romans had.[26]

La Cité des Morts

The Necropolis in Glasgow opened in 1831, a garden cemetery modelled on Père-Lachaise in Paris, with a remit to be 'respectful to the dead, safe and sanitary to the living, dedicated to the Genius of Memory and to extend religious and moral feeling'.[27] Intended to be interdenominational, the first burial was in 1832 of a Jew, Joseph Levi. In 1833 the first Christian burial was of Elizabeth Miles, stepmother of the superintendent. Famous residents include John Knox and Charles Rennie Mackintosh.

So what about Père Lachaise? A little background. In 1785, Louis XVI (guillotined eight years later during the French Revolution) decreed that the capital's burial grounds be emptied, due to a chronic shortage of space and a particularly unedifying stench emanating from the Cimetière des Saints-Innocents. The bones of six million Parisians were removed to the catacombs beneath the city.

King Louis was unable to oversee the project to its conclusion, as he was lacking a head, and so, in 1804, Napoleon Bonaparte took over and built Père Lachaise on the outskirts of Paris. To win over its citizens, the likes of Molière and Heloise were reburied in this new cemetery, giving it some status. When I first visited the City of Light in 1990, Père Lachaise was on my bucket list, mainly so I could visit the magnificent tomb of Oscar Wilde. At that time, you could get up close to the sculpture of the sleek, naked winged figure designed by Jacob Epstein. By 2011, this access had become such a problem that protective glass was installed to deter worshippers from further ruining the stonework with their lipstick kisses. Back then I was happy to stand quietly and reflect, reading the epitaph from *The Ballad of Reading Gaol*:

> And alien tears will fill for him
> Pity's long broken urn,
> For his mourners will be outcast men,
> And outcasts always mourn.

Wilde certainly was an outcast. Irish and gay, he died in 1900, in exile in Paris. He also died in poverty and his friends could only manage to bury him at Bagneux, outside the city. But, when an associate donated £2,000, he was reburied at Père Lachaise and the impressive tomb commissioned. It's been a place of pilgrimage for some time and the lipstick kisses weren't its first vandalism problem; the testicles of its angel were hacked off in the 1960s.

Wilde's is not the only shrine here, where, according to the website, 'nature and funerary art mingle'. Amongst the 70,000 plots lie the war dead, Holocaust victims, and the celebrated. Amidst names such as Chopin, Sarah Bernhardt, Edith Piaf, Balzac, Colette, Pissarro, Seurat, Bizet, Proust, Isadora Duncan, Marcel Marceau, Eugène Delacroix and Gertrude Stein, there is one of the infamous 27 Club. In July 1971, the body of *The Doors* frontman, Jim Morrison, was discovered in the bath of their Parisian apartment by his girlfriend Pamela Courson. His official cause of death was heart failure, thought to be a result of too much heroin, though a post-mortem was not carried out, unrequired by French law at the time. Conspiracy theories still abound and, whenever you visit his grave here, you will share the space with groupies playing the guitar, smoking and generally hanging out with their hero.

☠☠☠

The Magnificent Seven

Back to London and the Magnificent Seven garden cemeteries which encircle London like 'a bracelet around bone'.[28] Brompton, Abney Park, Tower Hamlets, Nunhead, West Norwood, Kensal Green and Highgate (Betjeman's 'Victorian Valhalla'). John Claudius Loudon (1783–1843), horticulturist, reformer and polymath, hated intra-mural burials and wanted cemeteries to provide moral edification – just as churchyards had previously done. They would be 'elegant showcases of wealth and taste, triumphs of landscaping and architecture… The sorrow of a graveyard visit might be lightened by the pleasure of a promenade. You would come to grieve and to be seen to be grieving.'[29]

His *On the Laying Out, Planting and Management of Cemeteries and the Improvement of Churchyard* (published posthumously in 1844) led to the development of these great London cemeteries, the first of which – Kensal Green – is his final resting place.

Founded in 1833, a rival to the Necropolis and London's answer to Père Lachaise, Kensal Green has been named by Julian Litten as 'the Belgravia of Death' due to its aristocratic and notable residents, including Thackeray, Trollope, W.H. Smith and Isambard Kingdom Brunel.[30] It offered such people the opportunity to 'continue their elitism in death'.[31] As long as you had the money, you could have a big plot or a whopper of a mausoleum, impossible in a London churchyard. These cemeteries were much more than spaces for the disposal of remains; they were 'Victorian Britain, ossified'.[32]

London Necropolis

London grew and spread and now needed to look further afield for their dead. Conceived in 1849 by the London Necropolis Company, a vast burial ground in Brookwood, Surrey, was designed to 'provide a last home for every Londoner'.[33] When it opened in 1854, it was accessible by rail, for both passengers and coffins, from the London Necropolis Railway Station – next to Waterloo station. The trains had separate carriages for dissenters and three different classes and ran straight into the cemetery grounds, where there were two stations – the North, which served the Nonconformist grounds, and the South, which served the Anglican. It never operated to the level expected and, after the LNC terminus was badly bombed during the Blitz of 1941, it was basically the end.

However, Brookwood is still an operating cemetery with all faith and non-faith burials, interment and scattering of cremated remains, woodland burials, green burials and community mausoleums. It even houses the disgraced anatomist, Robert Knox, of Burke and Hare infamy. And there are many more to come. In 2017, 50,000 bodies were dug up in St James burial ground to make room for the HS2 to go through Euston, the largest archaeological dig ever in Britain. An ongoing project, they will be reburied in earth in Brookwood in a dignified way; today, in archaeology, ethics is very much at the centre, the days of imperialist tomb-raiding behind us.[34]

The Hardy Tree

Back in central London, not far from Euston, a much earlier railway line also disturbed some old bones. A decade after the Burial Act of 1852, Thomas Hardy, then a young architect, was working for the firm in charge of clearing some of the graveyard of St Pancras Old Church, which stood on an ancient Christian site. Hardy oversaw the exhumation of remains, which were then reinterred elsewhere. But what to do with the headstones? He came up with the idea of overlapping them around an ash tree, safe from the railway's encroachment. A symbol of life among death. This became known as the Hardy Tree, which you can still see today.[35] While you are there, look for Mary Wollstonecraft's memorial. Author of *A Vindication of the Rights of Women*

(1792), not only was she the mother of feminism, but she was also the mother of Mary Shelley, tragically dying when baby Mary was just ten days old. It is said that Mary later planned her elopement with Percy Bysshe while visiting her mother's grave here.

Then there is the story of the boy poet, Thomas Chatterton, who is alleged to have walked here in August 1770 when, so absorbed in thought, he fell into an open grave. His companion helped him out, joking that he was happy to assist in the resurrection of a genius. Chatterton replied, 'My dear friend, I have been at war with the grave for some time now.' Chatterton died by suicide three days later (but this we will come back to).

In another literary connection, Charles Dickens lived close by as a child, and clearly took inspiration from his surroundings. In *A Tale of Two Cities* (1859), Jerry Cruncher and his son come to the graveyard of St Pancras to do some 'fishing' (body snatching; definitely the worst of times). Dickens's schoolmaster, Mr William Jones, is actually buried here – the teacher who informed the creation of the sadistic Mr Creakle, headmaster of Salem House School in *David Copperfield*. Dickens was concerned about much of Victorian progress and was horrified at the burial situation, discussed in his essay *The City of the Absent*. He referred to another City churchyard, St Olave's, as Saint Ghastly Grim, inspiration for his description in *Bleak House* – 'a hemmed-in churchyard, pestiferous and obscene, whence malignant diseases are communicated to the bodies of our dear brothers and sisters who have not departed'. Dickens also called it 'one of my best beloved churchyards'. St Olave's survived the Great Fire and the Blitz and still stands on Hart Street. And here lies our other friend, Samuel Pepys.

Back in St Pancras, the most striking tomb is a Grade I listed monument (one of only two in London). Built for his wife, this mausoleum[36] houses renowned architect and collector Sir John Soane (d. 1837) and his family. Giles Gilbert Scott, trustee of the Sir John Soane Museum, took inspiration from the tomb to design a telephone box for a competition to commemorate the jubilee of King George V. He also designed the awe-inspiring Anglican cathedral in Liverpool. Not wishing this new cathedral to be a mausoleum, Gilbert Scott asked to be buried outside and, unlike Wren, his wishes were followed. (But inside you will find one of his iconic telephone boxes.)

Giles came from a family of architects. His grandfather, George Gilbert Scott, designed not only the fancy St Pancras Station, but also the Prince Albert Memorial in Kensington Gardens. Influenced by the Eleanor Crosses,[37] a blingy sculpture of Albert sits beneath a fancy canopy, a Gothic revival ciborium, and was opened in 1872 by his widow, Queen Vic, with the statue seated four years later. The pedestal is made from the same Scottish granite that was also used for the Tay Railway Bridge.

All these connections in one burial site.

And a brief mention of another disused London graveyard, now public gardens surrounding the parish church of St George's, Hanover Square, Mayfair. When famed novelist Laurence Sterne died in 1768, he was buried here. But not for long. He was resurrected by anatomists and turned up on a dissecting table in Cambridge, where he was promptly recognised and sent back for reburial in St George's. When development took place here, he was buried for a third time and his skull and a femur taken to Coxwold in Yorkshire for burial outside St Michael's, where he once held the living.

God's Acre at St Lawrence's, Church Stretton

Ashes to Ashes

Victorian reformer, Mrs Isabella Holmes (1861–1949), visited every disused burial ground in London. She believed they should be turned into public spaces which would both preserve them and give people some green space in an overcrowded city. In 1884, thanks to her campaigning, the Disused Burials Act and Open Spaces Act was passed to prevent the erection of buildings on disused burial grounds. In 1896, her book *London Burial Grounds: Notes on their History from Earliest Times to the Present Day* was published, and by now over ninety burial grounds were dedicated public recreation grounds rather than old tips. Not all memorialisation was lost; many stones had already been moved, but those that were recovered were marked in a register.

Isabella Holmes hated the extravagance of Kensal Green, saying it was 'truly awful, with its catacombs, family vaults, statues, broken pillars, weeping images, and oceans of tombstones'.[38] She believed money would be better spent on schools and hospitals. A new rational attitude to death and burial was superseding the pomp instigated by Queen Victoria herself. And this is where cremation comes in. Mrs Holmes was a big fan, advocating cremation as a means of body disposal: 'I fail to understand how any serious-minded person can harbour the idea that burning the body can be any stumbling-block in the way of its resurrection, for the body returns earth to earth, ashes to ashes, dust to dust, whether the process takes fifty years or fifty minutes.'[39]

She and other cremationists faced opposition, not least with the Bishop of Rochester forbidding crematoria to be built on hallowed ground. But progress was inevitable. In 1874, the Cremation Society of Great Britain was formed. By 1892, 253 cremations had taken place. A crematorium opened in Manchester and four years later in Liverpool and, in 1901, the first municipal crematorium was opened in Hull. Finally, in 1902, cremation was legal, an Act of Parliament brought in regulation, and Golders Green cemetery was opened. 'Just as their remote ancestors were immolated in pits outside the city walls, their cremains buried in urns, modern Londoners choose a similar method of burial,'[40] paving the way for the direction of the disposal of bodily remains for the next century.

Double Deckers

What happens now, as these Victorian cemeteries and many of Britain's burial grounds are full or close to capacity? When they are no longer working cemeteries, no longer burying the dead, they are at risk. Highgate Cemetery is almost there but, to sustain the existing inhabitants, the landscaping and maintenance, the income from burials is needed. As Ross says, '[r]ecent grief is the pulse of a graveyard, the beat below one's feet. Without that, a cemetery is little more than a park or, at best, a tourist attraction that the public will pay to enter'.[41] But the price of a plot in London can be staggering. You need money – lots of it – to stand a chance of getting into a prestigious place such as Highgate, where burials cost close to £20,000. Ross compares this situation to the city's property crisis: 'those who can afford to bury in the city, or who are lucky enough to inherit space in a grave, will do so – most, however, will either cremate or be forced to seek a cemetery further out'.[42]

What can be done? We can look to Europe again, where it is common to reuse graves, taking back ownership of long abandoned plots and memorials. In London, graves over seventy-five years old can be used for new burials, as long as the cemetery has tried to contact the owner for permission. To 'lift and deepen' old graves, first the remains and any coffin will be exhumed and then the plot is dug deeper, before reinterring the remains with a new burial on top. In the interests of genealogy, records can be kept of earlier occupants.

Ashes to Ashes

Death is less personal now, and we are less acquainted with dead bodies. Since the advent of the NHS, people have tended to die in hospitals rather than at home, and, since the late 1960s, cremation has become the predominant form of disposal of the dead. And, because our remains are often scattered elsewhere rather than being interred in the community, the ritual of visiting and tending the grave of a loved one is also becoming less common, driving a further wedge between the living and the dead.

But the disposal of ashes is not just a practical, cheap, space-saving method; ashes have religious significance. For Christians, funerals include the words 'ashes to ashes, dust to dust'. On Ash Wednesday, the sign of the cross is smeared on foreheads with ash (from the burnt palm leaves from the previous year's Palm Sunday), to start the forty days of Lent that lead up to Easter, the ash representing Christ's death and our own mortality. *Remember that you are dust and to dust you shall return.*

Cremation is the norm in India, where both Hindus and Sikhs scatter their ashes on the Ganges; when in London this can be done in the Thames, at an Environment Agency-approved stretch of water such as Cherry Garden and Lambeth piers. The flowing river carries away the ashes to the sea, symbolising the passage from this life to the next. Other popular choices are the Severn, the Mersey, the Clyde and the Soar in Leicestershire.

Given Muslim traditions of burial, it is important that this form of disposal continues to be available to local communities in Britain. As in the Jewish faith, Muslims bury their dead as soon as possible, after the deceased has been washed and shrouded in cloth according to Islamic guidelines. A funeral prayer is then performed, and the person laid to rest in a grave on their right side, facing Makkah. All plots are identical, all Muslims created by the same God. During WW1, over one million troops from India and Pakistan fought for Britain, and the wounded were brought to special hospitals on the south coast of England. Those who died received appropriate burial rites but, whereas cremation was available for Hindus and Sikhs at special crematoria at Patcham, Netley and Brockenhurst, there was no special burial ground for Muslim soldiers until 1915, when one was opened in Woking, home to the only purpose-built mosque at that time.

For the Jewish community, burial grounds are sacred sites and must stay in perpetuity. They usually contain simple headstones with Hebrew inscriptions, though certain Victorians broke from tradition and commissioned large monuments such as the neo-classical Rothschild Mausoleum in West Ham Jewish Cemetery. Respect for the dead is integral to the faith, as is the connection between body and soul after death, and, in the Diaspora, the dead are buried with their feet facing Jerusalem.

As with Islam, ritual cleaning (*tahara*), shrouding (*tachrichim*) and prompt burial are required. To ensure these needs are met, Jewish burial societies (*chevra kadisha*) provide these services for free. In Israel, the dead are returned to the earth in a simple shroud – though it is very expensive for those from other countries to be buried there. In the UK, plain pine coffins are used, with stones rather than flowers left at the grave.

In death, some of us are more equal than others.

For Romany Gypsies and Irish Travellers, visiting the grave of a loved one is both a responsibility and a chance to continue their bond with the deceased. The generations can spend time together, collectively maintaining the grave, which reinforces family and belonging. But they face discrimination. According to Lane et al., Gypsies and Travellers may have different aesthetic values to the Church or local authorities and can find themselves as 'unwelcome strangers, in a time of considerable emotional and spiritual distress'. They go on to say:

> Yet, as the Black Lives Matter movement has reminded us, memorials are never politically neutral, and those who stand in the position of being 'arbiters of taste' in relation to memorial headstones can be seen to only represent the views of a specific section of society. Surely this approach to the arbitration of headstones is not fit for purpose in the modern world.[43]

In death, some of us are less equal than others.

☠☠☠

A Green Death

Not all green burials are the same. There are differences between natural green burial sites, and between funeral directors offering green options. A burial can leave behind traces of your existence long after you have been put in the ground, especially if you have been embalmed or have a coffin with screws, a plastic lining and brass (or more commonly plastic) handles. For a truly natural burial, your unembalmed body not only has to be in a biodegradable shroud or in a compostable coffin made of cardboard or willow, but you must also have any extras such as hip replacements or boob implants removed beforehand (by a doctor or the funeral director). There should also be no headstones, but you can have a tree planted instead. All this costs money.

Cremations might seem like less fuss, but the amount of CO_2 released during one cremation is equivalent to flying from London to Rome.[44] Some crematoria have tried to reduce their environmental impact by going electric, but so far this has not taken off. But you could at least source a coffin from sustainable or reclaimed material.

Resomation (also known as alkaline hydrolysis, aquamation, biocremation, biological or flameless or water or green cremation)[45] is the process of dissolving bodies inside a pressurised canister containing water and potassium hydroxide solution. When heated to 160 degrees Celsius for four hours, the body will 'dissolve', leaving only soft grey bones, which are then dried and ground up, leaving a white powder. This can be given to the family, as are ashes after a flame cremation. It uses less fuel, reducing greenhouse gas emissions by a third, and is cheaper than conventional cremation, but until it is more accessible there will be a carbon footprint if you have to travel some distance.[46]

Human composting (natural organic reduction) is not currently available in the UK, but in the USA it is legal in seven states. Not only does this process provide a low carbon footprint, but our bodies are used to replenish the earth.[47]

All Saints

As for me, I started with St Enodoc's and now I move up and around the rugged coast to a tiny Somerset village nestled between the Bristol Channel and the edge of Exmoor. Twice a year I make a pilgrimage here, to Selworthy, part of the National Trust's Holnicote Estate, where one of my forefathers was estate manager. Here sits the Grade 1 listed whitewashed church, shining out of the trees. Stand in its ancient doorway and you will have a breath-taking view across the valley to the moors – my favourite view in the world. Close by are a clutch of thatched cottages[48] with names from fairy tales. Periwinkle Cottage houses a café that caters for weary ramblers with cream teas and home-made cakes. Clematis Cottage is a gift shop with offerings from local crafts people. Selworthy Beacon rises behind the village and, if you trek upwards, you will come to Bury Castle, an Iron Age hill fort, a series of cairns believed to be the remains of round barrows and, then, the Channel with the Welsh coast beyond.

All Saints is where my paternal ancestors have been laid to rest, including my father and his father, grandparents and aunt. Here, I am connected to the Stenner family both known and unknown except for their names – the surnames with differing spellings, and the dates of their lives, short and long. My father's ashes are interred in the lower graveyard, in the ground next to his father's, erosion-defying lead lettering spelling out his name and dates in loving memory. And this is where I'd like to be laid to rest when my time comes.

Graveyards and burial sites are liminal, a space between life and death, a place for the living and the dead, the past and the present, for grief and loss, memorial and remembrance. This is where we meet the needs of the bereaved, the care of the dead. The flowers, stones and objects we leave at the graveside, on tombstones, connect the absent to the present. And we remember that one day we too shall pass from this life to whatever lies beyond.

Where once there was an immediacy with the dead buried in the local churchyard and burial ground, now edge-of-town cemeteries separate us from our forebears and from death itself. But this too will pass; now there is a drive for another way, a return to ancient traditions such as woodland burial and even barrows.[49] The future of disposal looks a whole lot more creative than the soulless cremation conveyor belt of the last century. But, before we examine how we say goodbye to the dead, we will consider how death has been represented creatively in art and literature.

E
IS FOR ELEGY

How We Represent Death and the Dead

elegy *noun*
(*Lit.*) a poem or song of serious reflection or sorrow,
typically a lament for the dead.

Speak me fair in death.
THE MERCHANT OF VENICE

Heare lyes
(expecting the second comminge of our saviour Christ Jesus)
the body of Edmond Spencer
the Prince of Poets in his tyme
whose divine spirrit needs noe othir witnesse
then the works which he left behinde him.
He was borne in London in the yeare 1553
and died in the yeare 1598.
POET'S CORNER, WESTMINSTER ABBEY

☠☠☠

The Subject of Death

From ancient Greek tragedies to medieval illustrations of the crucifixion and the *danse macabre*, through to the Romantic poets and Victorian novels, war poets and Agatha Christie's whodunnits, death has been a ripe subject. Through the ages, artists have known that death is important for the living, and that how they represent it will help us understand and accept our ultimate fate. Obviously, there are cultural and historical contexts to take into consideration but, for the purposes of this book, I'll be looking at Western representations of death in different media. If we time-travel from Old English oral storytelling to 1990s Brit Art, we will see that death is embedded in our culture. In art, death is not taboo.

Vikings and Monsters

Beowulf is the longest epic poem in Old English, the language of Anglo-Saxon England before the Norman Conquest. Handed down orally, *Beowulf* is believed to have been transcribed by two Anglo-Saxons working together to form one manuscript dated *c.*1000. The text is tricky to read in Old English – I should know, I studied it as part of my English degree. You can see the manuscript in the British Library, but there have been many translations from the likes of Tolkien and Seamus Heaney, and even in comic book form. Fascinating for those interested in death studies, the narrative begins and ends with a funeral and, in between, there is fighting.

Beowulf, the hero and king of the Geats, battles and kills a monster named Grendel, and then has to deal with Grendel's vengeful mother, which he does. Then he takes it too far and fights a treasure-hoarding dragon. This ends badly for Beowulf. His dead body is carried on a bier and laid on a pyre decorated with shields and helmets. The fire is lit and, in its heat, while Beowulf's bones are turning to ash, funeral dirges and wails of anguish can be heard above the sounds of spitting flames and wood, lamenting this great loss and the frightening prospect of invasion for the now-leaderless people. Afterwards, the warriors spend ten days constructing a barrow on the headland, a monument that will be visible from the sea. Inside they put their king's remains surrounded by treasure from the dragon's hoard which Beowulf will take with him to the afterlife, so you can't help but wonder what it was all for.

When a ship burial was discovered at Sutton Hoo in East Anglia in 1939, one of the greatest archaeological finds in the country, there were echoes of *Beowulf*. Lying near the River Deben, the warrior's ship would have been dragged to this graveyard and his remains buried inside it. The Sutton Hoo cemetery contained about twenty barrows belonging to people of high status, whose bodily remains or ashes were buried with grave goods, including those of a young man and his horse. Art enables us centuries later to understand a little of these funerary rites and rituals through reading manuscripts such as *Beowulf*. Though it would be a long and laborious process, those two scribes knew the importance of writing down the story. But they could not have predicted its longevity or its prime place in the literary canon or that a young Devonian woman would be introduced to it in a northern university in 1986 and how it would resurface in her mind years later, living on the Wirral, in the land of the Vikings, down the road from where King Canute got his feet wet and where, a thousand years later, Rory McIlroy won the Open.

Funeral of a Viking, Sir Thomas Francis Dicksee (1893)

The Art of Dying

Written in Latin in 1415 by an anonymous Dominican friar, *Ars Moriendi* was a guidebook for priests to share information with illiterate Christians on how to have a good death. At a time of plague, famine and war, this was extremely popular and, in 1450, a shorter version was produced with woodcut illustrations. Thanks to the printing press, *Ars Moriendi* was now a more accessible text.

Post-Reformation, in the seventeenth century, Jeremy Taylor wrote *Holy Living* and *Holy Dying* with a more C of E spin, and now, four centuries later, the Catholic Church has launched a website called *The Art of Dying Well*.[1] This resource updates the tradition of *Ars Moriendi* and offers practical and spiritual support to those facing death and dying. Using personal testimonies, poetry, music, stories, prayers and reflections, this website claims that '[t]he slope that we all have to climb is still the same slope, and although we might not fall in the same places as did our ancestors, we will certainly fall along the way.'

Dance of Death, Hans Holbein, 1523–25

Let's Get Metaphysical

> *Death be not proud, though some have called thee*
> *Mighty and dreadful, for, thou art not so,*
> *For, those, whom thou thinks't, thou dost overthrow,*
> *Die not, poor death, nor yet canst thou kill me.*

Here, in John Donne's Sonnet 10, we see the author speak directly to Death personified, arguing that, ultimately, Death is the one who will die; Death is just 'one short sleep' from which we will 'wake eternally'. This is a brave poem, one where faith in the afterlife shines through, its brightness eclipsing the darkness that Shakespeare's Hamlet fears so existentially, a terror of what lies within this sleep, possibly the stuff of nightmares. Quite different to Prospero's vision of a sleepy death in *The Tempest*; 'We are such stuff / As dreams are made on, and our little life / Is rounded with a sleep' feels more positive, maybe because we know that this play will be repeated again and again, or maybe because of the trippy IKEA advert for comfy beds.

In his sonnets, Shakespeare talks about what is left behind after death, immortalising the person he addresses, whether the Fair Youth or the Dark Lady, or maybe one and the same or maybe someone else entirely. In Sonnet 18, the speaker addresses another person, rather than Death itself and, though death is personified, this is an expression of grief for someone lost. Perhaps, because of the phrase 'thy eternal summer', Shakespeare could even be alluding to the death of his young son, Hamnet. In fact, there is a theory that all the sonnets are addressed to him. Sonnet 18 offers some hope; the youth will be immortalised not only by enduring love but also by the fact he is noted in this sonnet:

> *But thy eternal summer shall not fade,*
> *Nor lose possession of that fair thou ow'st;*
> *Nor shall death brag thou wander'st in his shade,*
> *When in eternal lines to time thou grow'st:*
> *So long as men can breathe or eyes can see,*
> *So long lives this, and this gives life to thee.*
> William Shakespeare, Sonnet 18, 'Shall I Compare thee to a Summer's Day?'

Graveyard School of Poets

Thomas Gray's 'Elegy Written in a Country Churchyard' was published in 1851, and some of us may well have had to recite it in school many moons ago. Gray reflects that we are all equal in death:

The boast of heraldry, the pomp of power,
And all that beauty, all that wealth e'er gave,
Awaits alike the inevitable hour.
The paths of glory lead but to the grave.
Stanza 9

But his focus is on '[t]he short and simple annals of the poor', wondering what their lives could have been if given the same opportunities as the rich:

Full many a flower is born to blush unseen,
And waste its sweetness on the desert air.
Stanza 14

Some mute inglorious Milton here may rest,
Some Cromwell guiltless of his country's blood.
Stanza 15

This poem, which gave Thomas Hardy the wonderful phrase 'Far from the madding crowd', is supposed to have been inspired by the churchyard of St Giles in Stoke Poges, Buckinghamshire, where Gray spent many summers with his mother and aunt and where all three of them are buried. It is a little ironic that this unpretentious man, who turned down the job of poet laureate, has a fancy marble tablet (below Milton's) in Poets' Corner[2] in Westminster Abbey and rather a large, pedestalled monument outside St Giles's, erected in his honour in 1799. No 'frail memorial' for Thomas.

New Romantics

Now let's hear it for Thomas Chatterton, the Boy Poet, (1752–70), who fell into that open grave in St Pancras. As well as anti-slavery poetry and satirical verse, he also wrote poetry inspired by the marvellous St Mary Redcliffe[3] in Bristol, under the name of Thomas Rowley, a fifteenth-century monk. Chatterton copied his poems onto parchment and passed them off as medieval manuscripts, which got him into some trouble. Although he died by suicide aged seventeen, he influenced the subsequent Romantic movement, a symbol of youth and neglected genius, inspiring the likes of Blake, Keats, Shelley, Coleridge and William Wordsworth, who called him 'the marvellous boy'. But, perhaps most famously, he has been immortalised in the painting *Chatterton* by Pre-Raphaelite artist Henry Wallis, a deathbed scene in a garret in the shadow of St Paul's Cathedral, where a red-headed, pale-skinned Chatterton lies prone, arm outstretched, a bottle of arsenic and shredded paper abandoned on the floor. *Chatterton* was displayed at the Royal Academy in 1856 accompanied by a quotation of Marlowe's: 'Cut is the branch that might have grown full straight'. It now hangs in Tate Britain and has always fascinated me (but more of that later).

One of John Keats's (1795–1821) earliest poems from 1815 is the sonnet 'Oh Chatterton! how very sad thy fate'. Keats goes on to dedicate 'Endymion' to him and the poem opens with:

> *A thing of beauty is a joy for ever:*
> *Its loveliness increases; it will never*
> *Pass into nothingness; but still will keep*
> *A bower quiet for us, and a sleep*
> *Full of sweet dreams, and health, and quiet breathing.*

Keats works on this epic in 1818, whilst he and his brother, Tom, are trying to recuperate from consumption in Teignmouth (in the chiropodist's house where I had my verruca gouged out).[4] They choose my seaside town as it was supposed to be a mild climate, but it rains the whole time. And, though 'Endymion' receives poor reviews, this period of rain and wind and Devon damp allows Keats to think about what he wants from his poetry. The following year, he writes both 'To Autumn' and 'Ode to a Nightingale', poems still studied by school children today. In these, Keats uses nature to illustrate life and death; death is natural and part of life.

> *Darkling I listen; and, for many a time*
> *I have been half in love with easeful Death.*
> From 'Ode to a Nightingale'

Following Tom's death, Keats is taken by friends to Italy in the hope that the drier climate will help his own tuberculosis, but he dies, aged twenty-five. Buried in the Protestant cemetery in Rome, his gravestone reads: 'Here lies one whose name was writ in water.' Writ in water? Hardly. What would John have thought if he could have foreseen the immortality he has achieved through his words?

Shelley certainly caught a glimpse of Keats's genius. Despite being one of those who criticised 'Endymion', he was much affected by his fellow poet's untimely demise and wrote 'Adonais: An Elegy on the Death of John Keats'. You could call this a pastoral elegy or graveyard Gothic, but it is most definitely a lament.

> *Where, like an infant's smile, over the dead*
> *A light of laughing flowers along the grass is spread:*
> *And gray walls moulder round, on which dull Time*
> *Feeds, like a slow fire upon a hoary brand;*

*And one keen pyramid with wedge sublime,
Pavilioning the dust of him who planned
This refuge for his memory…'*

He visits Keats's grave and, in the preface to 'Adonais', he writes: 'It might make one in love with death, to think that one should be buried in so sweet a place.' Oh, the irony, of Shelley's own death the following year. Aged twenty-nine, he drowns during a boating accident off the Italian riviera. When his decomposed body washes up on the shore ten days later, a copy of Keats's poetry is found in his pocket. Shelley is cremated on the beach and his remains later buried in Rome, in the same cemetery as Keats.

Keats's grave

We last saw Mary and Percy Shelley in the old burial ground of St Pancras, where they resolved to elope, where Chatterton had earlier fallen in a grave and where Thomas Hardy would save the gravestones from the railway. The couple have had an adulterous, tumultuous, toxic relationship full of dead children, illness, and depression but, oh, the macabre memento that Mary keeps, stashed in a drawer supposedly wrapped in a copy of 'Adonais': her husband's heart (though it might possibly have been his liver). And there it stays until her own death – small wonder she came up with something as chilling as Frankenstein's monster.

☠☠☠

Picture This

We have seen the importance of memento mori funerary art found on monuments within churches and churchyards, symbolic references marking an individual's life on earth which were also used as a warning to visitors to repent and prepare for their own death. For centuries, death has been one of the major themes in Western art, with Christ's crucifixion at the centre, whether it be in illuminated manuscripts or on Renaissance frescoes. Then there were the vanitas[5] of the Dutch painters of the seventeenth century and finally, after a long absence, Damien Hirst's 2007 diamond-encrusted skull – *For the Love of God* – which brought back death into mainstream art.

Going back to the eighteenth century, the popular press enabled Hogarth to take his own version of art as a warning to the masses with his pair of illustrations *Beer Street* and *Gin Lane* (1751). An advertising campaign on behalf of a Georgian CAMRA, these prints showed the benefits of drinking beer compared to the vice of getting smashed on gin, with its slogan 'drunk for a penny, dead drunk for two pence, clean straw for nothing'. Set in the slum of St Giles, *Gin Lane* is an action-packed representation of modern life – a bit like one of those Spot the Hazard pictures[6] – and includes an undertaker's, a pawnbroker's and a drunken mother dropping her baby to take a pinch of snuff. It accomplished its ends: the subsequent Gin Act of 1751 reduced the number of cheap gin palaces and increased the tax on importing Mother's Ruin. Meanwhile, over on Beer Street, all are happy and healthy. A success it might have been, but it is surmised that these representations are more nuanced, and that Hogarth knew that poverty was the cause of misery, not gin.

A little while later, over in France, Marie Tussaud starts out making death masks from the severed heads of the guillotine, including those of Louis XVI and Marie Antoinette. This is an ancient practice to preserve the image of the great and good, the beloved and despised, which Tussaud made her life's work. After the Revolution, she took her waxwork collection on the road, ending up in Baker Street in 1835. In 1975, my grandparents took me to Madame Tussaud's for the first time. Grandpa reckoned the queue was a quarter of a mile long; it certainly felt like an age standing there in the heat of a London August. It was worth the wait: I was entranced by the models – the Queen, Liza Minelli, Agatha Christie (more on her below), but I wish I had never stepped foot in the Chamber of Horrors. I'm sure it's tame by today's standards but, for a good six months after, I would lie in bed at night, replaying the tableaux in my head: Dr Crippen with his mean little spectacles, Christie wallpapering up his victims and Marat languishing in his blood bath.

A death mask is a cast or impression taken from a corpse's face soon after death, which before photography was the best way of capturing a likeness as a memento or to be used for portraits. I've mentioned the death mask of William Burke in Surgeons' Hall, Edinburgh, which I found somewhat creepy, streets away from where he committed his gruesome crimes. The National Portrait Gallery holds many death masks but only one of a woman, actress Ellen Terry. Actually, two if you count Tracey Emin, who has made her own death mask whilst still living (gotta love Tracey).

The Victorians

Recently, I went to the Walker Art Gallery in Liverpool, the National Gallery of the North, with a particular painting in mind: *The Funeral of Shelley* (1889) by Louis Édouard Fournier. There's nothing like seeing a painting in person, both up close and from a distance. Bigger than expected, my eyes were drawn towards the funeral pyre and Shelley's pale face amongst the smoke. His burning body is watched by his three friends, Trelawny, Leigh Hunt and the instantly recognisable Byron (although in reality Byron actually went for a swim at the time). We know from Trelawny's account that the funeral took place on a hot August day, but Fournier portrays it as cold and grey, reflecting the sombre, dark mood of the occasion.

The Funeral of Shelley

In the very same room hangs William Frederick Yeames's iconic painting *And When Did You Last See Your Father?* (1878). The fictional scene from the English Civil War depicts Parliamentarians interrogating a beautiful young boy – a symbol of truth and honesty – from a Royalist family. While his mother and sisters look on, we feel the suspense, the dilemma of the boy. Does he tell the truth and endanger them all or does he lie in the hope of saving his father? This painting was so popular that it even inspired a waxwork tableau at Madame Tussaud's.

And When Did You Last See Your Father

E IS FOR ELEGY

Yes, the Victorians loved a story in pictures. They also loved a deathbed scene. Not just good deaths, in the medieval sense, such as those painted of Prince Albert. Or Nelson fatally injured in battle, leading his men to the ultimate victory at Trafalgar in 1805, who lies in Hardy's arms, time to say his final words before taking his last breath. They also portrayed bad deaths such as Chatterton's.

Take another Pre-Raphaelite painting which hangs in Tate Britain: *Ophelia*, painted in 1852 by John Everett Millais. From Shakespeare's *Hamlet*, the character of Ophelia is driven to despair by grief and dies by drowning. The painting shows her floating in the river, a scene we could only previously imagine as, in the play, it happens offstage, recounted by Hamlet's mother, Gertrude, to Ophelia's brother, Laertes.

> *There is a willow grows askant the brook,*
> *That shows his hoar leaves in the glassy stream.*
> *There with fantastic garlands did she make*
> *Of crowflowers, nettles, daisies, and long purples*
> *That liberal shepherds give a grosser name,*
> *But our cold maids do dead-men's-fingers call them.*
> *There on the pendent boughs her crownet weeds*
> *Clambering to hang, an envious sliver broke,*
> *When down her weedy trophies and herself*
> *Fell in the weeping brook. Her clothes spread wide,*
> *And mermaid-like awhile they bore her up;*
> *Which time she chanted snatches of old tunes,*
> *As one incapable of her own distress,*
> *Or like a creature native and indued*
> *Unto that element. But long it could not be*
> *Till that her garments, heavy with their drink,*
> *Pulled the poor wretch from her melodious lay*
> *To muddy death.*
> Hamlet, Act IV, Scene VII

Maybe Gertrude wants to spare Laertes added grief. After all, if she died by suicide, Ophelia would be denied a full Christian burial. Instead, at her graveside, the priest grudgingly says:

> *Her obsequies have been as far enlarged*
> *As we have warranty: her death was doubtful;*
> *And, but that great command o'ersways the order,*
> *She should in ground unsanctified have lodged*
> *Till the last trumpet: for charitable prayers,*
> *Shards, flints and pebbles should be thrown on her;*

> *Yet here she is allow'd her virgin crants,*
> *Her maiden strewments and the bringing home*
> *Of bell and burial.*

'Virgin crants' were traditionally used in England at the funeral of a young unmarried woman: a bell-shaped crown of wicker, decorated with white flowers, ribbons and paper rosettes, perhaps with a verse written on a handkerchief or collar, and sometimes even a pair or pairs of white card or kid gloves. This crown was then carried in front of the coffin in the funeral procession, by a girl of the same age as the dead maiden. Afterwards, it hung alongside previous garlands from the beams over the nave of the church. A few remain from the eighteenth century. I've seen the collection of seven in Holy Trinity Church, Minsterley, Shropshire (where there are also some fine memento mori skulls over the front door).

Romantic poet Anna Seward (1742–1809) wrote about this rite in 'Eyam',[7] a poem from her collection,[8] which she sent to the Ladies of Llangollen, who she counted among her friends, as well as such glittering literati as Samuel Johnson, Walter Scott and Erasmus Darwin (grandfather of Charles). Seward, known as the 'Swan of Lichfield', was a prolific writer and deep thinker. In her sonnet, 'To Colebrooke Dale', she uses funerary imagery to comment on the impact of the Industrial Revolution on the landscape. A pioneer in anti-pollution.

> *Of black sulphureous smoke, that spread their veils*
> *Like funeral crape upon the sylvan robe*
> *Of thy romantic rocks, pollute thy gales,*
> *And stain thy glassy floods; — while o'er the globe*
> *To spread thy stores metallic, this rude yell*
> *Drowns the wild woodland song, and breaks the Poet's spell.*

Seward never married and I wonder if she had her own virgin's garland at her funeral. She is buried in Lichfield Cathedral, where she has a rather fine memorial.

> *Now the low beams with paper garlands hung,*
> *In memory of some village youth or maid,*
> *Draw the soft tear, from thrill'd remembrance sprung;*
> *How oft my childhood marked that tribute paid!*
> *The gloves suspended by the garland's side,*
> *White as its snowy flow'rs with ribands tied.*
> *Dear village! long these wreaths funereal spread—*
> *Simple memorial of the early dead.*
> *From 'Eyam'*

She's a Model

1848: a year of revolutions across Europe. Chartists aside, Britain largely avoids such turmoil. Nevertheless, there is an artistic rebellion, kick-started by a secret society of painters known as the Pre-Raphaelite Brotherhood, intent on shaking up the art establishment. These young male students, who include Dante Gabriel Rossetti, William Holman Hunt and John Everett Millais, take inspiration from the past (pre-Raphael), using literature, myth and legend to tell luminous jewel-coloured stories and, through this medium, they often address the social injustices of the Industrial Age.

There are also women involved in this movement, connected to the Brotherhood through their work as models, poets, and painters. Christina, sister of Rossetti, is a talented poet, author of the words of 'In the Bleak Mid-Winter', that atmospheric Christmas carol, but she starts out modelling for her brother in paintings such as *The Girlhood of the Virgin Mary*. And then there's Elizabeth Siddal, ultimate supermodel. Tall and willowy, with striking red hair and pale skin, Lizzie is most famous for 'sitting' for *Ophelia*, floating for hours in an iron bath heated only by candles. When the candles are gutted, Millais is too absorbed to notice and Lizzie too committed to mention the cold water. She develops pneumonia and almost dies.

For years she is embroiled with Rossetti as his muse and lover, and yet, despite their tumultuous relationship, he does encourage her artistic ambitions (as does Ruskin, who's not exactly known for being a fan of women). Lizzie produces over a hundred works in the last decade of her life, powerful dream-like pictures with a dark undercurrent, paintings which have been overlooked in favour of the Brotherhood's male gaze.

The Lady of Shalott by Elizabeth Siddal

But, when you read Lizzie's poetry, you will gain some understanding of her life's journey with ill health, laudanum addiction, post-partum depression following a stillbirth, and how this ultimately leads to her early death.

D IS FOR DEATH

I felt the wind strike chill and cold
And vapours rise from the red-brown mould;
I felt the spell that held my breath
Bending me down to a living death.
From 'Fragment of a Ballad'

Lizzie Siddal's story doesn't end there. After her death, Rossetti is filled with grief and remorse for his treatment of her. He buries her in the Rossetti family plot in Highgate with the only manuscript of his poems tucked inside her famous copper hair. Seven years later, under cover of darkness, he has her exhumed to retrieve his poems for publication. And it is said that her body was in perfect condition, no sign of decay, and that her wondrous hair had continued growing and filled the coffin. This secured her iconic place in both art history and popular culture and her famous face hangs in galleries all over the land, haunting us from beyond the grave, where hopefully she lies at last in peace.

☠☠☠

Off with Her Head

We go back a few years now to Paul Delaroche's *The Execution of Lady Jane Grey* (1833), a life-sized tableau displaying the terror of the death penalty. Although a politically charged event, this is a powerfully personal and poignant scene, portraying the distress of the ladies-in-waiting, whose exposed necks remind us of what is about to happen to their mistress, as does the black cloth draped over the scaffold, strewn with straw to soak up the blood that will soon be spilled. The two men here are shown as far more compassionate in Jane's death than the men in her life who brought her to the conviction of high treason: the blindfolded teenager is gently guided to the block by the Lieutenant of the Tower while the executioner waits patiently, the axe relaxed in his hand, discreetly by his side. We can only imagine the red of the blood against Jane's white satin gown and, for the initial viewers in Paris, it must have called to mind the recent end of Marie Antoinette. You can see the painting in London's National Gallery.

☠☠☠

Children and Animals

In addition to good deaths, bad deaths, consumption, suicide and execution, the death of infants was another common feature of Victorian painting, employing the metaphor of the empty cradle. But let's not forget those loyal animals such as Edwin Landseer's *The Old Shepherd's Chief Mourner*

(1837), which portrays a mournful dog resting its chin on his master's coffin. This calls to mind stories and myths of loyal dogs around the world such as Edinburgh's Greyfriars Bobby, who – whether urban myth or truth or a mixture of both – sat at his master's grave for fourteen years. There have been many books and films about such canines and fans will go on pilgrimages to visit their statues and graves. As for me, I have rubbed the nose of Bobby's statue in Candlemaker Row several times (which is naughty as it has to keep being restored – though at least I never kissed Oscar's tomb).

☠☠☠

Cold in the Earth

And now we leave the art world and return to literature, to Yorkshire and Emily Brontë (1818–48), whose *Wuthering Heights* and poems have death at the centre. As with Keats, she lingered over morbid thoughts, hardly surprising, the tragedy she had known; when she was only three, her mother died of cancer and, just before she was seven, her two eldest sisters, Maria and Elizabeth, succumbed to TB. Teenage girls might read *Wuthering Heights* as romantic fiction, bolstered by out-of-context internet memes such as 'Whatever our souls are made of, his and mine are the same'. But this is a dark, Gothic story, not of love but of jealous possession. Not even death can end Cathy and Heathcliff's co-dependent, toxic, destructive relationship. (I know it is literary blasphemy to say I dislike this novel but it does not sit well with me. That said, it is a work of teenage genius, not least because it sparked Kate Bush to do wondrous things.)

Emily continues the death theme with a series of stark poems such as 'A Death-Scene' which includes the stanza, 'So I knew that he was dying— / Stooped, and raised his languid head; / Felt no breath, and heard no sighing, / So I knew that he was dead.' But her poetry offers some hope, illustrating through powerful imagery her first-hand knowledge of the enduring power of nature and her belief that the spirit lived on after death.

> *There is not room for Death*
> *Nor atom that his might could render void*
> *Since thou art Being and Breath*
> *And what thou art may never be destroyed.*
> From 'No Coward Soul Is Mine'

We cannot help but dwell on those Brontë sisters – Charlotte, Emily, Anne – living in the vicarage close by the graveyard, all dead before their time, poor Emily so wasted by consumption that the town carpenter had to make the narrowest coffin he had ever constructed for an adult. Ann followed a year later. Charlotte was the longest-living sister, dying aged thirty-eight, possibly from dehydration and malnutrition due to hyperemesis gravidarum (extreme morning sickness), her chance of love and family thwarted.

These sisters achieved so much in so short a time and are immortalised in their remarkable literary works while, across the pond, another young Emily, Ms Dickinson (1830–86), wrote hundreds of poems on dying, grief and the afterlife, in repeated attempts to understand. She also used death as a poetic metaphor such as 'I felt a funeral in my brain', which describes mental health. Perhaps her most famous is '"Hope" is the thing with feathers'. As she was a fan of Emily Brontë, perhaps this was a homage to the Yorkshire woman's poem 'Hope', where hope 'stretched her wings and soared to heaven'. In fact, Dickinson chose 'No Coward Soul Is Mine' to be read at her funeral.

☠☠☠

Sparkling Cyanide

The sweet shop where we lived in the early 70s on Belgrave Road in Torquay was near the parish church of All Saints, where Agatha Christie was christened in 1890 and which was central to her life while she lived in the town. Opposite our shop was the chemist's where she worked as a Saturday girl, before she went on to be a wartime hospital dispenser. She employed her knowledge of poisons to construct her murders as well as taking a forensic approach to how they were solved: 'But surely the study of fingerprints, footprints, cigarette ash, different kinds of mud, and other clues that combine the minute observation of details – all these are of vital importance?'[9]

As well as her methodical approach to fiction, Christie was canny in her literary career, writing for the stage and using the pseudonym Mary Westmacott for romantic fiction. But how she handled her beloved Inspector Poirot's death was genius. *Curtain: Poirot's Last Case* was written during the Second World War but locked in a safe to be published after his creator's death – though it was actually published in September 1975, four months before Agatha died aged eighty-five. In the novel, an elderly Poirot returns to the house at Styles – where he first appeared – and calls on his long-term associate, Hastings, to help him find a murderer. But, after leaving behind some clues for Hastings (spoiler alert), Poirot dies (I won't tell you how or why). Following publication, the *New York Times* printed a front-page obituary of the Belgian detective, the only time they have done this for a fictional character.

The pioneer of English detective fiction proved that women could successfully write about murder and went on to inspire crime writers such as Patricia Highsmith, Ruth Rendell, and PD James (who disliked comparisons, being rather snooty about Christie's writing). Her title 'the Queen of Crime', trademarked by her estate, has caused some recent hoo-ha. Along with eleven other established authors, Val McDermid was commissioned to write a new Miss Marple short story for an authorised collection. Following publicity around the book, Christie's estate sent the Scottish writer's publisher a cease and desist, warning them not to use the phrase to describe McDermid. Now, McDermid has always claimed her love affair with crime began when she read *The Murder at the Vicarage* – the first Miss Marple and the only book in her grandparents' home apart from the Bible. She knows she owes her career to Christie. But she was somewhat surprised by the estate's reaction. Her own response was to rename herself 'the Quine of Crime'[10] and print it on a T-shirt. (Yas, Quine!)

Why do we like reading about murder? Why does crime pay? For Christie, it was all about solving a puzzle, and less about character; there is very little emotion in her books. While other writers might delve deeper into the psychology of murder, their books remain plot-driven, offering a structure and comfort that the crime will be solved. Whether it's Nordic noir or cosy crime, we can't get enough of murderous death.

The same goes for the telly, where we have a penchant for both dramatised and real-life crime, across the country from Shetland to Jersey via Hebden Bridge, across time from Crippen to Dahmer. The murder genre now involves the post-mortem as part of its story: 'The chalk outline of the murder victim has been fleshed out.'[11] This goes some way to explain why *Silent Witness* is the BBC's longest-running crime drama, currently in its twenty-seventh season. (Though it would be good to see them spend more time on forensics and less being Colombo.) Viewers want resolution, and this is where forensics step in, providing clarity through evidence; the right person will be punished, the dead given justice. Viewers also like to be reminded that our lives are (generally) far removed from such dangers. *Crimewatch* was a BBC programme that understood this, but its end came in 2017 when it was killed off aged thirty-three. Mark Lawson wrote the show's obituary, which included this:

> Although the show has undoubtedly solved many crimes (helping to apprehend, it claims, 57 murderers, 53 rapists and 18 paedophiles), it may be seen as symbolic that its most high-profile case – the murder of its own presenter, Jill Dando, in 1999 – remains officially unsolved, after the conviction of a man was overturned.[12]

A sad reminder that murder is real and that many families and friends have to live with the brutal loss of a loved one.

Thankfully, murder is a rare occurrence. So please don't have nightmares.

Grief Is the Price We Pay for Love

What are we left with when a beloved has died? How do we live without them? Memoirs on grief show us how individuals have coped, how they've remembered, how they've gone on to live and love. In *A Grief Observed*, T.S. Eliot writes about his dead wife, telling us, 'Her absence is like the sky, spread over everything.' Grief is all-encompassing, like breathing. (I recently watched *Shadowlands* (1993) and literally cried through the second half.)

In Dylan Thomas's poem 'Do Not Go Gentle into That Good Night', the speaker talks universally about death, that we should not approach it without a fight, that life is worth hanging onto. The final stanza is more personal, with the speaker addressing his father – maybe Thomas reflecting on his own father – asking him to 'rage, rage against the dying of the light'.

We've touched on Emily Dickinson's 'hope', which is 'the thing with feathers'. Max Porter takes this phrase and changes it to *Grief Is the Thing with Feathers*. In his remarkable little book that is anything but small, Porter explores the effects of the death of a wife and mother of two boys on the family she leaves behind. A crow comes to visit, a metaphor for overwhelming, messy, brutal grief. But somehow this crow's ministrations enable the shrunken family to move forward until they reach the place where they can spread the mother's ashes and that is when the father hears his wife in the voices of his sons. He hears 'the life and song of their mother. Unfinished. Beautiful. Everything.'

☠☠☠

'The thought of death is a good dancing partner.' Kierkegaard

We know about the medieval *danse macabre*, an iconography representing sinners – from princes to paupers – dancing to the grave, while Death watches on, playing his fiddle. Repent while you can. A more modern take is Matthew Hart's 'Dances with Death', performed by the Royal Ballet, with Darcy Bussell in red, dancing the part of the AIDS virus, a personification of death. In fact, death often takes centre stage in ballet, nowhere as much as in the nineteenth-century *Giselle*.

Giselle is a peasant girl deceived by aristocrat Albrecht, who pretends to be a commoner to gain her love. Poor Giselle has a weak heart and, when she finds out he is betrothed to someone else, she goes mad and dies. She becomes a *wili*, a creature from Slavic folklore, just as her mother warned her might happen. (Don't they always?) A *wili* is the ghost of a maiden who has died of a broken heart after a man's betrayal and any man who encounters a *wili* at night in a graveyard will die. In *Giselle*, the manner of death is more specific: the *wilis* kill men by dancing them to death. When, one night, Albrecht, filled with grief, visits the graveyard where Giselle is buried, she saves him from his fate. (Not sure I'd have bothered.)

I saw this ballet when I was a girl with my grandpa. While he snored most of the way through, I sat upright, holding onto my seat, and watched these *wilis* dancing through the atmospheric graveyard in the second act. I did ballet for about twelve years, until boys lured me away, so I was gripped. I got it. I get it.[13]

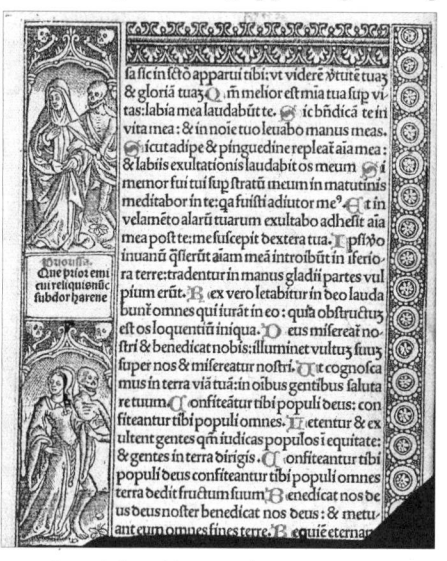

Death and the Abbess and Death and a Lady

As did Hans Christian Andersen, who wrote the cautionary tale *The Red Shoes* in 1845. In this story, a young peasant girl asks her stepmother to buy some red shoes to replace her old, tatty black ones. This means she can no longer go into church, because only black shoes are allowed in there. But far worse is the curse. Once she starts dancing in the shoes, she can never stop. The 1946 film of the same name takes the kernel of this story, where a pair of red ballet shoes become a metaphor for the ambition of the prima ballerina, who chooses her career over her lover, which ultimately (spoiler alert) dooms her to jump in front of a train.

☠☠☠

Grim Tales

Death would have been very real for children at the time of the Brothers Grimm, whose fairy tales featured orphans, dead mothers and stolen babies and children, reflecting the reality that death in childbirth and infancy was common. Jacob (1785–1863) and Wilhelm (1786–1859) lost their father in childhood, his death plunging them into poverty. Helped by family, they eventually went to university and, with their strong work ethic, dedicated the rest of their lives to collecting German folktales, which they rewrote. *Sleeping Beauty*, *Hansel and Gretel* and *Little Red Riding Hood* all have death as a constant threat. Terrifying. And, unfortunately, sometimes anti-Semitic, used by the Nazis as propaganda. Chilling. As is the story of *Snow White*, whose central character lies in a glass coffin while her beloved dwarves surround her in mourning. Unsettling from today's perspective to think of the prince falling in love with a corpse. Perhaps death here is more about change than about the end of life. But actual death will come to us all and such stories allow us to address it.

Moving Pictures

I could write so much about the big screen, but I'm not too much of a film buff. And it's hard to think of many films without at least one dead body or a mention of death somewhere along the line, either direct or indirect. So just some quick mentions.

1. *Carry on Cleo* (1964). For Julius Caesar's ides of March. Who can forget Kenneth Williams's exclamation, 'Infamy! Infamy! They've all got it in for me!'?
2. Ridley Scott's *Gladiator* (2000). Not just for its death-as-entertainment for Joaquin Phoenix's cruel Commodus but for the unexpected tenderness that Russell Crowe portrays through his character's grief. When Commodus asks for his name, the gladiator replies: 'My name is Maximus Decimus Meridius, commander of the Armies of the North, general of the Felix Legions and loyal servant to the true emperor, Marcus Aurelius. Father to a murdered son, husband to a murdered wife. And I will have my vengeance, in this life or the next.' And, oh, those wheat fields.
3. *Truly, Madly, Deeply* (1990). For the wonderful Alan Rickman (RIP).
4. Ingmar Bergman's black-and-white classic *The Seventh Seal* (1957). For its *danse macabre* end. Parodied brilliantly by French and Saunders.
5. *Bambi* (1942). For every Boomer and Gen-Xer who had to go through this rite of passage at the cinema. I was at the long-missed Riviera in Teignmouth with my mum when I heard the hunter's gunshots that killed Bambi's mother. I was stunned and couldn't even cry, though several other children could be heard sobbing. The crime of the century according to Edward Tudor-Pole and the Sex Pistols.

Art and literature help us consider death in general, our own death, and the death of those we love. And this brings us now to funerals. How we say goodbye to those we love. How we sum up a life.

F

IS FOR FUNERAL

Rites and Rituals.
Practice and Practicalities

funeral *noun*
1. the observances held for a dead person usually before burial or cremation.
2. an end of something's existence.
3. if your decisions or actions will have bad consequences: 'it's your funeral'.

Parting is such sweet sorrow.
R*OMEO AND* J*ULIET*

Hurrah! my boys, at the Parson's fall,
For if he'd lived he'd 'a buried us all.
F*ROM* T*ALBACH* C*HURCHYARD*, S*OUTH* W*ALES*

☠☠☠

'For a society to be healthy, people must significantly mark the milestones of life through ceremony and ritual.'
Carl Jung

I am at a death café in Frodsham, Cheshire, organised by a wonderful woman called Iris. We meet in a lovely café with fabulous coffee, in an upstairs room.

There are eight of us gathered around a refectory table. Over in the corner of the room, a woman taps away on her laptop. Behind us, a couple chat over coffee and bagels. We are here to talk about death, dying and bereavement in a safe and friendly space. No judgement. No counselling. Just comparing notes. And cake. I couldn't have picked a better group for my first death café. The collection of people is my dream team: a widow, a funeral celebrant, a funeral director, a soul midwife, a doula, a palliative care nurse and two women who offer free community services such as bereavement support and sessions on subjects such as anticipatory and complex grief, how to care for someone at the end of life and advance care planning. All women. All humans happy to share what has brought them here, now, today. All of us interested in talking about death over a cuppa.

Wow.

And why? Because death is unavoidable. Because about 600,000 people die in the UK every year. At least one child in every classroom is growing up without a parent. Almost 40 per cent of us will be diagnosed with cancer in our lifetime. Around 49 per cent over the age of sixty-five have a life-limiting illness. As Anna Lyons and Louise Winter say: 'These are stark, sobering statistics and yet we still don't talk about death or teach our children how to live with the inevitability of it.'[1]

I drive home, feeling I have found my tribe. These women get me. We are part of a movement that want to make the end of our lives a more positive experience, who want to make the farewells to our loved ones more individual, more sensitive, more appropriate, with far more choice than has ever been offered or available.

And that starts with the dead body of the deceased.

From Cradle to Coffin

Death is a rite of passage that most cultures from time immemorial have marked by a ceremony. Funerary rites and rituals connect generations and validate the continuity of life.

For centuries in England, these obsequies remained unchanged. This included the after-death care of the body, also called 'last offices' or 'laying out'. Soon after death, these procedures would have been carried out by the women of the family or by the local midwife. As Arnold says, 'The midwives who ushered new life into the world also prepared dead bodies for the next one.'[2] These women closed the eyes, undressed and washed the body. They plugged the orifices to prevent leakage, and laid pennies on the eyelids to keep them closed. To stop the mouth gaping, the chin was bandaged, or a Bible placed under it, though a nightcap would do the same job, whilst also giving the appearance that the corpse was sleeping. Then the body was wrapped in a shroud, or draped in a winding sheet, or dressed in grave clothes. These grave clothes might have been part of a woman's trousseau, along with a set of burial clothes for future children who might need them. Babies dying within a month of baptism were buried in their baptismal gown. Herbs such as rosemary would be tucked into the fabric, for its pungent masking smell, and yew for its symbolism.

'Caring for the Dead'

Once laid out, the family watched over the corpse. This vigil, known as the 'wake', was the tradition of praying for the departed and consoling the mourners and continued until the funeral. During this time, perhaps a couple of days, an important ritual was to offer hospitality to friends and neighbours who came to pay their respects. Candles were lit and placed around the open coffin – if they had one – and this would have sawdust to absorb liquid and more sweet-smelling herbs. If they could not afford a coffin, they might be laid out on a table or board and then they would be carried to church in a box ('chesting') or in the parish coffin and then buried in a shroud.[3]

The family carried the coffin from home to church on foot, perhaps using a bier. If the body had to be carried from a remote region to the parish church, possibly a long way over rough ground, the bearers would follow a corpse road (more of this in 'M Is for Myth'), with coffin rests at certain points. At the lychgate[4] – or corpse gate – at the entrance to the church, the coffin rested on a table[5] while the mourners waited for the priest to receive it. Under this covered archway, the pallbearers could rest on seats, or shelter from bad weather. Between here and the church, the burial rites began.

In Ireland, this tradition of waking the corpse is still carried out today. Windows might be left open to allow the soul to escape, clocks stopped, mirrors covered or turned round, and pets kept out. In England, the wake now tends to be after the funeral or memorial service. As for the last offices, these actions are more likely today to be performed by a nurse in a hospital or hospice. If the person dies at home, the laying out is done by a nurse or end-of-life doula or the body removed by a funeral director and the offices performed at their premises. Though procedures vary between hospitals and cultures, there are legal requirements and health and safety measures. But there is a choice now.

Undertakers

In a letter to the editor of *The Reflector*, the English essayist Charles Lamb (1775–1834) wrote about London burial societies, where you could pay into a fund to enable you to be buried, when the time came, in a 'genteel manner' (like today's pre-paid funeral plan). Lamb satirises, in some detail, what one could expect at a genteel funeral:

> A strong elm coffin, covered with superfine black, and furnished with two rows, all round, close drive, best japanned nails, and adorned with ornamental drops, a handsome plate of inscription, Angel above, and Flower beneath, and four pair of handsome handles, with wrought gripes; the coffin to be well pitched, lined and ruffled with fine crape; a handsome crape shroud, cap, and pillow... a handsome velvet pall, three gentlemen's cloaks, three crape hat-bands, three hoods and scarves, and six pairs of gloves; two porters equipped to attend the funeral, a man to attend the same with band and gloves; also, the burial fees paid, if not exceeding one guinea.

As he facetiously states: 'what sting is there in death, which the handles with wrought gripes are not calculated to pluck away?'

Lamb acknowledged that it was mainly the working classes who paid into these funds, 'clubbing their twopences to save the reproach of a parish funeral'. They had such horror of a pauper's burial that '[m]any a savoury morsel has the living body been deprived of, that the lifeless one might be served up in a richer state to the worms'. But it was the undertakers who took the brunt of his irony, caricatured as money-grabbing charlatans. 'He is bed-maker to the dead. The pillows which he lays never rumple. The day of interment is the theatre in which he displays the mysteries of his art.'[6]

Making profit out of death was not new. In 1666 the Wool Act was passed, making it law that one must be buried in wool rather than 'the linen of Christ' – apart from plague victims (note the date). This not only helped the wool trade but also protected the paper trade; newspapers were printed in recycled cloth – hence the term 'rag'. The Act was eventually repealed in 1814.

Before the emergence of undertakers as a profession, it was the tradesmen that offered goods and services: stable owners provided the hearse[7] or carriage, carpenters, joiners or cabinet makers constructed the coffins. The sexton of the church tolled the bell and dug the grave. Lamb's undertaker stepped in with a custodial role, coordinating different areas until the end of the nineteenth century, when he became more involved in directing the funeral and the disposal of the dead. As London expanded, so did the emergence of the new middle class and the concept of the family unit. This led to funerals becoming social events and also to the desire for lasting memorials.

We have already seen that, until the establishment of the garden cemeteries in the mid-nineteenth century, most burials took place in parish churchyards, with the Church of England providing burial space both for its own members and for those of different faiths, such as Nonconformists, Catholics and Jews, though burials had to be conducted by Anglican clergymen using the prayer book service. In larger towns and cities, non-Anglican groups set up their own burial grounds where they could hold the services according to their own beliefs. In 1880, after years of campaigning by Nonconformists, Parliament passed the Burial Law Amendment Act, which removed the obligation to follow the prescribed form of service for burial in Anglican churchyards, particularly important in parishes without Nonconformist, Catholic or Jewish burial grounds.[8]

A Highland Funeral by James Guthrie (1882)

Funeral Profession

Jessica Mitford, in the updated[9] version of her classic *The American Way of Death Revisited*, examined the big business of the funeral industry and came to a similar conclusion as Charles Lamb almost two centuries earlier:

> He [the funeral director] has relieved the family of every detail, he has revamped the corpse to look like a living doll, he has arranged for it to nap for a few days in a slumber room, he has put on a well-oiled performance in which the concept of death has played no part whatsoever – unless it was inconsiderately mentioned by the clergyman who conducted the religious service… He and his team have given their all to score an upset victory over death.[10]

Mitford was particularly horrified with the embalming process, comprehensively used by American funeral directors in the second half of the twentieth century, for which she saw no need, except in circumstances such as travelling long distances across a vast continent or repatriation (embalming is compulsory for a body to be conveyed in an aircraft). She uses vivid language to describe the process the corpse must go through:

> Alas, poor Yorick! How surprised he would be to see how his counterpart of today is whisked off to a funeral parlour and is in short order sprayed, sliced, pierced, pickled, trussed, trimmed, creamed, waxed, painted, rouged and neatly dressed – transformed from a common corpse into a Beautiful Memory Picture.[11]

Mitford believed that this preservation technique was employed purely to prepare the body for public display because of the North American tradition of having an open casket present at a funeral, with no legal or religious decree to forbid it. She went as far as to say, '[f]oreigners are astonished by it' whilst at the same time admitting that Americans were 'blissfully ignorant of what it is all about, what is done, and how it is done.' Add to this, the thick coffin liners and metal caskets,[12] and you have 'everything to avoid decay or an acknowledgment that this is what happens to the body in death'.[13]

And then there's the cost. The coffin displays and catalogues suggest to the recently bereaved that 'their loved one is worth it'. In fact, Mitford worked out that the cost of the funeral was 'the third-largest expenditure, after a house and a car, in the life of an ordinary American family'.[14] Not to mention the lack of transparency over the difference between the retail cost and wholesale cost of caskets and furnishings.

Mitford suggested a shroud or a basket was the best method of disposal

– cheaper, more environmentally friendly, more natural and actually more in keeping with tradition in many cultures. But she received huge opposition from the funeral industry, with perceived experts saying that embalming protected the living, calling it 'hygienic treatment'. Actually, corpses present less threat than a living body, even when the person has died of contagion: they don't breathe, sweat, or excrete. Town planning and sanitation are more effective in fighting infection than embalming. And anyway '…the organisms which cause disease live in the organs, the blood, and the bowel, and cannot all be killed by the embalming process'.[15] The hygiene argument is a cover-up to facilitate an open-casket funeral. It's all about the money. And bad for the environment as bodily waste and toxic embalming fluids such as formaldehyde are poured into sewers. The fancy metal caskets are also a concern because the body must be taken out of its expensive temporary home before cremation, as they can't be burned. And, because they are not allowed to be reused, the caskets are broken up and scrapped.

In the USA, the funeral home has become more of a focus, and often the wake will be held there. This only serves to disenfranchise those families who might have liked their loved one kept at home until the funeral or at least held a wake in their own surroundings or somewhere special. This happens less in the UK, with the funeral parlour's chapel of rest used for private viewings of the body by close family or just for the body to be cared for in the interim between death and disposal, rather than for funeral services or wakes.

However, embalming is on the increase in the UK, though not always possible, because a body cannot be embalmed until a death certificate is obtained and the death registered.[16] Because NHS doctors do not want to limit autopsies, they do not advocate embalming, which has to be done as soon as possible after death, before decomposition sets in.

Mitford wasn't the only one to object to the business hustle of the American system as it crossed the pond. She cites Boseley and Godwin's article about the 'creeping Disneyfication – and soaring prices – in the British funeral industry', as big-brand American funeral directors imported their business (aka McFunerals) with little transparency for costs so that, on top of the usual disbursement fees for third party services such as crem fees, venue hire, catering, and flowers, there would be pressure to have the fanciest casket and the biggest cortege. Because you're worth it.

> McDeath is on its way to a funeral parlour near you. The Americans are here, although you may not yet have noticed it. We British don't talk about these things. But there they are … gearing up to effect a huge change in The British way of death.[17]

In journalist Kate Berridge's book, *Vigor Mortis*, she follows up on this idea of the death industry and death's ultimate taboo:

The funeral parlour, like the massage parlour, became the establishment nobody wanted to be seen entering – plastic flowers and shaded windows, dingy discretion with Kleenex and credit cards – both premises conducting furtive commercial transactions for the relief of socially embarrassing situations.[18]

Berridge argues that death and sex are linked; if sex sells, then so does death. But the depletion of funerary rites and rituals of the second half of the twentieth century led to a deepening of this taboo: 'The fast funeral that is cremation suits a society crippled by fear of death, and turns death into waste disposal rather than a rite of passage.'

We'd do well to remember Mitford's thoughts on how we treat each other in death.

'The major Western faiths have remarkably little to say about how funerals should be conducted. Such doctrinal statements as have been enunciated concerning disposal of the dead inevitably stress simplicity, the equality of all men in death, emphasis on the spiritual aspects rather than on the physical remains.'[19]

Disenfranchised Death

It is a cold, bitter day. The dead time between Christmas and the dawning of the new year. The skies are dark and gloomy. Old snow shrouds the ground. Mainly dirty and slushy but frozen and lethal in patches. Most people will be hunkered down in their homes, watching *The Great Escape*, *The Bridge on the River Kwai*, *The Dirty Dozen* – the war is still fresh for some, though it has been thirty years since its end. A few mourners venture outside because they must. They make the treacherous journey across counties, down motorways, dual carriageways, B roads and country lanes, to reach the ancient church on the wooded hill, crouching between moor and sea.

The ancient service will not be a celebration of life. It will be a sad, difficult occasion for the meagre collection of family and friends. No one will know what to say. What can you say when someone has chosen death over life?

Today is my father's funeral.

I am ten years old and I am not allowed to go.

Felo de Se

For centuries, suicide was a crime in the eyes of the law and a mortal sin against God in the eyes of the Church – God gave life and only God could take it away – therefore those who died by suicide were denied a Christian burial in consecrated ground (remember the hoo-ha over poor Ophelia, grudgingly given her virgin crants?). If they were lucky, they might be allowed burial on the north side of the church, reserved for outsiders. Otherwise, they could well end up buried at crossroads, at night, on the edge of town, in unhallowed ground, a stake hammered through their heart to stop their spirit coming back to haunt the living and to prevent them from rising up to meet God on Judgement Day.

This tradition wasn't always the norm. In the fourteenth century, the Bishop of London bought a piece of ground called No Man's Land in Clerkenwell, which he consecrated and set aside for the plague dead to allow them a decent burial. A chantry chapel was erected for mass to be said for the pardon of their souls, dying as they had without the last rites and thus destined for Purgatory or worse. (This chapel also had a mural of the *danse macabre*,[20] so that was handy.) The graveyard was named Pardon Churchyard (from which Pardon Street in Clerkenwell takes its name) and continued to be used by St John's Priory and for the burial of suicides, along with executed criminals and heretics.[21] So, still not great, but better than what was to come with those crossroads.

This harsh treatment of the bodies and souls of suicides was ended in the nineteenth century after the foreign secretary, Viscount Castlereagh, died in 1822.[22] The inquest found that he had taken his own life whilst 'not of sound mind', and he was therefore permitted burial in Westminster Abbey. The following year, the Burial of Suicide Act was passed, allowing suicides private burial in a churchyard, but only at night and without a Christian service. A review of the law resulted in a new Act in 1882 allowing burial in daylight hours. But it wasn't until 1961 that Parliament decriminalised suicide. The Suicide Act was passed just seventeen years before my father's death on a snowy day in 1978.

As attitudes changed, the Anglican Church also had to examine how they treated suicide victims. The Book of Common Prayer, used since 1662 for the funeral service in an Anglican church, was not allowed 'for any that die unbaptized, or excommunicate, or have laid violent hands upon themselves'. In 1959, a Church report said that 'a person who attempts suicide must be in a state of mental distress and therefore needs special sympathy and understanding'. Although this led to a decree that an adapted funeral service could be used for suicides who were 'of sound mind' (hard to imagine anyone taking their own life being of sound mind), few bishops produced such services for their clergy and, for years, many used the full service. In 2015, Canon Michael Parsons told the Synod that 'We take funerals of murderers, rapists, child abusers and gangsters and we are happy to commit them to the mercy of God. But not, it seems, suicides... Do we want to be part of church that rejects vulnerable people?'[23] The Synod voted overwhelmingly for the canon to be amended so that those who take their own lives can be buried in accordance with the rites of the Church of England. This was put into canon law in 2017.

☠☠☠

Hierarchy of Death

Funerals are especially difficult for the loved ones of those who have taken their own lives. As are those of victims of well-publicised 'accidents' or of murder (a subject in 'T Is for Terror'). But the funerals of those who have died a natural or expected death can also be fraught with conflict. There is such a thing as a hierarchy of a funeral, with the deceased spouse or partner at the top, followed by children, parents, siblings, other relations and close friends. But what if you are a stepdaughter? Where do you stand then? Ralph was my stepfather for nearly twenty-five years. He was in my life far longer than my own father, seeing me through such rites of passage as O levels, sixth form, university, graduation, marriage, early motherhood. It wasn't always easy, but he gave me away at our wedding and helped out with a deposit on our first flat. I returned with my family to Devon to be with him and my mother when his Alzheimer's became advanced. I was there moments after he died and was with my mother for the funeral arrangements, for the viewing in the funeral home. But one night, in the run-up to the funeral, I couldn't stop crying. Another father figure gone. And what was my place at the funeral? I knew I wouldn't be in the hearse with his four children. I wouldn't be with my mother in the car because my older brother naturally took on this role. My other brother, being a minister, took the funeral service. But I had the conversation with Mum. I felt left out, with a sad loss of control, and my mum asked if I would like to read out Psalm 121. A psalm that had been important to Ralph from his childhood in Canada. When his parents were struggling during the Great Depression, his mother told him to say this psalm. And though he was a little boy, he always remembered this in his time of need.

> The LORD watches over you—
>   the LORD is your shade at your right hand;
> the sun will not harm you by day,
>   nor the moon by night.
> The LORD will keep you from all harm—
>   he will watch over your life;

the LORD *will watch over your coming and going*
 both now and forevermore.
From Psalm 121:5–8, a song of ascents

☠☠☠

Twenty-Four Funerals

Funeral customs and traditions have always varied in different parts of the UK and between different communities, and they have evolved and changed over the millennia. While there are elements that remain the same, such as the use of light and the continuing bonds between the dead and the living, 'death in custom and tradition continues dynamically to adapt to the times'.[24]

I have been to twenty-four funerals. The youngest was for a three-year-old. The oldest a hundred and one. One was a double funeral – my aunt and eight-year-old cousin. I have written and said three eulogies, one for my dear nan, one for her beloved second husband, and the other for my great-auntie Ruth. Some of these were memorial services with the body absent. Some were in crems, some in parish churches. One was in a village hall before a woodland burial. Secular, humanist, Christian, I've never attended one of a faith different to mine, though I have been to a Roman Catholic funeral, a different denomination to mine, where the noticeable difference to my Baptist roots was that the coffin of my uncle was sprinkled with holy water and incensed.

There are different forms of Judaism with varying funerary customs but what happens straight after someone dies is the same. A prayer is recited by a *shomer*, who takes care of the body until the burial, which should be within twenty-four hours if possible. The body is washed and purified by members of the *chevra kadisha* of the same sex as the deceased, then wrapped in a shroud and placed in the coffin. Although the deceased will not be viewed again, the *shomer* will remain with them. After the burial, mourners scatter earth onto the coffin, perhaps using a shovel which they will stick back into the ground for the next mourner to take out again, symbolising that this is an individual act. Then the group divides into two lines for the family to walk through, a symbol of being cared for by their community. After the funeral, the family sits *shiva* at home for seven days while friends and family visit, bringing food and offering comfort.[25]

Ritual washing is important in many of the world's major religions, as it represents the deceased being cleansed from sin. *Ghusl* (ablution) is an obligatory part of Islamic burial; a body must be purified ahead of meeting Allah. As in the Jewish faith, women wash women and men wash men. Then the body is anointed with attar, a perfume, before being shrouded. *Tayammum* is a dry ablution using dust from a special stone, performed over the top of a shroud when the condition of the body is too decomposed or damaged for washing with water. If a Muslim has died in a place where there are no Muslims, an absentee funeral prayer will be said, such as during the Covid-19 pandemic.

One type of funeral I would be interested to witness is for that of a magician, who would traditionally have a broken wand ceremony where either the wand which they used in performances, or a ceremonial one, is broken. First performed at Houdini's funeral in 1926, this symbolises the magician's death and that the wand has lost its magic. I'd also love to attend a New Orleans jazz funeral and pop over to Utah to eat some Mormon funeral potatoes. And I'm intrigued too by the traditional Cockney funeral used by the 'Pearlies' (who do a lot of good for the community in which they live) and by East End criminals such as the Krays (who did a lot of bad for the community in which they lived), harking back to the Victorians with their horse-drawn hearses, feathers and razzmatazz.

And then there is the fictional Polly Gray from *Peaky Blinders*. To mark her death, she is laid in a wagon, surrounded by her personal effects – including her gun, as she'll most probably need it in her afterlife. This is her funeral pyre. Her loved ones stand back and watch. (And plan revenge.) A moving end for her and of course for the late wonderful Helen McCrory, who played Aunt Polly.

Gypsy and Traveller communities have their own culture and customs regarding cemeteries and burying their dead.

> Irish Travellers and Romany Gypsies are distinct ethnic groups with their own belief structures, languages and customs… Many of the customs refer to the great respect that Travellers have for their deceased loved ones and allowing the spirit of that person to pass onto the afterlife without disruption. … Travellers maintain a strong connection with loved ones once they have passed. For Travellers death does not mark the end. The spirit lives on and the graveside is the place in which to grieve and show your respect for the deceased.[26]

Floral tributes are important and offer comfort to the bereaved, a token of their love for the deceased. But, according to the *Travellers' Times*, some churches and cemeteries make this difficult time even harder for Gypsy, Roma and Traveller families. For example, they reported a Romany Gypsy woman in Essex being told by the church to remove some of the floral tributes because they were 'gaudy' and 'Traveller-ish'.[27] A funeral director from Derby, Matthew Lymn Rose, has spoken about such attitudes: 'We understand the gravity of the stigma and discrimination that people from Traveller communities receive. A.W. Lymn are a funeral provider for all communities, backgrounds, and people, we never discriminate, and work hard to understand every culture, religion, and request.'[28]

According to Lane et al., historically, nomadic Gypsy and Traveller families had 'wayside burials' on unconsecrated ground, but today it is important for Gypsy and Traveller families to have a Christian burial, regardless of the family being nomadic or living in permanent accommodation.[29] The majority of Gypsies and Travellers are Christians[30] and, therefore, many of the death rites and funeral practices are informed by their religious and cultural beliefs and most families will usually choose a burial. Time and dignity are crucial and the 'Victorian way of death' continues for many Gypsies and Travellers in England today.

The expectation is that the dead should be given a 'good send-off' – a large casket, a large cortege, many mourners who have travelled a long way and who rely on hospitality. This can incur considerable expense, with many needing to pay for the funeral in cash, as they do not have a bank account or access to bank loans or credit cards.[31] While there is a cultural expectation of a large funeral, the majority of Gypsy and Traveller families live in poverty,[32] with funeral costs placing families under extreme financial pressure.

Most Gypsies and Travellers prefer the deceased to be returned to the family for the 'sitting up' or 'wake' prior to the funeral. Family and friends pay their last respects to the deceased and support the immediate family, sometimes hundreds of people, who will often have travelled long distances. Due to a lack of authorised stopping places, nomadic families will have to liaise with the local authority to be 'allowed' to stay in the area.

Gypsies usually drape special white sheets over the walls of the trailer or room for the sitting up. Some funeral directors will lend these to the family, as well as candlesticks, as candles will be kept alight during the sitting-up period to light the way to Heaven. As with the Victorians, some will cover the mirrors so that the soul will not see itself and want to stay in the home. To help the soul depart, the bereaved will open windows and keep doors unlocked.

For Romany Gypsies, the sitting up will take place at home after the funeral director has returned the body there. For Irish Travellers, the wake tends to be held the night before the funeral in the funeral parlour. However, if the deceased and family are nomadic, the funeral director will usually return the body in a coffin or casket to the family at an agreed place – in a field, at the side of the road, or in a permanent park. Here personal belongings of the deceased will be put into the caravan and burned – a purifying and transformative practice.

Nomadism is an integral part of Gypsy and Traveller culture, and the journey to the church and graveyard is an essential part of the funeral. The cortege will stop at meaningful places, which can mean the large cortege will move across a large area. The logistics of this requires a good funeral director, one who can coordinate relationships with other agencies. And not just for the cortege, but at the cemetery itself. Imagine the distress when there is a lack of attention to detail, such as the size of the casket being too big for the size of the grave. Sadly, this has happened.[33]

Cooperation

Co-op Funeralcare is the UK's largest funeral director. In 2018 they did a study into attitudes to death and dying in the UK to break taboos around talking about funeral plans. Director David Collingwood said:

> We know that talking about death is one of the hardest conversations people have to have and many choose to avoid it… But having to make lots of decisions under pressure can add to the stress and pain of bereavement. We would really encourage people to discuss or write down their wishes.[34]

As a result, they launched their direct cremation service, reflecting changing attitudes towards death and a shift from traditional funerals to celebratory gatherings (highlighted by the absence of a funeral for David Bowie in 2016). A direct cremation is where the deceased is collected from the place of death and cremated without a funeral service. No crem or church. No mourners present. No hearse. No flowers. You can pick up the ashes at a later date and perhaps have a memorial service. Or perhaps a party, or a shared meal. You can scatter the ashes somewhere with meaning. This will be less than half the price of a full funeral.

But it doesn't have to be one or the other, this or that. You have choices. Perhaps a cremation followed by a memorial service in a church or a community centre of some sort. Maybe a funeral with the coffin present in a church followed by a cremation at the crem or burial in a cemetery or churchyard or natural burial site. You can be buried in your garden – it is legal – though you need to check with the local authority and bear in mind that it might impact any future sale of the property. You can do the funeral at home and then have a cremation or burial elsewhere. More funeral directors are open to offering choice and flexibility, and there are an increasing number of forward-thinking independent and small chain companies now such as Poppy's, Poetic Endings and Full Circle.

It's Your Funeral

Tom Sawyer with his friends Huck and Joe secretly watch their own funeral and then reveal themselves, much to the astonishment of the congregation. How would you want your funeral to pan out? How do you want your family and friends to see you off into your long night? What would you like them to say about you? Thinking about this, discussing and planning it, will take away some stress for those you leave behind while they deal with practicalities alongside raw grief. If they know your wishes, they can not only honour them – feeling they have done something positive for you at this difficult time – but they don't have the anxiety of second guessing.

I've talked to people who say they don't want a funeral. I've asked them what their family think about that. Usually, they say they've never discussed it. If you do nothing else, have the conversation. One of my friend's daughters used to say that she wanted to have her ashes spread outside Frankie & Benny's in Dorking, but sadly that's now closed. However, they had the conversation. They joked about it. They put death on the table and looked at it, however obliquely. The very act of talking about such a taboo subject is good.

Contemplating your own funeral allows you to focus on how you live and what you will leave behind. And although your legacy will be much bigger than the funeral itself, the ritual can be life-affirming for your loved ones, helping them to grieve. Furthermore, if you play a part in the planning, your funeral can genuinely reflect who you were in life. As with writing wills, plan ahead; none of us knows when we are going to die and this takes away some of the unknown.

You're unique. You deserve a funeral that reflects that. So ponder what you'd like and let your family know what you want. After all, we make birth plans, so why not end-of-life plans? My birth plans didn't get followed to the letter, but the gist was there. If I die suddenly, my end-of-life plan won't go as expected but my family will know the heart and bones of what I want and that will hopefully be of some help and even comfort.

It's Your Life

- Where do you want your body to be laid out?
- Do you want to be buried or cremated?
- What type of funeral would you like? Religious or civil or humanist? Do you want an ethical funeral service which will look after you and the planet?
- Locations for the funeral: green or woodland burial site, a crem, a cemetery, a church. Did you know, for example, that you can have a C of E funeral in the parish where you live, whether you are a churchgoer or not?[35] There are choices.
- Officiant: a church minister can do the whole funeral service at any of these places or a combination of locations with a service in a church followed by prayers elsewhere. Or why not consider a celebrant? There are some fantastic, independent ones who will guide you through every stage of the journey, making the experience individual, intimate and unique. Involve family and friends.

D IS FOR DEATH

- Coffin: wooden, wicker, painted, cardboard that can be decorated beforehand by family or during service. Or a shroud.
- Pallbearers: this is a last act that members of your family or friends can do for you. Or maybe you are part of some community group. Or you can have the funeral directors.
- Transport: hearse, motorbike with sidecar, horse and carriage, cart.
- Who will you invite? Do you want them to wear certain colours? Or bring certain things?
- Flowers: strewing flowers on graves has been noted in sources as early as the 1770s, though in some areas of England this practice was banned in some churchyards right up until late 1880s. In Wales, flowers were often planted on top of graves to symbolise the time of life in which the person died: daffodils, primroses and violets for infants, roses for those who died in mid-life, rosemary for the elderly. In England, evergreen shrubs such as rosemary and box were planted; because they did not wilt, these plants symbolised remembrance and eternal life. It is only recently that wreaths have been put on graves.[36] You could opt for: a formal wreath, a bunch of wildflowers or dried flowers, a quirky arrangement, a garland. You could have pots of flowers in the aisles or around the room where the service is held. These can be carried to the graveside or taken home.
- Music: traditional or modern hymns, special songs, a string quartet, live or recorded, a choir.
- Readings: a poem, a religious text, a piece of writing from the deceased, a letter, individual or communal.[37]
- Eulogy/tribute: who will deliver this? A family member? A friend? A minister or celebrant? A pre-recorded message made by the deceased (think Denholm in *The IT Crowd*).
- Time for reflection: how long? Silence? Music? Do you want those gathered to do something such as write down a note/memory on a piece of paper (maybe heart- or leaf-shaped) and hang it on a tree or put in a box?
- A message of hope: a blessing, a prayer, some significant words that will send people off with something uplifting in their hearts.
- What do you want to do afterwards? Refreshments somewhere convenient where you can look after guests who have travelled and where people can talk and share memories. Have a guest book.

Discuss your thoughts with others, write them down and tell them where you will keep these plans. Or maybe keep with a solicitor. You should also aim to review it every now and then as circumstances change and as life goes on.

Knowing there are choices, knowing what those choices are and acting upon them is an important way to feel more in control of a situation.[38]

F IS FOR FUNERAL

When I Die/Death Wishes

There is a growing movement in the UK advocating for the care of the dead at home until the funeral, either if they have died at home or elsewhere when they can be brought home with the help of a funeral director. There is no legal amount of time you can keep a body at home, but there are decisions that need to be made. If you choose to lay out a body at home for an extended period, a funeral director or doula can help, for example with the supply of a cool blanket.[39]

Wherever I die, I'd like to be kept at home until the funeral. But this will involve me having some conversations with my family. I'd rather not be embalmed, just kept cold. However, if I still live a long way from Selworthy, then I'd like my body to be taken to Green Undertakings in Minehead. I'd like to be dressed in something of my own: some comfy pyjamas or a nice dress. Perhaps someone could take fingerprints as a memento.

My funeral:

- I'm not bothered about what cars should be in the cortege but people might need help getting to this remote place.
- All Saints Parish Church, Selworthy, Somerset.
- Minister: Jamie Redfern from Teignmouth Baptist Church.
- Whoever wants to come: refer to my list of people and how I knew them.
- Order of service: someone be creative and use funny photos or quotes of mine (from my life or from my books), whatever you want.
- Wear whatever you'd like: I don't mind if it's black. Maybe a yellow flower.
- I want my body to be present in a wicker coffin from Somerset Willow Coffins[40] with a garland of wildflowers and greenery (and burial in the churchyard afterwards).
- Tealights on the pews (to be lit later), jam jars of wildflowers in the aisle, pebbles in a basket (from Teignmouth beach).
- Music before the service: 'Breathe Deep (the Breath of God)' by the Lost Dogs and 'Everything' by Tim Hughes (to show my Christian beliefs) and *Brideshead Revisited* theme to show my literary love. Any others my family would like.
- Music for coffin to come into: Max Richter, 'Spring 1'.
- Pallbearers: chosen by my family.
- Welcome: Jamie to explain what is going to happen.

- Reading: whoever wants to do this can choose something they want.
- Hymn: Psalm 23 (modern version with harmony).
- Eulogy: whoever wants to do this.
- Light the tealights while 'Crossing the Bar' by the Long Johns is played. Or if you can get four or so people together, then it could be live! (Johnny? Rina Vergano? Nikki Racklin? Beth and Rob Porch?). A time for reflection. With photo slide, if tech allows.
- Jamie: message of hope.
- End with 'Bring Me Sunshine'. You can use my video with photos of my life (on my website) if tech allows.
- Coffin to be taken out by music of family's choice (but something uplifting like 'Lark Ascending' by Vaughan Williams or 'What a Wonderful World' by Louis Armstrong).
- As guests leave the church, they can take a jam jar of flowers or a pebble and follow the coffin down to the graveside. (These can be taken home afterwards.)
- Burial in churchyard: someone to say Christina Rossetti's poem 'Let Me Go':

> *Miss me a little, but not for long*
> *And not with your head bowed low*
> *Remember the love that once we shared*
> *Miss me, but let me go.*

- Committal, commendation and dismissal by Jamie at the graveside while earth to be cast on the coffin (or flower petals or pebbles).

> *We have entrusted our sister to God's mercy*
> *And we now commit her body to the ground:*
> *Earth to earth, ashes to ashes, dust to dust*
> *In sure and certain hope of the resurrection to eternal life*
> *Through our Lord Jesus Christ.*

- Jamie's blessing.
- Back to Northmoor House in Dulverton for the night/weekend if available, or else a nice country hotel for a cream tea and a glass of sherry/fizz (preferably English sparkling wine such as Huxbear).
- Choose a book of mine to take home.
- My family can decide on the headstone.
- Neil and children to decide on my social media and digital legacy.
- Donations to Samaritans.
- If I have a dog, I'd like them to be there if appropriate, like a therapy dog.

Digital Legacy

How would you like to be remembered? We can't all be the subject of an elegy by a romantic poet, but we will still be remembered by loved ones. Even those we clashed with in life will most likely be sad at our death; death has a habit of putting old disputes into context. A few years ago, I had a Facebook spat with a Scottish writer friend over independence. I didn't want the union broken up, but Alison did. By the time of Brexit, she was still resolute in the need for an independent Scotland. And, by now, so was I. Why wouldn't the Scottish people want to be in control of their own destiny? After all, they had voted to remain.

More importantly, I now put myself in my friend's shoes. She was Scottish and she wanted independence. She also had breast cancer. It had come back. To her lungs and to her brain. She didn't have long to live, but she used this time to blog about her cancer which really did put things in perspective. She was remarkable. A fighter who had always put her beliefs into action. She'd been on Greenham Common in the eighties protesting against nuclear weapons and now she was fighting for legislation for dignity in dying, while marrying her beloved long-term partner to make sure she was financially secure and because she loved her.

About sixteen months after her death, I had my own breast cancer to deal with. The same type of aggressive triple negative breast cancer. I re-read her cancer blog posts. Brutally honest and yet life-affirming. They helped. Not because she indulged in platitudes – not her style – but because she laid bare the truth of cancer. During my diagnosis and treatment, I couldn't face online forums, the natural choice during Covid lockdown. Chemo is difficult, and shielding meant I was isolated and far from my family. But I read her posts. They were what I needed. I don't want to say she fought her cancer, because you can't. The NHS do that on your behalf. But she was a warrior. A warrior who fought on behalf of others for a better world. She even wrote her own obituary a few weeks before she died. Wise words that have stayed with me: 'A good life is about the people we meet.'[41]

I am glad for Facebook, which kept me in touch with her life and death. But these days, I prefer Instagram and its pretty pictures of dogs, churches and post boxes. Our words and photos live on. Our final goodbye is not the end. Helen Frisby calls the 'internet ghost' a 'twenty-first-century kind of revenant… popping up often unbidden to surprise and sometimes distress relatives and friends'.[42]

Sometimes, something more than our words and photograph remains.

Websites and Articles

The Arbory Trust
The Barton Glebe Woodland Burial Ground, established on Church of England glebe land in 2000, offers an alternative to burial in churchyards or cemeteries. Coffins (or shrouds) must be biodegradable,[43] and embalming is not permitted. A non-profit-making organisation and member of the Association of Natural Burial Grounds.
https://www.arborytrust.org/

Association of Natural Burial Grounds
Established by the Natural Death Centre in 1994, the Association assists individuals in the process of establishing new natural burial grounds, provides guidance to existing burial ground operators and represents members who must comply with a code of conduct to assure best practice.

Coffin Club
Empowering people to take control of their final send off.
https://coffinclub.co.uk/when-you-go-go-green/

Poppy's Funerals
A fresh approach to funerals.
https://www.poppysfunerals.co.uk/talking-death/how-to-care-for-someone-who-has-died-at-home/

Natural Endings
Person-centred funeral services
https://naturalendings.co.uk/

Full Circle
Funerals your way. Yorkshire with partners in the North-West.
https://fullcirclefunerals.co.uk/

Present Ascent
Lucy Biggs, independent funeral celebrant in Cheshire and the Peak District. 'Lighting a path through the darkness.'
https://www.presentascent.co.uk/

A Quiet Revolution
A Scottish humanist charity that conducts meaningful funerals, tackles funeral poverty and promotes creative ageing.
https://www.aquietrevolution.org/

G
IS FOR GHOSTS

The Paranormal

ghost *noun*
1. the spirit or soul of a dead person, sometimes represented as a transparent image, that some believe appear to the living or haunt specific locations.
2. a memory, usually of something or someone bad.
3. a trace, e.g., *a ghost of a smile*.

other words for ghosts: phantom, apparition, wraith, revenant, spook, ghoul, spirit, manifestation, poltergeist, vision, shade, shadow, demon, spectre, appearance, banshee, daemon, visitor, zombie, vampire

If charnel-houses, and our graves, must send
Those that we bury, back, our monuments
Shall be the maws of kites.
MACBETH

In this churchyard lies Eppie Coutts,
Either here or hereabouts;
But where it is none can tell
Till Eppie rise and tell hersel'
FROM TORRYBURN CHURCHYARD

Dawlish, 2015

We had just moved into the central section of a two-hundred-year-old farmhouse in the seaside town of Dawlish, Devon. It is a building of note in the town. For a period last century, it was let by a cousin of Elizabeth Bowes-Lyon (later known as the Queen Mother), who used to bring her two young daughters to stay. (Yes, the late Queen, then a princess, might well have used the same loo.) Whatever its provenance, it was a house full of character. Quirky, the estate agent called it. Nooks and crannies and a lot of wood: floors, wall panels, shutters, cupboard doors, built-in wardrobes, hatches. So much wood that it made the house feel a little hobbity. Set over two wings, it was disorientating at first; you could feel quite alone, out of earshot, even though there might be several of us in the house.

Within a couple of days of moving in, I could smell soot, everywhere, especially when I was on my own. Then a few odd things happened. As I stood in the hall one evening, a wooden stool flew down the stairs, just missing me. Over the following week, both my seventeen-year-old daughter and I fell down a few stairs. We didn't trip, or slip; it was as if we'd been given a nudge. We were never hurt and none of these incidents felt particularly spooky, but I wondered if this was something we would have to get used to. I asked my Canadian cousin, a paranormal investigator, for advice. Why do I keep smelling soot? Did the house ever have a fire, he asked. Check it out. I checked it out. Yes, there had been a fire. In 1900. Quite a big fire actually. So big, it razed the cobb-and-thatch house almost to the ground (but it was rebuilt with a tiled roof that was to become the ongoing maintenance issue of future inhabitants). And where did it start? Oh, in our kitchen. Right, he says. But what do I do about the ghosts? Do you think there are ghosts? Of course, there are ghosts, he says. It's an old house. (I know 'old' takes on a different meaning in North America, but yes, even by British standards, this is an old house.) What should I do? Get an exorcism? Hold your horses, he laughs. First things first. The next time you smell soot or something weird happens, just tell them to go away. You live there now.

So, the next time I smell soot, I tell them.

Go away. We live here now.

I sound like I'm telling off a pesky kid. Perhaps it actually is the ghost of a child; it doesn't feel like a malevolent presence, rather a mischievous one. The next time something weird happens to my daughter, she also has this weapon up her sleeve. One day, alone in her attic room, she hears a scratching noise. It could be a mouse, but to be quite honest she'd rather it were a ghost. Calmly and firmly, she tells it to go away. She never hears that noise again. Even when we do have mice.

Pretty soon, the presence seems to have gone. We hope to a place of peace.

☠☠☠

In her book *The Ghost*, Susan Owens examines the cultural reach of ghosts in our ancient country, wandering through the centuries, discussing our evolving opinions of the spirit world.

> Ghosts are woven into the fabric of our lives: every village, town and great house has at least one spectral resident, sometimes a whole host of them… Today, anyone who lives in a very old house finds themselves asked frequently, and quite matter-of-factly, if it is haunted. Surprisingly often, the answer is yes; and it is perhaps a reflection of the phlegmatic British character that, by and large, we quietly cohabit with our resident ghosts – whether we wholeheartedly believe in them or not.[1]

She even asks if their prevalence has something to do with the British weather (doesn't everything?). 'Do the mists, fogs and rains of our climate play on our imaginations, suggesting uncanny presences out there in the murky darkness?'[2] Not forgetting our landscape:

> Had generations of people looked out fearfully towards the wild, lonely places – the marshes, the moors and the misty hills – and shuddered at what their imaginations conjured up, glad to close their doors and to reach the safety of the hearth … The idea of something not quite human lurking malevolently out there in the darkness is buried deep within our collective imagination and has a long history.[3]

Is that why we sit around the fireside telling ghost stories? From a safe, warm place, we can look at the world from a different perspective. We can close our eyes and picture revenants, zombies and the undead hovering in limbo, between this world and the next. And, however sceptical we might be, most of us know a ghost story.

The Red-Eyed Nun, Trinity School, Teignmouth, 1982

The White Lady is a ghostly archetype in many cultures, differing in character, often associated with the loss of a loved one. In Ireland and Britain, her screams are said to foretell death. But who has heard of the red-eyed nun? If you attended my school in the 1980s, you'd know all about her, as she struck fear into the hearts of us teenage girls. My school was a convent until the end of my primary years and, as I moved over the road into the senior school, the nuns left for Liverpool. But their legacy remained, not just from their graveyard in the grounds or the chapel tucked away inside the Gothic, red-bricked convent. It was the red-eyed nun in the science labs that kept their memory alive.

Although I was a day girl, there were also boarders, mainly children of the military or divorces. Students from all over the world, which meant that, although I came from a very white town, I mixed with children from Kenya, Nigeria, Liberia, Malaysia and Hong Kong, albeit privileged ones. And almost all of us were intrigued, morbidly so as only teenagers can be. Had anyone actually seen this spectral nun? Why did she have red eyes? Was she evil? Or simply a lost soul?

The story goes that she had been a chemistry teacher and not a very kind one, until one day an experiment went wrong and killed her off. She was said to roam the chemistry lab at night, doomed to float amongst the Bunsen burners and jars of pickled animal innards until she moved on to the next realm. (Purgatory was still well and truly a thing in our corner of Devon.) Looking back some forty years later, I can see some chinks in the narrative. The chemistry lab, for example, was a relatively new prefab and so the myth of it being haunted by a long-dead nun doesn't feel particularly authentic. Also, the boarders – the ones spreading the story – would have been unable to ghost-hunt; there was no way they could have escaped their dorms at night.

Perhaps the frisson of terror that swept through the school had something to do with the copy of Pan horror stories which was making its way through our clammy, ink-stained fingers. When it was my turn, I took it home, devouring it in a few hours, then was unable to sleep for months afterwards, particularly when I had chemistry the following day. Perhaps that's why I gave up the subject when we took our options. Or maybe that was because I got 23 per cent in my end-of-year exams. You decide. Anyway, while others progressed to Stephen King and James Herbert, I moved onto Jilly Cooper and Jackie Collins. I chose sex over death.

Torre Abbey, Torquay, 2012

In 1588, Sir Francis Drake captured the flagship of the Spanish Armada, taking prisoner nearly four hundred of the crew, which included the fiancée of one of the lieutenants, disguised as a sailor so she would not be separated from him. They were locked in a barn in the grounds of Torre Abbey, crammed together in awful conditions. She caught a chill and died. Since then, the ghost of the Spanish Lady has haunted the barn, crying for her lost sailor. There is also a headless cleric on a ghost horse and Lady Cary in a ballgown driven in a lit-up carriage by her coachman. They are everywhere these ghosts, and so this was the place where I did my first paranormal investigation, alongside my Canadian cousin, who also happens to be a corrections officer, which is enough to scare off the more faint-hearted ghosts.

G IS FOR GHOSTS

Equipped with EMF detectors and IR thermometers, we go to Torre Abbey at nightfall. Not much action is happening in the barn. It is a little disappointing. But then, unexpectedly, when we are alone in the darkened chapel, the candles on the altar sputter out. Then they light up again. Then out. Then on. They are of course electric lights. But still, there isn't an obvious explanation. But my ghost-busting sceptical cousin will not be taken in. Not until we reach the darkened parlour of the mansion and a few of us sit around a card table, a Ouija board at the centre, candlelight throwing shadows across our faces so we look like spectres. Not really my thing, not since trying this with my cousin, my Auntie Liz and Uncle Alan and their family friends, a nice couple. I was hoping to hear from my dad, but Eloise and I, the only ones with our fingers left on the glass, felt, saw and witnessed it move without our doing, spelling out I-R-I-S. 'Auntie Iris!' shrieked the friend. 'It's my Auntie Iris!' And, while she might have been delighted, I was both disappointed and discombobulated. Had Eloise been playing me? Later, she asked me the same. To this day, we both can't explain it. Teenage hormones perhaps? Or Auntie Iris? Anyway, it got me wondering about my father and if I could ever speak to him from beyond the grave...

Back at Torre Abbey, we have a finger each on the glass. There's palpable tension in the room. The EMF is going ballistic and the temperature has dropped. The glass moves. Almost imperceptibly at first. Then more definite. Stronger. Faster. It slides across the board. Our fingers, with only the lightest touch, follow it but it doesn't spell anything that makes sense to us. And, although there are no sightings of the Spanish Lady, the headless cleric or Lady Cary that night, there is definitely some crazy energy in Torre Abbey.

There is crazy energy all over Devon; from Dartmoor to the old fishing towns, stories of ghosts abound, none more so than at Berry Pomeroy Castle, a ruin now, but once home to a Yorkist family who had it fortified during the Wars of the Roses. Later, it was acquired by Edward Seymour, Duke of Somerset, brother of Jane and lord protector of his nephew, Edward VI. Ambitious building plans formulated by his descendants came to nothing. Lack of funds. By 1700 it had been abandoned. It is supposed to not only be the last castle built in England, but also one of the most haunted. Georgian visitors couldn't get enough of it. There was even a Gothic novel called *The Castle of Berry Pomeroy* (1806), 'a tale of jealousy, multiple murder and ghostly revenge'.[4] As for the ghosts, one of them is the White Lady, supposed to be the beautiful Margaret Pomeroy who died of starvation while held captive in the dungeons by her jealous sister.

It is said that most of the paranormal experiences happen by day, but then you wouldn't catch me going there by night.

A Visit to Tintern Abbey by Moonlight, Peter van Lerberghe, 1823

North York Moors, 1400s

In the early years of the fifteenth century, a monk from Byland Abbey in Yorkshire fills in some blank pages of a manuscript with local ghost stories. Centuries later, this text finds its way into M.R. James's hands and, in 1922, he transcribes the twelve stories into Latin.[5] According to Eleanor Jackson, the ghosts in these stories are not evil forces:

> They are mostly people from the community who have died without confessing sins, righting wrongs or otherwise preparing for a 'good death'. The ghosts cannot get to heaven until these issues have been resolved, so they rise from their graves to seek help from the living... They reveal medieval people's very real fear of death and the uncertainties of what lay beyond, but also a surprising compassion for the undead.[6]

Ghosts have been hanging around for a long time in this country. By the 1400s, they have made their way into church, where 'the Living and the Dead' is a common mural: three young men and three corpses in various stages of decomposition warn the illiterate congregations to repent now, while they still can. Especially with contagion lurking in every corner.

Such as I was you are, and such as I am you will be.

Scholars argue that the concept of Purgatory enabled belief in these ghosts; while souls were still loose in this liminal place, they could flit back and forth between here and there, both dead and undead. The Reformation aimed to put a stop to what was perceived as Papist nonsense. Now, after death, the soul would zoom straight up to Heaven or straight down to Hell. End of. No second chances. The pious reformers 'tidied ghosts away as part and parcel of the unwanted old paraphernalia of Catholicism'.[7] But, just as dust will keep on settling, so ghosts continued to be seen.

St Paul's Cathedral, 1666

Remember John Donne's 'Death Be Not Proud'. The metaphysical poet and dean of old St Paul's fixated on death and the afterlife and believed in the possibility of ghosts coming back to the living. So certain was he of the resurrection that, when he was dying, he put on a shroud and had an artist sketch him. He meditated on this picture whilst on his deathbed. After his death, the drawings were used to sculpt a full-size marble monument, which was placed in the choir of his beloved cathedral in 1631. A few decades later, when the medieval building went up in smoke during the Great Fire, Donne's was one of the few figures to survive relatively unscathed. The story goes that, during the inferno, the effigy slid off its pedestal and found its way into the crypt, where it remained until the end of the nineteenth century.[8]

The Old Rectory, Epworth, Lincolnshire, 1716–17

With the dawning of the Enlightenment, the reality of ghosts was debated further as reason was pitched against religion, science against superstition. Philosopher Thomas Hobbes stated that, apart from angels, ghosts were all in the imagination. This was rebutted by Joseph Glanville, scholar and chaplain to Charles II, who said that to deny ghosts or spirits – and witches – was to deny the afterlife and therefore the hope of the resurrection. John Wesley, the Methodist preacher of the evangelical revival, also rationalised the existence of ghosts and demons, seeing the paranormal as evidence of the spiritual realm. His beliefs were no doubt influenced by his childhood home, the Old Rectory, where for about two months, the household experienced the haunting of a poltergeist.

Referred to by the Wesley family as Old Jeffrey, the spirit's groans, knockings, footsteps and all manner of noises were heard by the servants, by all eight children who still lived at home, and by their mother, Susanna. The only one to remain sceptical – angry even, at the hysteria going on in the home – was the father, the Reverend Samuel Wesley, until, that was, he experienced Old Jeffrey for himself at family prayers at six o'clock one evening. This continued at the same time for the next few evenings, after which Samuel arranged for a vicar friend to be present the following day at family prayers but, when six o'clock struck, Old Jeffrey did not knock. He did not make himself known until later that evening, when a servant beckoned them upstairs, to the nursery.

Samuel led the way by candlelight and, once inside the nursery, where three of his daughters lay trembling and sweating in their sleep, the knocking moved next door. Once in that room, they heard the knocking back in the nursery, where it continued even after they had returned there, until Samuel was so angry he threatened to shoot the place of the knocking. His friend intervened. 'Sir, you are convinced, this is something preternatural. If so, you cannot hurt *it*: but you give it power to hurt *you*.' Samuel then went up to the site of the knocking and said in a stern voice: 'Thou deaf and dumb devil, why dost thou fright these children, that cannot answer for themselves? Come to me in my study, that am a man?'

The next evening, Old Jeffrey did exactly that and when Samuel opened the door to his study, it was thrown back with such force that it nearly slammed him over. Once inside, the knocking began and then, after a time, it moved to the room next door, where his daughter Nancy was. Samuel told the spirit to speak but it was quiet. Then he told Nancy to extinguish her candle as 'spirits love darkness' and perhaps it would then communicate. The knocking continued but there was no voice. He then sent Nancy downstairs, saying that two Christians were probably too much and that one-on-one it might speak. Once alone, he asked it to knock three times if it was the spirit of his son Samuel. It immediately went quiet and stayed that way all night.

The knockings continued for a while longer and several clergymen advised Samuel to leave the house, but he was adamant: 'No: let the devil flee from me: I will never flee the devil.'

Soon after, Old Jeffrey disappeared.[9]

William Hogarth satirised such Nonconformist thinking with his engraving *Credulity, Superstition and Fanaticism* (1762), which shows a Methodist minister bellowing fire-and-brimstone so animatedly that his wig flies off, revealing a tonsured head – suggesting the preacher is a Catholic in disguise. The picture includes many references to contemporary cases of alleged supernatural visitations: the preacher holds a puppet of a witch on a broomstick; at his feet lies Mary Toft, who said she had given birth to rabbits and the boy who vomited nails; three women in the congregation hold figures of the Cock Lane ghost; on the pulpit are the figures of three ghosts from popular literature – George Villiers, Julius Caesar and Mrs Veal; to the right of the pulpit is a figure of the Tedworth Drummer; and all the while the poor box grows cobwebs.

Credulity, Superstition and Fanaticism, William Hogarth, 1762

By the time of the Industrial Revolution and migration to cities, ghosts now had connotations of the 'rustic and poorly educated', but, according to Owens, the 'clear light of reason did not penetrate into every corner of the eighteenth century. There were dark, eerie places where owls shrieked, doors creaked and, if there was a moon, it was usually threatened by dismal clouds. It was an age of melancholy as much as it was one of enlightenment.'[10]

York, City of a Thousand Ghosts, 1989

When a final-year student at Lancaster, I was vice-captain of the rugby team. As part of Roses, the annual sports tournament with York, it was our turn to visit them – we alternated each year. Two of the original seven plate-glass universities established in the 60s, they have similar campuses and a collegiate system set up to be the Oxbridge of the North. Despite the rivalry, York was a home from home.

Lancaster has its fair share of the supernatural, what with links to the Pendle witches who were tried there. But York is supposed to be one of the most haunted cities in Europe. I had some spare time after my match (we won), so my mate Ruth suggested a trip to the York Dungeons – surely ghosts will be aplenty there. It will be a laugh and give our kidneys a couple of hours' reprieve from cider and British sherry (not mixed; we're not animals).

It wasn't a laugh. In fact, it was as terrifying as it had been in the Chamber of Horrors as a child. Ruth was no braver. We could offer each other no comfort but instead latched on to a group comprising mum, dad and two young children, hoping that by shadowing them we would get out alive.

This may be a family thing. When my sister-in-law, Sarah, took our oldest, Johnny, aged about ten to the London Dungeons, he only made it as far as the ticket kiosk. When Sarah took our younger two to the haunted house at the fairground in Teignmouth, I thought they'd be fine as they are less 'sensitive'. While Izzy had no problem whatsoever, Ed only made it slightly beyond the ticket barrier. As soon as he realised it was dark, he legged it back outside into the sun, without looking back. That was £2 well spent. (And that's what aunties are for.)

☠☠☠

Edinburgh, City of the Dead, 2011

It is autumn and my first visit to Edinburgh. A dip in temperature from Devon but clear skies. I am accompanying my Canadian cousin so he can indulge in his romanticism for his ancestors and so that we can do some paranormal investigations. If you're going to find something spectral, it will be here, in the Scottish capital; you can't walk around the city without being tripped over by a ghost. If you leave the bag pipes and the tartan and step off the bustling Royal Mile, you will find yourself dodging the dead who skulk along the cobbles of the closes and lie in wait in the nooks of the wynds. Edinburgh is a city of opposites. Old Town, New Town. Jekyll and Hyde. Dead and alive. And somewhere in between.

We have an evening investigation booked at the underground vaults, beneath the place where the gallows once stood at the Mercat Cross. In centuries-old caverns, we hear stories. Ghost stories. Historical stories. Burke and Hare, Deacon Brodie. Body snatchers, murderers, witches. Deals with the devil. All recounted by an actor who draws us in, cranking up the tension in the dark, airless crypts.

A couple of years later we are back in the city, this time to Mary King's Close, which was once a busy street, until it was built over by the Royal Exchange in the eighteenth century. It has always been known as a haunted place, perhaps because it was located close to the Nor Loch, the polluted marsh where the city's excrement was dumped, from which toxic gases escaped, creating spooky lights which could be mistaken for ectoplasm or could even have given hallucinations. We hear of Agnes Chambers, a sixteenth-century maid, and the seventeenth-century plague doctor. But it gets creepy when inside Annie's room.

When filming haunted places of Britain, Japanese psychic, Aiko Gibo, visits the Close. She is about to enter a small room when she feels such pain and sorrow she has to stop. She recounts: 'I cannot enter this roo... it is too strong... there is a child beside me, her little hand is clutching my trouser leg. I... I just cannot go into this room... she was separated from her parents. She wants to go home and see her family... her desire haunts this place very strongly.'[11] Eventually, she goes inside and communicates with the spirit of Annie, who has lost her doll. Then Gibo goes back onto the Mile and buys a doll from one of the tourist shops, which she leaves for Annie. She believes Annie is now at peace and, as long as the doll remains, her spirit will rest. Since then, visitors from across the globe have left dolls and toys. It's quite a moving, if macabre, sight.

But it is back in the vaults that we have our most creepy experience. We have a psychic Welshman with us. In one of the damp, dimly lit cellars, the ECT goes wild. Something is here. Something is happening. And while we sit quietly, so quietly you can hear your own heartbeat, quietly, gently, Colin talks to a spirit whose presence he can feel. He rests his hands on his knees, leaning slightly forwards, and the chain around his neck falls forward with him, its pendant swinging with the movement. Then he addresses the spirit more firmly, directly. If you are here, let us know, give us a sign. And, while this might all sound clichéd, the next few seconds could come right out of one of those Pan ghost story books. While Colin is very still, the pendant on his chain moves. It swings a little more, back and forth, independently. Yes, it could be a draught. But that doesn't explain how the pendant travels along the chain towards the back of Colin's neck, against gravity. Against the natural laws of the cosmos.

☠☠☠

We can't leave Edinburgh without visiting the tomb of the villainous George Mackenzie, in Greyfriars kirkyard. Known as the Black Mausoleum, it is infamously haunted by the Mackenzie poltergeist. Mackenzie was lord advocate during the reign of Charles II and, in the 1670s, he persecuted the Presbyterian Covenanters for their opposition to the Common Book of Prayer. This was an act of treason and over a thousand Covenanters were held and tortured in the Covenanters' Prison, in a field next to Greyfriars kirkyard. They were there for four months with no shelter and little food. Hundreds died, and many were executed. The lord advocate's vicious treatment earned him the nickname 'Bluidy Mackenzie'. After his death, he ended up buried next door to where his terror reigned; divided by a high wall and a locked gate, his Black Mausoleum is just yards from the prison, on the site of an old plague pit. And it is alleged to be very, very haunted. By a malevolent poltergeist, the cruel George Mackenzie. People have reported being bitten and scratched, kicked and pushed, with many actually fainting. After so many eyewitness accounts, the council keep the mausoleum locked, but you can go on an official tour. On their website, The City of the Dead, there is a warning: 'The Mackenzie Poltergeist can cause genuine physical and mental distress. Join the tour at your own risk.'

I haven't been on one of those tours; however, a few months ago I went with Johnny – braver now he's pushing thirty – on a Harry Potter tour which took in Greyfriars, not only because Mackenzie was supposed to be the inspiration for Harry Potter's Peeves but also because in another section of the kirkyard is the gravestone of a certain Tom Riddle. I recommend you go, if only to see the wonderful skulls and crossbones on the tombs and to see Greyfriars' Bobby's tomb. But now we leave this beautiful city of contrasts and head down south to the gentle downs of rural West Sussex.

The Swan, Fittleworth, South Downs, 2013

My great-auntie Ruth was born in the same year as the late Queen. She was also a teenage Wren towards the latter part of the war and was posted to Stanmore, to a satellite station of Bletchley Park, to work on the Enigma code-breaking machine. She had no idea what the bigger picture was, just that she played a very small part, legging it up and down corridors, clutching strips of paper printed with numbers. In 2013, her spirit is undeterred by age and frailty, and she continues to live alone as she has done since her parents' death in the 1960s, supported by friends, neighbours, community groups and the village church. But now, she is ill. She has had a fall and has gone into hospital. She needs her family. She never married, never had children, so, along with my two brothers and a pair of cousins, we are her next of kin.

We don't know how long Ruth will be away from her home. It could be a while as she has to stay in a nursing home for some rehab. So, my brother, Peter, drives Mum and me up from Devon to visit her in Bognor, to check she is her usual argumentative self (she is). We head into town to buy her nighties and toiletries before going to her home to make sure all is secure and to clear the fridge and larder. She has no sense of smell and ignores best-before dates, even if she can read them. Amongst the mouldering carrots and curdling milk, we find a jar of Marmite from 1992 and a packet of Golden Wonder crisps

G IS FOR GHOSTS

with packaging that hasn't been around since the 80s. I feel I am going back in time and imagine my father, Ruth's nephew, sitting in the corner of the dining room playing solitaire. But then I remember he never even visited this house. Even though she's been here since the mid-80s, that was several years after his death. But still. He would have touched certain objects. Family heirlooms and knick-knacks. I remember us playing Scrabble using the now-retro board with its wooden tiles and holders. Dad might even have eaten some of the jam that is lurking at the back of a cupboard. Errands done, we decide we don't want to stay the night here. There's enough room, but it's chilly and the beds will be damp. And there's a perfectly good inn down the road.

The Swan is a listed building which has been serving ale since 1382 (though sadly not since the pandemic). A coaching inn, the Swan offered rooms and a change of horses for the postal route from London to the coast. In later centuries, it became a draw for artistic sorts and has quite a cultural heritage. A previous art-loving landlord allowed impoverished artists to stay for free in exchange for paintings of the local area, including one by Constable – not John, but his brother Golding, although John did stay here in the 1830s. Kipling too signed the visitors' book, as did Hubert Parry, of 'Jerusalem' fame. In 1917, Elgar moved just outside the village, where he composed his last four major works, including Cello Concerto in E minor, and is said to have enjoyed the pub. And when I had a meal there twenty years ago with Ruth on her birthday, there was quite a famous BBC reporter having a tête-à-tête with an important-looking fellow.

The Swan's low beams and open fires give a cosy, intimate atmosphere, but with all those hundreds of years of previous guests, surely there must be the odd ghost knocking about? We are given a room each and are shown up the crooked stairs and along the uneven corridor. Peter grabs the first bedroom and then we offer the larger room with a four-poster to Mum. She walks in and then straight back out, saying she doesn't like it. It's too cold. She is far happier with the small double next door. So I take the four-poster, quite pleased to be sleeping in such grandeur. We settle down for the night.

I am woken suddenly in the early hours by the sound of rushing water. Is it raining? Is there a flood? A leak? Is someone in my bathroom? I get up to look, somewhat perturbed but not scared witless. In the small ensuite bathroom, the basin tap is turned on, full, gushing. I turn it off. The tap isn't loose: it's a few turns to stop the water flow. Odd. I definitely remember turning it off after I brushed my teeth, as it was a little stiff. No drips, no washer problem. Hmm. I go back to bed. Keep the bedside lamp on. Then the tapping starts. Above me. In the rafters. Is this a plumbing problem? Maybe, but the reason this room is cold is because it is single-storey. Why would there be water pipes above? It sounds like someone is sitting on the roof.

The next morning, I tell my story to Mum and Peter over breakfast. When I get the chance, I query the landlady. Is it haunted here? She looks a bit wary.

Is this a trap? I reassure her. I wasn't scared. And then I recount the previous night's escapade. She asks if I stayed in the four-poster room. When I nod, she says that strange things do go on in that room. Sometimes, after she has cleaned in there, she'll leave and turn off the light. If she has to pop back for something, the light will be back on.

Is this a ghost? Is it the ghost of a groom? A maid? A traveller? Or was it all explicable? The wind. Dodgy plumbing. My mind playing tricks? It can't be proved. It can't be disproved. Strange things happen that are beyond a yes or no answer. Strange things happen.

Jamaica Inn, Bodmin Moor, 2015

Cornwall has its fair share of haunted places and ghost stories. Jamaica Inn is probably the most well-known and the most haunted. Dating back to the eighteenth century, it was a coaching inn on the new turnpike road from Launceston to Bodmin, a changing point for horses on the Truro to London route, and a notorious pitstop for smugglers. When Daphne du Maurier's story of wreckers, *Jamaica Inn*, was published in 1936, it reached far beyond Cornwall and the West Country.

As well as two museums – one dedicated to du Maurier, the other to smuggling – this is a genuine pub where you can have a pint of Beast of Bodmin ale to go with your Cornish pasty. I've visited by day, when the place is full of coachloads of tourists tucking into fish and chips, and by night for a paranormal investigation. Knowing that the British Paranormal Association have declared the inn as a genuine haunted establishment, my cousin was obviously keen to go.

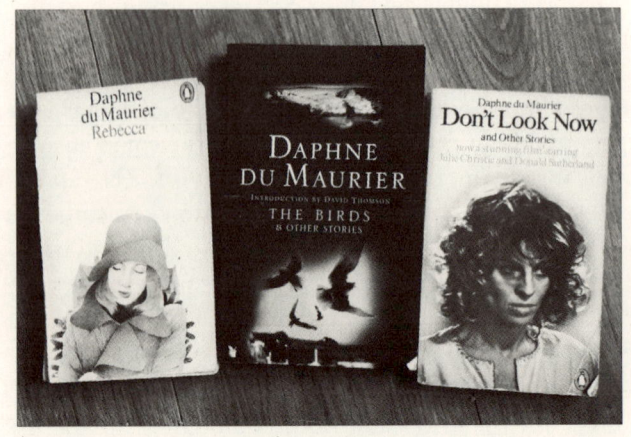

From my du Maurier collection, which sits on my shelves between my friend, Ruth Dugdall, and me

G IS FOR GHOSTS

In the evening, we join a group of investigators from Bristol. We have a meal and a drink or two. Not keen on warm beer, he goes for Korev, the Cornish lager, but we take it easy; we need a clear head before the investigation. Which is the thing. After spending time in the barn attic, where we hear about a hanged man, and some time in the museum, where we try out the equipment, not much has happened. But, after being in the gift shop for a while, I have a banging head and excuse myself for an early night; there's no way I can make it till three in the morning. I lie in bed listening out for the sound of hooves and coach wheels clattering across the cobbles outside. For the sounds of footsteps pacing up and down the corridor. For the sound of smugglers colluding in Cornish. But there is nothing except the wind and I fall into a deep sleep. As an insomniac, this is the most unusual thing to happen to me here. I'll take it. As will my bank balance. This ghost-hunting isn't cheap, but if it keeps remote pubs going, then why not? Ghosts are good business and, whether you believe in them or not, there's no denying that. And as long as we yearn to make connections with the other side, we will continue to be haunted.

H
IS FOR HEALTH;
I IS FOR ILLNESS

How a Bra Saved My Life.
The Art of Dying Well

health *noun*
1. a person's mental or physical condition.
2. the state of being free from illness or injury.
3. 'What is health? We use a broad definition of health that encompasses both physical and mental health, as well as wellbeing. This means we are not only interested in whether or not people are ill or have a health condition, but also in how healthy and well they are.' NHS

By medicine life may be prolonged,
Yet death will seize the doctor too.
CYMBELINE

illness, *noun*
1. a disease or period of sickness affecting the body or mind.
2. a condition of being unhealthy in your body or mind
3. 'Disease then, is the pathological process, deviation from a biological norm. Illness is the patient's experience of ill health, sometimes when no disease can be found. Sickness is the role negotiated with society.' *BMJ*

Last scene of all,
That ends this strange eventful history,
Is second childishness and mere oblivion,
Sans teeth, sans eyes, sans taste, sans everything.
As You Like It

Dúirt mé leat go raibh mé breoite
(I told you I was ill)
Spike Milligan
St Thomas's churchyard, Winchelsea

☠☠☠

June 2020

Covid deaths for this month in England and Wales: 4,091

Covid restrictions ban most indoor gatherings involving more than two people. Up to 30 people gather in the cabinet room of No 10 for Boris Johnson's birthday. Fines are later issued for Johnson, Carrie Symonds and Rishi Sunak.

A few non-essential shops have reopened with one-way systems and social distancing. You are excited because M&S is one of them and you need a new bra. Once inside, there is no browsing and you certainly can't try on, so you grab one in what you hope is your size. When you get home, it's not the best fit and, being underwired, not very comfortable. In fact, it hurts a bit under the wire in the lower inside quadrant of the right breast (over the next few months, you will become familiar with such terminology). You lie in bed and feel a lump. It's painful. You remember being told once that if it is painful it is unlikely to be cancer. That is your first thought. Cancer. You've been to the breast clinic before – once for what turned out to be a cyst. Another time, a blocked milk duct. You assume this will also be benign. But you call the surgery. After triage, you get a call back from the receptionist. The GP wants to see you today. At the appointment you tell her about the bad bra. She examines you, finds the lump straight away. It could be cancer, she says. Just like that. She fills in a referral form there and then. Torbay or Exeter? Exeter, you say. For no other reason than it is a teaching hospital.

July

Covid deaths in England and Wales: 1,603

The following week, your friend drives you to hospital. She lives in your household, your bubble, alongside your three adult children and your two Tibetan terriers. She waits in the car while you go in alone, masked and sanitised. You see the registrar. He takes your history. Over a woman's menstruating life, the more periods she has, the higher her risk of breast cancer. You are low risk because you have had three full-term pregnancies, you have breastfed three children for an accumulated thirty-six months, you started your periods at the relatively late age of fourteen and you had a hysterectomy at forty-two. In addition to this, you had a clear routine mammogram sixteen months ago, and there is no family history, though it is noted that your maternal grandfather had prostate cancer. The registrar examines you. He is kind. Reassuring. It's probably fat necrosis from the bad bra, but he sends you for a mammogram all the same. Twenty minutes later, after your breasts have been squashed between cold, hard metal plates, the rather distant radiographer asks you to wait outside. Soon after, she joins you. You need an ultrasound. She escorts you to another room, where two women are waiting, a radiologist, a nurse. The mammogram has revealed two lumps. One in the left breast that is probably a cyst. One in the right that is more worrying. The doctor squirts cold gel on your breasts, a reminder of happier pregnancy scans, little aliens floating in amniotic fluid. She probes and searches before showing you the screen. She points to a white lump. White is bad. It looks like cancer, she says. She measures it: 18mm. Small. Then she scans the lymph nodes in the armpit; if the cancer has spread, it will have gone here first. It looks clear. She takes a biopsy from each breast lump while the mammogram radiographer talks to you about your dogs. You shouldn't have judged her. She's kind. Once dressed, you return to the registrar, who introduces you to the breast care nurse. It is hard to breathe with the mask and your glasses have steamed up. She hands you a tissue. They will have the results in a few days, but it is likely you will need surgery and radiotherapy. You should stop taking HRT straight away. You message your partner. You talk to your friend in the car. Once home you tell your children, reassuring them. It is caught early. Highly treatable. Five days later, you are back, alone again. The registrar and nurse are joined by the consultant in Plastic and Oncoplastic Breast Surgery. She confirms you have cancer. A less common cancer. A more aggressive, fast-growing type called triple negative breast cancer. The bad cells have no receptors that hormones or a protein called HER2 can attach to. Hormonal or targeted therapy such as Herceptin or Tamoxifen will not work so, in addition to surgery and radiotherapy, you will need chemotherapy. You cry for the first time. A date is set for surgery. In three weeks, you will have a wide local excision (WLE) to remove the cancer and its surrounding tissue. Taking fat from below your breast, the consultant will fill the space left by the tumour. You must self-isolate for two weeks. Time is an issue and your house is full: three adult children, your friend, two dogs and now your husband – from whom you are separated – back from Qatar. Impossible to isolate, so you stay at your brother's empty house. Your super-cautious eldest son isolates with you. One day your husband brings round some shopping and your dogs, Millie and her daughter, Susan. Susan is excited, playful. Millie gives you the cold shoulder, sorry for herself, tail down. Socially distanced, you talk with your husband who you've been with your whole adult life. He is upset. It should be him looking after you. You can see he is hurting, but you are barely hanging on. He leaves with the dogs. For the next two weeks you and your son look after your brother's hens, the twenty-year-old cat and the garden. You lose half a stone. You have an appointment with the nurse, who discusses post-surgery bras, cold caps and wigs. She tells you not to Google.

August

Covid deaths in England Wales: 530

You have spent two weeks Googling before your partner arrives from the Wirral and tells you to stop. And now it is here: surgery day. Your anxiety is rife. The staff let him stay for an hour before kicking him out. You see the consultant, who introduces her team, one of whom is from the army, observing this MICAP flap technique which conserves the breast in the most natural, least invasive way. The previous day, blue radioactive dye was inserted into your veins to locate the sentinel lymph node, which will be removed to check for rogue cancer cells. The blue dye will stain your breast for the next year. But, for today, you are third on the list, taken down early afternoon. You start counting back from ten when, as if by magic, you are awake again, in recovery. Later, on the ward, the consultant tells you the surgery was a success. She removed the tumour with clear margins and the lymph node. Once you have had a wee, you are discharged with paracetamol and surgical tape for your wound. The next day is painful. You long for lovely morphine. Your GP prescribes codeine, which takes the edge off. Your partner stays for a few days to see you over the worst. He feeds you. Washes your hair. Changes your dressing. When he leaves, your old friend, Ruth, takes over. You watch *Ferris Bueller's Day Off* and reminisce about your student days, nostalgic for a time before all this. When she has to go, you feel alone. You are weepy and call the breast nurse, who listens and reassures.

September

Covid deaths in England and Wales: 769

Back at the hospital, this time with your partner. The consultant gives you good news: the lymph node was clear, the cancer hasn't spread beyond the breast. However, the tumour was high grade, grade 3, and had invaded the surrounding tissue, so she had to remove a lime-sized mass. She is confident she got it all but, in addition to radiotherapy, you definitely need chemotherapy, effective against any fast-growing cells that might have escaped. You explain that you want to move to the Wirral to be with your partner for treatment, and she refers you to a colleague in Liverpool. Then you see the oncologist. He explains your prognosis: surgery has given you a 70 per cent chance of living ten years; chemo will add another 7 per cent. But chemo will also push you through the menopause, which weakens the bones, so you need bisphosphonates for three years, delivered in six-monthly infusions to make the bones a dense, hostile environment for further tumours. This will add another 2 per cent. You'll take it. It is unlikely you have an altered BRCA gene because breast cancer doesn't run in your family, so you are not offered genetic testing. He will hand over to a consultant close to your new home. A tearful set of goodbyes with your mum, children and dogs and you set off with your partner. At Stafford services, the new consultant phones and runs through his treatment plan. Chemotherapy is set for three weeks' time. But five days later you return to Devon. Millie, the mama dog, has a tumour in her right shoulder and will be put to sleep the following week. You stay in the family home with your children, husband and dogs. For five days you all spoil Millie and each night she sleeps between you and your daughter. On the fifth day, when everyone has said their goodbyes, you and your daughter take Millie to the vets. They meet you in the car park and take her gently from your daughter's arms to give her pre-meds. A few minutes later, they let you both come in the side door to be with Millie as she crosses that rainbow bridge. You stay one more night, cuddling Susan, who is lost without her mother. In the morning, you head back to the Wirral, your scar pulling on that long drive north. Your heart pulling in the other direction.

October

Covid deaths in England and Wales: 3786

You have a PICC line inserted, a fine tube threaded into a vein in your left arm all the way up to a bigger vein in your chest. Not only is this the easiest way to have your weekly bloods taken and chemo given, but it also saves the veins in your arms from being destroyed by the harsh, toxic drugs. You will never again have an injection or have your blood pressure taken on the right side as you are at risk of lymphedema. You must keep the PICC line dry, the challenge of your daily bath ritual alleviated with plastic sleeves. The following week, alone again and masked up, you have your first session of paclitaxel whilst wearing a cold cap to limit hair loss. It isn't so bad. You get free sandwiches, tea and biscuits. Free car parking. You are not allowed to drive, so your partner waits in the car, working. You can't sleep that night. The steroids. You wake up to nausea, reminded of your babies swimming in your missing womb.

November

Covid deaths in England and Wales: 10,140

A new lockdown is announced in England. Indoor gatherings with other households are banned, unless for work purposes. Eight days later there is a farewell gathering for Dominic Cummings in No. 10.

Over the following weeks, there is a cumulative effect, the toxicity building, immune system sinking. You have a Covid vaccine, a flu jab, and shield alongside the vulnerable and the aged. You experience fatigue, nausea, insomnia. Everything tastes wrong, yet every week you put on a kilo. You have the cheeks of a hamster. Every day you take your temperature and must phone the chemo ward if it is raised. Sepsis is a risk.

December

Covid deaths in England and Wales: 11,945

Allegra Stratton resigns after joking about a party in No. 10.

No holidays for cancer: chemo two days before Christmas and two days before new year. The nurses are amazing. You have lost 20 per cent of your hair, so you are glad you persevered with the cold cap, which is painful at times. But now it is time for the red devil.

January 2021

Covid deaths in England and Wales: 30,157

A gathering is held in No. 10 to mark the departure of two private secretaries.

You will have high-dose AC, which stands for Adriamycin (doxorubicin) and cyclophosphamide – the secret weapon, the best chemo for TNBC but also the worst, hence the 'devil' part. The 'red' is because, well, it is red. You will have three cycles, two weeks apart, instead of the usual three. Your partner injects G-CSF growth factor into your tummy on day 2 to boost white cells. You have a twenty-four-hour hospital phone line and, one night, when you have chest pain, they tell you to come straight to hospital. In A&E, there are several cases of domestic abuse. Police are everywhere. Eventually you are seen and monitored. Next morning a chest X-ray checks for clots. They send you home with an extra week off between doses 2 and 3. You are part relieved, part worried this will impact the treatment. Day 8 and your hair starts coming out in clumps. You feel so sick and now this. Hairdressers are still locked down. Your partner uses his (personal) trimmers to clip your hair to an inch all over. You are not completely bald and, being winter, when out for your daily walk, you wear a hat.

February

Covid deaths in England and Wales: 20,004

Despite anti-nausea medication, the sickness is relentless and the nights wakeful. A list of ailments. Sore mouth. Exhaustion. Constipation. Bloating. Anxiety. Chemo fog. You can't read, let alone write. You want to give up, but you cannot. The end is in sight. After the last chemo, you ring the bell, a few nurses clapping. An anti-climax. A relief.

March

Covid deaths in England and Wales: 5,333

Five consecutive days of radiotherapy. A breeze after chemo. The long-term effects are potentially worse, though hard to measure. But one thing is certain: You will never be the same again.

April

Covid deaths in England and Wales: 1,606

Rules are eased in England on 12 April. Working from home continues to be recommended and socialising indoors with people from other households is not allowed. Meeting others outdoors is limited to six people or two households. Two parties are held at No. 10. The next day, the Queen sits alone at the funeral of her husband of seventy-three years.

May

Covid deaths in England and Wales: 482

You have physiotherapy for your right shoulder, which hurts following surgery and radiotherapy. You speak to the psychiatrist; your mental health has taken a hit. You miss your dead dog. You have not seen your mother or children for eight months until, finally, you reunite at the funeral of your great-aunt, who died in a care home, the same age as the bereaved Queen. You write and deliver the eulogy. An honour. A woman who as a teenage Wren worked on Enigma.

Since buying that bra in M&S, you have connected to old friends and to new, one of whom, despite never having met face-to-face, crocheted you a superwoman cape to keep you warm during chemo.

You see the best in people.

You were lucky.

I was lucky. I found the lump thanks to my bra. My treatment wasn't delayed. I had first class care under trying circumstances. I am still here but I am changed for ever.

Thank you, NHS.

Demographic Transition

'The early twenty-first century is the healthiest time ever to be alive.' So says Andrew Doig, professor of biochemistry at the University of Manchester. This is because, although there will be dips in life expectancy when bad things happen such as war or pestilence, there are more permanent increases due to antibiotics or vaccines or access to contraception. He goes on to say that '[e]ven the world's poorest countries have good life expectancies at present compared to rich countries in the recent past. All the poorest countries now are healthier than every country in the nineteenth century.' This huge recent change in life expectancy is part of the 'demographic transition' from a high birth rate/high death rate society to one with low birth and death rates.[1]

Interestingly, the USA has poor life expectancy despite spending far more on health than any other country.[2] This is because of the high administration costs of their healthcare system, as well as high rates of homicide and suicide due to the availability of guns. There are also high levels of child mortality and death in childbirth, which, in turn, lead to a higher death rate among young people. Health spending shows 'exceptional levels of inequality'.[3]

(Thank you, NHS.)

Doig dives deep into the history of mortality and argues that for at least 95 per cent of our time on earth we have lived as healthy, active hunter gatherers with infectious disease almost unknown, though the world was a dangerous place – accidents were common, as was being killed by wild animals or other groups. But once we began to live in permanent settlements living off agriculture, we were at risk of famine if crops failed. As settlements grew, we caught infection from contaminated water and from animals.

However, in 1600, there was a big advance in healthcare once we started collecting and analysing data. (Remember those bills of mortality in 'C Is for Contagion'.) In the following centuries, '[g]erm theory rationalised why we should drink clean water, wash bodies, clothes and living spaces, eat fresh food, perform operations in sterile conditions and so on.' (Thank you, science.) Today, our main causes of death are cancer, diabetes, stroke and heart failure, compounded by age, obesity, smoking, alcohol and sedentary lifestyles. There has also been a huge increase in the death rate from dementia, with Alzheimer's now the most expensive disease in the world; it is common, it leads to high caring and nursing costs, and there are no effective drugs, as yet.[4]

Doig goes on to say that healthcare is not always expensive or high-tech: vaccines, water filters, soap, and fluids for rehydration are cheap. Therefore, such treatments should be available to everyone, wherever they live. He is passionate about this:

> International borders are products of our imagination and are not respected by infectious microorganisms. Successes against polio, guinea worm, malaria and many others can only be achieved if every country participates in programmes ... Failed states or war zones that are inaccessible to healthcare workers are a danger to us all, as they will be reservoirs of disease... Similarly, groups of people who refuse to participate in vaccination, or other measures aimed at disease elimination, ensure that the diseases stay with us... We were fortunate that there was no substantial antivaccination campaign against the smallpox vaccines in the 1970s.

He goes on to say:

Despite 'flare-ups' such as Covid-19, infectious disease has been in retreat since the nineteenth century. If we continue with this progress, we can get more countries through the demographic transition, working together to reach a place where we all live long and healthy lives.[5]

Thank you, NHS.

☠☠☠

From Pit to Parliament

A cousin of my grandfather, Jim Griffiths, made the journey from pit to Parliament. When Labour won the 1945 landmark general election, Griffiths – former miner and now MP for Llanelli – was made Minister for National Insurance by Clement Attlee. He was responsible for creating the modern state benefit system, introducing the Family Allowances Act 1945,[6] the National Insurance Act 1946 and the National Assistance and Industrial Injuries Act 1948. Along with Nye Bevan, Griffiths was one of the chief architects of the welfare state.

But this is where my family story comes in, a few years later. As well as being party chairman, Jim was also Minister for the Colonies from 1950–51 (and much later, under Wilson, he was the first ever Secretary of State for Wales). While Callaghan describes him as 'one of the greatest sons of Wales', my own Welsh family never spoke well of him. Never. Presumably because they were Tory voters, possibly the only ones in Carmarthen. In fact, they said he was responsible for the disastrous Tanganyika groundnut scheme, which was supposed to address the post-war food shortage through the production of cash crops and the mechanisation of farming in rural Africa. And yes, it was a disaster. It was costly and ill thought out, in so many ways. There was no pilot scheme. There was crop failure due to the soil and the climate. There was no use of local knowledge or skills and 'the disregard of agricultural traditions was overhauled by the colonisers'.[7]

Now, while Griffiths was part of this government, he did not become Secretary of State for the Colonies until 1950, when he had to oversee the scheme's demise. So could the blame be laid at his feet? From minutes of the Cabinet meeting of 7 December 1950, we read that he thought it wrong to abandon the scheme, because he was 'seriously alarmed that the world's population was expanding faster than world food production'. He believed that 'the United Kingdom, as a great Colonial Power, had a special obligation to promote the expansion of food production'.[8] So, yes, no doubt he shares the responsibility, but to have his whole legacy blighted by his family was harsh and, though post-war colonialism failed abysmally, I am proud of his achievements building the welfare state in this country.

Clearly, not all legacies are positive. But there's always the NHS. In 1942, during the darkest time of the war, the Beveridge report called for a state welfare system to provide universal and free benefits to those in need. This included a National Health Service which would enable Britain to 'beat want, disease, ignorance, squalor and idleness'.[9] The NHS Act 1946 came into effect on 5th July 1948, with the aim of providing a comprehensive service funded by taxation, available to all and free at the point of delivery. 'With continued food rationing, a housing shortage, spiralling tuberculosis death rates and on the back of an exceptionally severe winter the inception of a welfare state could not have come at a better time for post-war Britain.'[10]

Thank you, sons of Wales.

The NHS brought better healthcare, better nutrition, immunisation, and new treatments such as antibiotics, kidney dialysis and chemotherapy. The generation born after the War, the Baby Boomers, were the first to benefit. They represent our very own demographic transition. Sandwiched between the Silent Generation and the Gen-Xers, they never had it so good. In 2018, the NHS celebrated its seventieth birthday. David Jarrett points out that this biblical three score year and ten is 'the natural length of a life' and that, during these seven decades, the 'big killers' have changed. While in 1948 one in twenty died of tuberculosis, death rates from heart disease and strokes have now almost halved, but cancer death rates have almost doubled and deaths from dementia almost quadrupled. Overall, people are now living thirteen years longer, though this varies according to wealth and postcode.

Alongside the increase in life expectancy, there was a behaviour change which, according to palliative care expert Kathryn Mannix, 'saw the sickest people being rushed into hospital for treatment instead of waiting at home to die'. She believes this change, evolving over the decades, has brought 'a point of futility' where 'technology is deployed in a new deathbed ritual that is a triumph of denial over experience … instead of dying in a dear and familiar room with people we love around us, we now die in ambulances and emergency rooms and intensive care units, our loved ones separated from us by the machinery of life preservation'.[11]

All this care costs money so, Boomers, take note and think of your Gen-Z grandchildren. Yes, they might have nice phones and enjoy a fancy coffee, but they'd swap all of that for a home of their own, a job with security and the chance to retire before their eighties with a full pension. And, while more and more of us are dying in old age, for the first time in our history, there are more old people than young. A big burden for those who have the least. But not just that. 'In a nutshell, the free NHS care, which was basic and took place in large wards, has been replaced by means-tested care in community homes.' No longer 'free at the point of delivery'. The cradle-to-grave care promised in 1948 has gone; people in some areas are eligible for NHS-funded social care while those in others are not.[12]

H IS FOR HEALTH; I IS FOR ILLNESS

☠☠☠

The Generation Game

My godmother's brother was born in 1943, so technically he was a member of the Silent Generation, but he lived the life of a Baby Boomer, which he would have been if born two years later. From humble beginnings, he became a bon viveur. A gastronome. He lived life to the full. Brought up in a council house in Somerset, his parents sacrificed a lot to send him to private school. He joined the army. When he left three years later – because they were 'mutually incompatible' – he worked in bars and kitchens until eventually he opened three restaurants in Bristol. As was a theme of his, he had to sell up and moved to the south of France, where he opened a restaurant, before returning to Bristol, where he once again opened a restaurant and wrote a cookery book. This got him onto the radio and then he blagged his way onto the telly, where, throughout the 80s and 90s, he was famous for cooking with a glass of wine in hand, often in unusual locations all over the world. A natural cook, a host of considerable charm, he faced bankruptcies and divorces (he believed the restaurant business was 'death to family life').[13] He also endured ill health – not surprising, considering his love of booze and rich food – but this bon viveur, this man who lived a somewhat chaotic life, was the George Best of cooking. He was Keith Floyd. In 2009, on a day when he'd luncheoned on oysters, partridge and champagne to celebrate his partner's birthday, he sat down with her in the evening to watch a documentary about himself made by Keith Allen, appropriately called *Keith on Keith*. But, before it aired, the maverick cook died of a heart attack aged just sixty-five. He left behind two children and a pool of inspiration for the likes of Jamie Oliver and Nigel Slater (hopefully without the booze).

His older sister, my godmother, might as well have been from a different generation, living a conventional life as a wife and mother. And, although some Boomers will take offence, well, I am going to say it anyway. They are a big generation and, as they are hitting old age, they should bear some responsibility for their grandchildren. Renowned geriatrician David Jarrett, a Boomer himself, recognises this: 'the responsibility of the old is to fight on behalf of the young against the continual erosion of the rights and privileges they have themselves enjoyed'. He knows they have had the biggest slice of the welfare state's cake – health and social services, the post-war rise in prosperity, cheap housing, free university education, jobs with pensions. No zero-hour or short-term contracts for them. Or living with their parents into their thirties.[14]

As the number of elderly and very elderly grows in proportion to working taxpayers, with the majority of money spent on healthcare in the last six months of life, how will this be sustained?[15] Already, only the very frail and ill have their care paid for by the NHS. Others are means-tested and pay for most of their care themselves. And, while the rich can afford it and the poor have it covered by their local authority, the 'middle' use their savings and sell their homes for care mainly provided by private companies in the community.

How will this be paid for in the future? Jarrett says that, although tax rises lose general elections, it is the price we pay to live in a civilised society. ('… Although we seem to be taxed at every turn … the overall tax burden in the UK is less than that of most other European countries and, many would be surprised to hear, lower than in the USA.')[16]

But this money needs to be spent wisely. 'There is something fundamentally wrong when the very elderly in one country are ending their days in an intensive care unit when a child is dying of malaria in another part of the world.'[17]

☠☠☠

Let's Talk about Death

No more of this collective amnesia about death. We need an *Ars Moriendi* for the twenty-first century. In short, let's think and talk more about death.[18]

Most of us will spend time unable to live independently in old age but, according to Atul Gawande, we avoid thinking about or planning for this and end up in institutions that do not address what makes life worth living, with doctors concentrating on 'repair of health, not sustenance of the soul'.[19] So we should talk about what we want to happen when we are old and frail. We should think about whether we really want a futile, costly treatment that will only prolong our suffering and upset our loved ones:

> Such decisions require courage… future generations will look back at some cancer treatments used in the opening decades of the third millennium with the same bewilderment we feel when contemplating the common treatments from the eighteenth century.[20]

Jarrett, Gawande and Mannix all urge us to talk about death so that we can reach a realistic understanding of ageing, dementia, frailty and terminal illness. Anna Lyons and Louise Winter also want this. (Me too. It's why I am writing this book.) They point out that over the last century we have lived through two world wars and two pandemics, which have impacted our relationship to death:

> During the wars, millions of people left home and never returned. Everyone knew they had died, yet no one was taught how to grieve or deal with the

difficulty and complexity of their emotions. The severity of the trauma was minimised. Society was taught to keep calm and carry on because, in order to survive, there was no other choice.

However, this stiff upper lip of the Silent Generation has shifted. We are getting better at dealing with our emotions.

> We go to yoga, we meditate, we eat consciously and we talk about our mental health. Life used to be about surviving, now it's about thriving. We want to live happy, contented, purposeful and meaningful lives.' [21]

We must keep the conversation going. Talking will help transform our approach to death and help us live fuller, more satisfying lives. As Philip Gould said:

> Only when you accept death can you free yourself from it, can you deal with it, can you move forward from it, so acceptance is the absolute key, at that moment, you gain freedom, and you gain power, and you gain courage. [22]

☠☠☠

Palliative Care

Kathryn Mannix has spent her career as a palliative care expert working with the dying to make the most of their living. She believes we no longer see death enough to 'recognise its pattern, to become familiar with life lived well within the limits of decreasing vigour, and even to develop a familiarity with the sequences of the deathbed'. Even doctors and nurses lack this familiarity, as 'their practice increasingly entangles technology with terminal care'.[23] And yet, we are all going to die.

As we know from 'A Is for Accidents', sudden, unexpected deaths have little chance for goodbyes and can be full of trauma. Mannix believes that possibly 25 per cent of all deaths are sudden and unexpected, but most of her patients are in the last months of their lives. However, there is still time to make the most of their remaining days. And, while the art of dying has become a forgotten wisdom, 'every deathbed is an opportunity to restore that wisdom to those who will live, to benefit from it as they face other deaths in the future, including their own'.[24]

The cancer charity Macmillan describes the lead-up to an expected death:

> The person you are caring for may drift in and out of consciousness. There may be times when they do not seem to recognise you or other people. They

may also talk to people they knew in the past or who died long ago. This may be because they are thinking of these people. For most people, the final moments of life are very peaceful. The person's breathing may become even slower and more irregular, with very long pauses between breaths. Their tummy (abdominal) muscles may take over control of breathing from the chest muscles, so that their tummy rises and falls with each breath. Finally, they will stop breathing altogether. This can take a long time for some people. For others, it will only be a few minutes. Sometimes it can be difficult to know the exact moment of death. Often, the person's body will relax completely, and they may look very peaceful. You may feel that you can sense when the person has died.

In the UK, half of us die in hospitals, a quarter in old people's homes, 20 per cent at home and about 5 per cent in a hospice.[25] As part of their *Life. Death. Whatever* manifesto, Lyons and Winter believe we should make links between the communities involved in end-of-life and after-death care – hospices, nursing homes, hospitals, carers, coroners, funeral directors, cemetery staff, therapists, etc. Death and dying are not separate, and yet as a society we separate them. For example, after someone has died, the care team hands over to another set of professionals. Instead of 'removing' them from their community after death, why don't we build facilities for after-death care such as a chilled room which could allow people to come together. Rather than hiding death away, let's acknowledge it. If we work together, we can create 'an emotionally intelligent, flexible and more holistic system that better serves and supports everyone'.[26]

Palliative and end-of-life care is more than symptom and pain management. Its raison d'être is to empower the dying to make the most of living. Part of this is naming death, reclaiming the language of illness and dying to reduce superstition and fear, 'when pretence and well-intentioned lies can separate us, wasting time that is very precious'.[27] It also allows patients and families 'to make choices based on truth, instead of encouraging the misleading, hopeless quest for a medical miracle that promotes futile treatment, protracts dying and disallows goodbyes'.[28] The questions Mannix asks are about priorities. For example, as you approach death, do you want to be awake or alert or sleepier and less aware of people around you? What is the balance you would like between time and quality of living? What are your plans for an emergency? These conversations are much better for everyone involved if held early on.[29]

In the USA, Atul Gawande has a similar view and asks similar questions of his patients: 'What do they understand their prognosis to be, what are their concerns about what lies ahead, what kinds of trade-offs are they willing to make, how do they want to spend their time if their health worsens, who do they want to make decisions if they can't?'[30] He knows from a lifetime's experience that accepting your mortality and understanding both your limits and medicine's possibilities is 'a process, not an epiphany'.[31] He also believes that 'the chance to shape our story is essential to sustaining the meaning in life… we have the opportunity to refashion our institutions, our culture, and our conversations in ways that transform the possibilities for the last chapters of everyone's lives'.[32] Mannix concurs: 'Even at this end time, the discovery of new things, making new friends, learning and growing are all still possible, still fulfilling, still worthwhile.'[33]

The USA has also seen a medicalisation of death. Gawande has spent his life working with the ageing and dying and believes that 'scientific advances have turned the processes of aging and dying into medical experiences, matters to be managed by health care professionals. And we in the medical world have proved alarmingly unprepared for it.' He goes on to say that, over the last few decades, 'medical science has rendered obsolete centuries of experience, tradition, and language about our mortality and created a new difficulty for mankind: how to die'.[34] Medicine's goal is to extend life, whereas palliative care helps people have the fullest life right now. What is surprising, perhaps, is that often people will live longer when offered the latter.[35]

Palliative care focuses on life, so don't think of it as a death sentence.

☠☠☠

Geriatrics

> 'Growing old is the greatest risk factor for most human diseases. The incidence of the majority of conditions increases, often exponentially, with age… By the time we are in our seventies and eighties we have death at our elbow.'[36]

The late Queen Elizabeth had 'old age' as the cause of death written on her death certificate. However, for most of us, old age is not the final diagnosis; it is one or maybe several illnesses. A geriatrician cannot fix problems, but they can manage them. Jarrett argues that these multiple pathologies are tricky to diagnose because not only do elderly patients 'present atypically', but often they are also confused, perhaps following a fall. In geriatrics, there is uncertainty and it is our inability to accept this uncertainty that leads to 'over-investigation, overtreatment and, ultimately, harm to patients, and to the waste of precious resources'.[37] In fact, Jarrett believes that hospitals are dangerous places for the elderly, 'precipitating confusion, falls and fractures with the added risk of hospital-acquired infection. It is very easy to admit a frail elderly person but often very difficult to discharge them. It is not unheard of for events to lead to a patient leaving feet first.'[38]

Jarrett has devoted his career to the healthcare of old people, but he believes the very term 'geriatric' has such negative connotations in the UK that it is 'the specialty that dare not speak its name'.[39] Marjory Warren (1897–1960) was the mother of geriatric medicine. In 1935, whilst working as a doctor at the West Middlesex Hospital in London, her practice extended to the nearby Poor Law Infirmary, with its 714 patients. She turned this infirmary into the first geriatric unit in Britain and, within a few years, she had reduced the number of beds to 240 and tripled the turnover. She pioneered multidisciplinary care, believing the old and sick needed diagnoses, treatment and rehabilitation. In the first decade of the new queen's reign, geriatrics was recognised by the young NHS as a specialty. It is now the largest in the UK[40] but, sadly, over the decades, it has been pushed out into the community with the other 'Cinderella' services such as forensic psychiatry, learning disabilities and substance misuse.[41]

According to Gawande, old age and infirmity are no longer a shared multigenerational responsibility but experienced largely alone or in institutions. Only 10 per cent of Europeans over eighty live with their children; almost half live completely alone, without a spouse. Even in China, Japan and Korea, the percentage of the elderly living alone is rising. He believes that the veneration of elders has been replaced by veneration of the independent self, but what happens if and when you can no longer live independently?[42] There is a difficult path to pick between neglect and institutionalisation. In the States, and increasingly in the UK, concern about lawsuits can mean safety takes priority. We worry about 'whether Dad loses weight, skips his medications, or has a fall, not whether he's lonely'.[43] In fact, Mannix argues that loneliness is 'a far harder burden than ill-health, and this is a sadness hidden in plain sight, a modern epidemic'.[44]

The medicalisation of death has failed. Instead of obsessing over mortality, Jarrett believes we should pay greater attention to quality of life. After all, '[m]edications that claim otherwise won't turn back the clock any further than a middle-aged man squeezing into leather trousers'.[45]

> The battle of being mortal is the battle to maintain the integrity of one's life – to avoid becoming so diminished or dissipated or subjugated that who you are becomes disconnected from who you were or who you want to be.[46]

There is no clear-cut answer but there is a better way.

☠☠☠

And Now for Something Different

> Doulas walk alongside you and bear witness to the experience. We'll never tell you what to do at the end of your life; we're only there to help you live it.[47]
> Anna Lyons

In the UK, we are going through a societal change, rejecting the institutionalised version of ageing and death, and going back to a more traditional view which will free the NHS from 'overseeing the time-consuming and costly overtreatment of those with little if anything to gain from it'.[48] We can then focus on what is most important, our priorities: no suffering, simple pleasures, daily routines, spending time with loved ones. After all, our endings are important not just for us but for those we leave behind.

The growing #deathpositive movement includes some very special people who want to enable this. End-of-life doulas, or soul midwives, bring death and dying back into the community so that death is once more part of life. Just as a midwife supports pregnant women and new mothers, a doula supports people who are living with dying and their loved ones. This can include walking the dog, creating a memory box, facilitating difficult conversations or working on living wills. They can liaise with the medical team, makes notes during consultations. They will find out what is important to their clients and they will support the bereaved in their grief.

The Long Goodbye

> Those with dementia die slowly, along with all their memories, insights and feelings. Without memory, we are nothing. The dead don't so much walk among us as sit, mostly out of sight, in our long-term care facilities.[49]

In September 2020, at the height of Covid, the Office for National Statistics (ONS) revealed that dementia and Alzheimer's disease were the leading cause of death that month – 11.2 per cent of all deaths in England and 11.1 per cent of deaths in Wales.[50] Alzheimer's is the most common form of dementia (around 60% of diagnoses in the UK), although it is comparatively rare for under-65s –[51] although, recently, we heard that broadcaster Fiona Phillips has been diagnosed with the disease, aged just sixty-two.

It is a cruel disease. My stepfather's decline was gradual. He was fourteen years older than my mother, and over the years this age gap became more apparent. He gave up golf and beekeeping, became anxious about travelling and his sleep was disturbed. This was exacerbated by deafness incurred from his time as gunner on a naval ship at the end of the war.

Then his memory failed. His grasp of words weakened. He no longer read. He wrote gobbledegook. On a visit, I realised he was no longer doing anything meaningful. It was sad. Devastating. Mum accompanied him on appointments with the consultant. He would give Ralph three words at the beginning of the meeting and ask him to remember them (apple, penny, table). Then he would ask questions – what day is it? who is the prime minister? etc. – and then he would ask him to draw a clock, marking in the numbers and showing ten past eleven. On one occasion, Mum primed Ralph in the car and said that the doctor would ask him to remember 'apple, penny, table'. (She doesn't know why she felt the need to do this other than she didn't want him to fail.) When he saw the consultant, the first thing Ralph said was 'apple, penny, table'. The doctor gave Mum a knowing look and smiled. She realised she wasn't the first spouse to do this.

As a family, we moved from Worthing to Teignmouth to be nearby. It was the right time as Mum was struggling and our oldest was in his penultimate year of primary school. After the move, I spent a lot of time with Mum and Ralph. There were escapes. From home, from a garden centre, from my home. Until, finally, the heart-breaking decision to put him into a nursing home for those with dementia. My children loved visiting as there was always something going on. A woman who ran up and down the corridor and then sprawled on a sofa. After a nap she'd do it all again. The man with two ties and two watches. The man waiting in the airport lounge for his flight. The two bickering sisters aged ninety-nine and one hundred and one. The escapologist who made it as far as the beach. The very kind Filipino carers, one of whom found love with the son of a resident.

Nine months later, Ralph had a fall and caught pneumonia, the old man's friend, dying a few days later.

☠☠☠

A Story of Hope for Old Age

No one is saying we should write off the old and frail. But nor should we normalise overly invasive treatment. We should enable the senior members of our society, our elders, to concentrate on what is important to them. And in so doing, this will stop money being used for pointless, distressing medical interventions and allow us to focus on making the most of their latter days.

Take Frasier the lion. In 1972, he is rescued from a Mexican circus at the grand old age of nineteen and taken to live out his days in Lion Country Safari, Orange County, California. The editors of *LIFE* magazine described him: 'He is underweight and splay-footed. His fur resembles an old moth-balled coat, and he sleeps 19 hours a day. The muscles in his tongue are so shot that it unreels from his mouth like a slobbery red carpet.' Once on a special diet, he puts on weight but then he surprises the keepers. Where other young lions have failed, Frasier is a hit with the lionesses. In fact, they worship him, accompanying him on his walks and bringing the best meat for him, waiting to eat only when he has finished. Within seven weeks, all the lionesses are pregnant and within sixteen months, he has fathered thirty-three cubs. When he dies of pneumonia, members of the Scottish Fraser clan perform traditional burial rites, in kilts, accompanied by a bagpipe lament. He is buried beneath a cross at Lion Country.

☠☠☠

The Future

> Perhaps it would become routine to go into hospital at the age of sixty to freshen up with new sets of lungs, kidneys, liver, pancreas and heart.[52]

It is hard to imagine just how the future will change health and illness. AI and monitoring systems will allow us to intervene at the earliest stages of disease. Treatment will be personalised. Genetic disease will be defeated at its source. Stem cells will grow new organs. My stepdaughter who has type 1 diabetes could have new pancreas islets cells to secrete insulin: 'By DNA editing as part of stem-cell-based organ-replacement therapy, we can give every organ the optimal DNA for its function. We could have hearts like Usain Bolt and lungs like Serena Williams.'[53]

But, oh, the ethics…

In the meantime, we need to remember that death, sickness and pain are part of life and medicine has limits. Healthcare professionals need to be clear with their patients. Politicians and journalists should be realistic in their claims. Schools should put death and illness and wellbeing into the curriculum. Families should be open about what they want to happen at the end of their life.

We're all in this together.

> Your legacy is planting seeds that you will never see flower. Your legacy is knowing that you've done better for the next generation. Your legacy is having the rebellious hope that the actions you take today will create a better society tomorrow.
> *Dame Deborah James*

Useful Websites

NHS
End of Life Care
https://www.nhs.uk/conditions/end-of-life-care/

Bowelbabe
The late Dame Deborah James's charity, raising money to fund cutting edge research into early detection and personalised medicine, raising awareness of signs and symptoms, and tackling stigmas around cancer to give more people more time with the people they love. 'Find a life worth enjoying, take risks, love deeply, have no regrets and always, always have rebellious hope. And finally, check your poo – it could just save your life.'
https://www.bowelbabe.org/

Age UK
The UK's leading charity for older people. Guidance on death and dying called 'Let's Talk about Death and Dying: To help everyone to feel empowered and confident to talk about death, to ask questions of each other, to listen, to be sure what all of our loved ones would like to happen when death comes.'
https://www.ageuk.org.uk/information-advice/health-wellbeing/relationships-family/end-of-life-issues/talking-death-dying/

Macmillan Cancer Support
All-round brilliant charity with loads of information on their website. When I was being treated for breast cancer, my breast nurse told me not to Google, just to look at Breast Cancer Now or Macmillan.
https://www.macmillan.org.uk/cancer-information-and-support/supporting-someone/coping-with-bereavement/if-the-person-you-care-for-is-dying

Marie Curie
The UK's leading end-of-life charity. From nurses to guidance on how to organise a budget funeral, a website packed with info.
https://www.mariecurie.org.uk/
https://www.mariecurie.org.uk/help/support/terminal-illness/preparing/end-of-life-care

Companion Voices
Singing for the end of life. Groups of people who meet to learn songs and prepare together for singing at the bedsides of people who are dying. On request and by arrangement.
https://companionvoices.org/

End-of-Life Doulas
Doing life differently. 'Doulas are the bookends of life - Just as a Birth Doula is there at the beginning, an End-of-Life Doula is there for the end. Meaning

that the last months or weeks or days are compassionate, calm, natural and as normal as can be.'
https://eol-doula.uk/

SWAN (NW England)
The SWAN model of end-of-life and bereavement care is used across the Northern Care Alliance NHS Foundation Trust and has been adapted by other NHS trusts around the UK. It supports and guides the care of patients and their loved ones at the end of life and after they have died. 'From handprints, memory boxes and support for those who are bereaved, the Palliative Care and Bereavement Services know that they only have one chance to get it right.'
https://www.england.nhs.uk/north-west/2021/12/07/raising-awareness-of-end-of-life-and-bereavement-care-in-the-north-west/

J
IS FOR JET;
K IS FOR KEENING;
L IS FOR LAMENT

The Victorian Cult of Death: Rites and Rituals

jet, *noun*
1. anaerobically fossilised wood of (probably and maybe not exclusively) *Araucaria araucana*, descendant of the monkey puzzle tree used for Victorian mourning jewellery.
2. an intense black.

Black, forsooth, coal-black as jet.
HENRY VI

keening, *noun*
Irish: *Caointeoireacht*
1. the action of wailing in grief for a dead person.
2. a traditional form of vocal lament for the dead in Ireland and Scotland

J IS FOR JET; K IS FOR KEENING; L IS FOR LAMENT

If you have tears, prepare to shed them now.
JULIUS CAESAR

lament, *noun*
1. a demonstrative expression of grief, sorrow or regret
2. a mournful poem; a lament for the dead
3. a song of mourning, composed or performed in memoriam

My grief lies all within:
And these external manners of laments
Are merely shadows to the unseen grief
That swells with silence in the tortured soul.
RICHARD II

Friend more than Servant. Loyal. Truthful.
Brave.
Self less than Duty, even to the Grave.
JOHN BROWN'S STATUE AT BALMORAL

☠☠☠

Northmoor House, Dulverton, Somerset, 2021

I don't think what the five of us did was keening. In fact, it wasn't. It was more like howling at the moon. We meant no disrespect. It was a communal response to our friend's loss. We were in the middle of a writing retreat and she'd just heard that a once close friend had died suddenly and quickly from cancer. She was unsure what to think or feel. She was also uncertain how to comfort the deceased's wife as they had been out of touch for a while. Someone suggested keening. So a group of us went outside into the cool spring night garden, the dark sky sprinkled with stars. We formed a tight circle, we held each other, and we howled. And as we howled, each one of us felt something fundamental shift inside. This doing-something-together, it was guttural. Animal. Deeply human. Our friend felt uplifted, joyous even, moved that her friend was now part of the great universe and that we five weird writers could connect with his soul under a big Exmoor sky. She also felt able to make contact with the widow and reconnect with her old friend.

The word 'keening' comes from the Gaelic *caoineadh*, meaning 'crying', and the tradition of keening was important in mourning rituals in Ireland and

Scotland. It has died out now, though you can access hours of recorded keening at www.keeningwake.com – a wonderful resource which has this definition:

> Keening was a vocal ritual artform, performed at the wake or graveside in mourning of the dead. Keens are said to have contained raw unearthly emotion, spontaneous word, repeated motifs, crying and elements of song.

A keen is different to a lament, which is a more structured response to death in the form of a poem, song, or piece of music – read, sung or played in remembrance at any time or place after the death. Keening, on the other hand, is 'the final farewell to the deceased, and was composed and performed live, often touching the coffin and addressing the corpse'. This was done by professional keeners (*mnàthan-tuirim*), generally experienced elder women, usually three or more, who paid respects to the deceased and expressed grief on behalf of the bereaved family. These 'cultural professionals' performed 'a skilled ritual artform at the meeting point between life and death, and received due respect, including payment'. An important, respected role, not only because the keener helped the family to mourn, but also because it was believed that the act of keening enabled the soul to leave the body.

That moonlit night in the Victorian garden of Northmoor House, our group made a communal, healing sound and hurled it into the stars.

Doing Right by the Dead

We have looked at Victorian cemeteries and the rise of the undertaker as a profession, but here I want to delve deeper into the funerary rites and rituals of this period and, more specifically, the mourning. We know that the Industrial Revolution brought about a huge population increase and mass migration to the cities and that this resulted in contagion and a high mortality rate, particularly of infants. Meanwhile, the trend for the medicalisation of death also grew, with vaccinations, pain relief and germ theory. However, according to Helen Frisby, 'the traditional understanding of an ongoing relationship with the dead, and sense of responsibility on the part of the living to see them safely into the after-life, persisted'.[1] Frisby argues that this was especially so in rural areas where folklore was still a fixture of daily living (and this will be looked at further in the next chapter).

From elaborate funerals to structured mourning, the colour black was everywhere in Victorian Britain, the outward expression of a constantly present death which, according to Kate Berridge, was 'the axis around which nineteenth-century British society spun'. And here is where the 'black job'[2] business came into its own, oiling those wheels, not necessarily for the common good. Sir Edwin Chadwick – the public health champion whom we met in 'D Is for Disposal' – estimated that there were over one hundred deaths a day in London in the 1840s (the 'hungry forties') and two hundred and fifty undertakers. This competition for business led to unscrupulous activity, so much so that the undertaker was 'little better than one of the dreaded Resurrection Men'.[3]

Although there were still pauper burials in unmarked common graves 'on the parish', the stigma was terrible. This was eased with the introduction of the 'guinea' grave, which allowed an entry on a headstone, even if it was shared with strangers. (Quite a contrast to the elaborate memorials in such cemeteries as Highgate.) There was an answer to this: burial clubs into which members would pay a weekly sum, a forebear of pre-paid funeral plans, but we know from Charles Lamb that this was still a burden for the working classes. In fact, Chadwick, while investigating the high cost of dying, examined these clubs and what he found was truly worrying. A child could be buried for a pound, and a burial club fee would cover this. However, a wicked parent could pay (illegally) into several clubs and, well, you get the picture.

At the other end of the scale was France and Banting, Undertaker by Royal Appointment to the Crown, who coordinated funerals of epic proportions. Historically, the public looked to the Court for guidance (remember how the British public wanted to see the Queen openly grieve for Diana?), and this was one trickle down that actually played out. But, for the discerning bereaved, there was always *Cassell's Household Guide*, which explained how the trade was divided up, and why an undertaker, though costly, could be needed.

> Besides the persons who make the coffin, there are the coffin-furniture manufacturers, the funeral robe, sheet, and ruffle makers, the funeral-carriage masters, and funeral feather-men. All these supply at first-hand the furnishing undertaker, who, in his turn, supplies the trade and the public. It is not usual for one house to represent all these different departments.

The guide also listed what you would get for your money, ranging from a £3 5s funeral to a more eye-watering £53 one. The latter amount was charged by a large London undertaking firm who guaranteed the best workmanship and quality, well-trained, attentive attendants and 'all funerals conducted with the strictest possible attention to respectability and decorum'. The extensive service included the following:

> Hearse and four horses, two mourning coaches with fours, twenty-three plumes of rich ostrich-feathers, complete velvet covering for carriages and horses, and an esquire's plume of best feathers; strong elm shell, with tufted mattress, lined and ruffled with superfine cambric, and pillow; full worked

glazed cambric winding-sheet, stout outside lead coffin, with inscription plate and solder complete; one and a half inch oak case, covered with black or crimson velvet, set with three rows round, and lid panelled with best brass nails; stout brass plate of inscription, richly engraved four pairs of best brass handles and grips, lid ornaments to correspond; use of silk velvet pall; two mutes with gowns, silk hat-bands and gloves; fourteen men as pages, feather-men, and coachmen, with truncheons and wands, silk hat-bands, &c.; use of mourners' fittings; and attendant with silk hat-band, &c.'

A family whose status dignified all this would also be obliged to fork out for items for the mourners: new kid gloves, new scarves and hatbands (crape for the relatives and silk for friends). They could borrow these 'fittings' off the undertaker, but they would be expected to give something to the minister of the cemetery or the vicar of the parish church, wherever the service was held, and according to their class.

Chadwick's 1843 *Report on the Practice of Interment in Towns* advocated reform because over £4 million was 'annually thrown into the grave at the expense of the living'.[4] Although the Victorian funeral industry has been much criticised for excessiveness, Frisby argues that 'industrial modernity was affording more people the opportunity to express feelings, bring communities together in the face of existential challenge, and, on a theme stretching back through time, to "do right by" the dead'.[5] This extended well beyond the day of the funeral into a significant period of mourning.

> In the acquisitive climate of upward mobility mourning dress flourished. Its heyday was the period 1840-1880. It was a complex code, clothes denoting not only the wearer's relationship to the deceased but also their social status according to the style of accessories and the quality of the fabric... But the most important factor governing mourning etiquette was the duration of the time it was worn, with strict rules dictating what was worn for whom, and for how long.[6]

Covered in Mourning

Queen Victoria, the Widow of Windsor, took mourning to the extreme. Not only did she wear black for the rest of her life after her husband's early death but also, for much of it, she withdrew from society, spending much of her time in Osbourne House on the Isle of Wight. Her subjects were expected to follow her lead in the wake of their own losses, with the hierarchy of grief strictly adhered to and widows weighted under the heaviest expectations, in full mourning for a year. The use of black was a visible way of showing your grief while also acting as a shield, protecting your bereavement from the world.[7]

Kate Berridge compared Victoria's black dress to Diana's, arguing that it is increasingly divorce not death that separates couples:

> Diana's little black dresses – notably the one she wore to the Serpentine gallery on the night her husband gave the most important interview of his life – give an impression of a woman locked in an impossible tug-of-love with a man to whom she was denied access. Victoria's big black dresses fulfilled a similar function… for what clothes they wore and how they wore them were richly expressive of their emotional states.[8]

Dilara Scholz believes that Victorian mourning attire had two key aspects – feel and *looks*. The 'black stuff' industry manufactured these fabrics. Dresses tended to be made of non-reflective paramatta[9] silk or bombazine, a matt twilled fabric of silk and wool. They were trimmed with crape (crepe), a scratchy crimped silk – a sort of sackcloth-and-ashes affair and Victoria's go-to. A dull, gauze-like fabric, crape could be layered and dyed deep black. Introduced by Huguenot refugees, crape was produced largely in Norwich and used for full mourning in such quantities that Courtauld's based their empire on it. Heavy for the wearer, so women were literally burdened by their grief, anchored by funeral lingerie, white broderie anglaise threaded with black ribbon.[10]

After the specified period, the crape could be removed – known as 'slighting the mourning' or half mourning. Lighter colours could replace full-on 'widow's weeds', such as purple, grey and black-and-white. A lighter weight of fabric was also acceptable – fabrics largely lost to us now and whose names mainly begin with the letter B: brilliantine, barathea, balzarine and barège, all slightly different in look and feel.

And then there was the headgear. Whilst withdrawing from society, a Victorian widow was expected to shroud herself with a full 'weeping veil' decorated with 'weepers' or black ribbons, covering her face whenever she left the house (not often) 'to hide tears and deter the curious'. Not without danger as the black dye of the crape could lead to asthma, catarrh and even cataracts. A lighter material called 'nun's veiling' was used towards the end of the century. As for the Queen, for the rest of her days, she sported a widow's cap à la Marie Stuart, inspiring European royalty.[11]

Hatbands varied according to the relationship to the deceased, with very specific measurements, so, from a glance, it was clear who the mourner was grieving.

When worn by the husband for the wife they are usually at the present time about seven inches wide. Those worn by fathers for sons, and sons for fathers, are about five inches wide. For other degrees of relationship the width of the hat-band varies from two and a half inches to four inches.[12]

While men only had to worry about these hatbands and a black armband with their normal dark suit, 'the social and emotional work of maintaining relationships with the dead fell most heavily upon women',[13] with huge pressure to conform.

And the expense. Because it was considered bad luck to keep mourning clothes in the house, it was often disposed of and then bought anew with a further death. A costly process, especially when people could spend many years, perhaps the majority of their years, in mourning. Arnold compares the death industry to today's wedding and baby business and says that 'high Victorian mourning demonstrated the ability of the Victorians to exploit an inevitable event. Victorian manufacturers seized upon the commercial possibilities of mourning with characteristic enterprise.'[14] Berridge says the sheer quantity of items needed was 'the budget buster for the bereaved'. She also states that, although fortunes were made on 'the back of black', they were also lost. She describes how, when Princess Amelia, daughter of George III, died, public mourning put pressure on the fashion trade, particularly coloured ribbon manufacturers who had to close mills. The cloth industry appealed for a lessening of the mourning period 'for a whole season's fashions could turn into a sad stockpile if a member of the royal family died, suddenly turning society black'.[15]

And where did you buy all this? At the *magasin de deuil*, the go-to place for all mourning matters. Located in the bigger cities, these department stores of the dead accommodated every income and every stage of mourning, supplying appropriate wear for all members of the family down to its servants. They satisfied 'the urge to express the love for the dead through material goods, to show how dear they were to someone, people outshining each other with every purchase'.[16] Jay's London General Mourning Warehouse opened on Regent Street in 1841 and dressed the Queen for the forty years after Albert's death. The shop was a bastion of quality as well as fashion. After all, as Arnold says, 'Grief was no time to be dowdy. Even in bereavement, women wanted to be stylish.'[17] Jay's understood the strict mourning rules and the need to hastily gather all the accoutrements needed for a funeral and thereafter: 'From shoes, to flowers and drapes, Jay's was a one-stop-shop for all things grief-driven.'[18] They even had travelling salesmen who would bring the wares to the home of the bereaved and, for those further afield, there were catalogues. According to Kate Cherrell, 'Jays were very much the Argos of grief'.[19]

J IS FOR JET; K IS FOR KEENING; L IS FOR LAMENT

Richard Davey discusses the *magasin de deuil* in A History of Mourning (1890) and sets out his early brand of Brexit, stating that, while such establishments were believed to be French, that was wrong because 'our quick-witted neighbours ... originated very few things'. (Ouch.) He says the French nicked the idea off the Italians:

> [A] brilliant and elaborate adaptation of the old *Mercerie de lutto* which has existed for centuries, and still exists, in every Italian city, where people in the haste of grief can obtain in a few hours all that the etiquette of civilisation requires for mourning in a country whose climate renders speedy interment absolutely necessary.

And then he really puts the boot in:

> Continental ideas are slow to reach this country, but when they do find acceptance with us, they rarely fail to attain that vast extension so characteristic of English commerce.

And who was the publisher of this book? Jay's. So much to unpack here, from advertising to anti-French rhetoric and xenophobia. Also, a complete lack of self-awareness – or any awareness for that matter – when he uses the word 'etiquette'. Brilliant.

As well as ready-made mourning clothes (thanks to the invention of the sewing machine), these emporia sold funeral tea services, funeral invitations, handkerchiefs embroidered with tears, and black-edged mourning stationery because even writing had strict rules to be followed. The mourner began with a thick black border around their writing paper and envelopes, which would then narrow over time. The recipient would respond accordingly with their own black-edged paper and envelopes, only with a very narrow black border. There were also funeral invitation cards which might be sent with a packet of funeral biscuits wrapped in black-edged paper printed with a verse, tied with black ribbon and sealed with black wax. 'Attending a funeral without having been thus invited was now an unthinkable offence against social propriety.'[20] In addition to this, the bereaved would later give their family and friends memorial cards, 'stating the name, age, date of death, where interred, and date of interment, and also a verse of Scripture appropriate to the occasion'.[21] These cards were just one of many keepsakes the Victorians hoarded to keep the memory of the dead alive.

'For life be, after all, only a waitin' for somethin' else than what we're doin', and death be all that we can rightly depend on.'
Bram Stoker

Whitby, the North Yorkshire coast: home of Dracula, goths and the ultimate in mourning keepsakes made from Whitby jet. Though technically a gemstone, jet is actually fossilised wood, probably – though arguably not exclusively – from *Araucaria araucana*, descendant of the monkey puzzle tree. Once carved, jet will last thousands of years and has been used in Britain since Neolithic times. Jet jewellery was very popular amongst the Romans both here and across the Roman Empire, as a fashionable adornment and because of its supposed magical and medicinal properties. In fact, Pliny the Elder wrote of a black stone used for protection against witchcraft and that it could be ground, burned and inhaled. Because jet can create static electricity when rubbed, this could have fostered beliefs in its magical qualities.[22]

After the Romans left, jet continued to be used for a number of purposes – as a powder for cleaning teeth, as a pain reliever for gout, for gaming pieces and dice, for religious amulets such as pendant crosses and rosaries and tokens for pilgrims to Santiago de Compostela. After fluctuations in fashion, its popularity resurged following the death of Queen Charlotte, George III's wife, in 1818,[23] and then following the death of her son, George IV, in 1830, when the Lord Chamberlain's office decreed that jet be used in mourning.[24] It was later displayed in the Great Exhibition of 1851, but the industry really took off a decade later, when Queen Victoria lost not only her mother, but also her beloved Albert, with jet her accessory of choice.

The Queen's state of mourning continued for decades, and this impacted the jet industry, which boomed during this time, with many workshops in Whitby providing employment for highly skilled craftsmen and work for jet miners who hacked it from the cliff face (whereas today Whitby jet has to be beachcombed). The railways brought in the tourists, keen to buy jet jewellery as souvenirs of this fashionable seaside resort. Jet inevitably became the preference for mourning jewellery. Not only could it be polished, but it could also be left matte, 'satisfying ancient superstitions that warned of shiny surfaces reflecting images of the dead',[25] and jet items were sometimes decorated with seed pearls which symbolised tears. Cheap imports and a move away from excessive mourning customs meant that, with the dawning of a new century, the jet industry was in decline – though it is currently having a renaissance, with many workshops once again established in Whitby.[26] (Thank you, goths.)

J IS FOR JET; K IS FOR KEENING; L IS FOR LAMENT

Hair, Hands and Other Relics

Tis easy for you
To be drawn by a single gold hair
Of that curl, from earth's storm and
Despair,
To the safe place above us.
Elizabeth Barrett Browning, 'Only a Curl', *Last Poems* (1862)

Mourning jewellery was also made of finely worked hair, making it both a very personal memorial but also a unique memento mori. There's something about keeping locks of hair that is macabre to me, even when the person is still alive. My mum still has my brother Peter's first curl (and some of our milk teeth; I have all the milk teeth of my three children in a box, and, while I don't find that macabre, my kids most certainly do. I also have the whisker of my cat, Trixie, and a tiny milk tooth from Millie, my dog.) Peter's curl is soft and blonde and probably not so different to when Mum first cut it off sixty years ago. Which I find funny: why would she cut off his first curl? Why not enjoy it on his head? Maybe this was a leftover from her family forebears, who might have done the same. A few years ago, I inherited two mourning brooches with hairwork (no idea whose hair) and found them creepy, so I sold them on eBay. Now, having learned a little of Victorian mourning culture, I wish I'd kept them. I also feel a tad guilty for selling what would have been someone's very dear possession. Hair was hugely significant as a memento for the Victorians. Having the hair of someone special close to one's heart kept a part of them with you always. 'By regularly looking at, touching and even wearing these items, people could reaffirm a sense of continued contact with their dead loved one.'[27]

Not only did Victoria have locks of Albert's hair worked into jewellery, but she also kept a coloured photograph of his corpse above her bed in each home. There was a dichotomy here: she knew he was absent and yet she treated him as if he were still alive by keeping his rooms at Windsor, Balmoral and Osborne as he had left them. When Lord Clarendon visited the Queen on the IOW in March 1862, he wrote about this:

> She talked upon all sorts of subjects as usual and referred to the sayings and doings of the Prince as if he was in the next room. It was difficult to believe that he was not, but in his own room where she received me everything was set out on his table and the pen and his blotting-book, his handkerchief on the sofa, his watch going, fresh flowers in the glass, etc., as I had always been accustomed to see them, and as if he might have come in at any moment.[28]

D IS FOR DEATH

Victoria also had casts of Albert's hands made by the sculptor William Theed, which she kept by her bed. Along with many portraits of the dead prince, these offered some comfort and 'served as the most vivid reinforcements to her belief that her husband was still watching over her'. She also sent the Crown Princess (Albert's favourite child and mother to Kaiser Wilhelm II) 'dear precious relics and hair' and even copies of his hand casts. The princess wrote about the moment she unpacked them:

> I thought my heart would break – I felt quite faint! They were the 1st thing that brought home to me the dreadful reality those dear hands I was so happy to kiss so happy to hold the rings I knew so well – all so like – and yet thin as I had never known him. Oh how dreadful to see them only in the cold plaster & to think I shall never kiss them again, it was an agony which I cannot describe![29]

The Queen commissioned statues and busts of Albert for the royal residences, and as gifts for family and faithful servants. She described the first posthumous bust, sculpted by Theed, as 'a living beautiful monument' – the use of the word 'living' quite telling. She took advantage of the modern invention of photography and posed alone and with her children around these busts, just as she had photographs taken of his death-bed corpse. In fact, post-mortem photography was a thing for the Victorians, one of the more mawkish customs. 'Once taken these images would be kept and viewed within the family album, thus keeping the person alive in the collective memory.'[30]

Historians Darby and Smith discuss how Victoria's mourning became a 'sort of religion' for her:

> Queen Victoria's worship of the Prince, her desire to preserve relics associated with him and their life together, and to fill her residences with his image, was an excessive manifestation of the nineteenth-century obsession with mourning... No one could replace Prince Albert for whom Queen Victoria's personal mourning never ceased, and for whom she ordered that official mourning should be 'for the longest term in modern times'.[31]

Lord Clarendon could vouch for this, writing that Victoria was 'very watchful about what people do and how the mourning is observed. She sent back the other day all the papers she had to sign because the black margin was not sufficiently broad.'[32] Queen Victoria really was extra in her mourning, expecting her subjects to mourn in the right way, and children, including her own, were certainly not exempt from this.

In Front of the Children

A quarter of all nineteenth-century deaths were of children under one years old. While all classes were affected, poor working-class children in northern industrial cities suffered the most. In 1840, Chadwick used statistics from nine different places to calculate the disparity in mortality; while one in five children of the gentry and professionals died, for the children of labourers, artisans and servants, it was one in two.[33] Parents and siblings took some comfort from the new idea of Heaven as a place where families would be reunited. A good death was still required to get to Heaven but, since the Enlightenment, some saw 'the concept of everlasting torment as incompatible with a just and loving God, and the doctrine of Hell was slowly eroded'.[34]

Children were not exempt from mourning. During the mourning period they also wore black, although infants could wear white. There are many photographs of Victoria's youngest child, Beatrice, dressed in black as a three-year-old. All over the country there were death customs which involved children. In Cornwall, for example, children would kiss the hand of the dead body, believing this would give them long life. In the North, children knocked on the door of a house in mourning to ask to see the laid-out corpse. In general, children attended deathbeds and funerals. Sometimes they would act as pallbearers at the funeral of a child, holding the white straps of the white coffin as a symbol of innocence. Because of the complicated funeral customs, all the extra work meant there was now more of a delay between death and funeral, perhaps up to a week. The body, unembalmed, was kept at home amid the living, in the family bed or on the table. While it might not have been pleasant, especially in the summer, it did mean death was familiar, a communal event. Before the funeral, mourners would assemble in the home to share biscuits and burnt wine. After the service there was a funeral tea. Because these rites and rituals took place in a domestic setting, they were part of life and children were used to them.

Berridge discusses the 'interplay between mortality and morality' as regards children and death. For the Victorians 'the requirement to die a good child was still being powerfully expressed ... a sanctimonious death is preferable to sinful survival.' Because of the high death rates, children were aware of their own mortality. There was much literature aimed at helping children live a good life so that they could have a good death. Juvenile obituaries focused on the child's demise and periodicals were full of death-related material including 'tips on taxidermy, poems about graveyards and human remains, funerary rites in far-flung places and woodcuts of catacombs'. This factual information appeared between stories 'where, instead of living happily ever after, the young heroes and heroines die happily, believing in the hereafter'.[35] Not exactly the *Beano*. The New Year message in *The Child's Companion*, 1824, was this:

You may not live to see the end of the year now just begun. How many little graves you see in the churchyard and whatever your age may be, you will see graves of children younger than yourselves. Will you not repent and pray to God?[36]

Dickens might have been a critic of the state of the churchyards and of the undertaking industry, but he was no stranger to grief, losing a daughter aged eight months and a son aged twenty-two. He also knew the power of a good death for a young person. Who can forget his description of Little Nell?[37]

She was dead. No sleep so beautiful and calm, so free from trace of pain, so fair to look upon. She seemed a creature fresh from the hand of God, and waiting for the breath of life; not one who had lived and suffered death. Her couch was dressed with here and there some winter berries and green leaves, gathered in a spot she had been used to favour. 'When I die, put near me something that has loved the light, and had the sky above it always.' Those were her words.

There were also morbid hymns. This is one from the sweetly named *Hymns for Little Children* (1848):

There are short graves in churchyard, round,
Where little children buried lie,
Each underneath his narrow mound,
With stiff cold hand and close shut eye.

This was written by a Mrs Alexander. She wasn't always this bleak. In fact, she wrote 'Once in Royal David's City' and the much more cheerful 'All Things Bright and Beautiful' (which was actually sung at my nan's funeral).[38] As Berridge says, 'There is something incongruous about the image of respectable children in comfortable parlours poring over accounts of putrefaction, stinking cadavers and endless variations on the theme of death.' But who are we to judge from our twenty-first-century viewpoint?

While we might not sing about child death in assemblies these days, we have lost something. As Berridge argues: 'The dramatic decline in the death rate for children in the twentieth century is a major factor contributing to the contemporary complacency and disregard of death.'[39]

Is Anybody There?

Intrigued by the supernatural, the Victorians invested emotion and time in ghost stories, fairy tales, myths and legends – some of which will be looked at in the next chapter. But it was more than stories that informed their interest; it was the modern world in which they lived: 'Disembodied voices over the telephone, the superhuman speed of the railway, near instantaneous communication through telegraph wires: the collapsing of time and distance by modern technologies that were transforming daily life was often felt to be uncanny.'[40]

In 1852, Spiritualism arrived from America, with the first Spiritualist temple opening in Keighley, West Yorkshire, a year later, a few miles from the Brontë parsonage at Haworth. Known as the 'Mother Church of British Spiritualism', it is still there today, in Heber Street. According to the website, Spiritualism is based on seven principles which came from the mediumship of Emma Harding Britten, who was inspired in 1871 after communicating with the spirit of Robert Owen, founder of the co-operative movement 'when on the physical plane'.[41]

The main belief of Spiritualism is that the spirits of the dead can communicate with the living through a medium who has supernatural gifts and thereby the living can continue their bonds with the dead. In the 1860s, Spiritualism became part of Victorian subculture, with its famous mediums, pamphlets, societies and seances, which included table rapping, table tipping, automatic writing, levitation and other communications with spirits.[42] This was at a time when Darwin published the *Origin of the Species* (1851), which, alongside other scientific advances, challenged the orthodox Christian view. Many lost their faith and replaced it with the occult – astrology, mesmerism, clairvoyance, hypnotism, magic, ghosts and Spiritualism. There were celebrity fans, including the Queen herself and writers such as Arthur Conan Doyle and Elizabeth Barrett Browning. A fangirl of Mary Wollstonecraft (mother of Mary Shelley, whose grave we encountered in St Pancras burial ground near Hardy's stricken tree), Elizabeth took opiates to alleviate head and back pain. And, while Spiritualism influenced her poetry, maybe there was some blurring of fact and fiction. However, although Elizabeth could reconcile her Christian belief of the resurrection with the afterlife of Spiritualism, it was a source of contention with her husband, Robert Browning.[43] Though there were frauds who exploited the bereaved, the movement gave solace to many following the loss of a loved one, so it is hardly surprising that Spiritualism peaked during the First World War. Even now there are more than three hundred Spiritualist churches in Britain. Including one in Teignmouth.

Fin de Siècle

As the century progressed beyond the 1870s, thanks to public health reforms, better nutrition, higher living standards and more control of contagion, there was a demographic transition with a decline in the death rate. The commonest time of death slowly moved from young age to old age. Jalland states: 'Within half a century death began to be perceived as the monopoly of the elderly and society's preoccupation with death receded.' The other major change was the gradual decline in Christian faith. From the 1870s, church attendance 'ceased to keep pace with population growth and Evangelicalism had passed its peak by the 1880s'. The system of belief and rituals which had helped so many Victorians to mourn was disappearing.[44]

As with any societal change, there are always factors, variables, contradictions and different opinions, but as the nineteenth century progressed – and not just in reaction to Victoria's excessive mourning – there was less need for such elaborate funerary and mourning customs. And while people, especially the poor, were no doubt burdened with the cost of death, this coping mechanism was about to be lost and would be gone for much of the following century.

Those keeners understood the importance of tradition and ritual. And they understood something about the transformational power of grief:

> Losses are alchemical by nature and the long-term effect of grief is influenced by how the grieving process is understood. Grief has the capacity to transform who we are and how we experience the depth of life. Though our losses will never leave us, our deepest wounds can become the gateway to our greatest gifts.[45]

Our rendition of keening that moonlit night on Exmoor might not have been traditional, but it was transformative. I think Geoffrey Gorer, the anthropologist who analysed the social impact of the disappearance of mourning rituals, would be pleased that they are making a comeback. We might no longer wear black 'weepers', but we do wear ribbons on our chest to show solidarity for causes such as AIDS/HIV and breast cancer. We might no longer wear locks of hair in brooches, but we do have the opportunity to turn cremated remains into jewellery or tattoos. As we progress into the twenty-first century, we are facing up to death once again. We will come to this all in good time. But, firstly, something about the myths and legends of our country, which has such a long-standing folklore tradition.

M
IS FOR MYTHS

Myths, Customs and Superstitions Surrounding the Dying and the Dead.

myth *noun*
1. a traditional story made up in the past to explain natural events, religious or cultural beliefs and practice, or the origin of social customs.
2. a commonly believed but false idea.

No common wind, no customed event,
But they will pluck away his natural cause
And call them meteors, prodigies and signs.
KING JOHN

December 23, 1664
This evening I being informed did look and saw the Comet, which is now, whether worn away or no I know not, but appears not with a tail, but only is larger and duller than any other star, and is come to rise betimes, and to make a great arch, and is gone quite to a new place in the heavens than it was before: but I hope in a clearer night something more will be seen. So home to bed.
SAMUEL PEPYS discussing the comet that many believed was an augur of bad news. Note the year.

D IS FOR DEATH

In Eyam churchyard, North Derbyshire, is the following, which seems to embody a superstitious belief respecting the death of one member of a family in seven years from the date of the death of another member of the family. Carved retrospectively, the safety of the prophecy was ensured.

> Here lise ye bodie of
> Ann Sellars
> buried by this stone
> who died on January 13th, 1731
> Likewise here lise
> Isaac Sellars
> my husband on my right
> who was buried on that same day seven years,
> 1738

☠☠☠

Anthropologist Nigel Barley says: 'Death is such an important event that most cultures encapsulate it in myth and ritual, give it at least a place in the world if not a justification.'[1] Myths swirl around the British Isles, the same old stories with regional variations, centuries old, stemming from myths and legends, common sense, the Church. In 1895, a collection of local folk tales, superstitions and rituals was published by Derbyshire lad, Sidney Odhall Addy. These included those related to death and burial. You can access it online, and there are some brilliant customs such as: 'If you bring dust downstairs after twelve o'clock you will soon have to carry a corpse down.'[2] (See, dusting can be lethal.) Another is: 'If three members of one family, being sisters and brother, or brothers and sister, marry on the same day, some person who attends the wedding will be sure to die.' (Hardly surprising if you mix all that family with booze and emotion.) A more well-known one perhaps: 'It's unlucky to pass someone on the stairs.' (I remember being told this as a child. It makes sense: remember, accidents are most common at home and, back in the day, those narrow, steep staircases, would have made it only too easy for one to take a tumble.) And this one most likely stems from the Church, harking back to the Last Supper which preceded the deaths of Jesus and Judas Iscariot: 'If thirteen dine at table together one of them is sure to die.'

☠☠☠

In the Home

Because people died at home, many rituals and beliefs were rooted there, from the bedroom to the parlour, from windows to doors. And many made sense. 'Spirit-rapping' was one of these, the noise made by the dying person in their last moments, indicating the spirit was leaving the body. We might know this as the death rattle. After death, the body would be laid out by the women, feet towards the rising sun, the window left open to enable the spirit to escape. Fresh air would also keep the room cooler, slowing decomposition. Ditto with the fire being extinguished. In later times, clocks would be stopped, 'suspending signs of life … to encourage the spirit to move on their way'. The curtains would be drawn or replaced with white sheets kept for this very purpose. Not only would this help keep the room cool, but also it would alert the neighbours that this was a household in mourning. (My mother, born in 1939, remembers the closed curtains from her childhood in Wales and Bristol.)

During the laying out, the women washed and shrouded the body. As well as the practical reasons, the shroud symbolically protected the dead person and recalled their baptism. Flowers and herbs, with special meaning, could be used to mask decay. The eyes would be closed to prevent rigor mortis setting them open; if the corpse eyeballed you, it could threaten you or your family. Pennies were placed on the eyelids to keep them shut, or they were bandaged, or, later, eye caps were used. A coin was also placed inside the mouth in the belief – lingering centuries after the Romans had left – that the dead could pay Charon, the ferryman, to take their soul across the river Styx to the afterlife. This practice is also associated with Wales and the North, 'a penny for St Peter', gatekeeper of Heaven. While the living believed they were helping the dead on their way, in reality it is more comforting to see the deceased in an attitude of sleep, rather than staring into the abyss.

If after shrouding the body did not stiffen, it was believed, as late as the industrial period, that there would be another death in the household.[3] And more specifically and macabrely, if the neck of a child did not stiffen shortly after death, another family member would pop their clogs. People, including children, were certainly used to corpses in the home, so it would be easy enough to touch one, to avoid bad dreams. They took it further in Yorkshire; you would never be afraid of the dead if you kissed the corpse.

> Such familiarity with the dead, and anxiety to be at peace with them, is better understood if we remember that this was still in the days before the funeral parlour, and when close proximity was unavoidable in often crowded homes.[4]

Mirror, Mirror

Perhaps because it lasted well into Victorian times, one of the more well-known customs involves mirrors, which would be covered when someone died, originating from the old idea that your reflection embodied your soul; you really did not want your soul to be trapped and taken off by the devil. There was also the belief that, if you saw yourself in a mirror in a room where someone had just died, you would die shortly after. Or maybe you would glimpse the dead soul. Belts and braces, a mirror could be turned to the wall or removed from the room. Sometimes other reflective surfaces, such as door handles, were also covered. Wearing matt black and veils not only protected you against your own death but would also confuse lurking demons.

Into the Light

Although wax forming a shroud down one side of candle was an omen of death, generally candles are sources of good. A candle was kept burning all night in the room where the person died, with maybe a candle or two placed around the body, to ward off the devil and to prevent the spirit from haunting the living (ghosts were believed to be afraid of light). Candlelight also offered the dead one of the comforts they had enjoyed in life. It showed that you remembered the deceased, ruling out any reason for them to attack you for forgetfulness. Instead, the light would remind the dead to guard the living in return.

Back in Eyam, the plague village in Derbyshire, the family would sit all night by candlelight with the laid-out corpse. Across the British Isles, 'watching' – or 'lich-waking' or the 'wake' – took place the night before the funeral, with family and friends watching over the deceased to protect them both physically and spiritually. A communal time where the bereaved consoled each other and recognised their own loss. Frisby says it was a liminal time between death and the funeral: 'The characteristics of both life and death were widely believed to be present during this in-between stage; there were folk beliefs that the dead could move around, and that a corpse could still sign a will if not yet cold.'[5]

Food and Drink

Food and drink have always played an important part at funerals, though in the past it was custom to leave some out for the deceased. For example, at Eckington, in Derbyshire, food was placed on a table within reach of the corpse. At Dore, a pewter plate of salt was put on the breast to keep away witches. In Cardiganshire, this was also done but to prevent swelling.[6] Although salt is a preservative – and where this idea might have originated – it has long been associated with death. Da Vinci's iconic mural of the Lord's Supper shows Judas Iscariot overturning the salt, an omen of his pending betrayal of Christ, which led to his crucifixion and Judas's own death by suicide. Some people today still throw salt over their shoulder if they spill it.

When you drank wine at a funeral, every drop was a sin committed by the deceased, so you were taking away their sins and bearing them yourself, a Christian belief, one that suggests a continued sense that the dead needed help to the afterlife. In some areas, in exchange for a small fee, food and drink were passed to a sin-eater, over the coffin of someone who had died without confession. Unlike the keeners, they were not respected, tending to be outcasts who lived on the periphery of village life. The sin-eater would eat this food, usually bread and ale, and make a short speech: 'I give easement and rest now to thee, dear man, that ye walk not down the lanes or in our meadows. And for thy peace I pawn my own soul.' This ritual allowed the sin-eater to absorb the sins of the dead, allowing their spirit to go to Heaven, which Frisby suggests could be a medieval tradition or a post-Reformation form of Holy Communion. It has also been argued that the sin-eater was like the biblical scapegoat:

> And Aaron shall lay both his hands upon the head of the live goat, and confess over him all the iniquities of the children of Israel, and all their transgressions in all their sins, putting them upon the head of the goat, and shall send him away by the hand of a fit man into the wilderness.[7] Leviticus 16

Richard Munslow (1833–1906), the last known sin-eater in England, is buried in the small country churchyard of St Margaret's in Ratlinghope, on the Long Mynd in the Shropshire Marches. Unusually, he was neither poor nor an outcast, but a respected farmer. On the tombstone[8] it says, 'Jesus said: Suffer little children to come unto me, and forbid them not, for of such is the kingdom of heaven' (Mark 10:14). If you read on, you will see that, although Richard died in 1906 and his wife Ann in 1913, this is a memorial to four of their children: George (11 weeks), who died in 1862, and Thomas (3), James John (6) and Elizabeth (1), who died of scarlet fever in 1870 all within one sorrowful week. Did this drive Richard to revive the practice?

Despite criticism by the Church for such practices as sin-eating and wakes, the latter could be jolly times, with drinking, smoking and parlour games taking place around the corpse. There are accounts from the seventeenth century of Hot Cockles, a somewhat bawdy game of Blindman's Bluff played around the corpse in Yorkshire. Trouncing on Trippets was another, played at Welsh wakes, but generally they were calmer here, with hymn singing and the sharing of memories.[9]

In some areas, before the funeral, wine was offered first to the pallbearers with the guests receiving it after the return from church. In Eyam, at home before the funeral, the mourners had 'burnt drink', an aromatic dark-looking ale spiced with cloves, nutmeg, ginger, and mace. They drank from a large tankard handed round to the mourners at the door of the house, before the funeral procession set off for church. At the same time, triangular cakes spiced with currants were handed round in a willow basket for the mourners to carry to church wrapped in a handkerchief. The same tankard and basket were used at all funerals.[10]

Clothes Show

In times past, people tended to make their own shrouds, often many years before their deaths. In Derbyshire, they often made their own coffins. In the Middle Ages, there was a Welsh custom of the wealthy being buried in the garment of a monk, protection against evil spirits – a nice priestly money-maker. Burial in a shroud was the norm, while the priest said words of absolution, which might also be written onto a scroll and put on the breast of the body.

Addy noted that, at funerals in the East Riding, women used to wear black silk hoods with a long piece of silk hanging over their shoulders and that when a young girl died she was carried to her grave by her friends, who wore black frocks, white silk shawls, white gloves, and white bonnets. 'A woman's wardrobe was not considered complete if it did not contain a white silk shawl.'[11] And, if you were not yet a widow, you would be ill-advised to put on a widow's bonnet – or you just might become one.

Teeth were also important. In Derbyshire, people kept their teeth in jars until death, when they were put into their coffins and buried with them. Mothers would also keep the teeth of their infant children. (Is this why I have all my children's?) Addy believes this was related to the old practice of burying the dead with their clothes, weapons, shoes and even food, because the dead needed these for the afterlife. Alternatively, it could be that you needed your teeth for the resurrection of the body, a belief that survived the Reformation in the form of superstition. Addy reports a man remembering his grandmother who would call out at a funeral: 'Have you got his teeth in the coffin?'

Part of the Coffin Path in the High Peak of Derbyshire

The Corpse Road

Now it is the time of night,
That the graves all gaping wide,
Every one lets forth his sprite,
In the church-way paths to glide.
Puck in *A Midsummer's Night Dream*.

A corpse was always carried feet first from the house. If upstairs, the body had to be carried down the stairs and, unless feet first, the deceased would be upside down, which was disrespectful. If carried feet first, the bodyweight would be lighter for the bearer at the foot end of the coffin. In time, practicalities can become superstition, so it would be unlucky not to take the dead out feet first; it might look back and want to stay or beckon another family member to follow. It was even believed that sleeping with your feet towards the door would invite death. Sometimes, the family placed shoes on the feet of the corpse or in their coffin, so they could continue their journey into the afterlife.

When it was time to leave, the door of the house would be left open or unlocked to allow the spirit to depart. The mourners walked in front of the coffin, which the bearers continued to carry feet first, so the body would symbolically walk away from its home, rather than towards it. In Wales they would sing hymns or say prayers all the way to the churchyard.[12] In Derbyshire, there was a superstition that whoever met the funeral party first would die next. Addy records a woman from Dronfield who followed corteges to see who this person would be.[13] A Victorian funeral chaser.

Many rural communities were scattered over a large area and, while there might be a local chapel-of-ease, the parish (or 'mother') church was the only authorised burial ground and could be some way off. So, the funeral party would follow an established track to the churchyard, with names including the bier road, the burial road, the coffin road, the coffin path, the corpse way or the lych way. It might also be the church-way path, the route parishioners took to worship at church. You can spot these tracks as they don't lead to markets or settlements, just to a church. On a satellite image you can see them crisscross places like Dartmoor and the Peak District. They tended to be straight – perhaps something to do with ley lines – to prevent the spirits of the dead from getting stuck on the road and haunting the living. If there was no cart or bier, the shrouded body might be carried on horseback or pallbearers might carry the coffin. But, however far and whatever the means, if the dead was not carried along the corpse road, its spirit might head home and haunt the family, and you really wanted to get the body to the churchyard so it would be ready for resurrection on Judgement Day.

Coffins often had to be carried for long distances, sometimes through tricky landscape. Spirits cannot cross running water, so there would be special rituals performed before crossing bridges or stepping stones to prevent spirits getting stuck and wandering the land as lost souls or animated corpses. The belief in revenants was widespread in medieval times, and it was assumed that corpse roads were passages for them.

If the party came to a crossroads, the Devil might show himself, so they would cross quickly, praying or performing a ritual in keeping with local custom. In Wales this would be the repetition of the Lord's Prayer to keep the body safe from the spirits of the dead criminals buried there, in case they were still lingering, hoping to cast their evil influence over the bearers' precious load. Along the route were lych stones or coffin stones, to rest the coffin while the bearers had a snifter. You can still see one of these on Dartmoor, part way up the hill near Dartmeet, set back from the B3357. This would have been a resting point on the way to Widecombe church. It is recognisable because it is split in two – legend has it – by a bolt of lightning.

One of the oldest superstitions surrounding these old tracks is that any land over which a corpse is carried becomes a public right of way, though this is not enshrined in law. As for the theory that if a dead body were carried across a field, it would affect the crops, I assume this is less likely. But who knows?

This brings us to corpse lights. These small eerie lights flitted at night along the corpse roads. An omen of death, they could signal either the souls who had already passed through the roads, or those about to. Also known as corpse candles, earth lights, fetch lights, dead men's candles, spook lights, death lights or, in Scotland, *deid lichte*. They were reported all over the isles and thought to be supernatural spirits with names such as Jack O'Lantern, Pixy-light, Spunkie, Jenny Burn-tail, Kitty wi' the Whisp, Joan of the Wad and, probably the most well-known, Will o' the Wisp. Others believed them to be the confused spirits of stillborn babies, or babies who, having died before baptism, were stuck in limbo.

There have been varying theories put forward to explain the phenomenon. Their flame-like phosphorescence could be caused by pockets of methane gas from decaying plants in bogland, deadly because they lured travellers from their path into the marsh. Or perhaps they were fungal bioluminescence, a blue-green glow known as foxfire or fairy fire. Some say glow-worms could be the source, others static electricity. My favourite theory is this: the feathers of barn owls have a luminescence, possibly from brushing against fungus. Found all over the British Isles, barn owls hunt at night, close to the ground. Could they be misinterpreted as corpse lights? Whatever the source, don't try and touch one – it might stray from the corpse path and cause the death of someone it meets.

Now we arrive at the church. At Kneesall, Nottinghamshire, Addy tells us, there were two entrances to the churchyard, the Bride Gate and the Corpse Gate. For obvious reasons, the bride would never enter the churchyard through the Corpse Gate. In Wales, at the funeral of a young newly-wed, it was customary to strew evergreens and sweet-scented flowers on the way to the grave, which was known as their marriage bed. Frisby describes the more general funerary rite of putting willow or hazel staffs ('metewands') into the grave, and maybe a small mortuary cross made of lead or wax, symbolic of the resurrection, before the priest cast earth onto the body, sprinkled holy water and censed the grave.[14]

But beware the gravedigger. In Wales, if he shook his spade at you, you would come under the evil influence of the spade and it would soon be your grave he would be digging. If someone was ill, another might ask: 'Has the sexton shook his spade at you?' And never carry a spade into a house on your shoulder, otherwise you might soon have to carry a coffin.

By the late 1940s, most of these customs had died out; now the dead were quickly removed by the undertaker. The coffined body might be brought home, but only to wait outside in the hearse before the funeral cortege set off. Even the hearses were different. Frisby argues that the mass requisition of horses in the Great War and the availability of cheaper motor cars meant a move from horse-drawn hearses to motorised ones. The carrying of herbs and flowers was replaced by wreaths delivered to the crem. Corpse roads fell out of use and are now heritage trails. We no longer have such opportunities to help the dead.

Fire, Fire

Fire is elemental, essential to sustaining life, and has played its part in death rituals. We know the home fire would be extinguished immediately after death, for practical and symbolic reasons. But did you know that, in days gone by, if a fire spat out an oblong (coffin-shaped) ember, it foretold death? At bedtime, the ashes from the household fire would be 'riddled' onto the hearth to prevent cinders catching fire and burning the house down. As with tea leaves, there was superstition in Yorkshire, cited by Frisby, that if any member of the household were going to die within the year, their footprint would be found in the ashes. In a similar vein, riddling the chaff after harvest could predict death. If you sieved it in a barn at midnight with the doors wide open and you saw two people pass by bearing a coffin, you would die within a year.[15]

Ding Dong

> No man is an island, entire of itself... Any man's death diminishes me, because I am involved in mankind. And therefore never send to know for whom the bell tolls; it tolls for thee.
> John Donne

Bells have a strong connection to death, and were even believed to have special powers. Many church bells have messages cut into the metal, such as 'I to the church the living call, and to the grave do summon all'. So important were they, bells were actually baptised. Before the Reformation, the priest would ring a handbell on his way to the deathbed, so people knew what was happening. Immediately after death, the living could help the dying by having a passing bell rung to frighten off evil spirits from claiming the soul. It was also a memento mori and would alert the poor to assemble in the hope of the dying person's last giving of alms. This was a reciprocal arrangement, the dead helping the living and the living helping the dead whizz through Purgatory. Although there were times the Church (for doctrinal reasons) and authorities (for morale reasons) tried to stop this, it continued for centuries. There were different patterns of ringing depending on where you lived, which would identify the age and gender of the deceased. In Eyam, it was believed that 'if the sound of the passing-bell be very clear there will soon be another death in the village'.[16] Perhaps this stemmed from the deadly visitation of the Great Plague.

Not only did bells warn of impending death and announce a death (the death knell), but a third bell – a dead (or *deid* in Scots), corpse, mort, lych or skellet bell – was tolled for a funeral. Funeral tolling, which still continues, is the slow sounding of a single bell, with a significant gap between strikes, from the tradition of 'telling' of the death. For some funerals and Remembrance Day, bells are half-muffled. The following is an extract from the guidance notes for Operation London Bridge (the code name for the protocol to follow upon the death of Queen Elizabeth II) from the Central Council of Bell Ringers:[17]

> Muffles are leather pads fitted to a bell's clapper to reduce the volume. They attenuate the bell's strike note whilst retaining the hum. By only muffling the clapper on one side (half muffled) you get an 'echo' effect as blows are alternately loud and soft. [This mournful sound with an eerie echo was heard at Princess Diana's funeral.] Bells are usually muffled on the backstroke as the handstroke gap emphasises the echo effect. Two muffles can be fitted, one on each side of the clapper, to fully muffle the bell. [This is reserved for the demise of the Crown and most of us would have heard this for the first time in September 2022.]

After the Funeral

Sharing a good meal after the funeral back at the house symbolised the resumption of normal life – a contrast to the understated refreshments beforehand – with the quality and quantity dependant on class. Frisby cites the funeral of a Yorkshire farmer: 'The better class were regaled in the parlour with wines, spirits and cakes; the smaller folk were offered ale or spirits in the front kitchen; the labourers had ale and bread and cheese in the back kitchen.' But it was always the best the family could afford under huge social pressure. If not, beware the judgy neighbours: 'They buried him wi' cowd ham. Now, I've putten away three childer, and they wor all buried wi' roast beef and plum pudding.' This was another reason put forward by funeral reform campaigners; money would be better spent on the living.[18]

High Days and Holidays

There are many customs and myths associated with special days. On the anniversary of the death of a loved one, candles were lit because it was thought that the dead would visit and the light would guide them home. Don't take a light out of the house on New Year's Day because someone in the household will die during the following year. Never do your washing then either because you will wash one of the family away. And, if you hang out the washing on Maundy Thursday, there will be a family death before the end of the year.[19]

On St Mark's Eve (24 April), some would keep a vigil in the churchyard for an hour either side of midnight, for three successive years (or for three successive nights in the one year). On the third occasion, the watcher might see the ghosts of those destined to die during the following twelve months, floating one by one into the church. But, if the watcher fell asleep during their watch, it was they who were doomed.

In the eleventh century, Abbot Odilo of Cluny realised that getting to Heaven was much easier for the rich, and so he founded All Souls' Day (Soulmas) so that, for one day, every person who had ever lived would be helped through Purgatory by the prayers of the living. Originally observed in February, All Souls' was changed to 2 November, the day after All Saints' (Hallowmas) on 1 November, when flowers were laid on the graves of loved ones. (You can work out where our modern Hallowe'en comes in.) Today, Catholics still light candles on All Souls' Day in memory of all the faithful dead.

And then we come to Christmas Eve, when some believed, if an east wind blew, it was blowing over the feet of corpses, because it blew towards the foot of the graves in the churchyards (bearing in mind the east-west orientation of the graves and the church itself). Addy records the custom of a candle or lamp being left burning all night on Christmas Eve, otherwise there would be a death in the house. In fact, grocers in Yorkshire would give their customers a candle at Christmas, especially made for this purpose.[20] (Makes a nice change from a calendar.)

The Black Dog

Animals are symbols of death in various cultures. Dogs are a common one. The black dog, with his huge burning red eyes and large teeth and claws, is found in folklore all over the British Isles. He appears at night near prisons, at crossroads and at the site of gallows. Known variously as padfoot, Bloody Tongue or shriker depending on the region, these dogs were believed to be an omen of death. In East Anglia, for example, the black dog was Black Shuck, and if you met him, you would die by the end of the year. Called Barghest in Yorkshire, it was an omen of imminent death if he lay across the threshold of your home. If he were invisible to someone, it might be they who die. The black dog can also shapeshift into the Devil or a ghost. In Devon he is the yeth or yell hound, possibly the inspiration for Conan Doyle's *Hound of the Baskervilles*. A headless dog, the hellhound is believed to be the spirit of an unbaptised child, whose howls can be heard in the woods at night. Also, Devonians believed that Sir Francis Drake had supernatural powers, defeating the Spanish Armada thanks to a pact with the Devil. His ghost rides across Dartmoor in a black coach driven by headless horses, led by twelve goblins and pursued by a pack of baying hounds. Any dog that hears the barking will die instantly.

Though these various black dogs are mythical, there is a black dog that is only too real: depression. Churchill, Samuel Johnson and Horace all referred to depression as the black dog. There is a mental health charity called My Black Dog,[21] offering adult peer-to-peer support. The mental health charity Sane run a Black Dog campaign.[22] And there is a video and book series called *I Had a Black Dog, His Name Was Depression*.[23]

(Don't even get me started on wolves and werewolves.)

☠☠☠

Pussy Cat, Pussy Cat

We know that in Ancient Egypt, cats were deified and mummified. But did you know that, in Transylvania, if a black cat jumps over a dead body, the corpse will become a vampire? Back in the West Country, a black cat is a symbol of bad luck being an omen of death. There is also an association with witchcraft; some believe cats are witches in disguise, others that they are witches' familiars. One old English superstition is that, if a cat sits or lies on a tombstone, the soul of the dead person buried there was possessed by the Devil. Two cats fighting near a dying person, or on the grave shortly after a funeral, are supposed to be the Devil and an angel fighting for possession of the soul. If a cat deserted a house where there was sickness and refused to be lured back, this was thought to foretell the patient's demise.

Bat!

In folklore, bats are witches' familiars or are associated with vampires. Nocturnal creatures, they often have associations with death or the underworld though, across cultures, some of the symbolism is much more positive.

The Birds

Firstly feathers. Because a feather bed did not help an easy death, feathers would be removed from the mattress. Or the bed could be moved under a beam, or the dying removed from the bed itself. Alternatively, there are records of feathers being put into the bed to hold back death until the dying received one last important visitor.

One for sorrow? We all know about the magpie. Some people still doff a pretend cap or salute Mr Magpie if he's spotted alone. In fact, a magpie (contraction of 'maggot-pie') is a type of crow, a carrion bird who feeds off the dead.[24] Ravens croaking near a house or alighting on your roof were a cause for concern. But it wasn't just carrion birds you had to worry about: any bird which flittered near a house, rested on a windowsill or tapped at a window foretold a death in the house. As did a cockerel crowing during the night. Or a swallow or jackdaw flying down the chimney. A few years back, in our old house in Dawlish, a pigeon flew down our chimney and my son and I had a horrific time getting it back outside. No one died.

Owls were particularly associated with death and Frisby says this belief persisted into the 1930s in Lincolnshire. Because of the owl's keen sense of smell, some thought it could detect early disease and this is why it could foretell death. Chaucer wrote in his *Parlement of Foules* of 'the owl eke that of deth the bode bringeth'.[25] The barn owl is the prominent owl in British folklore – maybe because its hoot is so atmospheric and its shriek quite something. Although since ancient times the owl has universally been considered wise, these death superstitions arose from our fear of the dark, the time an owl comes to life. According to my trusty *Observer's Book of Birds*, its haunts are 'barns, towers, ruins, woods and farm buildings', and 'by day it usually remains hidden'.[26] It has also been used as a meteorologist, its screech forecasting a storm brewing. Into the nineteenth century, an owl (dead, presumably) might be nailed to a barn door to ward off both lightning and evil.

Cuckoos are often maligned. Famed for its distinctive song, and for being a sign of spring on its return from Africa, the cuckoo is also renowned as a fake intruder, a con bird, laying its eggs in the nests of other much smaller birds such as the dunnock and robin, pushing out their own eggs and exhausting the parents. A great example of Darwin's survival of the fittest theory. The cuckoo has its place in the folklore of these isles: the number of its cries foretells the years of life left. Children in Victorian Yorkshire would sing around a cherry tree: 'Cuckoo, cherry tree / Come down and tell me / How many years afore I dee.'[27] And, of course, 'cuckold' was a term used to describe a man who had been cheated on by his wife (and perhaps the death of a marriage).

Some say the sound of a flock of flying geese, likened to a pack of baying hounds, is the 'gabble rachet' (derived from Gabriel's hounds). In North Yorkshire, the gabble rachet is the name for a nightjar, meaning 'corpse hound', and is associated with the souls of unbaptised children crying (these poor babies). Although beliefs vary, one thing is for sure, whatever it might be – and in some parts of Yorkshire and Durham it is a human-headed dog – the gabble rachet is a death omen.

Telling the Bees

There are many examples of bee, honey and beekeeper Egyptian hieroglyphs, and jars of honey have been found in their ancient tombs, to see the dead into the afterlife. Through the centuries, bees have been thought of as intelligent and even holy, with their wax used to make church candles, their honey a biblical image of plenty. My stepfather, Ralph, was a beekeeper and, though not superstitious, he had huge respect for his bees and their healing properties. He believed that, if you were stung, this would prevent arthritis. Because bee stings are par for the course for the apiarist, he was convinced that was why he never suffered from this ailment. He would rub honey on a cut, had a spoonful of honey in his tea and gave my son his local honey to help with his hay fever.

Addy tells us some of the customs associated with bees after their keeper had died:

> When a bee-master dies tins containing funeral biscuits soaked in wine are put in front of the hive, so that the bees may partake of their master's funeral feast. Two kinds of funeral cake are used, namely, biscuits and 'burying cakes', the latter only being given to the poor. The bees always have the biscuits, and not the 'burying cakes'. At Eyam, in Derbyshire, a portion of the 'burnt drink' and of the three-cornered cakes used at funerals is given to the bees of the deceased bee-keeper. Sometimes pieces of black crape are

pinned upon the hive. It is said that the bees must be told of their master's death, or they will all die.[28]

As the items were presented, words were said, with local variations, reminding them to work for their new keeper. The bees would hum their approval. In fact, because these tiny creatures were believed to be other worldly spirits, or perhaps the souls of the dead, you had to 'tell the bees' when there was any important event in the household, but especially when there was a death – otherwise the bees might desert the hive. According to Frisby, telling the bees still happens in rural north Yorkshire.[29]

Supernatural Beings

The bogeyman is used universally to scare children into good behaviour. In Lancashire and other counties, there is the legend of Jenny Greenteeth, a river-hag who pulls children into the water to drown them. This probably originated as an effective way to keep children away from the danger of duckweed-choked ponds. The grindylow is another water sprite to be found in meres and bogs in Lancashire and also Yorkshire, possibly related to Grendel from *Beowulf*. In *Harry Potter*, grindylows are aggressive water demons who live in the Black Lake at Hogwarts. Bloody Bones is another water-demon (aka Tommy Rawhead, Rawhead-and-Bloody-Bones, and Old Bloody Bones in Cornwall). Again, his name was a deterrent to scare children away from ponds and gravel pits.

And we must not forget the banshee (Irish: *bean sidhe*, Scottish: *ban sith*) or the 'woman of the fairy mound'. In Irish and Celtic folklore, this female spirit shrieks and wails at night under the windows of the house where a family member is close to death.

Sheela Take a Bow

Across the isles and in parts of Europe, mysterious stone carvings, called Sheela-na-gigs, can be found on medieval churches, castles, gateposts and houses – of a naked squatting old woman pulling open her enlarged vulva. Current thinking is that, rather than being pagan as previously presumed, they are actually rooted in medieval Christianity,[30] and while many were destroyed by priests or prudish Victorians, many remain, probably because people did not realise what they were. While to modern eyes they stand out for obvious reasons, paradoxically they can be hard to find. Some excellent examples survive in the Marches, the most well-known on Romanesque St Mary and St David's, Kilpeck in Herefordshire. The one I know is in St Lawrence's Church, Church Stretton, Shropshire. She is wonderful, made from older stone, probably from an earlier Norman chapel on the same site.

Barbara Freitag believes from her travels and research in rural Ireland – where there are over one hundred – that they were fertility symbols:

> In medieval times, there was such a high maternal mortality rate that you wanted a big vulva to ensure the child came out as quickly as possible, because a long, protracted birth could well mean the death of the child and the mother.

People would touch the Sheela in the hope of magical power for a good birth. But Freitag questions why these figures of fertility are also reminiscent of mortality. 'The answer is, of course, because life and death go hand in glove.'

Georgia Rhoades talks about my little friend in Church Stretton, where she sits above the north door,[31] through which the dead would have been carried in and out:

> The ideas of birth and death are essential to thinking about the vulva. To me, the Church Stretton Sheela is saying that you come out of the earth, you return to the earth, you come out of me and you return to me … You can ignore death as much as you want to, but death is going to come.

In recent times, these figures have been reclaimed by feminists. Project Sheela, which advocates for women's rights, has placed beautiful carvings around Dublin. One sits outside a former Magdalene laundry 'to honour the women who suffered there'. It is 'a symbol against misogyny – one of unapologetic female empowerment and sexuality'.[32]

All at Sea

While I write this, five people have recently died in the depths of the Atlantic, somewhere near the sunken wreck of the *Titanic*. The sea is a dangerous place. Fishermen and sailors know this only too well:

> Superstitions are often born in face of the unknowable and the uncontrollable, an attempt to make sense of the world through stories, or to allay very natural human fears of things we cannot influence or understand. With

that in mind it is perhaps not surprising that, as workers in a dangerous industry often at the mercy of the weather, seafarers have historically held many superstitious ideas.[33]

Sailors believed that the mysterious, mesmerising sounds they heard at sea were made by sirens, mythical creatures that are half-woman and half-bird, luring them to their deaths in dangerous waters. Others believed they were made by mermaids, half women-half fish.

Another maritime myth was that seabirds carried the souls of dead sailors. Although it was a good omen to see one, it was unlucky to kill one, particularly an albatross' as shown in Coleridge's poem, 'The Rime of the Ancient Mariner'.

The *Flying Dutchman* was a seventeenth-century Dutch merchant ship, captained by Hendrick Van Der Decken. In 1680, en route from Amsterdam to the Dutch East Indies, the *Flying Dutchman* was rounding the Cape of Good Hope during a bad storm. The captain cursed the gods and, as penance, was doomed to sail the Antarctic Ocean for ever, never able to make port. Redemption is only achieved if the captain can convince another captain to take a letter begging forgiveness. But anyone who sees the ghost ship is also doomed to bad luck, so this is impossible. There are many reported sightings, including one by Prince George (later George V) whilst a naval cadet serving on HMS *Bacchante*:

> At 4 am the Flying Dutchman crossed our bows. A strange red light as of a phantom ship all aglow, in the midst of which light the masts, spars and sails of a brig 200 yards distant stood out in strong relief as she came up on the port bow, where also the officer of the watch from the bridge clearly saw her, as did the quarterdeck midshipman, who was sent forward at once to the forecastle; but on arriving there was no vestige nor any sign whatever of any material ship was to be seen either near or right away to the horizon, the night being clear and the sea calm … at 10.45 am the ordinary seaman who had this morning reported the Flying Dutchman fell from the foretopmast crosstrees on to the topgallant forecastle and was smashed to atoms.[34]

The *Mary Celeste* is another ghost ship. She was found adrift, largely intact and with full cargo, four hundred miles off the Azores in 1872. The last log entry, ten days previously, positioned them in the Azores, within sight of Santa Maria. The seven crewmen, captain, wife and two-year-old daughter were missing.

I am going to finish not with a myth but with a true story connected to the *Mary Celeste* and, by association, to me. Almost a century later, in 1969, another boat was found, deserted, off the Azores, a boat that had set sail much closer to home, my home, the previous year, the year of my birth, 1968.

At this point in time, Britain was shivering her timbers because, just recently, Sir Francis Chichester had sailed the *Gipsy Moth IV* into Plymouth, after circumnavigating the globe with just one stop in Australia.[35] The *Sunday Times* launched a challenge: the Golden Globe round-the-world yacht race, for the first person to sail single-handedly – and non-stop – round the world via the Three Capes. Nine skippers would leave a British port between 1 June and 31 October 1968, and return to the same place, with a £5,000 prize for the fastest. Out of the nine skippers to set sail, Donald Crowhurst was the least experienced on his trimaran, the *Teignmouth Electron*. Charismatic and persuasive, he had little business acumen, a succession of failures behind him, but enthusiasm for the future. He persuaded local businessman Stanley Best to invest £1,000 to keep afloat his company, Electron Utilisation, which made electronic devices for yachts. In time, when Best wanted the loan repaid, Crowhurst had to come up with an idea, quick, and persuaded him to fund the construction of a new boat which would be a test bed for his inventions. To garner publicity, Crowhurst would enter the race. It was agreed, the loan guaranteed by Electron Utilisation; if the venture failed, the company would go bankrupt.

Crowhurst set off from Teignmouth a few hours before the deadline, on 31 October, his boat far from shipshape, with none of his clever inventions connected, with yet more money borrowed from Best and his home mortgaged to guarantee the loan. It did not start well: 'Crowhurst made a desultory figure scrambling about the deck of his trimaran as he set off on his great adventure – only to turn around within a few minutes to untangle his jib and staysail halyards, which were snagged at the top of the mast.' He continued to be plagued by trouble, but dropping out would mean financial ruin. 'He was Icarus, with an overdraft.'[36]

The boat's speed had been greatly exaggerated: there was no way he would catch up the other boats or win the prize money, unless 'something extraordinary happened'[37] and here 'a bizarre hoax becomes the stuff of myth as much as literature'.[38] Five weeks after leaving my hometown, Crowhurst took drastic action. Listening to forecasts for the areas he was supposed to be in, he created a fake logbook. As he hid out in the Atlantic, he recorded himself as rounding the Cape of Good Hope, sailing full steam ahead for the Indian Ocean. To avoid detection, he kept radio silence for three months, blaming the breakdown of his generator. On 9 April, he sent a telegram, suggesting he was approaching the Diego Ramírez Islands, south-west of Cape Horn. Back in the UK, it was believed Crowhurst had a chance of winning, but it seems he planned to finish a close second to Tetley, saving him from bankruptcy and without his fraudulent logbooks being scrutinised, as they would for a winner. Tetley, the leader, worried he might lose to Crowhurst. He pushed his boat onwards through bad weather and had to be rescued by a passing ship.

Crowhurst was now the favourite. Thousands of people were expected to welcome him home. But it wasn't to be. In the middle of June, Crowhurst reached the doldrums. 'On a boat clogged with the weeds and jellyfish of the Sargasso Sea, his imagination was driving him to the brink of madness.'[39] On 10 July, the floundering *Teignmouth Electron* was found by a passing ship (thank goodness for passing ships). On board, there was no sign of the skipper. He was never found, but his story was pieced together by the two logbooks he'd left behind, the real and the fake. And from the entries, it appears that Crowhurst must have seen only one way out. Knox-Johnston was the only person to finish the race and donated the £5,000 cash prize to Crowhurst's widow, Clare.[40]

A few years ago, this story once again became world-famous when Hollywood descended on Teignmouth, headed by Colin Firth as Crowhurst and Rachel Weisz as his wife. I went to the premiere in the town's art centre. Every time there was a local scene or an extra someone knew – including my friend's boxer, Hoopi – there was an eruption of whoops. Now Hoopi has crossed the rainbow bridge, she is forever memorialised in *The Mercy*.

☠☠☠

Poor Miss Bowles

In the medieval period, Frisby tells us that such was the fear of a bad death that 'people looked anywhere they could for death portents'.[41] Post-Reformation, Purgatory was banished but customs and rituals lingered, even if just in superstition – powerful enough in itself. The bereaved now took preference over the deceased, though many still wanted to assist them, 'thus this period saw a divergence between official and "folk" practice in relation to the dead'.[42] Although a passing bell hasn't been heard since 1915, when the Defence of the Realm Act banned it,[43] many traditional beliefs, such as opening the door to let the soul out, persisted until the 1940s. But after the war, 'with death becoming ever more predictable and medicalised, and therefore generally less visible in everyday life', such beliefs waned.[44] Back in Devon, at the time we moved there, and I saw poor Miss Bowles dead on her stairs, a howling dog was still a death portent.

But now that so many of us die in hospital, the bureaucracy of death has taken over somewhat, with beds being needed, and legalities such as death certification and registration. Though we might still light candles and pray for the dead, this has meant a decline in deathbed customs. Death has been hidden from view. However, the increasing number of death doulas and soul midwives, and a growing desire to die at home surrounded by loved ones, suggests times are changing. And the law has to keep up with this.

N
IS FOR NEXT OF KIN

The Law and Ethics Regarding Death and Dying

next of kin *noun*
a term used to describe your closest living relative or relatives.

Let's choose executors and talk of wills.
RICHARD II

On a barrister, who died insolvent:
Without effects died *Nolo Pros*,
How happens this? cries one and pauses—
His palm no fees were known to cross;
Effects can only spring from causes.

☠☠☠

Missing Persons

Two friends are working for an American company in Saudi Arabia. They have the weekend off and hire motor bikes to go into the desert for the day. An escape from their expat gated compound. As the sun rises, the two blokes, helmeted, clad in leather, whizz down highways, past date palm groves, and small villages where boys play games and old men sit and smoke, all eyes upon them as they pass through.

Night-time falls and they have not returned. They are not back by morning. Days pass. Search parties come back empty-handed. There are no sightings. They have disappeared. They are never found.

Several years later and one of the wives has long believed her husband to be dead. She has grieved for him. She has slowly put her life back together. In time, she meets someone. After all the grief, all the difficulties, she has a second chance at love. They want to get married. But, in the eyes of the law, she is already married. The law on marriage and civil partnership states that if a person has been missing for seven or more years – with no reason to believe they are still alive – they are presumed dead and the court can probably make a dissolution order. But, because seven years have not yet passed, she must divorce the husband she believes to be dead. The ultimate cruelty, divorcing a man she loved because he is no longer here.[1]

NB: I know about this story because the husband had previously worked with my stepfather in Indonesia. His widow kept in touch long after the disappearance and, to this day, we do not know what happened in that desert.

The Body

> Most ethical dilemmas and medicolegal problems seem to occur at the beginning and end of life ... People can be dying, or recovering, or brain dead, or potentially alive as a frozen embryo.[2]

In his book *33 Meditations on Death*, Jarrett discusses the ethics of medical treatment for the aged and frail:

> There is a concept in medical ethics, often overlooked nowadays, that medical investigations and treatment should reflect and be appropriate to the life the patient has led. Should a person from an age when cars were a rare sight be subjected to the terrifying might of advanced technologies? ... So often the context of a person's life is ignored in the planning of treatment. Elderly people with an old-fashioned deference to doctors are particularly vulnerable to the excesses of modern medicine ... Too often they become the passive recipients of a technology they can barely comprehend, for little or no health benefit and potentially much harm. I'm not convinced that hospitals are for everyone.

Jarrett goes on to discuss the dilemmas a doctor can face:

N IS FOR NEXT OF KIN

In reality nothing strikes more fear into a hospital's trust board than the threat of reputational damage. With feeding issues and other end-of-life decisions, there is a very fine line between being thanked by grateful relatives and helping the police with their inquiries. In fact, you would have difficulty getting a fag paper between the two.[3]

He discusses the four 'time-honoured principles of medical ethics': *primum non nocere* (first do no harm), beneficence (try to do good), autonomy and justice. He explains that 'autonomy' is the opposite of paternalism and that 'justice' means treating people equally – 'transplant organs, for example, are for everyone, not just the rich'.[4] Instead, he proposes a return to Aristotle's ethics, based on courage. 'Courage rooted in a genuine concern for humanity.' This means the courage for doctors to have open conversations with patients and relatives about the efficacy of treatment and quality of life.[5]

Ethics is important. As is the law. In UK law, there is no statutory definition of death.[6] The Triad of Bichat defines death as 'the failure of the body as an integrated system associated with the irreversible loss of circulation, respiration and innervation' and is used to determine death.[7] Medical advances mean courts will also accept evidence that you are dead when there is brain stem death. You will not regain consciousness or be able to breathe without support and will be legally confirmed as dead.[8] Basically, in law, you are dead when a doctor says you are dead. Obviously, checks must be in place to prevent wrongdoing – let's not forget the biggest serial killer in this country was Harold Shipman, a GP.

What are these checks? Firstly, there is certification of death. This is carried out by a doctor who issues a medical certificate of cause of death (MCCD). To certify that you are dead, the doctor listens to the heart for one minute, then feels for the pulse for one minute, examines for signs of breathing, shines a light into the pupils to check for a response. Their job is to say if you are dead, not how you died. If they have seen you in the last two weeks and death was expected, they can sign immediately. If not, they must report to the coroner. The Notifications of Deaths Regulations came into force in October 2019, making it a legal requirement for certain deaths to be reported to the coroner.

A coroner is a government official responsible for investigating violent, sudden or suspicious deaths, or if your identity is unknown. The coroner has temporary legal control of your body while they do this. The coroner may request a post-mortem examination (autopsy) of the corpse by dissection to determine how, when and where you died. A family member will be asked to formally identify your body. The coroner will determine the cause of death: suicide, accident/misadventure, unlawful killing or natural causes. They will release your body for burial or cremation as soon as possible. A coroner's investigation is not a criminal investigation. They do not find someone guilty. Sometimes a coroner might want an inquest to find out the facts in a court with witnesses. Then your next of kin will need an interim death certificate to notify the registrar of your death. After the inquest, the coroner will confirm the cause of death to the registrar, who will register the death. Then your next of kin can get the final death certificate from the registrar.

Jarrett discusses post-mortems for geriatric patients who die with unanswered questions. An autopsy can give a deeper understanding of the illness and its symptom management and the impact of their treatment which can benefit future patients, help research and offer comfort to the bereaved. 'But if we fear discussing death, how can we ask permission for this last, definitive exploration of a person's dead body and the impact their illness had?'[9]

Next of Kin

In UK law, there is no clear definition of who your next of kin is, except for children under eighteen who should have a parent or legal guardian with the legal authority to make decisions on their behalf.

If you go into hospital (or take part in a dangerous activity), you will be asked to name a next of kin. Hospitals usually allow you to choose anyone, such as a partner or friend. If, however, you are unconscious on admittance, the hospital will choose the closest relative they can contact. A next of kin does not have any legal right or responsibility to make decisions on your behalf. Instead, think about getting a lasting power of attorney legal document, whereby you can appoint someone to act on your behalf if you lose mental capacity in the future. The nominated 'attorney' can make decisions about your medical care and/or finances.

After you die and within five days (eight in Scotland), including weekends and bank holidays, your next of kin must register your death with the registrar at the register office, a local government office where deaths, births, marriages and civil partnerships are recorded. The registrar will issue a free 'certificate for a burial' (known as the green form) to give to the funeral director or direct to the burial ground. Or they will issue an application for cremation to be completed for the crematorium.

If there is to be an inquest or if the funeral will be a cremation following an autopsy, the green form is replaced by a document from the coroner issued directly to the funeral director or crem. If the funeral is to be overseas, other forms are needed instead of the green form. If you were in receipt of a state pension or other benefit, the registrar will issue a 'certificate of registration of death' (the white form) to be sent to the Department of Work and Pensions along with any pension books. As legal proof of death, the registrar also issues a certified copy of an entry of death known as the death certificate. This is required to settle your affairs and estate. This form must be paid for and it is recommended that your next of kin buy several copies there and then, an original one for each bank, insurer, pension company, etc.

☠☠☠

Disposal

If you die intestate, the next of kin may have to arrange and pay for the funeral. If you made a will, the executor is usually responsible for dealing with the funeral arrangements. (An 'executor' is the person(s) named in the will as having the responsibility of administering the estate, making sure your written wishes are followed.) Usually, the executors work closely with the next of kin to arrange the funeral. If there is a family dispute over the disposal of your body, the executor is legally entitled to decide the funeral arrangements – which can come as a surprise if they are not a family member.

If you die alone, without family or friends to claim you, the hospital or local authority will try to track down a next of kin. This could even be a spouse from whom you were separated but not divorced – though this spouse may choose not to claim responsibility. If you are unclaimed, the local authority overseeing the place where you died arranges a public health funeral (a pauper's funeral), abiding by Section 46 of the Public Health (Control of Disease) Act 1984.[10] There is no statuary guidance, but non-statutory guidance was issued in 2020 for local authorities. They should protect public health, ensure individuals are treated with dignity and respect, show consideration for the bereaved, make efforts to find the next of kin and inform them of arrangements, and recover costs as far as possible. In all this they must be transparent.[11] Evie King has written about her job as a council funeral officer in *Ashes to Admin*.[12]

Contrary to popular belief, it is not a legal requirement for a coffin to contain a dead body. While your body must not be exposed, either naked in public or to deliberately shock anyone, there is no legal requirement to hide it from view. Your body can be taken to a funeral in ordinary clothes, a shroud, a blanket, a cardboard box; it is up to the person responsible for the disposal as to how they do this, as long as you are decently covered. If no coroner is involved, the person with this right can take possession of your body as soon as death happens. If you die at home, you can be kept there. If in hospital or hospice, they can bring you home. Evansaboveonline.co.uk has a body collection form to give the hospital if there is any resistance (check it is the latest one).[13]

Your skeleton or human remains cannot be sold. (eBay forbids it.) The Human Tissue Act 2004 regulates the removal, storage and use of human tissue. Its key principle is that all bodies, body parts or tissue should be treated with respect and dignity. The Human Tissue Authority (HTA) recommends that the disposal of bones is done sensitively. This can include by incineration, separate from other clinical waste, or burial, or by donation to a medical school for teaching purposes with an HTA licence.

The law varies across the different countries in the UK and the Crown Dependencies of Jersey, Guernsey and the Isle of Man but generally it will be considered that you agree to be an organ donor when you die unless you have recorded a decision not to donate (opted out).[14] But only about 1 in 100 people who die in the UK can usually be donors because of the circumstances of their death. The sooner the donation, the better the outcome for the recipient.

Posthumous reproduction involves the use of a person's sperm or eggs after their death. In some cases, it also involves their retrieval very shortly before or after death.

If you die abroad, your death must be registered according to the law of the country. It should also be reported to the British consul. The cost of repatriation may be covered by travel insurance or by the tour operator. If you die on a foreign ship or aircraft, the death must be registered in the country where the ship or aircraft is registered.

Certain aspects of disposal are heavily regulated, such as the minimum depth of graves and the siting and management of burial grounds and crematoria, but other aspects are less so. For example, there are no set time limits for disposing a body and you can choose where you wish to be buried: every inhabitant of a parish and every person dying within the parish has a common-law right to be buried in the parish churchyard or burial ground.[15] You can also be buried in a cemetery, in a meadow or woods, at sea (in a certain coffin) or in private land such as a garden (with permission from the council). You do not have a legal right to be cremated, and cremation can only take place in a licensed crematorium. Some may insist on a coffin to facilitate handling the body. Hindu and Sikhs are now allowed funeral pyres, in an enclosed building. Under English law, there is no legal requirement to use a funeral director or to embalm, unless you are being repatriated. But remember, the 'no property in corpse' rule limits your right to have your disposal wishes carried out.[16]

Exhumation is the removal of a body from its original burial ground either for relocation purposes, or if new evidence challenges the original cause of death and another autopsy is required. Exhuming a corpse or interred ashes requires legal permission. In England and Wales, the likelihood of securing permission depends on where the remains have been buried. For unconsecrated ground, an exhumation licence is required from the Ministry of Justice. For consecrated ground, a grant of permission is required from the Church of England – much harder to obtain. (In fact, in 2015, the Church of England spoke out against 'exhumation on demand' where families wish to relocate a loved one's grave when moving house.) Many municipal cemeteries have both consecrated and unconsecrated areas, so there are different laws for bodies and ashes buried within a few metres of each other. Some religions are opposed to exhumation within their own cemeteries.

☠☠☠

Estate

A grant of probate gives someone the legal right to deal with your estate. If you had a will, the executors apply for probate. If not, the next of kin applies for a grant of letters of administration. (After your death, the next of kin is your closest relative(s).) Your estate might not require probate if, for example, you only had savings, owned shares/money with others or land/property as joint tenants. The executor/next of kin must contact the banks etc. to find out if they need probate to access your assets. Every organisation has its own rules.

An estate is the money, property, belongings and all assets[17] you owned at death, after payment of debts etc. When you die without a will, the rules of intestacy in England and Wales define how the inheritance will be distributed, with a next-of-kin order of priority. Under current English law, your surviving spouse or civil partner is at the top of the hierarchy, followed by children, then parents and siblings, working down through the family. Cohabitants do not qualify, regardless of how long they were living with the deceased. Where two people fall within the same category (for example, siblings or parents) and there is a dispute, the courts will decide on a case-by-case basis. In a will, a beneficiary is a named person who is bequeathed (left) an asset or share of the estate. This is a bequest or a legacy.

It could be left in a trust or in life insurance.

And, of course, there is the old saying commonly attributed to Benjamin Franklin: '…in this world nothing can be said to be certain, except death and taxes'. And sometimes these two come together in the form of inheritance tax. Yes, you might still have to pay tax after your death. Your executor or next of kin will have to find out if there is inheritance tax due. This means your estate must be valued before anyone can apply for probate.[18]

☠☠☠

Assisted Dying

Dying people are not suicidal – they don't want to die but they do not have the choice to live. When death is inevitable, suffering should not be. Along with good care, some people believe that dying people deserve the choice to control the timing and manner of their death.[19]

The Campaign for Dignity in Dying believe the right law for the UK is one that allows a dying person, with six months or less to live, the option to control their death, safely and comfortably at home, if they decide their suffering is unbearable. In England, Wales and Northern Ireland, assisting a suicide is a crime, and those convicted face a custodial sentence of up to fourteen years. There is no specific crime of assisting a suicide in Scotland, but helping someone to die could lead to prosecution for culpable homicide. The Campaign does not support a wider law that would allow anyone to end another's life. Assisted death must be completely voluntary and limited to terminally ill and mentally competent adults. It should require the dying person to end their own life, not allow someone to do it for them. There should be a waiting period for reflection and assessment by doctors and high-court judge. The law prevents a dying person from asking for medical help to die. Some travel abroad to die where it is legal with medical assistance, where they can control their death. Not only is this very expensive but it might be earlier than they would like. Others take their own lives at home and risk a lonely and perhaps painful, violent death because they do not want their family to be implicated.[20] Many more are suffering and dying without dignity because the law does not allow any meaningful choice.

The Campaign also states that any law should respect that some healthcare professionals may not wish to support assisted dying. The choice of assisted dying should be carried out alongside palliative care. Doctors, patients and the public need confidence that the law on assisted dying will work in practice, will be safe and will not be repealed, such as in Oregon, USA, where the law has remained unchanged since 1997.

Geriatrician David Jarrett says that he used to oppose medical assistance in dying, such as in Canada, where, within strict guidelines, a patient can either self-administer a lethal ingestion or a doctor can administer a lethal injection on their behalf. This must go alongside good palliative care, which, on its own, used to be enough for Jarrett. However, he now believes individuals should be able to decide for themselves. 'Autonomy to the highest level.' Though of course this becomes hazy with dementia patients. While Jarrett would never criticise a doctor for assisting death within such parameters, he could not do this himself: 'Most of my working life has been spent trying to relieve human pain and distress but for me the injecting of a lethal dose of anaesthetic, and watching someone stop breathing and die, is a step too far.' Instead, he suggests 'we all need to decide, and document with our families, what type of old age, and what trajectory of decline, we want and what we do not want'.[21]

Atul Gawande also discusses assisted dying: 'At root, the debate is about what mistakes we fear most – the mistake of prolonging suffering or the mistake of shortening valued life.' He goes further, believing so passionately in high-quality palliative care: 'Assisted living is far harder than assisted death, but its possibilities are far greater, as well.'[22]

Preparation

Putting your affairs in order, even when you are perfectly healthy, is a great legacy for your loved ones. Death admin makes everyone's lives easier. Anna Lyons suggests the five most important things you can do:[23]

1. *Fill in an advance directive/advance decision (living will)* – a legal document setting out your wishes for healthcare if you are later unable to explain them, e.g. refusing certain treatments such as CPR. https://www.nhs.uk/conditions/end-of-life-care/advance-decision-to-refuse-treatment/ accessed 17/7/23
2. *Sign a DNR or DNACPR form* (do not attempt resuscitation/do not attempt cardiopulmonary resuscitation), which says that if your heart or breathing stops your healthcare team will not try to restart it. It is recorded on a special form, varying between doctors and hospitals but with the same purpose, and is kept with your medical records. It can also be printed and kept at home/in a care home. You will still receive the care and treatment you need. Tell your family. For it to be legally binding, you need to put it in your advance directive.

    Some facts about CPR: it is an emergency procedure that attempts to restart the heart, involving chest compression, inflating the lungs, and defibrillation. Only 3 per cent over 80 years old will survive CPR and 1.9 per cent of people with secondary cancer. 40 per cent might survive briefly but only 10 per cent of those will be well enough to go home.

    While CPR can be successful in younger people with heart conditions, it rarely is for those with multiple long-term conditions or for palliative patients. Without a DNAR, many will have pointless traumatic interventions. Dr Mark Taubert: 'The values we are currently using to dictate necessary measures when someone is close to death and dying, or actually dead, are biased towards defensive medicine practices. They are aggressive and often based on fallacious logic sequences. We can do better.'[24]

    A story. My step-brother-in-law once administered CPR on a man in his sixties who collapsed in the street. He started his heart and kept his breathing going until paramedics arrived. The man survived but only for a few weeks. However, his family were grateful for the time it bought them to spend with him.
3. *Write a will.* A will is a document that sets out what you want to happen to your property, possessions and money on your death. To make it legal, it must be signed and witnessed. If you die intestate, the law might override your wishes. It is especially important to decide who will be the guardian of your children.
4. *Instruct a lasting power of attorney.* An LPA is someone legally allowed

to make decisions on your behalf about your welfare and care if you become unable to do so. While you still can, appoint someone you know and trust to look after your best interests. They must be over eighteen and compos mentis and can be a family member, partner, friend or a professional.
5. *Plan your digital legacy plan*. Much of your personal life will be online after you die, and the law is hazy. Record who you want to access your data and talk to them about your wishes. While social media accounts can continue bonds with the dead it can be distressing for others. Elaine Kasket says: 'Throughout your life be an unapologetic curator. Tidy up your digital house frequently.' This will help your loved ones when they sort out your digital estate. Don't rely on the cloud or digital legacy websites to look after everything – keep back-ups.

NB: I am not a lawyer. All this information is accessible online via the websites below. Laws and society change and evolve. It does no harm to keep up to date. I wrote my will this year and my funeral plan. I'm making my way through Anna Lyons's list.

Useful Links and Websites

End-of-Life Planning

Age UK is the UK's leading charity for older people with guidance on death and dying.
https://www.ageuk.org.uk/services/information-advice/guides-and-factsheets/guides-about-death-and-dying/

Marie Curie – a charity that offers support and care through terminal illness and all aspects of death and dying.
www.mariecurie.org.uk

Alzheimer's Society – advice, information, support in England and Wales, to people with dementia and their families/carers.
www.alzheimers.org.uk

Compassion in Dying – information to help you be in control of your end-of-life decisions.
www.compassionindying.org.uk

N IS FOR NEXT OF KIN

Death Café – talking about death over tea and cake.
www.deathcafe.com

Dying Matters – Hospice UK's campaign to create an open culture in which to talk about death, dying and grief.
www.dyingmatters.org

Gov.uk – Lasting Power of Attorney – download the forms and guidance to make and register a lasting power of attorney.
www.gov.uk/government/publications/make-a-lasting-power-of-attorney

Office of the Public Guardian – information on making a power of attorney or applying to the Court of Protection
www.gov.uk/government/organisations/office-of-the-public-guardian

Human Tissue Authority – information about donating your body to a medical school
www.hta.gov.uk

Organ Donation – the NHS Organ Donor Register is a secure database keeping a record of your organ donation decision
www.organdonation.nhs.uk/register-your-decision

MedicAlert – provides medial ID jewellery with medical information for an emergency.
www.medicalert.org.uk

Message in a Bottle – order a free one (charge for P&P) from Lions Club International to keep your advance statements in your fridge so paramedics know where to look.
https://lionsclubs.co/Public/?s=message+in+a+bottle

Keylu – an online store for your important information which makes it available to the appropriate people when you die – bank accounts, savings, insurance etc. You can also list who you want to bequeath personal items to.
www.keylu.com

Free Wills Month – charities offer a free will for over 55s.
www.freewillsmonth.org.uk

National Will Register – register your will so it can be found easily
www.nationalwillregister.co.uk

D IS FOR DEATH

After Death
Tell Us Once service allows you to inform multiple government departments all at once. It is offered by most local authorities on behalf of the DWP. It is free to use and saves much time and effort.

DWP Bereavement Service – in England and Wales, the DWP allows the next of kin to report your death in a single phone call which will cover any of your DWP benefits. The Bereavement Service will also do a benefit check to see if the next of kin can claim any benefits and can take a claim over the phone for bereavements benefits or a funeral payment.

The Good Funeral Guide has lots of facts and offers some clarity on the law. https://www.goodfuneralguide.co.uk/your-legal-rights-and-responsibilities/

Law Society – independent professional body for solicitors
www.lawsociety.org.uk

The Coroners Support Service
https://coronerscourtssupportservice.org.uk/

Government guide to coroners
https://www.gov.uk/government/publications/guide-to-coroner-services-and-coroner-investigations-a-short-guide

www.advicenow.org.uk – you can download a free NHS Next of Kin Card to fill in and carry with you in your purse or wallet.

Citizen's Advice Bureau – advice on what to do after death, dealing with financial affairs, funerals, wills etc. www.citizensadvice.org.uk

https://www.gov.uk/funeral-payments – for those on benefits

Books
Conway, H., *The Law and the Dead*, Routledge, 2016
Chapman, S., *Funeral Arranging and End-of-Life Decisions*, The Book Guild, 2022

O
IS FOR
OPERATION LONDON BRIDGE

The Passing of Famous People and How This Has Affected Our Attitude to Death. Absent Death

Operation London Bridge *proper noun*
the funeral plan for Queen Elizabeth II, including the announcement of her death, the period of official mourning, and details of her state funeral. Created in the 1960s and revised many times before her death on 8 September 2022.

All the world's a stage
And all the men and women merely players.
As You Like It

In death, no difference is made
Betwixt the sceptre and the spade.
JOHN CUTHBERT, ob. 1711
From Inverness

☠☠☠

When I wrote *Betsy and Lilibet,* my fourth novel, I knew I wanted to set the book against the life of Elizabeth II, a long life. But the story was Betsy Sunshine's, born into a family of funeral directors on the same day the late Queen was born into a family of royalty. I felt I knew these women, born in 1926, the same year that my great-aunt Ruth was born in Croydon. She died in 2021, in a care home during Covid, but not of Covid. It came as no surprise that the Queen would die, but it was still a shock when it happened because, for most of us, she had simply always been there. It was a time for reflection. After all, the deaths of royals and other famous people can affect how we see ourselves, our family, our own death.

☠☠☠

A Right Royal Death

Obsessed by the details of death, Queen Victoria planned her own funeral, leaving instructions for burial to her doctor, Sir James Reid. Instructions included what would go into the coffin with her: Albert's dressing gown and a plaster cast of his hand, a lock of her personal attendant John Brown's hair and his mother's wedding ring, photographs (including one of Brown) and letters (including some of Brown's). As for Victoria herself, she wore white and her wedding veil.[1]

After decades of the self-induced purdah of his mother, when Edward VII ascended the throne, he revived royal display, infusing occasions such as the state opening of Parliament and Trooping the Colour with full pomp and circumstance. When he died in 1910, after a reign of just nine years, the medieval ritual of lying in state was resurrected. Hundreds of thousands filed past his coffin, which was displayed on a catafalque in Westminster Hall. Following George V's death in 1936, his four sons revived the Prince's Vigil, in which members of the royal family arrived unannounced and stood watch around the coffin. The late Queen's children and grandchildren, including women for the first time, did the same, reminding us that Elizabeth Windsor was an old woman, a mother, aunt, grandmother and great-grandmother.

Elizabeth was the first British monarch since 1760 to have her funeral in Westminster Abbey, a state occasion with two thousand guests. Images are still fresh in our minds; for me, it was the lone piper processing slowly from the chapel at Windsor, the haunting sounds gradually fading. The piper who woke her up daily, now performing an eternal lullaby.

☠☠☠

Elizabeth II
Born: 21 April 1926

O IS FOR OPERATION LONDON BRIDGE

Bruton Street, Mayfair, London
Died: 8 September 2022, aged 96
Balmoral Castle, Scotland

> The Queen is Britain's last living link with our former greatness – the nation's id, its problematic self-regard – which is still defined by our victory in the second world war.[2]
> Sam Knight

The only monarch most of us have ever known died during the writing of this book. I had planned this chapter, with this heading, and somehow did not believe it would be written in retrospect. The day the Queen died, I was in my caravan, with my elder son, Johnny. We put on BBC News when we saw on our phones that – even though just a couple of days previously she was broadcast to the world shaking hands with Liz Truss – the Queen was ill. And by ill, the inference was, dying.

The last monarch to die, in 1952, the Queen's beloved father, George VI, will only be remembered by the Silent Generation and older Boomers. The second episode of *The Crown* was titled 'Hyde Park Corner', the code word for his demise, employed so the switch board operators would not find out first. For Elizabeth II it was 'London Bridge Is Down', to be spoken by civil servants on secure lines. Sam Knight sums up the enormity of this for us, whether monarchist, republican or indifferent:

> From the Foreign Office's Global Response Centre, at an undisclosed location in the capital, the news will go out to the 15 governments outside the UK where the Queen is also the head of state, and the 36 other nations of the Commonwealth for whom she has served as a symbolic figurehead – a face familiar in dreams and the untidy drawings of a billion schoolchildren – since the dawn of the atomic age.[3]

When the BBC used to broadcast to the British Empire, they were the first news outlet to be informed of a royal death. These days, a news flash will go simultaneously to the Press Association and global media. At the same instant, a footman in mourning clothes will 'emerge from a door at Buckingham Palace, cross the dull pink gravel and pin a black-edged notice to the gates', announcing the demise of the Crown.[4] The BBC's radio alarm transmission system ('Rats' aka 'royal about to snuff it') will be activated. Commercial radio stations will light up their network of blue 'obit lights' to alert DJs to play inoffensive music until the news.

For the Queen, ITN used the code word 'Mrs Robinson'. The BBC News presenter Huw Edwards announced her death at 6.30 in the evening, wearing a dark suit and black tie. The national anthem was played showing a photo of the Queen. Soon, flags would fly at half-mast. There would be 'ritual proclamations, a four-nation tour by the new king, bowdlerised television programming, and a diplomatic assembling in London not seen since the death of Winston Churchill (Operation Hope Not)[5] in 1965'.[6]

Operation London Bridge had been practised for decades in government departments, the police, the army, the church, at Westminster, the Palace and Royal Parks, local authorities, cities and embassies. In the event, the Queen died at Balmoral, and so Operation Unicorn was also brought into effect to run alongside London Bridge, being the code name for the plans if she were to die in Scotland. Thursday, the day of the Queen's death, would have been D-day or D+0, but this changed to Friday, due to the announcement being in the early evening. The Queen's body remained at Balmoral until Sunday, 11 September, D+2, when Anne, the Princess Royal, the Queen's only daughter, accompanied her mother's body by car to rest in the Throne Room at the Palace of Holyroodhouse in Edinburgh until Monday afternoon, when they processed up the Royal Mile for the dead queen to lie in state at St Giles's, where fire-brand John Knox preached against Mary Queen of Scots four and a half centuries before. Then on D+4, on to RAF Northolt, London – under the guidance of Operation Overstudy because a flight was used rather than the Royal Train – before being driven to Buckingham Palace for the coffin to rest in the Bow Room. On D+5, the Queen was taken by gun carriage to Westminster Hall to lie in state until Monday, 19 September, D+10, when the pallbearers placed the coffin back on the green gun carriage that was used for Lilibet's father, his father and his father's father. Then 138 naval ratings pulled her to Westminster Abbey, following the tradition started by necessity at Victoria's funeral in 1901, when her white horses threatened to bolt at Windsor Station and the junior sailors stepped in and saved the day.

Because this was not just the demise of the Crown but also the making of a king, running in tandem with London Bridge was Operation Spring Tide, the plan for the accession of Charles III. On D+1, the flags went back up, and at 11 a.m., Charles was proclaimed King. The Accession Council convened in St James's Palace, a tradition harking back to the Anglo-Saxons. Four days after Penny Mordaunt was appointed Leader of the House of Commons and Lord President of the Privy Council, she presided over the Accession Council ceremony, the first to be televised. Alongside senior politicians both past and present, archbishops and judges, the new Queen Consort and the new Prince of Wales, Mordaunt became the unexpected star of the show, as she was to be at the coronation of the King. (We can just be thankful it wasn't Jacob Rees-Mogg, the previous Lord President.) Charles III was now officially king, and he set off on his tour of the home nations, a new queen at his side.

One of the biggest headaches will be for the Foreign Office, dealing with all the dignitaries who descend from all corners of the earth. In Papua New Guinea, where the Queen is the head of state, she is known as 'Mama belong big family'. European royal families will be put up at the palace; the rest will stay at Claridge's hotel.[7]

According to David Cannadine, British ceremonial occasions did not always run so smoothly. In fact, 'the majority of the great royal pageants staged during the first three-quarters of the nineteenth century oscillated between farce and fiasco'. In 1817, at the funeral of Princess Charlotte (more of her in a bit), the undertakers were drunk. A decade later, at the burial of the Duke of York, St George's Chapel was so cold that Canning, the foreign secretary, contracted rheumatic fever and the Bishop of London died. And reporting on the funeral of George IV in 1830, *The Times* said, 'We never saw so motley, so rude, so ill-managed a body of persons.'[8]

The only hiccup during the ceremonies of 2022 seemed to be Charles's annoyance at a pen or two.

☠☠☠

Horatio Nelson
Born: September 29, 1758
Burnham Thorpe, Norfolk.
Died: 21 October 1805, age 47
HMS *Victory*, Battle of Trafalgar,
Atlantic Ocean, off the southwest coast of Spain.

> [A]n Admiral whose military brilliance combined with human fallibility made him extraordinarily popular in his own lifetime.[9]

Vice-Admiral Horatio Nelson commanded the British fleet during the Napoleonic Wars. On 21 October 1805, during the Battle of Trafalgar, whilst walking the quarterdeck of HMS *Victory*, in full dress including medals, he was easy pickings for a French sniper. Third time unlucky perhaps – he'd already lost an eye and an arm in other campaigns. Now, he was fatally injured, carried below deck by his men only to die three hours later. Long enough to hear from Hardy, the ship's commander, that the British fleet had been victorious. Nelson was able to have a good death, leaving messages for Emma Hamilton and their (publicly unacknowledged) daughter, Horatia, and to give final directions for the fleet. 'Thank God I have done my duty' were his last words.

On 22 October, Nelson's body was put into a cask of brandy and transported on his flagship to Gibraltar, arriving on the 28th. The brandy was replaced by stronger spirits of wine to preserve the remains, which were laid in a small coffin made by a ship's carpenter using the timbers of Nelson's old bunk. As for his injured men, they were nursed on the peninsula and the dead buried in Trafalgar Cemetery, where their graves are still maintained.

On 4 November, the ship continued its journey. By the 6th, news had reached a shocked Britain, with the hero finally arriving home on 4 December, when HMS *Victory* was moored at Sheerness. After a post-mortem a week later, Nelson's body was placed in a lead coffin filled with yet more brandy (so much booze). On the 21st, the body was removed from this coffin and placed in another, as were his wishes, constructed from the mainmast of the French ship *L'Orient*, which the British fleet had destroyed at the Battle of the Nile. (The coat which Nelson was wearing when he died was returned to Lady Hamilton, as requested.) The coffin was then placed in another made of lead and put inside another of wood (so many coffins). This was collected by the *Chatham* two days before Christmas and taken up the Thames to the Royal Naval Hospital at Greenwich, where he was kept in a small domed room designed by Hawksmoor, locked away and guarded while funeral preparations were made. On 4 January, Nelson's body lay in state in the Painted Hall[10] for three days, during which time over 100,000 people paid their respects. On 8 January, a flotilla of boats followed the coffin on Charles II's state barge upstream to Whitehall and then to the Admiralty in preparation for the grandest state occasion of the era (the first of three state funerals at St Paul's for non-royalty, the other two being Wellington's and Churchill's).

On the day of Nelson's funeral, 9 January 1806, the streets were lined with weeping crowds. The procession – with Nelson's coffin in a funeral 'car' modelled on his ship, complete with a figurehead and topped with black plumes – was so long that the leading Scots Greys reached St Paul's before the rear had even left the Admiralty. 7,000 mourners attended the service, including 'seven royal dukes, 16 earls, 32 admirals and over 100 captains together with 48 seamen and 12 marines from HMS *Victory*'.[11] During the five-hour-long service, the coffin stood centre stage draped in the *Victory*'s flag. At its close, the casket was lowered into the crypt to rest in a marble sarcophagus[12] – originally intended for Cardinal Wolsey (whom we met earlier dying from the Sweat, a blessed relief to the alternative, being hacked to death on Henry's commands).

It seems that this grand affair pretty much went without a hitch, except perhaps for the sailors from Nelson's ship, who, it was reported, ripped its flag into pieces to keep as mementoes.

It was without precedent in British history that someone outside royalty… would be commemorated in such a way, such was the appeal of Nelson and his significance to the nation… He was considered by many as the figurehead of the struggle against the invading forces of Napoleon, an invasion threat not experienced since the Spanish Armada in 1588.[13]

Neither Emma nor Horatia was invited to the funeral; back then it was uncommon for women to attend such ceremonies – even Victoria did not go to Albert's. And, despite Nelson's wishes that Emma be generously provided for, she died in poverty in Calais in 1815, never acknowledging that she was Horatia's mother. Horatia lived until she was eighty-one; her gravestone is marked 'the beloved daughter' of Nelson, and today she is officially recognised as 'the child of the father she adored and the mother who denied her'.[14]

Every year at St Paul's, a 'sea service' is held on the Sunday closest to Trafalgar Day, when wreaths are laid at his tomb. In 1840, the iconic 170-foot-tall Nelson's Column, with the admiral's statue on top, was erected in Trafalgar Square. HMS *Victory* can be visited in Portsmouth. When my children were small we visited the ship alongside the *Mary Rose*. For some reason, my daughter, about three years old, stashed all her birthday money into her My Little Pony purse (around forty quid!) and dropped it somewhere near a life-sized model of Henry VIII. We didn't realise until we got back to Worthing that evening. The next day I phoned up the site and was told that the naval police had it. So, another day trip to Pompey, where we managed to retrieve it after getting through security. The other memorable quote from the trip was Ed asking us about the ship in his best five-year-old discourse, 'Who rid it?' Translation: 'Who rode it?' Meaning, 'Who was the captain?' We still ask this question, whenever we get the chance.

Napoleon Bonaparte
Born: 15 August 1769
Ajaccio, Corsica
Died: 5 May 1821, age 51
Longwood, St Helena

> Death is nothing, but to live defeated and inglorious is to die daily.
> Napoleon Bonaparte

St Helena, 1821. Family legend has it that six-year-old Mary McCallum, daughter of a soldier, granddaughter of a slave and slave-owner, is placed into a coffin. She is not dead, but very much alive. So why this macabre action by her father? So little Mary can tell future generations that she was here, sitting in the coffin, before the intended occupant could be laid inside. Mary grows up. She gets married to another solider, who also has an illegitimate child by a slave. But Mary bears him four children on the island and a further six in England, after they return in the 1830s to her husband's country of birth, somewhere she has never known. Her last child is named for her, born in 1856 in Clifton, my great-great-grandmother.[15] Mary McCallum died aged ninety by the seaside in Devon, in 1946, when my own mother, Mary, was seven. Every generation since the time of the coffin incident has had a girl with the middle name Helena. My daughter Isabel has it as hers. And, if you hadn't guessed, the intended occupant was one Napoleon Bonaparte.

After defeat at the Battle of Waterloo in 1815, Napoleon was exiled to the middle of the Atlantic Ocean, to St Helena, an island under British control. He'd already escaped his first exile on Elba,[16] off the coast of Italy. This time the Brits were not taking any chances. Over several years of exile, the ex-emperor's health deteriorated, living in a damp house in one of the most isolated spots of the world. He developed stomach trouble and died on 5 May 1821. Conspiracy theories have surrounded his death, such as arsenic-laced wallpaper, but it is agreed now that he most likely died of stomach cancer, exacerbated by bleeding stomach ulcers and bad medicine.

It was a couple of months before news reached Europe, and even then not everyone believed it, because his death had been reported many times before. Indeed, sightings of him continued to be reported – like Elvis or Tupac. Doppelgangers appeared all over the world and his face was even seen in the moon. All this fed into the cult of Napoleon. And while his will requested that he be buried in Paris on the banks of the Seine, 'in the midst of the French people, whom I have loved so well', this was thwarted by Sir Hudson Lowe, British governor of the island.

I am interested in what happened after Napoleon's death. It is well documented that, once his death mask was cast, and once he was sewn up following the autopsy and dressed in his battle uniform, his body was placed in three coffins: one of tin soldered shut, inside one of wood screwed shut, inside another of lead soldered shut. Two vases of viscera were placed in the innermost coffin. On 9 May (my birthday), the outer lead coffin was placed in a mahogany coffin.[17] Family legend has always had it that little Mary's father made the coffin and that is why he was able to sit Mary in there. When our family historian visited St Helena (no mean feat as this was before there was an airport), he could find no evidence of this. Which coffin could Mary's father have made? We know it wasn't this final mahogany one, as that was down to the upholsterer and undertaker, Andrew Darling. In his journal, Darling recorded the instructions for the construction of the coffins. It was decided that the exterior coffin would be made from the best mahogany on the island. Darling does not say where he found it, but according to Mrs Owen, daughter of a Captain Bennett, the coffin was made from her father's dining table. Others say the wood was from the stores in Jamestown. Perhaps Mary's father, a soldier, was part of the furnishing team. Perhaps he helped with the construction, as it would have been quite a feat to get all those coffins made. But I do like to think of little Mary sitting in one of them before Bony.

The interment took place in the Valley of Geraniums, in a tomb lined with stone slabs, three metres deep inside a brick-lined pit and sealed on top by a giant stone slab fixed in place by cement. The grave was then covered with two metres of stones and clay and topped with three stone slabs. (Beats the old mort safes used to deter the bodysnatchers.) Later, railings were placed around the site, which was under a weeping willow tree. Cuttings from this tree were taken as far away as New Zealand, and one of these relics – known as 'Napoleon's willow' (*Salix napoleona*) – lives on in Akaroa.[18]

In 1821, Napoleon's mother wrote to Castlereagh, the foreign secretary, to beg for her son's coffin to be exhumed and brought to France. She never received a reply. Finally, in 1840, Napoleon got his wishes. Darling returned to St Helena to oversee the exhumation of his remains, which took place on 15 October before French and British witnesses who had been present at the burial. The coffins were opened, and Napoleon's well-preserved corpse allegedly looked 'as if he were asleep'. According to Darling's diaries, discovered in 1915, he 'worked incessantly with others at the coffins, which were all ready for delivery by 1 a.m. on the Monday morning. Then apparently for the first time since he had risen on the Saturday morning, he was able to snatch a rest.'[19]

The outer mahogany coffin was replaced by another lead coffin brought from France, and this was enclosed in one made of ebony, also from France. During transit across the Atlantic, the coffins were enclosed in a case of oak, which was no doubt removed before the final interment in Paris, where Napoleon was given a state funeral and entombed in the crypt of Les Invalides. All the construction suggests a team of workers, and maybe my ancestor, John Bradshaw, little Mary's father, was one of these the first time round in 1821.

'Death and Bonaparte, the Two Kings of Terror'[20]

D IS FOR DEATH

Where Were You When…?

Diana, Princess of Wales
Born: 1 July 1961
Sandringham
Died: 31 August 1997, age 36
Pitié-Salpêtrière Hospital, Paris

> A girl given the name of the ancient goddess of hunting was in the end the most hunted person of the modern age.
> Earl Spencer

It is early on a Sunday morning at the end of August and I have been sleeping beside Edward, my one-year-old, whose itchy eczema makes night times difficult for him. My husband comes in to check on us and deliver a cup of tea. He has been watching children's television with our two-year-old. Johnny was upset because *Teletubbies* was interrupted by a news flash.

Diana is dead.

Diana is dead?

The news is hard to believe, but what is even more astonishing is the week to come, when the nation will act out of character, when 'a country known to quail at emotional expression was suddenly incontinent'.[21]

The world had seen Diana just weeks earlier comforting Elton John at Gianni Versace's memorial service in Milan. Who could have predicted that the singer would be performing at her funeral so soon after, or that Diana would have been 'transformed from mourner to mourned, from comforting to being the object of grief herself'.[22]

Her death was to become the most high-profile of the twentieth century and a watershed moment in the English way of death which lasted well beyond her funeral. Our behaviour changed because the media showed us how others behaved in grief. Berridge cites sociologist Tony Walters, who believes that this change had started the previous decade when a million people visited Anfield to lay flowers and football scarves in the wake of the Hillsborough disaster. This informed our response to Diana, so that now a mass of flowers, candles, poems and pictures were left at the gates of Kensington Palace, Diana's home. But not just there. Her face was everywhere in death as it had been in life. 'Suddenly, Diana's image on postcards and keyrings was memento mori… Her smiling face, oblivious of her fate, underscored the fragility of the present, and cheap souvenirs made tourists cry.'[23]

O IS FOR OPERATION LONDON BRIDGE

Why did we react as we did? Diana was so familiar that for many people it felt like a personal bereavement. Berridge suggests that as a divorcee and outcast from the Royal family, the portrayal of her alone at the Taj Mahal and then dying in a French hospital 'seemed to distil the sadness of every dysfunctional family, the loneliness of the broken home, and in this there was something symbolically modern about the nature of her demise'.[24] Some of us wept because we believed we knew her. As Tony Blair, the new prime minister said, 'she was the people's princess and that's how she will stay, how she will remain in our hearts and in our memories forever'. Others wept because her death made them remember other personal losses. Either way, Berridge points out that the reaction was genuine, not just a result of mass hysteria: 'Other people's deaths are filtered through a prism of personal experience; it is not right to say the tears are not "real".'

Many wanted to be part of a communal response. My mother-in-law took her nine-year-old granddaughter, Hannah, to the gates of Kensington Palace. Ronnie remembers the pungent smell of thousands of flowers and how many children were there. I was teaching and had two small children at home, so I was unable to go, even though I was living in London at the time. But I remember another teacher from my school jogging up there from Plumstead. She wasn't a monarchist by any stretch, but she felt compelled to go, just as my auntie Liz, living in Harpenden, rushed with her husband to a bridge over the motorway to Althorp to throw flowers onto the hearse. I felt a similar compulsion when the late Queen Elizabeth died. I got a lift to London and jumped the Tube to Heathrow, to stand alongside the trolley dollies and ground staff and a very rude, entitled woman who pushed me out of the way even though I'd been queuing for ages, counterbalanced by a lovely Japanese family who welcomed me into their group. We saw the hearse, the coffin covered with the Royal Standard, flowers, crown, orb and sceptre. For a fleeting moment she was in front of me. The only other time I'd seen her was almost half a century earlier, in Bristol, during a summer holiday visit to my grandparents. I always thought it was for the silver jubilee of 1977, but my brother Rhys is sure the occasion was in 1973, the six-hundredth anniversary celebrations of Bristol's city charter, when she stood up in a car crossing the Downs. Now, I saw her in death, the second and last time.

D IS FOR DEATH

As for the Queen, so for Diana, the press provided continuous coverage. But, for Diana, her life did not end in old age. It ended in trauma, unexpectedly, horrifically. So, for her, the news updates were a mixture of obituary, post-mortem and crime investigation, mixed with 'a measure of bereavement counselling'.[25] And the greatest of ironies: special memorial issues ran concurrently with demands for reform of the press and privacy laws. For the first time, the internet took on an important role, a medium of global mass mourning spinning Diana's death and legacy into that of a saint. In fact, Berridge points out that Mother Teresa died the day before Diana's funeral and the press linked the two women by the image of sainthood: 'In the reverential atmosphere of queues and crowds with the air heavy with the scent of flowers and the flickering of hundreds of votive candles around a multitude of individual shrines, Kensington Palace started to feel like Lourdes.'[26]

On the day of the funeral, the country stood still. Although I had two small boys, I managed to watch the funeral on the television. I assume their father took them out at some point. London was certainly quiet. Even central London by all accounts, despite the crowds. It wasn't like the wedding back in 1981. Even shops closed, 'the ultimate mark of respect from a nation of shopkeepers who normally don't allow even Good Friday to interrupt the kerching and swipe of sales'.[27] We watched on, saddened at the sight of two grief-stricken boys trying to be brave, following their mother's coffin. Prince Harry, looking back, spoke about how it was for him:

> For me, the thing I remember the most was the sound of the horses' hooves going along the pavement. Along the Mall, the red brick road. By this point I was, both of us were in shock. It was like I was outside of my body and just walking along doing what was expected of me.[28]

Despite being one step down from a state funeral, once inside the Abbey, once we acclimatised to the pomp and the rituals and the glitterati, the ceremony itself – and the burial afterwards – was a modern affair. 'A pop song, a warts-and-all address by a family member, being buried in one's own clothes (in Diana's case a Catherine Walker dress) a woodland burial site – these elements characterise the modern preference for personal relevance, a trend which has been gathering momentum since the 1980s.'[29]

In the aftermath, once she stopped being in the headlines, Diana's death was 'a reminder to remember death'.[30]

Two Roses

Diana's death echoed the death and mourning of another Princess of Wales. Charlotte, the daughter (and only legitimate child) of the Prince Regent (later George IV) was second in line to the throne, but on 6 November 1817, after a two-day labour, she gave birth to a still-born son and herself died shortly after. She was twenty-one. Berridge compares the public's responses to the two deaths. Charlotte, a champion of British fashion with an unhappy background, was also the people's princess, famed for her looks and empathy for human suffering. Charlotte's doctors were blamed and there were rumours of foul play and cover-ups. There was commemorative merchandise and references to Charlotte as a rose. While for both princesses the nation went into mourning, the greatest difference between the mourning rituals for Charlotte and Diana was the religious response to the death of the first and the secular response to the latter. In addition to newspapers and pamphlets, it was through church sermons that the country learned more about the death of Charlotte, whereas for Diana it was the rolling news of television and the early stages of the internet.[31]

By chance this summer, I was in Croft Castle, Herefordshire, in a small room dedicated to Princess Charlotte, telling the story of the sixth baronet, Sir Richard Croft, the male midwife (*accoucheur*) who attended her. After the deaths of the princess and her child, Richard was very upset, though the autopsy cleared him of blame. As did the statements from the other doctors and both Prince Leopold, Charlotte's widower, and the Prince Regent. But the wider public were savage, calling for a public inquiry. On 15 January 1818, Richard took his own life. These events became known as the 'Triple Tragedy'.

Absent Death

'Most English people die in old age, out of sight, in hospital or nursing and residential homes. These are the all too frequent unseen deaths of the confused elderly, victims of strokes, or in coronary care or suffering Alzheimer's.'[32] If you are famous or made famous by a violent or unusual death, following the initial news of the disaster, there will be a focus on grief and the search for causes. But, for us mere mortals, we might have a death notice in a local newspaper or, more likely, online.

Shelley (whom we last saw on a funeral pyre on an Italian beach) wrote about the death of Charlotte in a pamphlet, in striking words that foreshadowed Diana's death:

> Mourn then people of England, clothe yourselves in solemn black. Let the bells be tolled … shroud yourselves in solitude and gloom of sacred sorrow… Weep, mourn, lament. Fill the great city – fill the boundless fields with the lamentation and the echo of groans. A beautiful princess is dead; she who should have been the Queen of her beloved nation, and whose posterity should have ruled it for ever. She loved the domestic affection and cherished arts which adorn and valour which defends. She was amiable and would have become wise, but she was young and in the flower of youth the despoiler came.[33]

Berridge calls the poet's words 'a searing critique of the cult of celebrity' because the point of his writing was absent death. The day before Princess Charlotte died, three men were executed for their part in a demonstration. This appalled the poet. But what appalled him more was the obsession of Charlotte's death over theirs:

> The execution of Brandreth, Ludlum and Turner is an event of quite a different character from the death of Princess Charlotte – men shut up in a dungeon with fear of hideous death… nothing is more horrible than that man should for any cause shed the life of a man.[34]

We know that in death, as in life, there is disparity.

Yemen, the Arab world's poorest country, has endured eight years of civil war which shows no sign of respite. This is one of the world's worst emergencies, with children and families in urgent need of food, clean water and basic healthcare. According to UNICEF, as of December 2022, more than 11,000 children have been killed or maimed, figures verified by the UN but likely to be much more. Malnutrition is at an all-time high, with more than half a million children at risk of death. Outbreaks of disease, including one of the largest cholera outbreaks ever recorded, place greater demand on already scarce resources such as gloves, soap and ventilators. No place in Yemen is safe for children.[35]

It is hard for foreign journalists to gain access to Yemen, but in July 2023 Orla Guerin reported from there, showing us images of starving children that should have been left in the 1980s. Journalists such as Guerin make it their mission to bring absent deaths to our attention. But such humanitarian emergencies soon get knocked off the top spot of the news cycle to be replaced by stories closer to home.[36]

In the summer of 2023, five rich men died on the *Titan* submersible en route to the view the wreckage of the *Titanic* deep on the ocean floor of the North Atlantic. News coverage portrayed them as adventurers, whereas the concurrent story of the ship that sank in the Med (one of too many) with unnamed, uncounted victims, received far less attention and the rescue operation far less resources. Jennifer Allsopp reported that the migrants appealed for help 'multiple times, countering the narrative of the Greek coastguard'. She compared this first-hand evidence to that given by passengers of the *Titanic*, 'women and children not seen as credible sources'. For decades, these survivors were similarly gaslit when they testified that the ship split in half. They were consistently told that this was not possible, 'until the first visit to the wreckage proved otherwise'.[37]

The Lead gives stark reasons for this disparity:

> The people on the boat are many and therefore anonymous; the people on the sub are few and identifiable, and therefore easier to humanise and to take an interest in... And then, of course, the people on the boat were poor and brown, whereas the majority of the people on the sub were white and/or rich... Empathy is a finite resource, and every little degree of alienation that helps us to switch our attention away from vicariously experiencing someone else's trauma helps.[38]

Disparity, accountability, viewpoint, perspective.

Back in Yemen, since 2015, according to David Craig, a Saudi-led air campaign to defeat Houthi rebels has killed at least nine thousand civilians. And yet, the US government has defended its approval of tens of billions of dollars' worth of weapons sales to Saudi Arabia and its regional allies during this time. 'They insist there is no reason to believe that American-made arms are commonly used in such strikes.'[39]

Should we be surprised at this? After all, there is a long-standing gun epidemic in the USA. In 2017, the US was the only country with more civilian-held guns than citizens, with an average of 120.5 firearms per 100 people, the highest rate in the world. Yemen, a country in the grip of a devastating civil war, came in a distant second at 52.8.[40] For Brits, this is hard to comprehend.

D IS FOR DEATH

According to the Gun Violence Archive (GVA), in the first four months of 2023, at least 13,959 people died from gun violence in the US, an average of about 115 deaths each day. Of those who died, 491 were teens and 85 were children.

No place in the USA is safe for children.

In the same period there were 184 mass shootings, defined by the GVA as an incident in which four or more victims are shot or killed. These mass shootings led to 248 deaths and 744 injuries.[41] Despite these staggering stats, only 22–31 per cent of Americans say they personally own a gun, with the majority of gun deaths occurring in Texas, California, Florida, Georgia, North Carolina, Illinois and Louisiana.[42] A reminder that the US is a huge country made up of many parts and many people.

But let us not forget that deaths by suicide account for the largest number of gun deaths in the USA, with an average of about 66 deaths per day.

From the UK to you across the pond, I ask you to wrestle with your outdated obsession with the Second Amendment.[43] And, while you think about that, ponder this: why did you vote in the first African American president, who cried over the dead children of Sandy Hook elementary school, only to have his best attempts at gun control thwarted?

And yet, as ever, he had hope for change.

Remember his words, spoken to mark the tenth anniversary of this senseless school shooting:

The good news is that, of late, I have sensed that slowly, steadily, the tide may be turning. That we are not just condemned to repeat the mistakes of the past and that real change is possible. Ten years ago, we would have all understood if the families of Sandy Hook Elementary had simply asked for their privacy and closed themselves off from the world. The temptation must have been powerful, but instead they took unimaginable sorrow and channelled it into a righteous cause and in the face of cruel conspiracy theorizing and nasty partisan politics, and, worst of all, inertia and indifference and the TV cameras shifting to the latest distraction. They just kept on going and set an example of strength, resolve, and grace, which makes me very proud.[44]
Barack Obama

P

IS FOR POTTER'S FIELD

My Dad

Potter's Field *proper noun*
1. *Historical* a cemetery where paupers or the unidentified were buried.
2. *Biblical* land with clay soil owned by potters bought by priests used for burial.
3. *New Testament* land bought by the Sanhedrin with the thirty pieces of silver paid to Judas for the betrayal of Jesus, which Judas returned after Jesus' conviction, as it is 'the price of blood', before dying by suicide. Because it was blood money, it was illegal to keep, so the priests bought the potter's field to be used as a burial ground for strangers and paupers, known as the Field of Blood (Matthew 27).

Yet here she is allow'd her virgin crants,
Her maiden strewments and the bringing home
Of bell and burial.
HAMLET

He lived and died
By suicide
ON A CORONER'S STONE AT WEST GRINSTEAD CHURCHYARD, SUSSEX

Trigger Warning

...unanswered and unanswerable questions.
Julia Samuel[1]

This chapter talks about suicide. I aim to follow the Samaritans guidance for media[2] so will be careful about how I tell the story of my father, but I will be honest when I recount how his suicide has affected me and my life.

If you or someone you are concerned about is having a mental health crisis that requires an urgent response, then contact the person's GP, or the GP out of hours service or call NHS on 111. Or call Samaritans on 116 123.

If you have serious concerns for their immediate safety, then they can go to Accident and Emergency or phone the emergency services 999.

Your mental health is as important as your physical health. You will not be wasting anyone's time.

https://www.nhs.uk/every-mind-matters/urgent-support/

Stephen Nigel Stenner (1933–78)

Nigel to his first family. Steve to his friends and to my mum and her family. Dad to me and my two older brothers. I knew him for a short while, but I spent good quality time with him as he was at home a lot with a bad back. We played cards, backgammon, Scrabble. He read to me. If I couldn't sleep, I'd come downstairs and sit on his lap and watch *The Rockford Files*. He never got cross with me, because my eyes would well up and he couldn't tell me off. If I was off school, he made me sardines on toast and small cups of coffee. He whistled. He pottered about in the garage having cheeky cigarettes. He played golf, really well, until he had to give it up. Until he got ill.

Dad was born into a well-known Tiverton family, sawmill manufacturers who employed many in the mid-Devon town. He went to the local Blundell's School and then, aged sixteen, joined Dartmouth Royal Naval College as a cadet. During his time in the navy, he had an accident, falling down an onboard ladder, and was pensioned out. He moved to Bristol and worked as an electrician, a trade he had learned in the navy, and worked for the General Electric Company. The day he met my mother, an electric cooker demonstrator, he came into work grimy with smoke, with singed hair and no eyelashes. There had been a fire at his lodgings, and he'd got everyone out of the house. Mum and Dad's first date was to Wookey Hole in Somerset. They got married on 1 September 1961, in Redland, Bristol, and had the reception in my grandparents' home. They went on honeymoon to Spain, flying (with their car) from Bournemouth. They had a kitten called Sammy. My brother Peter was born ten months later, and his first winter was the coldest for over two hundred years, the Big Freeze. When he was one, they moved to Thornbury, a market town a few miles north of Bristol, into a brand-new Wimpey home. My brother Rhys was born there in 1964, and I turned up four years later, born in the same bed. When I was three weeks old, we relocated to Swindon with Dad's work and, two years later, we moved to Devon, to Teignmouth, where my mum and Peter still live and where I brought up my children. Family legend has it that we owned the first colour telly in town, as Dad worked for an electrical company. We had a two-year stint in Torquay when my parents ran a corner shop – newsagent's, tobacconist's, sweet shop and grockle shop – which we lived above (inspiration for my debut novel *The Generation Game*), down the road from the Boneyard, which was our back garden.

In the winter of 1975, we moved back to Teignmouth into a draughty old house with eight bedrooms which my parents ran as a guesthouse. Families from all over the country and students from all over the world came into our home and shared our lives for a brief time. This is the home I walk through in my dreams.

Sunday was the day we would drive to Tiverton to see Dad's aunt for high tea with bread and butter, scones and cake. (I have her bone china tea set.) Fay was more like a mother to him than his own mother had been. Betty, my grandmother, died of cancer aged sixty, when I was a baby. Stanley, my grandfather, died of cerebral malaria in 1958 aged fifty-seven. Theirs was not a happy home. Betty was twin to Ken and younger sister to Tom (who wanted to leave his body to medical research and who solved the mystery of typhoid from canned beef). Their mother, Mabel,[3] died in childbirth in 1909, when Betty was six. She grew up without a mother, passed from aunt to aunt, while her brothers went to boarding school. She took this sadness with her, unable to grieve because she had never been allowed to grieve. She married Stanley – who wore spats at their wedding – and had her two children within thirteen months of each other, Shirley and Nigel (Dad). After she had done her duty, Stanley looked elsewhere for 'comfort'. Betty became a headteacher and captain of the ladies' golf club.

But she was unable to mother properly as she had not been mothered herself.

I think that Dad had taken on the unhappiness of his mother.

D IS FOR DEATH

My great-grandparents' wedding, 1899, Colombo.
Mabel is sitting down with the biggest hat, George to her left.

My grandparents' wedding, 1932, Croydon.
Stanley in his spats next to a tall Betty.
Fay, Stanley's sister, is the bridesmaid back left. Ruth,
Betty's half-sister, is the little one.

P IS FOR POTTER'S FIELD

Dad, September 1978

Julia Samuel believes that traumatic grief – which comes from sudden or unexpected death – can be overwhelming. The bereaved can experience shock, both witnessed or imagined, with flashbacks triggered by sensory stimuli. They can alternate between extreme emotions and a shutting down. Samuels discusses secondary transmission of trauma. This is where children of those suffering untreated PTSD do not have memories onto which they can focus grief, but their lives are nonetheless pervaded by loss, 'haunted by the ghosts of people who haven't been mourned'.[4] She goes on to say that, if many families examined their history, 'they would have a sense that there were secrets that hadn't been told, their toxicity trickling down the generations'. She believes that, however difficult the truth might be, it is better than a lie or cover-up. 'We can't deal with what we don't know, so we can fully process an event only once we understand the "what", the "how" and the "why" of it.'[5] Our capacity to manage this burden is based on our social environment, how we communicate with those around us and our genetic predisposition. We need to understand all these aspects to help ourselves navigate this grief and trauma.

When I read this recently, aged fifty-five, everything made sense. As a child, long before Dad died, I experienced a sadness, carried a heaviness about with me. I was cripplingly shy, did not like leaving home to go to school but always worked hard, avoided being told off and hated any conflict. I didn't like large groups of girls, just had a couple of close friends, and this has all pretty much carried on into adulthood, though being a mother has made me braver. (Just wait till I'm a grandmother.)

Some of my character traits are innate. I'm an introvert. An INFP, according to Myers-Briggs (introversion, intuition, feeling, perception, these are my personality traits). One of the rarer types, I am a mediator and an idealist. I tend to be quiet and unassuming. A people-watcher. A daydreamer. A sensitive soul. I cry easily. I can feel adrift in the world but am self-aware enough to know this (therapy has helped). I am a good judge of character. Compassionate. I try to be non-judgemental, open-minded, and to walk in other people's shoes, but can despair at other people's words and actions. People confide in me, tell me their stories, and I am a good listener. An empath. Sometimes the world lies heavily. I take on other people's woes. Other people's bad vibes. It can be overwhelming. Exhausting. But my creativity has bloomed in the darkest days. I know that the cracks are where the light gets in (thank you, Leonard).

Some of my character traits are learned. I am risk averse. I am careful. I am a worrier. An insomniac. Sensitive and emotional. These cross over with my innate traits but have been exacerbated or added to by my family upbringing, especially so since the day my father died. The day when everything changed. When I stopped being a child and yet part of me remained, and has always remained, that ten-year-old girl consumed with disenfranchised grief.[6]

(An hour after writing this, I started reading Cariad Lloyd's book,[7] where she says on page 2 that the day her dad died, when she was fifteen, she stopped being a teenager and became a grown-up but also froze, 'the eternal adolescent'.)

Christmas 1978

My one and only white Christmas, slam bang in the middle of the Winter of Discontent. Boney M are on *Top of the Pops* singing 'Mary's Boy Child' and Morecambe and Wise have taken their sunshine to the other side. At some point, Rhys and I brave the cold to play with my best present ever, a Swingball, on the front lawn. I can't remember Boxing Day. As I go to bed on 27 December, I say goodnight to Dad. He is sitting in his armchair in the lounge. There is a coal fire. Orange flowery carpet. A real Christmas tree with coloured lights. The television is on, but I can't remember what programme or if Dad is watching. I ask him if he can pick me up from my friend's house the next afternoon. She lives out in the sticks and I have to be back in time for the evening's performance at the local theatre. I am part of the dance troupe in the pantomime. A blackbird baked in a pie. He says he will. There is something about him. Something I cannot put my finger on. Perhaps it is distraction. A sadness. Tiredness or maybe pain. Ever since his accident in the navy, he has had a lot of pain. It has been getting worse. No one can do anything about it. He has recently been told that he might end up in a wheelchair. Whatever it is this night, whether remembered or imagined, those are the last words we speak to each other. I never see him again.

The next day, my friend's dad picks me up in the morning, by which time Dad has already gone out somewhere. I spend the day at her house and when it is time to be collected I am ready. We watch the television. Dad is late. Mum phones my friend's dad and he says he will drop me back. Once home, Mum tells me Dad is still out. She seems a little worried, but I am focused on getting to the theatre. Mum drops me down. Afterwards, in the dressing room, where I take off my makeup and get changed, I am expecting Dad to pick me up but my brother, Rhys, now fourteen, turns up instead and walks me home. He says Dad is still not back. I can tell he is worried, but we don't really speak about it. I go to bed that night, knowing Dad will be here in the morning. He did this last year. Disappeared for weeks. A 'nervous breakdown'. But he came back. He will come back.

Only he doesn't. Instead, when I go downstairs, my grandparents are here, having travelled down early from Bristol. Soon the doorbell rings. We are all standing in the hall, and I can't remember who answers, only that it is the police and a neighbour. Rhys and I are sent upstairs (Peter is away fishing in Cornwall). We wait, pacing the landing, listening out for grown-up words. My tummy feels awful. Rhys looks sick. Eventually, we are called downstairs and into the lounge. Where I last saw Dad, only now he is gone. Mum tells us Dad has died. He is gone for good. I stare at the last photograph of him. He is standing on a pebbly Cornish beach, and I know with a deadly chill that I will never see him again and that never is a very long time.

Dad was just forty-five.

We hear whispers. *Suicidesuicidesuicide*. At some point we are told. Dad took his own life. We are told how this happened. I will not tell you as you don't need to know. You only need to know that it happened and that it was the worst thing that has ever happened to me, to my brothers, to my mum, and that it has been a shadow over us for much of our lives. Forty-five years on, I still yearn for him, but I have learned to live alongside the grief of his loss. I continue bonds with him. I visit his grave at Selworthy, where I wish to be buried. I have a few precious photographs of him. An old cine film of his wedding. My love remains. His love remains. I can touch it in his things. I can see it in my children.

The Good Samaritan

On 2 November 1953, Chad Varah, a vicar and writer-cartoonist living in London, answered the first ever telephone call to a new helpline for people contemplating suicide. He described the service as 'a man willing to listen, with a base and an emergency telephone'. Now, in over 200 locations across the UK and Ireland, Samaritans has 22,000 highly trained volunteers with the vision that fewer people will die by suicide. 'The power of volunteers – to listen, confidentially and without judgement – turned out to be the real strength of the service.'[8] Available every day and every night of the year for anyone struggling to cope, they respond to a call for help every ten seconds. Samaritans also works with schools, prisons, hospitals and the workplace, with the military and the media, at festivals and in the community, alongside

Network Rail to reduce suicides on the railways, and they campaign for and research into online safety. The Samaritans is co-chair of the National Suicide Prevention Alliance (NSPA).[9] The charity continues to invest in new technologies to reach as many as possible.

Globally, the availability and quality of data on suicide is poor, but the WHO recognises suicide as a public health priority whilst believing that, given its sensitivity and the illegality of suicidal behaviour in some countries, 'it is likely that under-reporting and misclassification are greater problems for suicide than for most other causes of death'. It also argues that improved monitoring is needed for 'effective suicide prevention strategies'.[10]

In the UK, Samaritans monitor suicide statistics to make sure they reach those most at risk to prevent suicide. Around 6,000 people die by suicide in the UK and Republic of Ireland each year. You can visit their website to see the complexity of how stats are made and for comparisons between the two countries.[11] You can also see the stats recorded in Parliament.[12]

What Is Suicide?

Suicide is the act of intentionally taking your own life. Suicidal behaviour includes suicide, suicidal ideation and suicide attempts. Suicidal feelings might be abstract thoughts about ending your life or that people would be better off without you. You might think about methods of suicide or make clear plans to take your own life. This can be scary or confusing. Many people think about suicide at some point in their lifetime. For every suicide, twenty-five people make a suicide attempt and many more have serious thoughts of suicide.

You are not alone.[13]

Different people have different experiences of suicidal feelings. You might feel unable to cope with difficult feelings such as pain, uselessness, desperation, disconnectedness or low self-esteem. You might feel less like you want to die and more like you cannot go on living your life right now. You might feel the urge to self-harm. These feelings might build over time or change from moment to moment. You might be tearful, overwhelmed by negative thoughts, such as people being better off without you. You might struggle to sleep, not look after yourself. Eat too much or not enough. You might avoid other people.

Anyone can feel like this, any age, gender or background, at any time.

Difficulties in life can cause us to feel suicidal: mental health problems, bullying, prejudice or stigma, abuse, bereavement, including the loss of a loved one to suicide, a break-up, long-term pain or illness, a big life change such as retirement or divorce, debt, housing issues, isolation or loneliness, prison, addiction, pregnancy, childbirth or postnatal depression, doubts about sexual or gender identity, cultural or societal pressures or expectations, trauma, and some medications, such as SSRIs, particularly for those under 25.

Whatever the reason, if you are feeling suicidal, there is support.
Talk to a GP, phone 999, go to A&E. Phone a helpline.

I'm a Survivor

> 'Families bereaved by and dealing with loss from suicide may also have to face agonising questions, intrusive public scrutiny and cope with extra emotions such as guilt, shame and self-blame. Children and young people may need extra support to help them cope with their grief.'
> *Winston's Wish*

> 'Every life lost represents someone's partner, child, parent, friend or colleague. For each suicide approximately 135 people suffer intense grief or are otherwise affected. This amounts to 108 million people per year who are profoundly impacted by suicidal behaviour.'[14]

A survivor is a family member or loved one left behind by the person who has died. I am a suicide survivor. I have never attempted to kill myself, but I have had fleeting suicidal feelings. Something has kept me here on this earth, even when I have had further losses – my amazing grandpa, who died four years after Dad, from prostate cancer; my little cousin and aunt, who were killed when I was a student. This was the first time I tried therapy, but it didn't work out. I didn't know how to talk about my grief. Weirdly (or not weirdly), it was when my nan died in 2009, when I was forty-one, that I first went to my GP for help. After an episode. (More on that later.)

Julia Samuel talks about the guilt and shame you can feel when a loved one dies by suicide.[15] This is on top of all the grief you already have. The stigma of suicide can also lead to isolation for the bereaved; people do not know how to approach you so might say nothing at all. You might even be branded as a 'bad daughter' or whatever, as if you did something wrong to contribute to the death.

Shock is another response. It can last a long time, an unending repeat of the story that never ends well. Samuel calls suicide a 'heart attack of the brain'. I find this helpful, even now, after four and half decades of living with the story. 'The person who took their own life was not functioning normally: they weren't thinking rationally and their mind attacked them – had a "heart" attack, with the devastating consequence of taking their own life.' This viewpoint takes away the blame and shame attached to 'choosing' to take one's own life.

Samuel also says a few more things about suicide that I will summarise here.

- Bereavement is a risk factor for suicide.
- When someone says they are suicidal they are not 'attention-seeking'. Take them seriously.
- A previous suicide attempt is the single biggest risk factor for suicide. Up to 50 per cent of people who take their own lives have previously attempted to harm themselves. Up to 20 per cent who made a suicide attempt try again within a year. As a group, they are 100 times more likely to go on to kill themselves than those who have never tried.
- Around 4,400 people end their own lives in England each year. One death every two hours. Ten times that number attempt suicide. Approx. 75 per cent are men. In almost all cultures the rate rises with age – the highest rate in UK is among people over seventy-five. It remains a common cause of death in men under thirty-five.
- Those who suffer from alcoholism, clinical depression or schizophrenia are at high risk.
- Young people are also at risk, especially if they have been bullied, or have family trouble, poor mental health, are unemployed or have a family history of suicide. 80 per cent are male. One in three young people are drunk at the time of death.
- For older people, the risks include poverty, poor housing, social isolation, depression, illness.

According to Samaritans, there is some evidence that suicide rates are unequal between different ethnic groups, with the highest rates among the White and Mixed ethnicity groups. But suicide is complex. It is important to avoid generalisations, because 'ethnicity is just one part of someone's identity. We know that age, sex and poverty, for example, are also really important when it comes to suicide risk.' Samaritans is committed to being more diverse and inclusive, to breaking down barriers to reach a wider range of communities.[16]

The Aftermath

After the police and neighbour leave, Nanny, Grandpa, Mum, Rhys and I stay in the hall and on the lower stairs. The grown-ups have a glass of sherry. My nan's hand is shaking so much I set down the glass for her. Mum tries to get hold of Peter in Cornwall. She phones the cottage where they are staying, the three young fishermen. They have been there a few months, living off the fish they catch and cauliflowers nabbed from the neighbouring field. One of the men has his girlfriend staying and it is she who answers the phone. She has to tell Peter, when he returns from the sea. At some point that day, Grandpa identifies Dad's body. That evening we watch a *Carry On* film. I know it is wrong, but we still manage to laugh at the silly bits.

I don't know when Peter gets home – I think it might be the next morning – but I worry about him alone on the train. Meanwhile, a friend who lives up the road comes by with her two older siblings. While her mum stays with my mum, the kids take out Rhys and me into the snow and we get so cold that it takes away some of the pain. Because the pain is too much to carry.

DadisdeadDadisdeadDadisdead.

My friend's mum is one of only two people to check in on my young, widowed mother, the other being the local Baptist minister from the church where Rhys has recently started going.

Suicidesuicidesuicide.

Because it is considered too upsetting, Rhys and I do not go to the funeral. We watch Mum in her black coat and black woolly hat. We watch her go with our older brother and our grandfather. I think my nan stays with us, but I can't remember. I just know that my dad has gone, and I cannot say goodbye.

And then it is school. I go back with a letter from my mum. I hand it to my teacher. She reads it. She says nothing to me. No one speaks of it. It is too shameful. Too embarrassing. Too difficult.

I am alone.

Mum doesn't know how to pay a bill. Dad has always dealt with the finances. Rhys helps her. There is no one to help me with my maths homework.

We are alone.

We cannot speak of it. We don't talk about dad. We can't. We just can't.

I don't speak of it for five years until I tell my boyfriend. He is kind. Lets me cry. Lets me say the words. But we are too young to know what to do with my frozen grief.

I am alone.

Help

> To anyone out there who's hurting — it's not a sign of weakness to ask for help. It's a sign of strength.
> Barack Obama

Dad might still be alive today. But, if he had still died, we would have had help. Precious help. You have help. Helplines to call, text or message, if you are having a difficult time or are worried about someone else.

Samaritans:
The leading suicide prevention charity. Whatever you are going through, a Samaritan is available to chat to 24 hours a day.
Call 116-123 (UK wide, free from any phone) or 116 123 (ROI)
Samaritans Welsh Language Line: Call 0808 164 0123 (7pm–11pm every day).
https://www.samaritans.org/

Papyrus:
Papyrus campaigns to reduce the number of young people who take their own lives, by 'shattering the stigma surrounding suicide and equipping young people and their communities with the skills to recognise and respond to emotional distress'.
If you are under 35 and having suicidal thoughts or are concerned for a young person, you can contact HOPELINE247 for confidential support and practical advice.
Call 0800 068 4141 or text 07860 039967 or email pat@papyrus-uk.org 24 hours a day, every day of the year including weekends and bank holidays.
https://www.papyrus-uk.org/

Childline:
Call 0800 1111
It is free, confidential and will not show up on the bill. For anyone under 19 in the UK. 24/7
https://www.childline.org.uk/

The Mix
Free helpline for 11–25-year-olds 0808 808 4994 open 4-11 pm, Monday to Friday
https://www.themix.org.uk/
Or Text SHOUT to 85258 (UK-wide) if you prefer not to talk but want mental health support, a free, confidential 24/7 text service providing support if you are in crisis and need immediate help. For children, young people, and adults. Messages will not appear on your phone bill.
https://giveusashout.org/

YoungMinds Crisis Messenger
For people under 19.
Text YM to 85258
https://www.youngminds.org.uk/young-person/shout-85258/

Community Advice & Listening Line (C.A.L.L.)
Mental Health Helpline for Wales, offering a confidential listening and support service.
Call 0800 132 737 (Wales only, 24/7) or text 'help' followed by a question to 81066.
https://www.callhelpline.org.uk/

SANEline:
A national out-of-hours mental health helpline offering specialist emotional support, guidance and information to anyone affected by a mental health problem or supporting someone else.
Call 0300 304 7000 (4.30pm–10.30pm, every day, over 16).
https://www.sane.org.uk/how-we-help/emotional-support/saneline-services

National Suicide Prevention Helpline UK:
Offers a supportive listening, non-judgemental, confidential service to anyone with thoughts of suicide over 18.
Call 0800 689 5652 (6pm to midnight every day)
https://www.spuk.org.uk/national-suicide-prevention-helpline-uk/

Campaign Against Living Miserably (CALM):
If you are struggling and need to talk and are 15 or over.
Call 0800 58 58 58 (5pm–midnight every day, all year)
Or try the CALM webchat service.
https://www.thecalmzone.net/get-support

SOS Silence of Suicide
For everyone.
Call 0300 1020 505 (4 pm to midnight everyday)
Email support@sossilenceofsuicide.org
https://sossilenceofsuicide.org/

Cruse Bereavement Support Helpline:
To help you make sense out of how you are feeling after a bereavement.
Call 0808 808 1677 (check website for opening hours)
https://www.cruse.org.uk/get-support/helpline/

Suicide and Co.
Provides support needed for those bereaved by suicide, whilst opening the conversation and addressing the stigma. One-to-one professional support through talking therapies, a counselling service and helpline staffed by bereavement counsellors. Website has resources to explore (see below). Suicide and Co advocate the power of shared experience and provide a safe space to share stories by writing and sharing letters to the lost. 'Expressing your feelings can make all the difference when going through suicide-related bereavement.'
Bereaved by suicide and want to talk to someone: call 0800 054 8400 9 am to 9pm. Monday to Friday
https://www.suicideandco.org/

Winston's Wish
Provides emotional and practical bereavement support to children, young people and those who care for them. Specialist suicide bereavement support for families, children and young people (up to 25) when someone important has taken their own life. Member of the Suicide Bereavement Support Partnership. Information, guidance and resources on how to talk to children about suicide and support them when their mum, dad, brother, sister or other important person has died by suicide.
Call 08088 020 021(8am-8pm, Monday to Friday)
Email: ask@winstonswish.org
https://www.winstonswish.org/supporting-you/supporting-a-bereaved-child/suicide-bereavement-support/

The Matthew Elvidge Trust
A national organisation campaigning for support for those at risk of and bereaved by suicide. The main objectives are to increase awareness and understanding of the importance of wellbeing and good mental health and to reduce the stigma of mental illness and fund and support organisations that work in the fields of suicide prevention.
Email: info@thematthewelvidgetrust.com
https://www.thematthewelvidgetrust.com/

Support After Suicide Partnership
UK wide network of over 70 members and supporters bringing together national and local organisations involved in delivering suicide bereavement support across the UK, to address the need for formal, multi-agency, proactive suicide bereavement support. A special interest group of the National Suicide Prevention Alliance (NSPA) based at Samaritans. Vision: everyone bereaved or affected by suicide is offered timely and appropriate support.
https://supportaftersuicide.org.uk/

Facing the Future
Safe online support groups for people bereaved by suicide where they can talk through their feeling with others who have similar experiences. Supported by Samaritans and Cruse.
email: ftf@cla.org.cuk
https://www.facingthefuturegroups.org/

Gambling with Lives
Support for families bereaved by gambling-related suicide, raise awareness of devastating effects of gambling disorder and campaign for change.
If you or someone you know has been bereaved by gambling-related suicide, get in touch with Judith for an informal chat at support@gamblingwithlives.org or on 07774 617771. (If outside working hours, they will respond as soon as possible.)
Or go to https://www.gamblingwithlives.org/help/ for a list of external organisations and services for advice about a gambling related issue for yourself, a family member or a friend.
In an emergency, call Samaritans on 116 123 or 111 or your GP or 999

Survivors of Bereavement by Suicide
The only UK-based organisation run by the bereaved for the bereaved. Peer-led support to adults over 18 impacted by suicide loss in safe, confidential environments, in face-to-face groups and online. A national telephone helpline (for information, help or to simply talk) an online community forum and email support.
Call 0300 111 5065 (9 am to 9pm, Monday to Sunday)
Email admin@uksobs.org
https://uksobs.org/

Andy's Man Club
Men's suicide prevention charity, offering free-to-attend peer-to-peer support groups across the UK and online. To end the stigma surrounding men's mental health. To help men through the power of conversation. Talking groups just for men who have either been through a storm, are currently going through a storm or have a storm brewing in life. Face to face meetings every Monday (except bank holidays) 7–9pm. Currently there are more than fifty groups across England and Scotland. Check out the website for a branch near you.
https://andysmanclub.co.uk/

Barnardo's Child Bereavement Service
National support for bereaved children and young people in care. Provides individual and group support to children and young people up to 18 years old

who have been bereaved and their parents/carers. Consultancy and training to professionals working with bereaved children.
Call 028 90668333
Email: cbsreferrals@barnardos.org.uk
https://www.barnardos.org.uk/what-we-do/services/child-bereavement-service-general

Breathing Space Scotland
A free, confidential, phone and webchat service for anyone in Scotland over the age of 16 experiencing low mood, depression or anxiety or feeling suicidal.
Call 0800 83 85 87 (Monday–Thursday 6pm–2am, Friday 6pm–Monday 6am)
Free and won't show up in telephone bills.
https://breathingspace.scot/

3 Dads Walking
Three dads who lost their young daughters to suicide. They walk to raise awareness of suicide – the biggest killer of those under 35 in the UK – in the hope of preventing other families from begin devasted by suicide. Wherever you live in the UK, suicide is a tragic part of so many people's lives. By walking between the parliaments of the four nations, they aim to highlight the help PAPYRUS can offer across the UK.
https://www.3dadswalking.uk/

Resources
https://www.mind.org.uk/information-support/types-of-mental-health-problems/suicidal-feelings/about-suicidal-feelings/
https://supportaftersuicide.org.uk/wp-content/uploads/2019/05/MIND-how-to-cope-with-suicidal-feelings_2016.pdf
An alphabet of suicide conversation guide: https://www.suicideandco.org/conversation-guide/alphabet/a

Words Unspoken – a collection of 100 letters written to loved ones who died by suicide, collated by Suicide and Co. who advise you to practise self-care when reading them as some are hard to read and could trigger you. They are there to speak to on 0800 054 8400 (9am to 9pm. Monday to Friday)
https://www.suicideandco.org/words-unspoken

Samaritans: whatever you are going through, a Samaritan is available to chat to 24 hours a day. Call 116-123.
Samaritans Welsh Language Line: 0808 164 0123 (7pm–11pm every day).
https://www.samaritans.org/

Q

IS FOR QUILT;
R IS FOR RAINBOW;
S IS FOR SCARVES AND SHOES

Inclusion in Death and Bereavement

quilt *noun*
from the Latin *culcita*, meaning 'a stuffed sack',
a warm bed cover made of two layers of cloth filled with padding
such as down or wadding, held in place by decorative stitching.

This above all: to thine own self be true.
HAMLET

rainbow *noun*
an arc of colours seen in the sky when rain is falling and
the sun is shining.

D IS FOR DEATH

Grief fills the room up of my absent child,
Lies in his bed, walks up and down with me,
Puts on his pretty look, repeats his words,
Remembers me of his gracious parts,
Stuffs out his vacant garments with his form.
KING JOHN

scarf *noun*
a broad band of cloth worn about the shoulders, around the neck, or over the head, for warmth, protection or decoration.

shoe *noun*
a covering for the foot, made of a strong material with a sturdy sole and not reaching above the ankle.

I'll note you in my book of memory.
HENRY VI PART I

In memory of
Mrs Phoebe Crewe
Who died May 28, 1817,
Aged 77 years.
Who during forty years
practice as a midwife
in this City, brought into
the world nine thousand
seven hundred and
thirty children.
FROM THE OLD MEN'S HOSPITAL, NORWICH

☠☠☠

Q IS FOR QUILT; R IS FOR RAINBOW; S IS FOR SCARVES AND SHOES

> As the twenty-first century unfolds there is an increasing reaction against the institutional control, and practically convenient but emotionally unsatisfying funeral customs of the late twentieth century. Continued bonds between the dead and the living – and indeed the fact of mortality itself – are starting to be acknowledged again.[1]
> Helen Frisby

Helen Frisby argues that since the 1980s there have been great numbers of 'disenfranchised deaths', notably from the AIDS epidemic, which led to the reinvention of funeral traditions and memorialisation. In this chapter, I want to look at those deaths that could be considered disenfranchised and those that lead to 'disenfranchised grief' – when society doesn't validate your personal grief because it doesn't fit in with your community or wider society's attitude to death and loss. Kenneth Doka introduced the concept of 'disenfranchised grief' in 1989, a decade after my dad died. He defined it as 'the process in which the loss is felt as not being openly acknowledged, socially validated, or publicly mourned'.[2] Feeling unable to express and manage your grief, plus a lack of support during your grieving process, can prolong emotional pain. It can become complicated grief (see 'U Is for Unfinished'). Central to the grieving process for every bereaved person is the memory of the dead.

☠☠☠

Over the Rainbow

> Thousands of people have died in San Francisco, millions in the world. The point of the National AIDS Memorial Grove is to remember them, one at a time.
> Nancy Pelosi

The Grove is a ten-acre memorial site in San Francisco's Golden Gate Park, 'a dedicated space for healing, hope, and remembrance' of those who died from HIV/AIDS. It tells the story to current and future generations. Associated with the Grove, though it has been exhibited in other cities and countries, is the AIDS Memorial Quilt, thought to be the largest community arts project in history, remembering those who have died. Each quilt panel is three feet by six feet[3] and is made by individuals and groups to celebrate the lives and stories of loved ones.

The Quilt was conceived nearly forty years ago by activist Cleve Jones.

Since the 1978 assassinations of gay San Francisco Supervisor Harvey Milk and Mayor George Moscone, Jones had helped organize the annual candlelight march honouring these men. While planning the 1985 march, he learned that over 1,000 San Franciscans had been lost to AIDS. He asked each of his fellow marchers to write on placards the names of friends and loved ones who had died of AIDS. At the end of the march, Jones and others stood on ladders taping these placards to the walls of the San Francisco Federal Building. The wall of names looked like a patchwork quilt.[4]

A year later, Cleve created the first panel in memory of his friend Marvin Feldman. To date, there are about 50,000 panels dedicated to more than 110,000 people. It is also used as a campaign tool; a new initiative called Change the Pattern brings sections of the Quilt to communities in the southern states, where AIDS disproportionately impacts communities of colour. 'There, the Quilt honours Black and Brown lives lost to HIV and AIDS and strives to reimagine the response to the epidemic in the region.'

Now you can also visit the Interactive Aids Quilt online.[5]

By sharing the story of the struggle against HIV/AIDS, we remember, in perpetuity, the lives lost, we offer healing and hope to survivors, and we inspire new generations of activists in the fight against stigma, denial, and hate for a just future.

An American Tradition

Death and loss sever our real time connection with someone we love, but memorial quilts restructure that pathway to connection through a beautiful, tactile, intensely personal object.[6]
Lori Mason

Quilting is an American tradition from the days when scraps of fabric were used to make warm bed coverings. Quilts are sustainable, reusable, circular. They used to be stitched together, in the home, a communal activity. Zak Foster has taken the tradition and, like the AIDS Memorial Quilt, both honours and subverts it. (You should check out his *O, America* political quilt, crafted in response to Trump's election in 2016.) What interests him most about quilting is 'not only that intersection between art and utility, but also how quilts can be comfortable messengers for uncomfortable truths'.[7]

Foster makes unique burial quilts from the clothes and fabrics of loved ones to be used as a shroud, instead of a coffin. The bed, a place of expressiveness and individuality, the most private place of all, is covered by the quilt, offering warmth and rest. Your quilt, which has been with you all your life, can see you into death, taking with it 'the continuity of habits and patterns'. So why, he asks, would you choose a coffin from a catalogue rather than have something that reflects who you are? (Though he points out that if you are woodworker, then of course it would be appropriate to construct your own casket.) Foster has made his own burial quilt. He looks at it first thing every morning when he wakes up, a memento mori, the image of being wrapped in it giving him comfort and beauty. 'A companion to the end.'

He also makes funeral quilts to be used for the ceremony itself. These quilts, made long in advance, take centre stage, a beautiful backdrop on which the casket can be laid. Then, rather than the deceased using it as a burial quilt, their loved ones can keep it. Foster even makes the quilts modular, with temporary stitching that can later be unpicked to separate the quilt, so that, for example, each child can keep a piece.

Foster mainly makes memory quilts. He believes that the clothes we inhabit in life, and the fabrics they are made from, are 'changed by our presence'. After someone has died, their loved ones will give Foster a selection of significant items. As well as using 'pretty bits', he looks for the parts that might be discoloured or faded or frayed which reflect an aspect of their lives. He talks about the headscarf of a woman which she always wore knotted under her chin. Two of the corners were worn, where she tied them, and so he stitched the scarf in a way that you could see all four corners, including the two that were misshapen by everyday use. Such pieces 'occupy, create, sustain a physical presence of someone that we love and hold so dear'. He says that the bereaved often approach him a couple of years after the death, when the initial grief has subsided and those around them have moved on. Their collaboration with Foster presents further opportunities for storytelling, allowing them to continue their bonds with the dead. 'What we touch, touches us.'

When I had breast cancer, a dear writer friend made me a quilt. Anne is American and has come later in life to quilting, using a sewing machine to stitch wonderful soft fleece on the underside and beautiful fabric strips for the design on the front. My quilt is made up of a spectrum of seaside colours, from yellows through to blues, to remind me of my home in Devon, which I had to leave to have my treatment up north, also by the sea, but not the seaside as I know and love it. (Thank you, Anne.)

In addition to the Quilt, the red ribbon was created in the USA. One of the most recognised symbols of recent times, it was conceived by twelve NYC artists in 1991. Taking inspiration from the yellow ribbons tied on trees to show support for the US military, the red ribbon would be a visual expression of compassion for those living with HIV. Relevant and accessible to everyone, the loop design was easy to make and the colour red, associated with the heart and love, was bold.

In the UK, this symbol has both raised public awareness of HIV and inspired other charities to use their own, such as the pink breast cancer awareness ribbon. But we lag behind the Americans in terms of memorialisation. Although there are several AIDS memorials throughout the country, such as the Beacon of Hope in Sackville Gardens in Manchester, there is yet to be a national one. However, there is a campaign for a London- and UK-wide memorial to be located on Tottenham Court Road, a significant location to the HIV and AIDS movement, close to the former Middlesex Hospital, which had the UK's first AIDS ward opened by Princess Diana in 1987 (with the ground-breaking photo of her shaking the hand of a patient). The memorial will pay tribute to more than 21,000 people who have died in the UK and 3.5 million worldwide. It will also highlight the road taken so far and the journey still to come.

The death taboo is being broken. Berridge argues that:

> In the 1980s the dance of death assumed a different tempo. Without warning, the carefree and confident mood of that decade changed dramatically when AIDS gatecrashed life. After nearly seventy years of taboo and crisis management, we were jolted into a forced awareness of our own mortality. Reminded to remember death, we were reminded of our invincibility. The reverberations are still being felt in many ways.[8]

Just as Diana changed attitudes to AIDS and homosexuality, so her funeral and burial, as with the generation of (mainly) men who died in their prime during the 1980s and 90s, showed us it was possible to change tradition.[9] According to Jessica Mitford, initially, most mortuaries in America refused to accept cases where it was believed that the deceased had been exposed to HIV. Those that did, refused to wash or embalm them.[10] Diana's photograph was key. And then her death, according to Berridge. 'In her dying, she has conferred on people cultural permission to express their feelings. This is an important legacy. Like sex, death is a social minefield – a minefield which, in death, Diana, Princess of Wales, has helped to clear for us all.'[11]

NB: Queerly Departed[12] is a tour in Brompton Cemetery in London where you are shown the graves of people known or believed to have been LGBT+. In death they can be fully who they were. In Henbury, Bristol, in the graveyard of St Mary's church where my grandparents married, lies Amelia Edwards (1831–92) – writer, Egyptologist and intrepid traveller. Ellen Braysher, Amelia's partner of thirty-two years, is buried beside 'the godmother of Egyptology', whose grave, marked with an obelisk and ankh, was designated in 2016 as a landmark of English LGBT+ history by Historic England.[13] They lived together in Westbury-on-Trym, where my grandparents had their final house. (A fan of graveyards herself, in 1857, Amelia visited our friend Shelley's grave in Rome. I just love these connections.)

☠☠☠

The Queer Funeral Guide

Written by Ash Hayhurst in 2019, *The Queer Funeral Guide* is really useful. Did you know that, when registering a death in the UK, you do not have to give the name as it is written on the birth certificate, passport or medical card? It does not even need to match the name on the medical certificate issued by the doctor. You just have to make sure the information you give the registrar is 'believed to be true at the time of death'. Therefore, a trans person without a gender recognition certificate or who has not changed their name by deed poll can still have their death registered in their new name and gender. However, if you are registering a death with a different name from the one on the medical certificate or the person's bank details, you should also give their previous name(s) to avoid any confusion with the will or estate.[14]

As ever, planning is key.

☠☠☠

Crossbones

Crossbones, an unconsecrated burial ground on Redcross Way near Borough High Street in Southwark in London, was traditionally used for prostitutes who were forbidden Christian burial by the Church. From the twelfth century, the area was part of the 'Liberty of the Clink'. This meant it was not subject to the laws that governed the rest of the City. Near where Chaucer's pilgrims set off for Canterbury and where Little Dorrit was born in Marshalsea Prison, this area south of the river has always been seedier. Bear-baiting, plays, sex workers. The Bishop of Winchester oversaw the Liberty and licensed the brothels ('stews'). The working women were known as Winchester Geese.

By the eighteenth century, it was a general burial ground for paupers, many of them Irish. By the nineteenth, Crossbones was in one of the worst slums in London, crammed with cholera victims and a haunt of bodysnatchers.[15] It finally closed in 1853. Just thirty by forty metres, there are an estimated 15,000 people buried here. But no headstones. In 1992, work to extend the Jubilee Line required a partial excavation of the site. Archaeologists removed 148 skeletons from the mid-nineteenth century. A third were children. Two thirds of the adults were women. 'These people had it hard; cheap coffins, bent bones, lives lived in smog and slums,' says Peter Ross.[16] One of these skeletons belonged to a young teenage woman who has become known as Crossbones Girl. Tiny, at four foot seven, and damaged by syphilis, she was probably a child prostitute, possibly Elizabeth Mitchell, who died of pneumonia in St Thomas', a charity hospital. Her last days would have been spent in the Magdalen ward where victims of venereal disease were treated. As Ross says, 'Those who rest in unmarked graves are often those on whom life has left its cruellest marks.'[17]

Today, the Church apologises annually for the way it formerly licensed these women but forbade them or their babies Christian burial. A short walk away is Southwark Cathedral. Every year its clergy process to Crossbones to say sorry. Other people are drawn to Crossbones, to what is now a garden of remembrance for the 'outcast dead': the homeless, the abandoned babies, the suicides whose lives are memorialised and celebrated by 'a community of people who see themselves as outsiders, margin-walkers, freaks'.[18]

Previously, Crossbones was known as the Invisible Garden, created by Andy Hulme, a security guard living in a caravan in situ, who also gardened for Vivienne Westwood. Security was needed because of the heroin addicts congregating there. 'That's Crossbones,' writes Ross, 'a place linking catwalk and shooting gallery.'[19] Since 2014, the graveyard has been cared for by volunteer gardeners from Bankside Open Spaces Trust, a charity that leases the ground from Transport for London. The raised beds did not disturb the dead. Any bones found were reburied.

Ross describes Crossbones as 'a weird liminal space right in the heart of corporate London... a place of skulls, stories, sadnesses; an oddball Golgotha'.[20] Its value must not be counted in square feet; its importance is in healing and tolerance. 'Where the poor were once dumped is now rich with meaning.'[21]

Visit https://crossbones.org.uk/history/ to find out about John Crow and the other friends of Crossbones. Attend a vigil on the 23rd of every month to remember 'the outcast dead'. Tie a ribbon or leave a memento at the gate. Visit the *mizuko Jizo* (more on them below) and Redcross Mary, a statue of the Virgin holding a goose.

☠☠☠

Beyond the funeral or memorial service, people have always found creative and individual ways to memorialise the dead. Remember Père Lachaise cemetery in Paris, where the red lipstick kisses damaged the tomb of Oscar Wilde's grave, where the hippies hang out with Jim Morrison. In Highgate, pilgrims are a little more intellectual when visiting the grave of George Eliot, leaving pens in the soil. Go to the British Library and you can see scraps on which John Lennon wrote the lyrics to 'Strawberry Fields' and where, in the vaults, lies what is believed to be the only existing literary manuscript written in Shakespeare's hand, *The Booke of Sir Thomas More*. This text, in draft form with revisions and edits, is a collaborative piece and Shakespeare could well be one of the playwrights involved, writing the emotional scene which pleas for tolerance towards immigrants.

> Their babies at their backs, with their poor luggage,
> Plodding to th' ports and coasts for transportation,
> And that you sit as kings in your desires,
> Authority quite silenced by your brawl… (sc. vi, 84–88)

Handwriting is infused with individuality. I have a postcard which Dad sent to me in 1974, one of my most precious belongings, his handwriting, his words reaching out to me across time.

For millennia, oral tradition was the way we told the history of our people, and for the last century audio recordings have allowed us to hear voices from the past, talking in clipped received English or in strong dialects. I wish I had my dad's voice, caught in a phone message, on a cassette, but his was a previous time. Though sometimes, when I least expect it, I can hear his voice. Certain words and phrases and it is like he is whispering to me.

Fingerprints are not only used for capturing criminals but can also be used for memorialisation, as they are unique. Handprints and footprints both make keepsakes, just as the Victorians used hair and mourning jewellery in remembrance. Now you can have a container or piece of jewellery made to hold a small amount of a loved one's ashes. You can even mix some of the ashes (less than a tablespoon) with ink for a tattoo in their memory.[22] You can memorialise someone in the stars.[23] In sculpture. You can eat food that tastes of memories – sardines on toast, Yorkshire pudding, sherbet lemons. You can plant a garden, even a virtual memorial garden, though, for me, nothing beats the blousy scent of wallflowers, catapulting me back to our first home in Teignmouth next to the house of poor Miss Bowles. I am a two-year-old again, not a care in the world.

Heirlooms. I have the full set of Agatha Christies that Grandpa bequeathed me. I have my great-grandmother Mabel's wedding ring inscribed with the date of her marriage to George. I have my mum's charm bracelet that Dad bought her, with the charms she got each birthday and Christmas. I have many things. Much stuff. Somewhat of a hoarder, not uncommon for someone who has suffered sudden loss as a child. These things bring comfort, some permanence in a transient world; touching them connects me to loved ones who have gone before. They remind me who I am and where I have come from.

What is more poignant than a worn-through-love teddy bear? I have mine, though Mum reupholstered him when I was at university so that he is now unrecognisable from the tatty one hidden inside – though that is another story and another memory of how we howled with laughter when she handed new Ted to me.

And remember those teddy bears left at the gates of a school in Dunblane, for the children who never came home.

Out of Order Death

> One in five parents has a child die before them. The child may have been an adult, perhaps even in late middle age, but the devastating effect is the same. I can often spot some underlying heartache when taking an elderly person's history in the outpatients clinic. These patients have an almost imperceptible air of sadness about them, as if the thermostat of their life has been turned down a notch or two.[24]
> David Jarrett

When I was seven years old and in the first year of junior school, there was a girl called Lucy. She was in the year above and would come into our classroom when her own form had PE. She brought a book and sat quietly reading while we got on with whatever lesson we were currently enduring. Lucy was very thin. I remember looking at her shoes and wondering at their narrowness. Part way through the year, Lucy stopped coming to school. One day our teacher, Sister Marie Joseph, told us she had died. I think it was leukaemia. Lucy's life and death have always been in my mind, and I have often thought about her parents who wanted her to live as normal a life as she could, going to school for as long as she was able. Lucy even became inspiration for a character in my first novel.

Q IS FOR QUILT; R IS FOR RAINBOW; S IS FOR SCARVES AND SHOES

Lucy. You lived. You mattered. You are remembered.

We were the last class that Sister Marie Joseph taught because she died soon after. I still visit her grave from time to time in the grounds of what used to be the convent and is now an independent school. I wish she had been my teacher when my father died three years later, because I think she would have been kind.

Today, according to Kathryn Mannix, the odds of being cured of cancers in childhood are much better than for those in adulthood. Children's cancer specialist nurses work with newly diagnosed children and their families to support them through surgery and treatment. They support community children's nurses and GPs because they may only deal with one or two children with cancer throughout their whole practice lifetime. They advise schools on how to give pastoral support to classmates and how children can keep in touch with the absent pupil, because most teachers will never teach a child with cancer. But some children relapse or do not get into remission in the first place. Then these nurses offer palliative care to keep life as normal as possible for as long as possible, offering support to the family and team that surround them.[25]

I hope Lucy and her family got the support they needed. The teachers had their faith and community to support them. I'm not sure about Lucy's young classmates. Lucy was never mentioned again, but I have never forgotten her.

Lucy, Lucy, Lucy.

When Dad's sister, Auntie Shirley, had her first child, Stephen, he was born healthy and fine. Her second baby, Susan, had a blood transfusion that saved her. But, when Shirley had her second son and third child, he lived just a few hours before he died of rhesus disease. Rhesus disease happens when the mother has rhesus-negative blood (RhD negative) and the baby in her womb has rhesus-positive blood (RhD positive). The mother must have also been previously sensitised to RhD-positive blood (usually during a previous pregnancy with an RhD-positive baby). The woman's body responds to the RhD-positive blood by producing antibodies which recognise and destroy the foreign blood cells. Shirley, already sensitised, was exposed to Paul's RhD-positive blood. Her body would have produced antibodies immediately and they would have crossed the placenta, causing rhesus disease in Paul in utero. Unfortunately, this was just before medical advances would have given Paul a better chance of survival.

But Shirley still came home with a baby. She was allowed to foster a newborn and looked after her for a year until she was adopted. Shirley continued to foster babies for a few years. I don't know how this helped her grieving process, but I imagine it injected her life with meaning, enabling her to love alongside her loss. But it must have been very hard to give back those babies.

D IS FOR DEATH

☠☠☠

In previous centuries, stillborn children in England were buried before sunrise or at night, in order for them to go to Heaven. In Ireland, unbaptised babies could not be buried in consecrated ground, so they were buried in a graveyard beyond known as a *cillín* (little church). A double loss for the parents who had lost their child and would not be reunited with them in the afterlife.[26] As with Crossbones cemetery, in these *cillíní* were also buried the disenfranchised: still born babies, women who died in childbirth, suicides, unknown bodies washed ashore, murderers, the excommunicated and the loved ones of families who couldn't afford their burial.[27] Those without a name. These liminal spaces reflected the limbo that their souls would inhabit: 'neither one thing nor another, a borderland between within and without, land and sea, divine light and infernal fire'.[28] Ross points out that even Limbo itself is now, theologically speaking, 'an uneasy marginal place … on the tideline of faith, somewhere between belief and disbelief'.[29]

Now there are much better ways to remember lost babies, though we have no specific word for them. The Japanese, however, have the word and concept of *mizuko* ('water children'). Viv Mayer says this gives all life in the womb 'a unique and equal status' which cannot be 'denied or categorised by gestational dates' or by how the *mizuko* died. Mayer went to Japan and visited Buddhist temples with rows of baby-like statues called *mizuko Jizo* ('water child Buddhas') to whom parents offer prayers, douse with water[30] and leave gifts. Jizo is the protector of *mizuko*, smuggling them to paradise in the folds of his kimono.[31]

Mayer compares this to the UK, where 'it's either a baby, worthy of grief, or it's not'.

> And therein lies one of the biggest challenges to acknowledging pregnancy loss in all its forms in the UK – the problem of how to acknowledge the nameless. Words make sense of life; perhaps it is impossible to acknowledge this loss properly until we are brave enough to agree on what it is we have lost and name it.

Instead of a specific word, we add 'lost', as in *lost* baby. But what noun should we use? 'Some women feel 'baby' is too emotive or medically inaccurate, especially for earlier miscarriages. On the other hand, words like (lost) embryo, or foetus sound too clinical for some women and devoid of the humanity required for grief to seem appropriate.'[32]

The importance of a name.

☠☠☠

Still Born is an art and poetry project initiated by artist Adinda van 't Klooster in 2017, following the stillbirth of her first daughter, Elvira, in 2010, 41.5 weeks into what appeared to be an uncomplicated pregnancy. This tragedy could have been prevented with more routine scans in later pregnancy, 'an injustice that motivates her to date to help break the taboo on stillbirth, which prevents more funding from being allocated to pregnancy care to avoid similar preventable stillbirths from recurring year after year'.[33]

According to Alexander Heazell, consultant obstetrician and director of Tommy's Stillbirth Research Centre in St Marys Hospital, Manchester, globally there are approximately two million stillbirths a year (at or after twenty-eight weeks of pregnancy; if stillbirths were counted after twenty-two weeks, the number would likely be 50 per cent higher). He says, 'When confronted with a figure of that magnitude it is challenging to appreciate the individual consequences of the death of a baby.'[34] Heazell believes the power of parents' stories will help break the stigma and taboo surrounding stillbirth. This in turn will improve care for parents and help prevent stillbirths. Visual and written art will aid the conversation around stillbirth, allowing families to grieve and bringing awareness to wider society.

> It is by understanding different narratives that one can truly appreciate the stories which underpin women's experiences of stillbirth which the numbers struggle to convey. As human beings we respond to human stories in a way that most of us do not react to figures and numbers.[35]

I met Lucy Biggs at my first death café in Frodsham. She was there partly because she is an independent funeral celebrant and part of the #deathpositive movement, but what had really brought her along was her son, Reuben. Lucy writes beautifully and touchingly about the stillbirth of her first child. She'd had a normal pregnancy until the end when, without warning, Reuben died in her womb. No reason was ever found. Nothing prepared her or her husband, Stephen, for what was to come.

Lucy describes how she felt in those first days.

> I wanted to feed him – my breasts were full of milk and excruciatingly painful. I looked for him everywhere – desperate for comfort. I drew the stars from our bedroom window. I studied the freckles on my chest, hoping for a map of my future. On the day of his funeral, a single poppy flowered in our garden. He was there.

But in the days, weeks and months that followed, she took comfort from the words of others – letters, conversations, cards, texts. Better to say something than nothing at all.

> They say there are no words for stillbirth, because your baby has died, but there are many words for stillbirth, because your baby was here. We will

always speak of Reuben. We will always write his name. He will always be ours, but he will always be gone.[36]

When their second child was born in 2019, a daughter, Lucy searched for 'an alternative working path', wanting to be as present as possible for her. A year later, pregnant with their third child and second son, she realised she could draw on her experience. She completed her funeral celebrant training in 2021 and took her first funeral in 2022, a month ahead of what would have been Reuben's fourth birthday. And what was remarkable and special was that it was for her beloved grandfather. Including live music, open time for contribution and drawings from all his great-grandchildren, while their Pop lay in his coffin among them. 'It was everything that I had envisaged during my training, and a benchmark of what I hoped to provide to families: ceremonies reflecting their hopes and wishes, tailored to the beauty of the life lost.'[37]

Reuben, Reuben, Reuben.

☠☠☠

Rainbows

The symbol of the rainbow is often used by members of the baby-loss community to refer to a baby born after a previous loss, symbolising hope and light after a dark time. The arrival of a rainbow baby can evoke conflicting feelings – happiness, grief, even guilt. There is no 'right' way to feel.[38] However, some parents find the term rainbow baby problematic, as they do not like to think of their lost baby as the storm. And some parents might not go on to have another baby. Kirsty Liddiard from the Department of Education at the University of Sheffield suggests that you ask the parents what their preference is.[39]

The rainbow is also used for Pride and for the NHS. But here I am referencing rainbows with regard to pets, who are said to cross the rainbow bridge when they die. I've lost several cats over the years: Sammy, Suki, Trixie, Eric, Bert, Ernie, Jessie, Buzz. Some were lost in childhood. Sammy was Mum and Dad's kitten when they got married. He lived a good life and died in old age when I was about seven, though for the last few years he had lived with my grandparents in Bristol as we were living in a caravan park between selling the Torquay shop and buying the Teignmouth guest house. They had a large garden and Sammy spent his retirement years treated like a prince. He was a lovely cat, gentle and affectionate and very purry. Suki was just a kitten when she had to be put to sleep as she was riddled with ringworm. I was eight and cried a lot. The fearsome Trixie was the next cat in our lives. Her father was feral and sired half the cats in Dawlish. She would sit on the stairs and not allow anyone to get past her. She would chase dogs, jumping on their backs.

She was the best hunter, leaving bloodied gifts of rabbit feet and guts by our back door, which my stepfather likened to a butcher's shop.

Trixie lived until she was fourteen. I was married by then and we had our own cats, a pair of tabby kittens who we called Eric and Ernie. Eric was run over when he was two. We got Bert from the Cats Protection to be a companion for Ernie. Bert was a real character, would sleep under the bedclothes between us, but he was also killed on the same road. Then Ernie got sick with FIV and died when he was five. By now I had a baby and, while the loss was inevitably sad, it was not overwhelming as the others had been. When the children were a little older we took on two more tabby cats, Jessie and Buzz (yes, *Toy Story*). Jessie was sweet but died of cancer aged eight. Buzz was Trixie reincarnated. I lost count of how many people he scratched. In fact, when Izzy had a swollen lymph node, the doctor sent her for blood tests. An Australian registrar tested her for 'cat scratch'. It was positive – *thank you, Buzz* – and Izzy was treated successfully with antibiotics. Buzz moved with us to Teignmouth, where he lived happily, scaring the neighbourhood for a decade. Eventually he succumbed to kidney failure, and we made the decision to have him put to sleep. One thing the vet said was: if it is a tough decision, it is the right decision. I took comfort from that. The last thing he did was scratch Niall.

By now we had a dog, Millie, a Tibetan terrier. We chose her because, being an atopic family, we needed a dog who would not shed. TTs are brilliant dogs. In Tibet they are known as 'little people' because they think they are human. They are stubborn. Intelligent. Hard to train because they have a mind of their own. But they love with all their soul. Millie was my dog, never happier than when curled up with me. She had seven puppies, though the first was stillborn. We named her Pixie and buried her under the cherry tree alongside two guinea pigs, Barry and Smoky. We kept Susan. Susan loves everybody who pays her attention.

I've written about my cancer and how Millie died just before I started treatment. She had cancer too. A tumour in her shoulder. We didn't want her to have her leg amputated or to go through chemo. She was almost fourteen. And I truly believed she was happy to go. I was leaving Devon. She would have been lost without me, and I couldn't bring her or Susan, because I was moving to a flat and didn't want to take them away from the family I was leaving behind. I think of her every day. I can still smell her if I close my eyes. I have her ashes and her collar in a drawer. She is my phone screensaver alongside Susan. Susan is now ten and lives with Niall in Devon. I see her when I go home to Mum, but she is not my dog now. She is happy to see me, but no more than she is happy to see anyone else. And, because I love her, I am pleased about that. I don't think Millie would have coped without me.

I miss her so much.

I know she will be waiting for me across that rainbow bridge.

And presumably Trixie and Buzz with their claws at the ready.

D IS FOR DEATH

Recently I went to Agatha Christie's home, Greenway, on the Dart. In her stunning gardens, there is a small pet cemetery where all her dogs and cats are laid to rest. It's very touching. And in the grounds of Edinburgh Castle, the most besieged place in Britain, there is a corner which is a dedicated dog cemetery, memorialising the four-legged friends of soldiers from the reign of Victoria.

We have our pets for such a short time. But such a precious time.

Millie and me

Pet cemetery at Greenway

Scarves

I write this as my partner goes off to Liverpool, to Goodison Park, home of Everton FC, a mile from Anfield, where, following Hillsborough, the first two-minute silence outside Remembrance Sunday was held.[40] (This ritual at football matches tends to be a clap now, for obvious reasons.) In the immediate aftermath of the disaster, flowers and scarves were left at the Shankly gates and filled the Kop goal and pitch. But they weren't just red scarves; they were intermingled with blue, from Everton fans. Later, a mile of red and blues scarves – 'the chain of unity' – linked the two grounds. (When the initial estimate of 2,500 scarves was not high enough, an appeal went out and a 'scarfmobile' toured Merseyside to collect more.)[41] In 2014, to commemorate the twenty-fifth anniversary of Hillsborough, 3,000 football scarves were donated to LFC as a sign of global unity for the families. For the memorial service, they were laid on the pitch at Anfield in the form of 96. (Since then, the number has become ninety-seven.)[42]

NB: Andy Burnham, whom we saw in 'A Is for Accidents' campaigning with the Hillsborough families for justice, is an Everton fan.

Just recently, a young man was killed during construction work on the new Everton stadium. Counselling was provided for fellow workers, and at the match against Liverpool following the tragedy, Klopp laid a wreath and fans held the blue flag for Michael. This flag was then taken to Everton's away game at Aston Villa, where the Everton players wore black armbands. (The manager wore a white shirt with a black armband and, when two Sky commentators referenced that he looked like a croupier, there was uproar.)

☠☠☠

For Sale: Baby Shoes. Never Worn.[43]

Red shoes, ruby slippers, glass slippers, shoes have been used as a motif in folk tradition. People who know me probably associate me with Birkenstocks, sandals which accommodate my inherited bunions. My auntie Ruth would ramble for miles across the West Sussex countryside in her Dr Scholls. Carrie Bradshaw's Manolo Blahnik and red-soled Louboutins were icons of the noughties. Ginger Rogers famously did everything Fred Astaire did but 'backwards and in high heels' – a feminist mantra for women who achieve everything their male counterparts do but with the double burden of traditionally female work. It is also said that, before you judge someone, you should walk a mile in their shoes.

The symbolism of shoes resonates throughout the world. In some religions, you must remove your shoes before entering a place of worship. In some cultures, it is offensive to show the soles and, the greatest insult, to throw a shoe at someone. Empty shoes placed outside a Greek home used to tell others there had been a death in the family, usually a son who had died in battle. To mark the second anniversary of 9/11, approximately 3,000 shoes were placed on the town common of Stoneham, Massachusetts, to remember those who had been killed.

As part of Scotland's To Absent Friends Festival,[44] shoes have been used to highlight the deaths of the homeless in Glasgow. On 1 November 2019, in memory of the forty-seven homeless people who had died on the streets of Glasgow the previous year, forty-seven pairs of shoes were placed on the steps of the Royal Concert Hall. They remained there for two hours before being scattered across the city, with clues to their stories. Emblems of human life.[45]

But, to many, the shoe is a reminder of the Holocaust. Piles of shoes were evidence of genocide in the Nazi death camps.[46] A poignant motif of innocent lives snatched away with the utmost cruelty. In Budapest, sixty pairs of shoes sculpted out of iron mark the spot on the banks of the Danube, where 20,000 Hungarian Jews were shot by fascists and thrown into the river during the winter of 1944–45. They were first forced to remove their shoes, so valuable during the war. The shoes are all different in style, reflecting the people who wore them:

> Some have worn-down heels, others have shabby uppers; some have laces, others have straps left open; some are classic women's pumps, others are workmen's boots; some are standing straight up, while others have fallen over, as though they were hastily taken off. And then there are the tiny shoes of the children. All these different shoes represent the different individual Jews who were murdered on the riverbanks.[47]

We have seen in a previous chapter how Travellers are discriminated against in memorialisation in cemeteries and, at the start of this chapter, how the gay community found new ways to be remembered. And we think of the six million Jews who were killed during the Second World War. All these groups – Sinti and Roma, disabled, homosexuals, Jews – were othered by Hitler's despotic regime in his reign of terror. And terror is the subject of the next chapter.

☠☠☠

Information and Support for LGBTQ+ people

Action for Trans Health
www.actionfortranshealth.org.uk

LGBT Switchboard
0300 330 0630
www.switchboard.lgbt

Press for Change
www.pfc.org.uk

Help and Memorialisation Ideas Following Baby Loss

Wave of Light
15 October at 7 local time. Light a candle and burn for at least one hour, individually or in a group, at home or in a communal space. You will be joining a global Wave of Light in memory of all babies who lit up our lives for such a short time. Post a photo of your candle to FB, Twitter or Instagram using #WaveOfLight

Remember my Baby (RMB)
A UK based charity which offers a free gift of baby remembrance photography to all UK parents experiencing the loss of their baby before, during or shortly after birth.
https://remembermybaby.org.uk/

Sands
Supports anyone affected by pregnancy loss and the death of a baby to offer understanding and comfort. Works to improve the care, discover why babies are dying and reduce inequalities in healthcare. They also provide free memory boxes to UK addresses.
Call 0808 164 3332 (Mon–Fri 10am–3pm or Tuesday, Wednesday, Thursday 6pm to 9pm)
email helpline@sands.org.uk
https://www.sands.org.uk/

Miscarriage Association
Offers support and information to anyone affected by the loss of a baby in pregnancy, raises awareness and promotes good practice in medical care.
Call: 01924 200799 (Mon–Fri 9am–4pm)
info@miscarriageassociation.org.uk
https://www.miscarriageassociation.org.uk/

Aching Arms
A charity which offers a beautiful comfort bear to fill your arms and a community to support you as you grieve. Each Aching Arms bear is given as a gift from one bereaved family to another, to let you know that you are not alone. Supporting Arms service is run by bereaved parents and gives you the opportunity to talk to someone who has an understanding of what you are going through.
Call or text: 07464 508994 (a call-back service for anyone in the UK). Available to pick up messages Mon-Fri. If you need to talk to someone urgently, check out other charities such as Samaritans (You are not alone).
Email: support@achingarms.co.uk

Supporting Arms for Dads
Email: bereavementcare@achingarms.co.uk
https://www.achingarms.co.uk/

Antenatal Results and Choices
ARC is the only national charity helping parents and healthcare professionals through antenatal screening and its consequences. They provide independent, accurate, unbiased information so that parents can take the decisions that are right for them.
Call: 020 7713 7486
https://www.arc-uk.org/

Association for Postnatal Illness
Get in touch for some friendly advice, or just to talk through how you are feeling.
Call: 0207 386 0868 (Mon-Fri 10am-2pm or leave a voicemail outside these hours which will be picked up on the next working day)
Chat using the Chat box on the website.
https://apni.org/

Be More Ben
A diverse programme of support to parents and families affected by the death of a child.
Email: info@bemoreben.org
Call: 07554 01381
http://bemoreben.org/

Cherished Gowns
Creating beautiful items of clothing for babies who have passed away.
Call: 01304 201154
https://www.cherishedgowns.org.uk/

Child Bereavement UK
Confidential support, information and guidance for children, young people, parents, families and professionals throughout the UK to rebuild lives when a child grieves or when a child dies. support team available to respond to calls, live chat or email from 9am–5pm, Monday–Friday (except bank holidays). Messages can be left via telephone, email or live chat and they will respond on next working day.
Email: helpline@childbereavementuk.org
Call: 0800 02 888 40
Live chat: via website
https://www.childbereavementuk.org/

Child Funeral Charity
Assist families financially in England and Wales who have to arrange a funeral for a baby or child aged 16 or under. Whilst many funeral directors, the clergy and most celebrants do not charge fees, there are other funeral related expenses that bereaved parents struggle to find. Financial support is available to help with such funeral costs, together with practical advice and guidance.
Email: enquiries@childfuneralcharity.org.uk
Call: 01480 276088 (Mon–Fri, 9am–5pm)
https://www.childfuneralcharity.org.uk

Memory Ideas
Ideas for children to create memories.
https://fullcirclefunerals.co.uk/bereavement-support/continuing-bonds/
https://fullcirclefunerals.co.uk/wp-content/uploads/2022/12/Grief-Series-Dia-De-Los-Muertos-activity-pack.pdf

Handmade by the Haytons
Teddy bears made from a loved one's clothes.
https://www.facebook.com/handmadebythehaytons

Poppy's Funerals
Funerals for Babies and Children: Your Questions Answered.
https://www.poppysfunerals.co.uk/talking-death/funerals-for-babies-and-children-your-questions-answered/

Support after Pet Loss

Blue Cross
Animal charity offering bereavement support following the loss of a pet
Call: 0800 096 6606 (8.30am to 8.30pm every day)
Email: pbssmail@bluecross.org.uk (will respond within 48 hours)
https://www.bluecross.org.uk/pet-bereavement-and-pet-loss

Cats Protection
UK's leading cat welfare charity. Offers grief support service following the loss of a cat.
Call Paws to Listen grief support service: 0800 024 94 94 free and confidential (9–5, Mon–Fri, exc. bank holidays).
https://www.cats.org.uk/what-we-do/grief

Living with Pet Bereavement
Pet bereavement support following the loss of a pet. Offers a free one-hour phone support session. A list of creative ideas for memorialising a pet from funerals to shrines to ashes made into diamonds.
Call: 0845 46 55 999
https://livingwithpetbereavement.com/

Check out:
Before I Die Wall
A memento mori for the modern age. A global participatory art project enabling us to reimagine our relationship with death by writing a message on a wall. Originally created by Candy Chang in New Orleans after the death of a loved one, there are now over 5,000 walls around the world, in seventy-eight countries and thirty-five languages. 'Each wall is a tribute to living an examined life.' You can download resources from the website and plan one in your own community.
https://beforeidieproject.com/

Quaker Social Action
'Down to Earth' (help with funeral costs)
https://quakersocialaction.org.uk/we-can-help/helping-funerals/down-earth/why-we-run-down

T

IS FOR TERROR

Murder, Execution, Atrocity

terror *noun*
1. overwhelming fear.
2. a period of bloody massacres and public executions by guillotine (1793–94) known as 'the Terror' (*la Terreur*) during the French Revolution.
3. 'War on terror', the term used by George W. Bush, president at the time of the 9/11 terrorist attacks that killed 3,000 people in the USA. This changed intelligence and counterterrorism practice, launched two major wars, and altered attitudes and aspects of daily life.

O villain, villain, smiling, damned villain!
MACBETH

You villains! if this stone you see,
Remember that you murdered me!
You bruised my head, and pierced my heart,
Also my bowels did suffer part.
FROM THE HEADSTONE OF JOSEPH GLENDOWING, IN ST MICHAEL'S CHURCHYARD, WORKINGTON.
Killed on 15 June 1808; his murderers were never found

Huddersfield, 2023

This week, I started my post as Royal Literary Fund writing fellow at the University of Huddersfield. I spent some time one afternoon visiting the Holocaust Centre North, an independent charity based on campus. It tells the global history of the Holocaust through local stories of twelve survivors and refugees who made new lives in the North, before, during and after the Second World War. Amongst the recorded testimonies and eyewitness accounts of this reign of terror, there is personal memorabilia, precious belongings smuggled out of Europe – documents, letters, photographs. There are also artefacts on display from other museums such as a shoe on loan from the Buchenwald Memorial Collection. This wooden clog is typical of the footwear given to Jewish prisoners in concentration and forced labour camps. A prisoner's chance of survival could depend on having shoes that protected their feet. If they had difficulty walking, they were more likely to be judged 'unfit for work' and killed.

In the camps, the SS stripped each prisoner of their belongings, clothing, hair, name. They were reduced to a number stitched on their uniform; in Auschwitz it was tattooed on their skin. In Buchenwald, it was a label – yellow for Jews, red for communists, green for criminals, maroon for homosexuals. All they had was a uniform, a bowl and a spoon.

Six million Jews killed. Two million never identified. Most with no graves. No place for loved ones to remember their lost families. Because Nazis destroyed so many of their records in the final months of the war, many survivor families have a lifelong search for the lost. The International Tracing Service, established in Germany in 1948, holds millions of records. They receive over a thousand requests for help each month. Here, in Huddersfield, families from the north of England can remember their loved ones in a digital memorial.

It is a place to remember. The dead were more than numbers. More than labels. They were living breathing people who had their lives stolen in the most brutal, systemic way.

Another part of my week was spent on the usual training courses, including health and safety, GDPR, unconscious bias and safeguarding with regards to radicalisation – the latter in response to the Counter-Terrorism and Security Act (2015) and its impact on higher education. The Prevent strategy aims to reduce the threat of terror to the UK by stopping people becoming terrorists or supporting terrorism. Schools and universities have a Prevent duty to protect the vulnerable from messages of all violent extremism including, but not restricted to, those linked to Islamist ideology, or to far-right/neo-Nazi/white supremacist ideology, various paramilitary groups and extremist animal rights movements. Radicalisation is seen as a form of grooming, harm or abuse of vulnerable people and should be dealt with as for any safeguarding concern.[1]

Terror is not just a thing of the past.

This former mill town of Huddersfield is in the shadow of the Pennines, surrounded by soft-watered rivers which were perfect for textile treatment in the large weaving sheds which housed the power looms of the Industrial Revolution (some of which became the scene of Luddite revolts). The town was home to film star James Mason, the first female Doctor Who, Jodie Whittaker, and former PM Harold Wilson, whose major achievements included the abolition of the death penalty (1965) and the Sexual Offences Act (1967), which decriminalised some homosexual offences. The imposing Victorian neoclassical buildings, including the most stunning railway station, are testament to its former glory. The outward-looking university with its impressive modern architecture and diverse student population is testament to the way Huddersfield is now.

The soft Pennine rain falls all week.

Driving home across Saddleworth Moor, I think of those children buried there – Pauline, John, Lesley Ann, victims of Ian Brady and Myra Hindley, the Moors murderers. And poor Keith, whose body has never been found, despite his mother never giving up the search in the hope of giving him a Christian burial. She died in 2012, forty-eight years after little Keith's murder. The boy in the glasses with the cheeky grin.

It is bleak.

Terror comes in so many ways.

☠☠☠

War on Terror

The 9/11 terrorist attacks became defining moments for Tony Blair and his legacy. He allied with the USA and President Bush over the need to confront militant Islamism, first in Afghanistan in 2001 and then, much more controversially, in 2003 with the invasion of Iraq. The case for war in the UK had been built around the widespread belief that Saddam harboured weapons of mass destruction (WMD), which were not subsequently found.[2]

On 7 July 2005, terror came to the streets of our capital. London had seen terror before, notably during the Blitz, when, during eight months of nightly bombing, 43,000 civilians were killed by the Luftwaffe.[3] Later, during thirty years of the Troubles, the IRA killed fifty people in the city. Early on this summer day in 2005, as people were commuting to work, three explosions occurred at around 8.50 a.m. on the Underground between Aldgate and Liverpool Street, at Edgware Road and between Russell Square and King's Cross. At 9.47 there was a fourth explosion on the upper deck of a London bus in Tavistock Place. Fifty-two people were killed, several hundred injured. The bombers, Islamic extremists, also lost their lives in these suicide attacks.

D IS FOR DEATH

State-sanctioned or not, terror comes in many ways.

☠☠☠

Off with Her Head

> England under the Tudors was a police state, and there was no telling where the axe might fall.[4]
> Catharine Arnold

Public execution was a common pastime in sixteenth-century London, with beheading by axe the method of choice. When Anne Boleyn, Henry VIII's second wife, failed to give the king a male heir, she was accused of trumped-up charges, a triple whammy of witchcraft, adultery and incest. On 2 May 1536, Anne was carried by barge from Greenwich down the Thames, following the same route she had taken to prepare for her coronation. But this time it was to Traitor's Gate, where she was handed over to the Constable of the Tower and imprisoned in the Lieutenant's lodgings. After a show trial on 15 May, she was acquitted of incest (which would have meant being burned at the stake) but condemned to death for treason. On 19 May, Anne went to the scaffold on Tower Green – rather than a public execution site outside the walls. She famously had a small neck, and Henry was gallant enough to allow her to have an expert swordsman from Calais. She was killed with one stroke. Her body and head were put in a chest and interred in the Chapel Royal of St Peter ad Vincula within the grounds of the Tower – the resting place for executed nobility. She was later joined by her younger cousin and Henry's fifth wife (who had to make do with the axe). And later by the Nine Days' Queen, Lady Jane Grey, whom we last saw as a fifteen-year-old waiting on the scaffold in Paul Delaroche's painting.[5] Nearly seventy years after Anne was executed, and after a forty-four-year reign, her daughter, Elizabeth I, was buried in Westminster Abbey in one of the most elaborate funerals in English history. Gloriana, the Virgin Queen, lies in a tomb shared with her half-sister and nemesis, Bloody Mary.

☠☠☠

Off with His Head

After seven years of bloody civil war, Oliver Cromwell imprisoned Charles I[6] at Carisbrooke Castle on the Isle of Wight. When Charles refused to accept peace or submit to the republicans, he was convicted of treason, and in January 1649, outside the Banqueting House in Whitehall, the king was executed. He was later buried at Windsor in the Royal vault alongside Henry VIII and Jane

Seymour (in the space where Catherine Parr would have lain if she had not remarried). It's a long time since I went to Windsor Castle with my grandparents, but I do remember them taking me to Sudeley Castle, where Charles had been the last royal occupant during the Civil War. I remember seeing one of the several waistcoats he allegedly wore as he went to the block; such a freezing cold day, he didn't want to shiver and appear afraid. I've never forgotten that waistcoat, so small it looked like a child's.

After Cromwell died of kidney failure in 1658, he was interred in Westminster Abbey. But, when the monarchy was restored in 1660 and Charles II came to the throne, Cromwell was posthumously tried for regicide. In January 1661, his remains were dug up and, on the twelfth anniversary of Charles's execution, his corpse dragged to Tyburn and hung up on a gibbet until late afternoon, when it was taken down and decapitated. It is said that it took eight blows to hack off Cromwell's head. His body was buried in a pit beneath the gallows, his head displayed on a spike outside Westminster Hall.

Clifford Brewer, author of *The Death of Kings*, says there are several accounts that state that Cromwell had taken steps to prevent such a desecration. One says he was buried on the battlefield of Naseby, another that he was buried in the Thames, others that his body was substituted for Charles's at Windsor. Or possibly, Brewer suggests, while his body was at the Red Lion in Holborn on the night before being taken to Tyburn, the guards may have accepted bribes to substitute another body for his. There is also an account of his daughter, Mary, having a burial at Newburgh Priory, but the owners have never allowed the tomb to be inspected. Maybe, after all, the body really is beneath Tyburn, near Marble Arch.

But what of the head? It remained on its spike until it blew down in a gale in the early reign of James II. A guard took it home and later his daughter sold it. After passing hands several times, the skull was given to Cromwell's alma mater in Cambridge, Sidney Sussex College. In the 1930s, the skull was examined and believed to be that of Cromwell, whereupon it was buried near the chapel, the exact whereabouts a secret. However, the original postmortem carried out by Dr Bate documented that the cerebral vessels were more engorged than normal, implying he had removed the brain as per usual.

> For him to do this, he would have made an incision through the scalp across the top of the head from ear to ear. The scalp would then be reflected forwards and backwards, revealing the whole of the top of the skull. The top of the skull would then be removed, in the same way as removing the top of an egg, and the brain extracted. Finally, the skull and scalp would be replaced and stitched closed. From the reports [in the 1930s] there seems to be no evidence that the skull in question had been so opened. If Dr Bates's report is correct, the head may not be that of Cromwell.[7]

Dance with a Stranger

In 1955, Ruth Ellis was the last woman to be executed in Britain. Her hanging played a major role in the abolition of the death penalty, though it wasn't until December 1965 that it was finally abolished (thank you, Harold Wilson). Soon after her execution, the *Observer* wrote about the ethics of the death penalty – a life for a life – urging people to 'consider the task of explaining to the late Mrs Ruth Ellis's 11-year-old son, now at a boarding school, what has happened'. (Indeed.) 'This boy, who is also fatherless, has had something done to him that is so brutal it is difficult to imagine. We should realise it is we who have done it.' Powerful stuff. Especially when you also consider that Ruth's son, Andy, took his own life in 1982.

In 2018, American film-maker Gillian Pachter made a documentary for the BBC which re-examined Ellis's case, believing the story has a relevance today. She spoke to Donald Campbell in the *Guardian*:

> I guess the ongoing tragedy of gun violence as well as the persistence of state execution in the States made me interested in the impact of the Ellis case. I don't think we've had a case that changed the conscience of [the US] in quite the same way, and I'm wondering what it would take. Another timely aspect is the way that her violence and sexual violence was framed by the authorities who investigated and tried her case. Her experience of violence at the hands of men unfortunately still resonates today.[8]

For fifty-five years and for more than 800 executions, most for murder, some for treason, the Pierrepoint family were the country's executioners. Henry, his brother Thomas, and Henry's son, Albert. Albert hanged Ruth Ellis, one of many, many others sentenced to death, including twenty-two for war crimes. In his autobiography, *Executioner* (1974), he expressed his regret: 'The fruit of my experience has this bitter aftertaste: that I do not now believe that any of the hundreds of executions I carried out has in any way acted as a deterrent against future murder.'[9]

☠☠☠

Fire Burn and Cauldron Bubble

Back to the seventeenth century, and witch-hunting mania is sweeping across Europe, consuming James VI of Scotland. When he escorts his bride, Anne of Denmark, from her homeland in 1589, their ship is almost wrecked in a storm. James believes the tempest has been brewed by a witch intending to murder him and his new queen. Agnes Sampson, healer, midwife, widow, mother, is one of the accused. She is shaved, stripped, tortured, brutalised, with James insisting he be present. She is finally tried and convicted and then strangled and burned on Castle Hill in Edinburgh on 28 January 1591.[10]

It doesn't stop here. During what will become known as the North Berwick witch trials, over a hundred people are accused of trying to kill James by sorcery, many confessing during horrific, drawn-out torture. James goes on to write *Daemonologie*, which was published in 1597. This *Dummies Guide to Witches* discusses biblical evidence for witchcraft. Witches are enemies of God. Devil worshippers. Anyone can be a witch, but women are less able to resist Satan's temptations. Christians must hunt them down and, once caught, it is acceptable to bend the rules at a witch trial.[11]

By torturing and killing so many, James helps spread fear throughout Scotland, which has one of the highest rates of convictions and executions of witches, four times the European average. The most accurate figures comes from research at Edinburgh University, which estimates that 3,837 were accused, of whom 625 are unnamed. (Compare this to nineteen in Salem.) Many died before they went to trial. The convicted were strangled first and then burned, so that there was no record of them.

Claire Marchant sums up why there was such a dark period in Scottish history:

With the reformation, civil war looming or at large, and increased jurisdictional powers given by the Scottish State to the localised Kirk Sessions of the Church of Scotland, the male dominated parish elite were to see their Calvinistic Godly discipline meted out with fervour and ruthlessness… Catholic practices, the practice of carrying faith charms, folklore, fairies and many beliefs, which had previously brought comfort and had been part of Scottish culture for centuries, became the focus of the new system.[12]

Marchant has worked with others for Remembering the Accused Witches of Scotland (RAWS) to raise awareness of this great injustice. The founders were inspired by the stories of the West Fife accused witches, in particular, Lilias Addie. In 1704, Lilias was accused, imprisoned, tortured and deprived of sleep. She was 'persuaded' to confess to being a witch, but she refused to name anyone else. So brutal was her treatment that she died in prison, before her trial. Because she had not been convicted, she still had the presumption of innocence, so she was buried, hurriedly, on the shoreline at Torry Bay in the Firth of Forth, beneath a large sandstone slab. This heavy stone would keep Lilias in and, even if she did somehow get out, witches could not cross over water, so there would be no maleficence from beyond the grave.

From a distance, as the sand is dangerous, you can still see the stone, there in the mud, at low tide.

Lilias Adie.
The importance of a name.

Following discussions with RAWS, in March 2022, the Scottish Government formally apologised to the persecuted under the historic Witchcraft Acts, which ran from 1563 to 1736. This was followed two months later by an apology from the Church of Scotland for their involvement.

Why were these apologies so important, now, so long after the event?

They were mothers, daughters, cousins, sisters and living a hard life in a tumultuous early modern Scotland. Female inequality and persecution continue around the world to this day and in some way, the recognition of these historical injustices and the victims themselves, can shine a light for all women.[13]

'She lived in the Forest of Pendle, amongst this wicked company of dangerous witches.'[14]

Did the cattle sicken and die? The witch and the wizard were the authors of the calamity. Did the butter refuse to come? The 'familiar' was in the churn. Did the ship founder at sea? The gale or hurricane was blown by the lungless hag who had scarcely sufficient breath to cool her own pottage.[15]
Thomas Baines

It began with an altercation on a road near Pendle Hill, where Alizon Device asked a pedlar, John Law, for some pins which, at this time, were often associated with witchcraft, particularly with love magic. When John refused, Alizon cursed him. Soon after, he collapsed, probably from a stroke. He blamed Alizon. Alizon, convinced of her own powers and feeling guilty, accompanied Abraham Law to his father's bedside to beg his forgiveness and to attempt to reverse the curse she believed she had placed upon him. Her belief meant that she was admitting to the crime.

1612. At this time of religious persecution and superstition, witch-hunting frenzy has arrived in Lancashire, revealing itself in what will become the most notorious witch trials in English history: the Pendle Witch Trials. Witch-obsessed Protestant James VI is now also James I of England, having succeeded his Catholic mother's executioner, his aunt Elizabeth I, in 1603. In 1605, James survives the Catholic Gunpowder Plot, a foiled act of terror to blow up the Palace of Westminster with all the great and good inside. Consequently, Catholics and anyone suspected of witchcraft are watched more closely than ever. James even brings in the death penalty for those found guilty and has compelled every justice of the peace in the country to compile a list of locals who refuse to attend church or take communion (a criminal offence). In Lancashire, a county sympathetic to Catholicism and regarded as somewhat lawless,[16] Robert Nowell JP believes a successful witch trial will ingratiate him to the king. So, when he receives the complaint about Alizon Device, he seizes the opportunity.

This is a dangerous time to be a woman, especially one from a family whose income depends on offering cures to their fellow villagers. Especially when witchcraft is seen as hereditary, when members of the same family can be accused together. Alizon's grandmother, Elizabeth Southerns, is the matriarch of one such family. The widow, known as Old Demdike, lives with her daughter, Elizabeth Device, and Elizabeth's children James, Alizon and Jennet. The family has been accused of cursing their neighbours before, but now this is serious and has a knock-on effect to another family with whom they have feuded for years, headed by Anne Whittle, known as Mother Chattox.

Alizon confesses to Nowell: she told the Devil to lame John Law. From there, it snowballs. Upon further questioning, she accuses her grandmother, Old Demdike, of witchcraft. Nowell questions members of both families. The two matriarchs – blind, vulnerable octogenarians – confess to selling their souls to the Devil. Mother Chattox's daughter, Anne, denies her involvement but her own mother accuses her of making clay figures to practise witchcraft. After hearing all this 'evidence', Nowell sends Alizon, Anne, Demdike and Chattox to Lancaster Castle to await trial at the next assizes. A further eight people are summoned for questioning and then trial, accused of attending a meeting where they plotted to blow up Lancaster Castle and free the prisoners. Seven of these are also sent to Lancaster. The eighth, Jennet Preston, lives over the border, so is sent to the York assizes, where she is found guilty of witchcraft and hanged on 29 July. Conditions in Lancaster prison are cramped and filthy, so appalling that Old Demdike dies before the trials, which start on 17 August.

Because James has suspended the normal rules, the accused are denied witnesses to plead their innocence, there is no counsel for the defence and children can take the stand. This is how nine-year-old Jennet Device comes to testify against her mother, sister and brother.

> My mother is a witch and that I know to be true. I have seen her spirit in the likeness of a brown dog, which she calls Ball. The dog did ask what she would have him do, and she answered that she would have him help her to kill.

Why does she say this? Is it because she has been poorly treated by her family? Or is it pressure from the powers that be? Whatever it is, her evidence is damning. Added to the confessions already given, and with the vigour of the prosecutors, after just three days the trial is over. Alice Grey is the only person found not guilty. On 20 August 1612, the remaining nine are hanged.

But what became of Jennet Device? In March 1634, a woman of her name was one of twenty tried at Lancaster for witchcraft, accused of the murder of Isabel Nutter by a ten-year-old boy, Edmund Robinson. He later admitted to fabricating his evidence, and the twenty avoided execution. But it is believed that, despite being pardoned, Jennet died in Lancaster Castle, just like Old Demdike.

The last execution for witchcraft took place in England in 1684, by which time over five hundred had been killed. James I's statute on witchcraft was repealed in 1736 by George II.[17]

By the beginning of the eighteenth century, the hysteria might have dissipated, but the Pendle trials have left a mark on the landscape of the north-west. Talk of witchcraft is still whispered throughout the locality. Meg Shelton lives in poverty on the Fylde near Preston. Known as the Woodplumpton Witch or the Fylde hag, Meg has a reputation for witchcraft and mischief. Limping, old and said to be ugly, she is treated as an outcast. Her neighbours believe she can make cattle sick, make crops fail and shapeshift into animals. Any misfortune in the village is blamed on Meg with one story claiming that she transformed herself into a sack of corn and hid inside a barn so she could steal some food. When the farmer noticed there was an extra sack, he prodded each one with a pitchfork. When he struck Meg, she screamed, turned back into human form and ran off.

Sometime in 1705, Meg has not been seen for a few days and, after her cottage door is forced open, there she is, crushed between a barrel and a wall, dead. Whether an accident or murder, it is declared that the Devil has claimed her. However, she is allowed burial in consecrated ground, at the western end of the churchyard of St Anne's at Woodplumpton. But her spirit will not rest. She claws herself out of the grave, twice. Some locals suggest her body be turned upside down; if she tries again, she will dig her way down to Hell. So, during a midnight ceremony, Meg has a deviant burial, headfirst, and a large boulder is placed on top of her grave. You can still see the boulder. Some say if you walk round it three times reciting the words *I don't believe in witches*, Meg's hand will emerge from the ground and drag you down. Others suggest you make a wish and maybe it will be fulfilled. You decide. But if you do visit the grave, you will probably see flowers placed there in her memory. Or maybe the footmarks of those who have previously walked around it.[18]

'Leaving Behind Nights of Terror and Fear / I Rise'[19]

Slavery is when one person is 'owned' by another. A slave is not treated as a person. Instead, they are treated like property that can be bought and sold. The people who think of themselves as slave 'owners' force their slaves to work for nothing. Slavery has existed throughout human history and across many different civilisations. Slavery existed in Africa before the arrival of Europeans, but the Transatlantic slave trade *massively* changed the scale of the trade in human beings and the way it was done.[20]

In 2012, the 'witch county' of Lancashire commemorated 400 years since the trials. Over the centuries, Lancaster, where most of the accused were executed, has been known as 'the hanging town', having hanged the most people in England apart from London. Its castle was still used as a prison until 2011. The city has a long, dark history but it's a place I fell in love with as a student, especially during my third year, living on the banks of the Lune in the heart of town.

1988, St George's Quay. Our student house, in a row of wonky Georgian terraces, has a cellar that floods during a supertide and is just a few doors down from a local landmark, the Wagon and Horses. In the future, it will be a jazzed-up hotel, but now there is sawdust on the floor and men in cloth caps sit at the bar with their tankards and tolerate the students as long as they drink Old Peculiar. But the Quay is a place in transition. Along either side of our row of terraces are warehouses, some derelict, others in the process of being converted into yuppie flats. One regenerated townhouse is the European headquarters of Reebok. If you stand still and look up and down the cobbles, you can see evidence of a former industrious town of wealth.

The most imposing building on the Quay is the former Custom House, now home to the Maritime Museum. I visit one day with my Canadian cousin, who is visiting the UK for the first time. Wide-eyed and innocent, we stumble into the past and discover that Lancaster owes much of its wealth to the transatlantic slave trade. The Custom House in which we stand was constructed to accommodate Lancaster's expanding role in the gruesome trade, the place where merchants paid taxes on the 'goods'. The architect, Richard Gillow, was one of the city's biggest slave traders.

Slave traders, here, in Lancaster.

I mean, I know about slavery. As a child, I watched *Roots*. But here, now, a decade later, I understand that the slave trade operated much closer to home. This building, this quay, this town prospered from the blood of Africans wrenched from their homes thousands of miles away.

The transatlantic slave trade, also known as the Triangle Trade, had three stages. Firstly, manufactured goods from Europe, such as cloth, beads and guns, were taken to Africa and exchanged for kidnapped people. Secondly, these captured Africans were transported to the Americas. Thirdly, raw material and goods produced by slave labour – cotton, sugar, rum, mahogany, tobacco – were brought back to Europe and imported by the city's traders and merchants. Lancaster, on the west coast, was in a strategic place, and the damp conditions of the county were perfect for cotton production. Lancaster became the fourth biggest slaving port in the UK – after Liverpool, Bristol and London – involved in the capture and trade of around 30,000 people, with over 120 ships sailing from the town to the coast of Africa during the eighteenth century. Its slave-trading families and their descendants invested their blood money in mills and business. Small wonder it was one of the few British towns to petition the government in favour of slavery.[21] Lancaster, a vibrant university city with students from all over the world, has been making efforts to have open conversations about its past. In 2005 a memorial was unveiled, a tribute to the enslaved people intended to make us 'reflect on the human cost of our shameful slavery heritage'.[22] But *Captured Africans*, as it was called, had little publicity and was only recently included on the city centre map. Though there are several memorials countrywide celebrating abolitionists, as far as I can make out, *Captured Africans* is one of only two memorials to the victims of slavery in the UK (the other being in Plymouth). Though I only lived there for a short time, it was an important time in my life, a coming-of-age time, so I feel an affinity to Lancaster, though an affinity tinged with shame, all those nights danced away in the student union club, the Sugarhouse.[23]

I also have connections to the other major slave-trading ports. As an adult I lived and worked in London for eleven years. For nine years, we lived in Southwark, known for the docks where sugar was imported and stored. My three children were born at King's College Hospital in Camberwell, and two of them were regulars at St Thomas' for their allergies. During the Black Lives Matter protests of 2020, Guy's and St Thomas' health trust released a statement in conjunction with King's regarding statues in their grounds.

> We absolutely recognise the public hurt and anger that is generated by the symbolism of public statues of historical figures associated with the slave trade in some way ... We see the pervasive and harmful effects of structural racism every day through our work. Black people have worse health outcomes, and this inequality is one of many ways racism permeates our society. We are fully committed to tackling racism, discrimination and inequality, and we stand in solidarity with our patients, students, colleagues and communities.

Over the river, in a museum in Docklands, there was a similar response to a statue outside the building.

> Two centuries after the trade was abolished, Britain's economy and cultural heritage remains inextricably tangled with the after-effects of slavery; a tangle which we are only beginning to recognise in full... The

over-representation of black children among child poverty statistics, and their under-representation among university graduates, for example, are not random coincidences, nor are they caused by 'innate' racial characteristics. The structural racism with which British society grapples today is a direct consequence of cultural attitudes, economic policies and social constructs rooted in the slave trade.[24]

London mayor Sadiq Khan also responded by launching a diversity commission to review similar statues in the capital and committed £500,000 for a monument to be built to 'memorialise those who were enslaved and the impact of slavery on generations of Black communities, as well as recognising London's fundamental role at the heart of the slave trade'.[25]

These days, I am back in the north-west, living across the Mersey from Liverpool, home to the International Slavery Museum, where you can hear the untold stories of enslaved people and learn about historical and contemporary slavery. Controversial statues remain in the city, though in 2021 they were reclaimed for a time, Victoria redressed in a sari and Gladstone in a Pride outfit. Nelson, who we last saw buried in the vault of St Paul's, is increasingly recognised as a supporter of slavery. His statue still stands in the Exchange, complete with men in chains, a reminder that this was an area enmeshed in the slave trade. The late Eric Lynch was a tour guide who spent decades educating people about Liverpool's history, long before the city's formal apology in 1999.[26] An honorary Ghanaian chief, his parents were born in Barbados, descendants of enslaved Africans. (Barbados removed the statue of Nelson on their island in 2020.) 'It's important that we don't forget the slave trade,' he said in 2018 when he was made a citizen of honour. 'The Jewish people will, rightly, never forget what happened to them during World War Two, and black people should not forget the African holocaust.'[27]

As well as the statues, Eric's tours included less obvious reminders such as the depictions of enslaved African children on the entrance to Martin's Bank. I was there recently, to see them for myself. Three sides of the bank are bordered up at present as the building undergoes renovations by a property investor. On the fourth side, I found the entrance, where a young man with dreadlocks was trying to raise money for his fashion designs. We got chatting. He told me his dream was to open a clothes shop in Liverpool. I told him I was there to take a picture of the African children and explained why. He said he'd been looking at the children because they 'have hair like me' and pointed out that the child on the left had hair like the Senegalese lads you see around the city on their bikes delivering food. And that the child on the right had East African hair. But he was taken aback to see the moneybags the children were holding and what this meant. All this hidden in plain sight.

Lancaster, London, Liverpool. So much to answer for.

But it is my mother's home city, where I spent so many childhood holidays with my grandparents and where two of my children currently live, that we go to now.

The entrance to Martin's Bank

☠☠☠

Set in Stone

> From Cecil Rhodes to Edward Colston to William Gladstone, the backstories of the men our statues depict (and the vast majority of them are of men) and the forgotten stories of why those statues were erected in the first place, and by whom, have bust into the national conversation. In the midst of the so-called 'statue wars' the question of what should become of the men cast in bronze or set in stone has never been more urgent.[28]
> David Olusoga

In 2020, during the #BLM protests following the murder of George Floyd by a white American police officer, protestors toppled the statue of Edward Colston and threw him into Bristol harbour. Known across the city for centuries as a philanthropist with his name everywhere – streets, a concert hall, the school where my uncle and stepbrother went – in the 1990s, there was a growing awareness that much of Colston's wealth was earned from the slave trade. Born in the city in 1636, Colston grew up in a wealthy merchant family, before moving to London, where he established himself as a wool and textile trader. In 1680, he joined the Royal African Company (RAC), which had a monopoly on the west African slave trade. Headed by James II, the company branded 'RAC' on the chests of the slaves, including children. The company sold about 100,000 people in the Caribbean and the Americas, and here Colston made his fortune, eventually selling his shares to William III in 1689.

The toppling of Edward Colston's statue sparked fresh debate on how we deal with our colonial past. Historian and Bristol resident, David Olusoga (alumnus of Liverpool University), argued that tearing down the statue was a cultural and political act rather than an act of 'thuggery', which is how then home secretary Priti Patel described the protest. Olusoga believes this to be a racist response: 'The word "thug" has long been used in this country as a dog whip for attacks on black people; it's a word that drips with racism, but it just doesn't stand up to scrutiny.'[29]

In the days following the statue's demise, Olusoga wrote about Colston's role in shaping the slave trade, helping to oversee the transportation of 84,000 Africans, 11,000 of them children.

> [I]t is believed, around 19,000 died in the stagnant bellies of the company's slave ships during the infamous Middle Passage from the coast of Africa to the plantations of the new world. The bodies of the dead were cast into the water where they were devoured by the sharks that, over the centuries of the Atlantic slave trade, learned to seek out slave ships and follow the bloody paths of slave routes across the ocean. This is the man who, for 125 years, has been honoured by Bristol. Put literally on a pedestal in the very heart of the city. But tonight Edward Colston sleeps with the fishes.[30]

Patel pursued the Colston Four through the criminal justice system for criminal damage. During the eleven-day trial, Olusoga gave expert evidence to the jury, arguing that history is vital in deciding such a case. He said that, at one point, Bristol was Britain's largest slaving city, involved in the transportation of over half a million people, more than its current population. He explained how young people were kidnapped from villages in the African interior, babies and elders massacred in front of them. How they were branded before being packed in and chained to the decks of ships bound for the Caribbean. How, if they rebelled, owners had the right to torture and kill them, bodies nailed to posts on the plantations as a warning. He explained that, when slave-owning was eventually abolished in British colonies in 1834, the government raised £20 million to compensate slave-owners for their loss, £16–17 billion in today's money, the largest government bailout of an industry until the financial crisis of 2008. He pointed out that everyone in the courtroom would have unwittingly contributed to the payment of the debt through their taxes, as it was not paid off until 2015. Members of the Windrush generation would have paid towards the debt used to compensate the owners of their ancestors. 'It is a very emotionally charged issue for people of Afro-Caribbean decent.'

In his evidence, one of the defendants, Sage Willoughby said: 'Imagine having a Hitler statue in front of a holocaust survivor – I believe they are similar … Having a statue of someone of that calibre in the middle of the city I believe is an insult, and I will continue to believe that whatever the outcome of this [trial].'[31]

Despite the prosecution arguing that it was irrelevant who Colston was or what he did, the four protestors were acquitted.

> This verdict is a milestone in the journey that Bristol and Britain are on to come to terms with the totality of our history… For 300 years Edward Colston was remembered as a philanthropist, his role in the slave trade and his many thousands of victims were airbrushed out of the story… The toppling of the statue and the passionate defence made in court by the Colston Four makes that deliberate policy of historical myopia now an impossibility.[32]

And what happened to the statue? Recovered from the water, it was temporarily displayed in M Shed Museum,[33] but is now in store. Following a survey in which four out of five Bristolians said that, instead of lording it over the city, they wanted Colston on display in a local museum, in time it will be part of a permanent collection.

Meanwhile, back in Lancaster, days after the felling of Colston, 'slave trader' was painted on a memorial to a local Quaker family in Lancaster Priory. The Rawlinsons made their fortune from the transatlantic slave trade in the 1750s and 60s. Abraham Rawlinson, MP for Lancaster between 1780 and 1790, opposed abolition. Imogen Tyler at the university argues that 'it is difficult to find a Lancaster elite from the eighteenth and nineteenth century whose wealth and power wasn't derived in part from what is often euphemistically referred to as the West-Indies trade'. From her involvement in the Lancaster Slavery Family Trees Community Research Project, she argues: 'What we can see in Lancaster, if we trace these histories, is how the profits from slavery and the slavery business in the West Indies and the Americas, financed the industrialisation of the city and the development of its civic infrastructure, welfare estate and later universities.'[34]

A university from which I received both my first degree and my master's.

But, as of just recently, I discovered my connections to slavery are far more personal and far more shocking.

T IS FOR TERROR

Rawlinson's memorial in the churchyard of Lancaster Priory

Family Tree

> Colonial slavery shaped modern Britain and we all still live with its legacies. The slave-owners were one very important means by which the fruits of slavery were transmitted to metropolitan Britain. We believe that research and analysis of this group are key to understanding the extent and the limits of slavery's role in shaping British history and leaving lasting legacies that reach into the present.[35]

About ten years ago, I decided to do some family history research. I started with my paternal grandmother, Betty. Betty who was not the best mother to my father. Whose own mother, Mabel, had died in childbirth when Betty and her twin brother, Ken, were just six, their older brother, Tom, nine. Betty's maiden name was Gillespy with a Y. Easy enough to trace, I reasoned. And it was. I found a book written by a Victorian ancestor from Leith, the family genealogist. He had traced the family all the way back to William the Conqueror, through an ancestor Jane (or Joan) Beaufort. Now, I realise many of us are descended from royalty, but what was fascinating to me was that my heritage was written down, a direct line from me to Eleanor of Aquitaine, from whom I am twenty-six generations directly descended. A line that goes through both male and female, so it's not like I'll be getting the call to be queen any time soon. But pretty cool for someone who loves history and has visited all the castles, including Berkeley, where my direct ancestor (twenty-two generations ago) allegedly had a poker shoved up his bum. Royal connections aside, I had always been proud of the Gillespy side of the family. I gave the eulogy at Auntie Ruth's funeral (my half-great aunt). Pioneer of composting. Relief dairy farmer. Council gardener. Teenage Wren who fought terror through her work on Enigma. Her half-brother, Tom, had solved that typhoid case, working all his life in the canning industry on food safety. Socialist. Scientist. Crossword solver. I never knew Betty, as she died when I was a baby. And none of us ever met Ken, as he was married to a 'difficult' woman (a whole other story for another time). I only knew good things about the Gillespy family.

One day, my son, Edward, tells me he has put some family surnames into a database set up by UCL, more specifically by the Centre for the Study of the Legacies of British Slavery. A database of people who had been compensated after abolition. One of the names has a result.

'No.'

'Yes.'

My first thought goes to my maiden name, Dad's name. A Devon/Somerset family.

'Is it Stenner?'

'No,' he says.

Second thought. My married name, the name of my three children.

'Duffy?'

'Definitely not,' he says. The family are from County Mayo, servants and labourers.

I think of my mother's maiden name. Morris. A Welsh name said to derive from 'Moorish' or 'dark-skinned'.

'No,' he says.

I'm now thinking about my maternal grandmother's maiden name, a Bristol family. Bristol.

'Is it Box?'

I hold my breath.

'No result,' he says.

That leaves Gillespy.

'Tell me,' I say.

'There were two results.'

I feel sick.

'Who?'

'Thomas Gillespy and Thomas Gillespy Junior.'

Ed sends me the link. After a stiff drink, I click on it.

There it is. There they were.

From what I can make out, Thomas, the son, was a merchant ship and insurance broker and had shares in the Clermont Estate, in the parish of Trelawney, Jamaica. He and his father made a claim for £2,384 0s 4d. Though this was contested, it says in Parliamentary papers that 'the award was split: £1192 0s 2d went to each of (1) Gillespys & Longcroft (2) Wilkinson & Temple'. Compensation of the equivalent of approximately £110,500 in today's money – for the loss of labour of 109 enslaved people.

Thomas Junior, my great-great-great-grandfather, who died in 1872. I have his portrait. It used to hang on the wall, but now it is hidden in the wardrobe. The family skeleton.

My flesh and blood made money from the flesh and blood of others.

Auntie Ruth, who fought her whole life for social justice, had no idea. I feel her horror from beyond the grave.

Hidden in plain sight.

My flesh and blood.

In 'O Is for Operation London Bridge', I wrote about the other side of the family, who had lived on St Helena. I explained that one of my direct ancestors (seven generations) was enslaved there, one of the most remote places on earth. She was called Mary.

I have no other name than *Mary*.

She 'married' Captain Patrick Killin. Their granddaughter, another Mary, was born on the island, and reputedly sat in Napoleon's coffin as a little girl. When she married, she had several children on the island and several more when they came to the UK. My mother (another Mary) remembers one of these children, another Mary, because she was her great-grandmother – my great-great-grandmother. So, to be clear, my great-great-great-grandmother sat in Napoleon's coffin and my great-great-great-great-great-grandmother was Mary, an enslaved woman.

This happened such a long time ago, but we just have to reach out our hand and we can touch it.

We just have to reach out our hand.

And so to the Gillespy's. Easy to trace with a Y.

My great-great-great-great-grandfather and my great-great-great-grandfather profited from slavery.

How do I process this?

Descended from an enslaved woman.

Descended from a father and son who profited from slavery.

What does that make me? Does it change who I am? Does it change how I got here? To this place, now?

Everything is connected.

We have to have the conversation.

We just have to reach out our hand.

Laura Trevelyan left her job as a journalist at the BBC to campaign for reparations. Along with her cousin John Dower, they apologised to Grenada for their family's historic role in the slave trade, agreeing to donate more than £100,000 to education projects on the Caribbean island in reparations for the family's involvement in slavery. In 1835, the Trevelyan family received compensation of around £30,000 (about £3,000,000 in today's money). 'The enslaved men, women and children on their plantations received nothing, and were forced to work a further eight years unpaid as "apprentices".'[36]

Labour MP, Clive Lewis, has been working with Trevelyan to campaign on the issue of reparations. He can actually trace his family back to Grenada, where the Trevelyan's owned more than 1,000 slaves. She said of this that it is 'entirely possible that his ancestors were owned by my ancestors ... so in that sense, we represent both the pain of Britain's colonial past but also the promise – as we're now working together. I hope that by the two of us talking about that link, that will show people in Britain and indeed around the world, that this isn't something that's abstract.'[37]

Lewis's father was born and raised in Grenada and has welcomed the Trevelyan family apology, saying there has 'never been a conversation in this country about our role in the world for good and for bad... there are black people in this country who've been talking about this for many decades.' He added that the power structures in the UK created by the slave trade are 'part of the reason why those voices don't have access in the media... A white family who benefitted from slavery have decided to show real leadership on this, which is something that hasn't been done before.'

Although the cities of Liverpool and London have both offered apologies, the British government has never formally apologised for slavery or offered reparations. Trevelyan argues that repayment is due for what Barbadian historian and chair of the Caricom Reparations Commission Sir Hilary Beckles has called 'Britain's black debt', which left Caribbean nations with nothing when slavery ended. Following the death of George Floyd, Trevelyan, who lives in New York, pondered how her ancestors had 'sat sipping tea in England, profiting from an inhumane system of slavery more than 4,000 miles away'. She realised that 'the past was informing the present in ways that had to be confronted' which meant confronting her own white privilege.

> My own social and professional standing nearly 200 years after the abolition of slavery had to be related to my slave-owning ancestors, who used the profits from sugar sales to accumulate wealth and climb up the social ladder... If one of the legacies of slavery in America was police brutality towards black men, what was the legacy of slavery on Grenada, I wondered? I had to find out. Even if it was going to open me up to accusations of being a white saviour trying to salvage her conscience.[38]

So she visited Grenada, more than her ancestors had ever done, and, with a journalist's quest for knowledge, she talked to the inhabitants about reparations:

> The arguments for and against reparations are controversial and complex – the moral imperative of making amends, versus questions about whether this is the most effective way to tackle racial inequality. And is it right to

expect those who weren't responsible to pay the price for decisions made hundreds of years ago?[39]

She grappled with the philosophical question of whether she personally owed anything and consulted Beckles about whether she should give money to help Grenadian students with higher education. He said:

> Slavery is not in the past. Our grandparents remember their great-grandparents who were slaves. Slavery is part of our domestic present. Slavery denies you access to your ancestry. It leaves you in this empty void…What you are trying to reconcile is privilege on one side of the ledger and poverty on the other. We inherited poverty, illiteracy, hypertension, diabetes, racial degradation – all the negative dimensions. You inherited wealth, property and prestige … Think of the impact if every one of the slave-owning families did the same thing.[40]

Now, that's really something to ponder.
But where do I sit in all this?
A descendant of an enslaved woman.
A descendant of a father and son compensated for their shares in the transatlantic slave trade.
The pain and the promise.
Where do I sit in this reign of terror?
I don't exactly know but I want to be part of the dialogue.
I want to offer an apology on behalf of the Gillespy family.
And Mary, here I remember your name, whether it is one you were born with or one you were given. *Mary.*
You lived. And because you lived, so do I.
Thank you, Mary.

Mary Box (born McCallum), my great-great-grandmother.
Whose mother sat in Napoleon's coffin.
Whose great-grandmother was an enslaved woman on St Helena.

Useful websites

Heirs of Slavery
A small group of British people who have researched their family histories, and learned that their ancestors made significant wealth from, or helped organise, more than two centuries of industrialised enslavement of Africans in the Americas. Join the conversation.
https://www.heirsofslavery.org/

Remembering the Accused Witches of Scotland (RAWS)
A campaign to raise awareness of the ordinary women and men accused of witchcraft during this dark period of Scottish history and for a national monument to remember and honour the more than 4,000 accused.
https://www.raws.scot/

Holocaust Centre North
Charity that raises awareness of one of the darkest chapters in contemporary history. Tells a global history through local stories to inspire others to value human rights, freedom and equality.
The University of Huddersfield
Schwann Building
https://hcn.org.uk/

Advocacy after Fatal Domestic Abuse
Independent organisation offering specialist advocacy and peer support to families and friends bereaved after fatal domestic abuse.
https://aafda.org.uk/

U

IS FOR UNFINISHED

Grief and What I Have Learned about Loss

grief *noun*
1. a feeling of intense sorrow or distress, esp. following a loved one's death or a deep loss.
2. trouble or annoyance (*informal*).

Grief makes one hour ten.
RICHARD II

Lo, she lies here in the dust,
and her memory fills me with grief;
Silent is the tongue of Memory,
and the hand of elegance is now at rest
Gone forever is the sound of mirth;
The kind, the candied, the meek, is now no more.
Who can express our grief?
Flow, ye tears of woe!
FROM A HIGHLAND EPITAPH, IN THE GRAVEYARD OF
GLENORCHY KIRK, DALMALLY, ARGYLE AND BUTE
Translated from Gaelic

Unchosen

> When someone dies, it can be like finding ourselves in a play, having never read the script, or sitting an exam we've never studied for. We have to try to make sense of something that often makes absolutely no sense.'
> Lyons and Winter[1]

> Bereavement is what happens to you; grief is how you feel; mourning is what you do.
> Dr Richard Wilson[2]

> As humans, we naturally try to avoid suffering, but contrary to all our instincts, to heal our grief we need to allow ourselves to feel the pain; we need to find ways to support ourselves in it, for it cannot be escaped ... grief is a process that has to be worked through – and experience has taught me that grief is work, extremely hard work; but, if we do the work, it can work for us by enabling us to heal.
> Julia Samuel[3]

☠☠☠

Unspoken

Devon, 1979

> Deaths that are wrapped in tragedy or traumatic events aren't just grief: they are trauma and grief combined.[4]
> Cariad Lloyd

It is September, a new academic year. I have left junior school behind and crossed the road (literally) to the seniors. New shoes, new uniform, new bag. New type of school too. No more nuns. Now it is an independent Christian school. With a headmaster. Strict. Scary. Unapproachable.

Since Dad's death, money is more of an issue than ever.[5] Before the nuns left, Mum went to see the Mother Superior to say she could no longer afford to keep me at the school. Sister Kathleen was compassionate. She wanted me to stay. She understood that I needed familiarity and continuity at a time of such personal chaos. She searched for a charity that could help financially and found the Royal Pinner School Foundation (now the Royal Pinner Educational Trust),[6] who provide assistance in the education of the children of commercial travellers where need can be shown. Because Dad had been an electrical salesman, they offered to pay all my school fees plus a little money each term to go towards uniform etc. After O levels, when I attended the local comp for sixth form, this small grant continued. It continued until I left university.

(Thank you, Sister Kathleen.)

Almost nine months since Dad died and still no one has spoken to me about it. When new friends ask about him, I tell them he is working away from home. I can't physically say the words: *He is dead. He died.* I can't do it.

I don't speak to anyone about him until I am fifteen and have a boyfriend. Simon. He listens and comforts me as I cry. By now, Mum has remarried. I have a stepfather, Ralph. He has four grown-up children who all went to boarding school so he isn't used to having a teenager at home. I'm not a bad teenager. All I want is to be able to go out with Simon – to the cinema, his house, bowling. But I have to be in by 10.30. I even have to leave *The Return of the Jedi* before the end just so I can meet my curfew. Even when I turn eighteen, I am told when to be back. So I cannot wait to go to university. I choose northern and London universities so I can go far away. Make my own life. Make my own decisions. Have some control over a life which doesn't really seem to be mine.

After my A level results, I am offered a place at Lancaster, six hours on the train. Ironically, at the time I am old enough to live my own life, the boy who has saved me emotionally will no longer be with me. He gets into Chester, which isn't so far, but we don't last long. Not even until Christmas (though we are still friends, even now). I meet a boy I fall in love with. But we are young. I don't know what to do with this love. Nor does he. I can feel myself getting in too deep and end it. And that is when I meet my future husband. A cool, political Londoner who is JCR president. After ten weeks we get engaged and a few months after graduation we are married. I have a family. I am safe.

☠☠☠

Unique

> Celebrate the uniqueness if you can. It's not a negative, it's just how it is, it's what made up your relationship with them.
> Cariad Lloyd[7]

Just like death itself, grief is universal, a part of life, but we all experience it differently. And therein is the heart of the matter – we are all individuals, we are all unique, we all grieve in our own way. Models of grief have not always reflected this. Freud advised the bereaved to get over it and move on (or words to that effect). Swiss-American psychiatrist Elisabeth Kubler-Ross wrote about the five (or seven or nine) 'stages of grief' (1969). But this was in reference to people living with life-limiting illness – the model was not meant to describe grief following the death of a loved one. Without considering individuality or culture, this model became ambushed by many in the grief community. It also made people believe they were doing grief wrong. Then there was the 'dual process model'[8] (1999), where the griever moves back and forth between two different modes of functioning: the 'loss-oriented' mode is where they focus on the loss and process emotions connected to the loss and the 'restoration-oriented' mode is where they focus on adjusting to life after loss. This model is more flexible, but there are others which offer still more flexibility, such as Lois Tonkin's 'growing around grief' model, which says that your grief will not go away in time; it will stay the same size. But you can grow a new life which accommodates the loss.[9]

Tonkin's Model of Grief
Growing around grief

Your life → Time →

[Three pots labeled "Grief" with increasingly large plants growing out of them]

https://www.cruse.org.uk/understanding-grief/effects-of-grief/growing-around-grief/

At some point, we will all lose a loved one. Every day, whether expected or unexpected, thousands die, half a million a year in England alone. Julia Samuel says that, on average, each death affects at least five people, and so millions will be faced with grief:

> They will forever remember where they were when they heard that parent, or sibling, or friend, or child was dying or had died. It will impact on every aspect of their world for the rest of their lives and ultimately alter their relationship with themselves. How successfully they manage their grief will, in turn, come to touch all the family and friends around them.[10]

And yet, death is the last great taboo and grief is profoundly misunderstood and 'it is so frightening, even alien, for many of us that we cannot find the words to voice it'.[11]

This silence is deafening. I know. It is all you can hear when grief visits. People might use euphemisms for death such as 'passed away', 'lost', 'in a better place', but this does not help. But, if we face up to death, we can deal better with our grief. It is not the actual pain of grief that damages us – that is a normal process through which we all must go. But rather it is the things we do – 'even whole families, sometimes for generations' – to avoid that pain.[12]

And it's not always a 'loved one' that we grieve the loss of. Life is complicated. We don't always have good relationships with the people around us so when someone dies, it can throw up complex feelings. 'We can grieve the relationship we wanted to have, rather than the one we actually had.'[13]

Whatever you do, be gentle with yourself. 'Self-care might feel too ambitious. Self-maintenance is doing whatever it takes to get by. Some days, that might be just getting out of bed and opening the blinds.'[14]

☠☠☠

Untimely

Lancaster, 1987

> Research studies show that unresolved grief is at the root of 15 per cent of psychiatric referrals.[15]

Grief is messy. Nearly a decade after Dad's death, I am still stuck in the thick of it. I am yet to find a new normal. I don't actually know what 'normal' is. It is so painful I cannot feel, like coming in from the snow. Frozen. I'm still frozen; I haven't even begun to thaw out.

When I return to Lancaster after the Christmas break of my second year, I bring with me a new grief, a double grief, following the loss of my aunt and cousin in a road traffic accident. Added to the grief of my dad and that of my grandpa, this adds up to a really big 'grief-mess'.[16]

Trauma, multiple losses, unresolved grief has made my response to bereavement complicated. Suicide has added a whole range of other emotions to navigate. Out-of-order (or untimely) death – my little eight-year-old cousin – has deepened my trauma to the depths where I am struggling to manage everyday life. I have never consciously looked for answers to my predicament, but now I wonder if I should. Haven't I spent long enough, squashing down the feelings, the words to express them? Is it time to share my story with someone who might actually help?

I go to the doctor at the campus health centre. I tell him I can't sleep. He prescribes sleeping pills. They don't work. I still lie awake for hours at night and find it difficult to function in the day. I go back. He prescribes stronger sleeping pills. They take the edge off. I get a few hours of oblivion. And this begins a skirmish with sleeping pills that will turn into full-scale war later in time.

Niall suggests I see a counsellor. I agree to go if he comes with me. The counsellor is a nice man, but I can't voice my emotions, I can't even find my emotions they are so wrapped up in a tangled mess. He says I should come back when I feel able to talk. He says he'll put a message in my pigeonhole in a few weeks to see how I am doing. He never does. I don't go back to therapy for another twenty-four years.

I take up rugby instead.

Unsaid

London, 1990s

> Words left unspoken can disrupt and damage, they can become bigger and more troublesome as silent intruders in our minds. We need to find a way to release them, to say them or to write them.[17]

When most of our peers are enjoying the hedonism of Britpop, Niall and I are busy – he with politics, me with babies. By the time we have packed in three children, I have given up teaching, as childminder fees are more than my salary. Niall is head of the regeneration of Peckham and becomes the youngest leader of a council. We are skint. He is out most nights. I am alone with three babies, one of whom is sick. This period of my life is a blur. Looking back, I can see I was depressed, but I didn't know it then. I go to see a doctor after I have millennium flu as I am not getting better by the end of spring. She offers me anti-depressants, but I don't know why. It is my body failing, not my mind. It's lack of sleep. It's not having enough support. I can't be depressed. I have everything I ever wanted. I don't deserve to be depressed.

But at seven stone, with gaunt cheeks and visible bones, no sleep, exhaustion, I am burnt out. I am ill.

Unexplained

Teignmouth, 2007

> No one ever told me that grief felt so like fear. I am not afraid, but the sensation is like being afraid. The same fluttering in the stomach, the same restlessness, the yawning. I keep on swallowing.
> C.S. Lewis[18]

Many psychologists and therapists believe that trauma is held in the body. My lived experience concurs. Since having the flu, in the depths of which I wanted to die, I have never fully recovered. We live in Worthing now. We have no family near apart from my great-auntie Ruth, who has never had children, and some neighbours who can be called on in an emergency. No one who can take the burden. I have phases of complete lethargy, exhaustion. I have sleepless nights. Not run-of-the-mill-baby sleepless nights; I can barely make more than twenty minutes of sleep in any stretch of the night. I am never fully awake. Never fully present. I live a half-life of fog. Brain fog. Body fog. All over, top-to-toe fog. And I feel alone in this fog.

In 2005, we move to Devon to be nearer Mum, who is caring for my stepfather, who has advancing Alzheimer's. Following a long period of anticipatory grief[19] for the family, Ralph dies in 2007. I take this surprisingly badly. Despite my eighteen-year-old being desperate to leave family life behind for the freedom of university, Ralph clapped at my graduation. He walked me down the aisle. He has played an important part in my life for nearly twenty-five years. But now, in death, the hierarchy of grief hits me. I feel I don't have the right to grieve. I'm not a proper daughter. I don't know where I fit.

In 2009, my lovely, amazing nan dies. Weighing just three-and-a-bit pounds at her birth in 1918, baby Barbara Box wasn't expected to last the night. She made it to ninety-one, after an adventure-filled life, though not without her own losses. After forty-two years of marriage, Grandpa died of cancer in 1982. In time, she met and remarried David. But, just weeks after their wedding, her world was rocked when her little granddaughter Siobhan died.

Eventually, after Nan's death, I reach out for help. I accept the antidepressants offered by my GP. I take the zopiclone to help me sleep, to get me through. After weeks of numbness, my mood lifts, just enough. I sleep, just enough. But the fog, the fatigue, they carry on. And there is the pain. Unexplained pain in my hands, my feet, my neck, my shoulder. Headaches. Sore throats. I always feel like I am on the cusp of a cold, an infection. I fall over sometimes, loss of balance and vertigo. One day, I wake up and cannot move my head. I think I've had a stroke, but it is labyrinthitis. But I must get up every morning. I must take the kids to school, to ballet, to music lessons, gymnastics, friends' houses. I must keep going.

Over time, three years, the dosage of my antidepressants has been increased to the maximum, but then I am told there is new evidence that the top dose of citalopram can cause heart problems. Because the lower dose hadn't been enough, it is decided that, because the drugs are both SSRIs and work in the same way, I will do a direct switch – stopping the citalopram one day and starting sertraline the following day. In retrospect, a cross-tapering would perhaps have been better; as soon as I stop the citalopram, and because I am not starting on a high dose of sertraline, I have immediate withdrawal symptoms.

D IS FOR DEATH

Unremitting

'Prolonged grief disorder or complicated grief is when intense, long-lasting symptoms of grief, together with ongoing problems and difficulties in coping with life, go on for more than six months after someone dies.'[20]

Complicated grief (CG) can follow an unexpected or sudden death of someone close to us – a partner, a parent, a child, a sibling, a close friend. We can feel overwhelming pain as we fixate on the deceased. We can feel bitter and isolated. We can struggle with life. It impacts our health, school, work, relationships. We might even feel it is not worth living without that person when all we can think about is them. It doesn't get any better.

This prolonged grief differs from the usual grieving process, affecting about 7 per cent of bereaved people. It affects the amygdala and can cause avoidance behaviours. You are numb. Detached. Unable to trust. As with major depression, complex feelings can lead to hopelessness and suicidal thoughts. But, whereas depression is a mood disorder caused by chemical imbalances in the brain, complicated grief is caused by the death of a loved one. And, whereas depression has different forms, there is only one type of complicated grief. Behaviour might also differ: people suffering from depression might not seek help, but people suffering from CG might want to talk about their loved one. And CG should be easier to recognise as it is connected to a specific event, i.e., a death – though, if a long time has passed, others might not make the link. Not forgetting that depression/anxiety can happen at the same time as bereavement.

So what are the risk factors that make 'normal' grief complex?

If our loved one died in a sudden or traumatic way.

If we were disconnected from them when they died.

If we have experienced other losses, particularly at an early age.

If we have multiple bereavements or other losses, such as the loss of a home or marriage.

If we have difficult family relationships, especially when we were young.

If we experienced childhood trauma.

If we suffer from anxiety, depression or insomnia.

Complicated grief can also increase our risk of chronic disease or substance abuse.

Nothing is normal. But there is help. There are people to talk to and cry with. Family, friends, community, a support group can all help us feel less isolated and give us a new perspective.

Bereavement counselling can help us explore emotions and deal with our thoughts. Grief therapy can help us retell the story of our loved one's death to enable us, not to move on, but to find a way of living alongside our grief.

If we already suffered from depression, GP-prescribed anti-depressants can help rebalance the brain.

Significant dates might always trigger grief, but if we know that we can work on being kind to ourselves as those dates approach.[21]

As Samuel says: 'Love from others is key in helping us to survive the love we have lost.'[22]

☠☠☠

Undone

Selworthy, 2012

> Traumatic grief comes from a sudden or unexpected death which may be through suicide, murder or war. It can be overwhelming.
> Julia Samuel[23]

Driving across Saddleworth Moor has reminded me of the medieval belief in the importance of a body. Poor Keith Bennett's little bones still buried out there in the bleakness. His brother, Alan, has talked about the 'pain, anguish and distress' that 'runs right through all Keith's siblings and then filters down through the next generations'.[24]

Traumatic, complicated grief.

Largely alone, I have carried the burden of my traumatic, complicated grief for nearly thirty-five years. A year before, I had a hysterectomy after months of heavy blood loss. Now, in the dark days of January – always difficult for me (unsurprisingly when you remember the Winter of Discontent when that ten-year-old girl returns to school after the holidays, a dead dad hidden inside her) – as my serotonin plummets during my medication switch, I have what can only be described as a breakdown.

I do not remember which dark January day it was, but let's say it's a Tuesday. When the kids are home from school, I give them their tea. Because they are now seventeen, sixteen and fourteen, I can leave them for a while until Niall is back from work.

I write a note. I can't remember what it says exactly. Just that I am going away for a bit and that I love them all. I do remember writing it inside a card with a picture of the seaside on it. I remember putting it in an envelope and leaving it next to Niall's side of the bed.

I put on my coat, get in the car and drive away. I can't even remember if

I say goodbye. All I remember is driving. I don't know where I am going. I just drive. Northwards. Past Exeter. Past Tiverton. Through Dunster. And then onto Exmoor. Across Exmoor. And I find myself driving up the hill, a familiar hill so, although it is in almost total darkness, scattered houses, no traffic, I know my way to the white church at the top. I park in the car park. I sit still for a while. With the car heating off, it is getting cold. I get out into full darkness, the wind whipping around me. I head to the bottom graveyard and find my dad's stone. I touch the leaded letters that Mum ordered all those years before so they would not erode in the harsh Exmoor weather up on this exposed hill. Stephen Nigel Stenner. I lay down, my head on his stone like a pillow and my body folds in on itself.

I don't know how long I have been here. But it is very cold. So cold. (January, I really do not like you.) The wind whistles through the trees. An owl hoots. My ancestors comfort me. And then there are headlights. Voices. The clunk of a gate latch. And there is my husband and best friend with a flask of tea and custard doughnuts. They have found me even though I had no idea I was lost.

☠☠☠

Understanding

> The grieving process can be hindered by (often unspoken) feelings of blame, insufficient information and understanding about suicide, and others not knowing what to say or how to help. Family members are left isolated, pondering questions such as: 'If you loved me, how could you do this to me and leave me with this mess?' In addition, the loss of whatever the future might have held has a more powerful impact when a death is by suicide, as a decision was made by the person they love to have no future at all.
> Julia Samuel[25]

The morning after, my friend takes me to my GP, who decides to bring in the crisis team. I visit them in their office that afternoon. I can't remember much except that this happens in a building I have passed so many times over the years and had no idea people like me were helped here. They decide I am not at risk of suicide – mainly because I am a mother and I know the havoc suicide wreaks on children. They can see a drop in serotonin has affected me. They up the dose of sertraline and visit me the next day at home, where I am feeling a little better, though the events of the last couple of days feel surreal and I am turned inside out. Did that really happen? How did I end up in Selworthy? On Dad's grave? At midnight?

The crisis team is happy to sign me off as long as I continue to see my GP weekly and start therapy. But, firstly, I am referred to a psychiatrist. Because

Niall has private health insurance at work, I am seen quickly. A nice bloke. He says I can carry on with the zopiclone. You're only supposed to take it for a couple of weeks, but it has been three years. Not every night, but three or four a week, so I have some good nights. The benefits outweigh the drawbacks. This is reassuring, as it is something that gnaws at the edge of my consciousness. I am nearly the age Dad was when he died. The psychiatrist tells me I am not at risk of suicide, but suggests a local psychotherapist who he believes will be a good fit.

And she is. After one session, I am finally able to talk. We go back to the start.

Unfinished

> Believing life has some meaning is a significant factor in happiness, and provides protection in adversity. People who can find meaning by keeping a sense of the presence of the person who has died inside themselves, often feeling them in their spiritual being, are better able to continue living, even without their loved one's physical presence.
> Julia Samuel[26]

> You can still love the person who has died in their absence. The feelings you have for them have not died, your relationship with them has just changed. You can continue your connection to them by establishing rituals that mean something to you.
> Lyons and Winter[27]

The theory and practice of 'continuing bonds' was developed in 1996 by Klass, Silverman and Nickman as a response to the current grief models, which advocated the grieving person detaching themselves from their lost one and building a new life without them, in particular with reference to children grieving the loss of a parent. Love carries on. If you loved them in life, this is your connection to them in death. You are separated physically but, in their absence, you can still connect with them emotionally. Your love hasn't changed. Love doesn't change. It cannot die.

What can you do to continue bonds with your lost person?
- Cook a favourite meal you used to share.
- Nurture your memories. Take time over them.
- There is some evidence that the actions in rituals may release endorphins, which can ease anxiety and provide a sense of well-being.[28] Wear a special piece of jewellery, or an item of clothing that belonged to them, travel to a special place.

- Light a candle. Put your hand on your heart and speak to your person, tell them how much you love them.
- Carry them with you. Take a photo or an object that belonged to them.
- Make a quilt, a piece of artwork, a garden.
- Plant a tree. Watch it grow. Feel the earth in your fingers and under your nails. Remember everything has its season.
- Play music – it might be raw, but you will *feel*.
- Write a letter to them. What did you most appreciate about them? Read the letter out loud. Watch it float away on water on its journey somewhere. Or burn it as an offering. Were there things that you are angry about? Write it down, then burn it as a symbol that these negative feelings have no more power over you. Bury the ashes in the ground. Plant something beautiful over them.
- Say their name. Breathe deeply as you feel their love.
- Remember those who went before. They are in your eyes, the way you walk, your smile.
- Remember what you learned from them. Then think about yourself, those qualities and gifts you have inherited and how these impact others.

Unbounded

On Boxing Day 2008, Harold Pinter's *No Man's Land* reopens at the Duke of York in the West End. As the title suggests, the play is set in a mysterious limbo between reality and dream, life and death. The actors pay tribute to Pinter from the stage following his death from cancer on Christmas Eve. To a tearful audience, Michael Gambon, who is playing Hirst, says his monologue about the faces in a photograph album, while, on the other side of the Atlantic, Broadway will dim its lights.

I studied *The Birthday Party* during my first year at Lancaster as part of the unit on post-modern British plays, but knew little about Pinter. The only son of Jewish immigrants, he was a giant of the theatre, and became a political activist in later years, outspoken on matters of war and terror: 'What would Wilfred Owen make of the invasion of Iraq? A bandit act, an act of blatant state terrorism, demonstrating absolute contempt for the conception of international law?'[29]

The previous August, during the run of *No Man's Land* in Dublin, the famed playwright sat down with his wife Antonia Fraser and selected the readings for his funeral. During dinner one night, Pinter asked Michael Gambon if he would read the monologue. The following January, during the intimate graveside gathering at Kensal Green, his chosen pieces are read out. They reflect Pinter's 'abiding concerns' of 'memory, mortality, passion, politics and cricket'. Michael Gambon – whose death has been announced on the BBC as I write this – reads four of them, including that monologue which pays tribute to the ghost faces in a photo album.

> You might even see faces of others, in shadow, or cheeks of others, turning, or jaws, or backs of necks, or eyes, dark under hats, which might remind you of others, whom you once knew, whom you thought long dead, but from whom you will still receive a sidelong glance, if you can face the good ghost … They possess all that emotion, trapped. Bow to it. Assuredly it will never release them, but who knows what relief it may bring to them, who knows how they may quicken in their chains, in their glass jars. You think it cruel to quicken them, when they are fixed, imprisoned? No, no. Deeply, deeply, they long to respond to your touch, to your look, and when you smile, their joy is unbounded. So I say to you, tender the dead, as you yourself would be tendered, now, in what you might describe as your life.[30]

Continuing bonds. The importance of a photo. We can continue our relationships with the 'good ghosts' of our past.

☠☠☠

U Are Not Alone

> It helps to hear other people, helps us to connect with each other. When we find those crossover moments, we are no longer isolated, we are no longer alone, we are not the only person this has happened too. What happened to us isn't weird or unfair, it's human. Grief is human. Grief is the price you pay for life.
> Cariad Lloyd[31]

> [A]cknowledge, listen and simply give them time.
> Julia Samuel[32]

What can you do for or say to someone who is grieving?
- Acknowledge the death. Say something, even if you're not sure what. Say something clichéd, rather than nothing at all.
- Write a message in a card, a note, an email, a text.
- Send flowers or a comfort box.
- Offer practical help but be specific – you could pick up the kids from school, walk the dog, do the shopping or take them shopping, put the bins out.
- Remember we all grieve differently.
- Remember it's not about you.
- Don't judge.

- Listen. Listen more than you talk.
- Let them cry.
- Be present.
- Be patient.
- Walk with them.
- Ask open-ended questions.
- Talk about the deceased.
- If they died by suicide, don't ask them 'how?'. Instead, ask about the person who lived.
- Say their name.
- Share good memories.
- Remember special days.
- Gently encourage them to take care of themselves.
- Remember you can't fix it, but you can accompany them.

Until

> 'Time doesn't necessarily heal but it can give us a different and new normal, one that we can fill with life and living to allay the intense pain of our grief. We may even be able to find joy and happiness again.'
> *Lyons and Winter*[33]

If you are struggling, there is help.
And there are things you can do to help yourself.

- Take a break from grief – watch a funny film, read an absorbing book, go for a windy walk and breathe deep.
- Focus on things you can control – how you think, how you care for your body, having some routines. This can be comforting.
- Take some time to live in the moment. Watch the clouds. Walk in the park. Smell the coffee.
- Do something you enjoy without feeling guilty.
- Remember it's OK to have a bad day.
- Cry for as long as you need.
- Let it rain.
- Fill some of the emptiness with volunteering or joining a support group.
- Do a random act of kindness. Helping others can lift your spirits.
- As you move forward through grief, celebrate the small changes of a healthy grief process. Be proud of yourself.
- It's OK to be happy sometimes.

Cruse Bereavement Support Helpline:
To help you make sense out of how you are feeling after a bereavement.
Call 0808 808 1677 (check website for opening hours)
https://www.cruse.org.uk/get-support/helpline/

Griefcast is a podcast hosted by Cariad Lloyd 'that examines the human experience of grief and death – but with comedians, so it's cheerier than it sounds'. Each week she talks to a different comedian about their experience of grief. In her book *You Are Not Alone*, she describes her first episode where her guest was able 'to talk about that person without shame or embarrassment or fear about bringing death into the room. Death was welcomed in and given tea and cake.'[34]

At a Loss
UK's bereavement signposting website, helping bereaved people find support and wellbeing. From bereavement to funerals. Local and national.
https://www.ataloss.org/

Bereavement Support Payment
https://www.gov.uk/bereavement-support-payment

Unsaid
You can email your unsaid words to submissions@lifedeathwhatever.com and they will be displayed anonymously on the website or socials.
https://www.lifedeathwhatever.com/unsaid

Five Things
A collection submitted by people with lived experiences of illness, cancer, dying, funerals, grief, suicide, baby loss, addiction and so much more.
https://www.lifedeathwhatever.com/five-things

V

IS FOR VALHALLA

The Afterlife

Valhalla *noun*
1. hall of the fallen, the great hall in Norse mythology where the souls of heroes slain in battle are received.
2. a place of honour, glory or happiness.
3. heaven.

But that the dread of something after death –
The undiscover'd country, from whose bourn
No traveller returns – puzzles the will.
HAMLET

Here lie the remains of
JAS. PADY, brickmaker,
late of this parish,
in hopes that his clay will be remoulded in a workmanlike manner,
far superior to his former perishable materials.
Keep death and judgment always in your eye
Or else the devil off with you will fly.
And in his kiln with brimstone ever fry.
If you neglect the narrow road to seek,
You'll be rejected like a half-burnt brick.
IN AWLISCOMBE CHURCHYARD, DEVON

V IS FOR VALHALLA

[T]he history of the afterlife is the history of our hopes that there will be something after death and of our fears that there will be nothing.
Philip Almond[1]

Believing your person survives in some form in the afterlife can be comforting in your grief when everything is chaotic and out-of-sorts. In 'B Is for Bone', we looked at how Christians from the Middle Ages would pray for the dead, hoping to help them on their way – preferably – to Heaven. They could even pay money to have prayers said for themselves after death, maybe even in a special building called a chantry. And in 'D Is for Disposal' we saw how Sikhs and Hindus scatter their ashes on a flowing river which will carry away the ashes to the sea, symbolising the passage from this life to the next. Religions and culture play their part in how we see ourselves, the world, the afterlife. This can be a help or a hindrance.

☠☠☠

Northumbria, 627

In his *Ecclesiastical History of the English People*, the Venerable Bede writes of King Edwin of Northumbria, who, in 627, discussed Christianity with friends and counsellors. One of his men came up with an image of the afterlife which nicely illustrates our ignorance of it: a sparrow flies in one end of a candle-lit hall and then out the other. For its brief time inside, the bird is safe from the cold winter. But all too soon it disappears back outside. 'So this life of man appears for a little while but of what is to follow or what went before we know nothing at all.'[2]

Academic Philip Almond says that in the West, since the time of the Ancient Greeks and Hebrews (*c.* seventh century BC), we have imagined the afterlife – both after our individual deaths and after the end of history. Belief was that the fate of the dead was the same whether you were good or evil in life – 'a shadowy half-life in Hades beneath the earth or its Hebrew equivalent Sheol'. By the time of Christianity, there were two narratives of the afterlife, both arguing that the way you lived in life determined your fate. The first was that life continues immediately after an individual death when the soul was judged and sent either to 'the bliss of Abraham's Bosom' or 'cast into the pit of Hades'. The other narrative argued that our eternal destiny would be determined at the end of the world, when Christ returns to judge both the living and the dead. This meant that there was 'a constantly fluid series of negotiations, contestations and compromises between these two versions of our futures after death'.

Running alongside was the idea of justice after death. A reckoning 'where the righteous would receive their just recompense and the wicked their just deserts, and of punishments and rewards proportionate to vices and virtues'.

But what if you were 'occasionally good but not very good at being really bad'? Should you go to Heaven or Hell? By the fifth century, it was believed that most of us deserved a place between the two. Enter Purgatory. Over the next few centuries, the idea developed of a liminal place between Heaven and Hell 'where the not too wicked could be purged and purified in preparation for Heaven after the Day of Judgment'. This lasted until the Reformation when the ultimate judgment was left to God: Heaven or Hell.

But it was also argued (e.g., by Augustine in the fifth century), that 'God apportioned eternal happiness or everlasting torments merely as the arbitrary act of his own sovereign will, regardless of any person's virtues or vices'. This became a central feature of Calvinist belief from the time of the Reformation so that some made the most of the here and now, while others saw it as 'an incentive to piety, sobriety and accumulation of wealth as proof of election to salvation'. Whichever way you lived, there was no mistaking God's power.

From the seventeenth century, there was a 'gradual transition from a Heaven focused on the vision of God with much playing of harps and casting of crowns upon glassy seas, to Heaven as a place of ongoing activities, moral improvement, travel and reunion with family, friends and pets – a kind of ethereal Club Med'. By the middle of the nineteenth century, Hell 'with its dark fires and gnawing worms, its tormenting and tormented demons' was becoming a less popular idea. Almond argues that this was in part the result of 'the diminution of the public spectacle of punishments, torture and pain in the secular sphere'.[3]

We now live in an increasingly secular world which places its faith in scientific progress. In *Vigor Mortis*, Kate Berridge asserts, 'As the parameters of exploration expand, our stature is continuously diminishing; in relation to the rest of the cosmos, we are confronted by our own insignificance.'[4]

And for some, there remains an existential issue of salvation angst. (More of that to come.)

☠☠☠

Bali, 1993

We've spent the last few days in Bali and, thanks to my stepbrother who lives and works on Java, we've been staying at the Padma, upgraded to the presidential suite with our own swimming pool. Unbelievable and quite unlike our usual holidays in tents or on friends' sofa beds. One night we go to a nightclub at Kuta beach – nine years before it becomes a scene of terror. Back on Java, yesterday, we took a small (and somewhat terrifying) plane from Jakarta to Yogyakarta in the interior of the island. Today we awaken in darkness at a local hotel. A taxi driver takes us through the Kedu Valley to a remote hilltop where we plan to see the famed sunrise from the Borobudur Temple.

V IS FOR VALHALLA

Built in the ninth century, the Borobudur is the world's largest Buddhist Temple, forty-two metres high with ten levels stacked on top of each other. The six lower terrace walls are decorated with stone bas-reliefs illustrating the life and teachings of the Buddha, and details of daily life in ancient Java. The three upper tiers have seventy-two lattice-work stupas,[5] each containing a Buddha – you can see them if you peek inside. Starting at the bottom level, you go anti-clockwise from one platform to the next, from one symbolic plane of consciousness to the next, the journey to enlightenment, until you reach Nirvana, the large central stupa at the top.

Soon after we reach the summit of this sacred place, dawn breaks. The sun rises in spectacular fashion revealing a staggering view – lush green vegetation, volcanos, rice terraces, tropical forest. The silhouetted stupas gleam in the light and we are silent in the grandeur.

Borobudur, Indonesia, 1993

After Life

Our imaginings about the afterlife, both after death and after the end of history, are a testimony to the hope that many have had, and still do, for an extension of life beyond the grave. They speak to the desire for light beyond the darkness of death; for ultimate goodness beyond present evils; and for final justice over earthly inequities. They give voice to the faith that the drama of history, and the minor role that each of us has played in it, has an ultimate meaning and purpose, one that is discernible from the vistas of eternity if not from our present perspective.
Philip Almond

Sigmund Freud said there will always be religion where there is fear of death, and perhaps he was right, given that most religions (and mythologies) have defined beliefs on what happens when and after you die. However, that doesn't mean the concept of the afterlife isn't still debated.

In this chapter, I have some questions. And I can't say that I have the answers because, as of now, I am not dead.

Can belief in an afterlife help us face our own death or the death of loved ones?

Will we be reunited with those who have gone before?

Will we be punished or rewarded for our time on earth?

Can we make amends?

Will our lives continue straight after death, or do we have to wait till the end of time? What will it be like?

Is this it?

NB: These are my thoughts. Forgive me for any misinformation or lack of nuance. I do not want to offend anyone. This is just me, thinking things through, sharing ideas. For this reason, and because it is the text I know the most about, I am focusing on what the Bible has to say about the afterlife. And, because the focus of this book is the UK, there are centuries of history regarding Christianity and the afterlife.

But first, for a little context, back to Bali to start a whistlestop tour of some of the world's religions.

Life After Life

Now a UNESCO world heritage site, the Borobudur is a place of pilgrimage for Mahayana Buddhists, on a par, perhaps, with St Peter's in the Vatican City, the Western Wall in Jerusalem or Stonehenge on Salisbury Plain. As with other global religions, there are different beliefs, concepts, rituals and practices within Buddhism. So, a generalisation: what does the Buddhist tradition say about the afterlife? Most Buddhists believe in *samsara*, the cycle of death and rebirth; after death you are reborn as something and someone different, dependent on your behaviour in life, on good or bad *karma*. Death isn't an end, but rather a continuation. Life to life to life. Ultimately, the greatest hope for Buddhists is liberation from *samsara*, so that *nirvana* can be achieved, an end to suffering (*duhkha*).

Most of us understand death in an abstract way, but only comprehend its reality when someone close to us dies. They are here and then they are not. Buddhists know this life is temporary, that every moment of every day we are undergoing birth and death and rebirth. We are constantly changing. The world around us is constantly changing. There is nothing permanent. So, if there is nothing about us that remains the same, there can be no persisting self. And, if we don't have a separate self, death cannot take anything from us. Death is just one more change. Death is just death. You can't conquer it – even the Buddha (awakened one) couldn't avoid physical death. But if you can be aware – through the practice of mindful meditation – that this is what it is, right here, right now, then you can let go of fear and regret and anxiety.

But if there is no self, what gets reborn life after life? Some say it is helpful to think of a candle that you light from another candle before it burns out. The candles are not identical, but not completely different. But the flame that comes from one candle lives on for a time in the other candle. There is continuity without identity. And then there are those stories of people – often children – who believe they have lived another life. Perhaps they have scars or birthmarks in the same place as the deceased. Perhaps they can describe how the person died. Perhaps they know stuff that they really cannot be expected to know. (When Ed was about four, he asked me 'where is my other family?' I was taken aback, unable to answer straight away. After a moment I asked which family is that, but by then he was busy playing with his Playmobil rubbish lorry, telling me he wanted to work at the tip when he was grown up. Maybe he meant *where were his grandparents?* – they lived far away in Devon and we didn't see them very often. Maybe he meant something else. Who knows?)

Mahayana Buddhism is also practised in Tibet, where some Buddhists, to give them an awareness of death, will closely observe a decaying corpse, applying what they see to their own body, their inevitable future state. Focusing on death and living mindfully in each moment enables you to live fully. And, because death is the ultimate state of impermanence, Buddhists are also encouraged to observe the moment-to-moment of their own dying; instead of worrying about the afterlife, they attend to the dying process. Dying is also an opportunity to influence future birth; a positive state of mind can ensure a good rebirth. As death approaches, someone whispers the name of the Buddha, so this will be the very last word the person hears.

After death, relatives wash the body, wrap it in white cloth and place it in the corner of the family's home until the funeral a few days later. During this time, the first *bardo* state[6] can happen – when the deceased becomes conscious of being dead and the next form of rebirth is decided. For one lineage of Tibetan Buddhists, the *Tibetan Book of the Dead* is read for forty-nine days after death while the deceased goes through a series of *bardo* states, still capable of being influenced.

Because Tibet is mountainous, burying the dead is not easy, and so sky burial (or celestial burial) is the most common method of disposal and an integral part of Tibetan Buddhist beliefs, emphasising impermanence and symbolising the release of the soul from the physical body. The family picks a lucky day for the professional body carrier to take the deceased to the burial site in the mountains, where they dissect it with a blade – done with laughter because Tibetan Buddhists believe this will guide the dead to the next life. Smoke is burned to attract vultures, while lamas chant sutras to redeem the sins of the soul. When the flesh is eaten by vultures (this happens quickly, maybe within an hour), the body breaker smashes the bones into pieces and mixes them with *tsampa* (flour) to feed the 'holy birds', so that nothing remains and the soul can move on.

There are other types of burial in Tibet: fire burial (cremation), water burial, tree burial, and cliff burial – used for those of a higher status, in places without vultures, for children, or in different regions. Earth burial is inferior and now rarely practised, reserved for those who die from infectious disease or murderers, as these bodies are not clean enough to be presented to the vultures, which are holy birds.

Stupa burial is reserved for those of the highest status such as the Dalai Lama. The embalmed corpse is dehydrated, wrapped with rare herbs and spices and placed in the stupa, which can be elaborate or simple, depending on the deceased. The Buddha himself instructed that his body be cremated, and the relics distributed amongst his followers and enshrined in various burial mounds. (The largest stupa in the world is the Borobudur.)

Hinduism is the largest religion in India, home to the majority of Hindus worldwide. Most Hindus also believe in samsara, that when a person dies, their atman (soul) is reborn in a different form, human or animal. Some believe rebirth happens directly at death, others that an *atman* may exist in other realms. Hindus do believe in distinct places – *swarg* and *narak* – where souls go for a period before rebirth, but they are different to the Judeo-Christian Heaven and Hell. These are higher and lower worlds, physical places bound by time and space, not somewhere for souls to reside forever. Hindus also believe in *karma* – that good or bad actions in life determine the soul's rebirth.[7]

Death is part of the cycle to attain oneness with Brahman, when a soul achieves complete contentment and separates from human desires. So, death is something to celebrate, not mourn. If the soul has not learned how to separate itself from its humanness, then the *atman* is reborn so it can continue learning.

☠☠☠

Like Hindus, Sikhs believe in reincarnation and *samsara*. The purpose of life is to move closer to *Waheguru* – God who is genderless and eternal – and to gain enlightenment through meditation and the teachings of the gurus. Many believe there are millions of different possible life forms that they might have to experience before liberation (*mukti*) from the cycle of *samsara*. To reach *mukti*, a Sikh must get rid of bad *karma* and focus on gaining good *karma* so they must live their lives with *Waheguru* always in mind.

After death, the physical body is no longer needed so cremation is the norm, with the ashes scattered over water. Burial is possible, but without headstone or monument. Sikhs do not believe in Heaven or Hell, but that good or bad actions in this life determine the life form into which a soul takes rebirth.

Towers of Silence

Towers of Silence (*dakhma* in Farsi) are architectural structures where Zoroastrians traditionally perform their last rites. As with Tibetan sky burials, corpses are exposed for vultures to pick the flesh off the bones. Zoroastrians believe that the body is impure following the last breath, because death is the work of Angra Mainyu, the evil spirit. The earth is a beautiful work of God, so contaminating it with decay is sacrilege. No trace must be left.

In the West, where exposure is either impractical or illegal, Zoroastrians must compromise their traditions and usually opt for cremation. In Mumbai, where over half of India's Parsis live, the *dakhmas* of Doongerwadi are in a fifty-four-acre area of exclusive Malabar Hill. But there is a big problem: not so much the threat of urbanisation, but the rapid decline in the vulture population, which has almost been wiped out by a toxic livestock drug (now banned). The alternative is to use solar concentrators which desiccate the corpse but, although this process helps maintain the religious importance of the land ('real estate goldmine'), it is not as fast as a flock of hungry vultures. 'No Parsi would want the mystic eye of the vulture to be replaced by the rapacious one of the land shark.'[8]

Muslims believe that this life is temporary and that there is an eternal life after death when a person's soul moves on to another world. Islam means submission. Submission to God's will is the way to earn God's blessing. Muslims are reminded constantly of the eternal consequences of how they live. According to Mark Berkman, no scripture devotes as much attention as the Quran in describing the torments of Hell and the delights of Paradise. You must never forget about God; rituals such as prayers are a reminder to return to God. In this fleeting life, the only constant is God, who is compassionate and merciful and from whom we can take hope that we will be brought back to him in the end. The moment the spirit of life is blown by an angel into your embryo, the day of your death is written. Only God permits you to die, therefore suicide and euthanasia are forbidden.

When you are dying your face is turned towards Mecca, and when you breathe your last, the angel of death takes your soul from your body until the resurrection. Your body belongs to God and must be treated with dignity. After ritual washing, you are dressed in a shroud, preferably the one you wore to perform Hajj (pilgrimage), funeral prayers are said and you will be buried quickly, on your right side.

While you are in the grave there is an intermediate period – pleasant or unpleasant (unless you are a martyr, when you go straight to Paradise). Two angels visit every grave and ask two questions: whom have you worshipped? Who was your prophet? If you answer correctly, you can rest in comfort, with a view of Paradise, until the Day of Judgement. If you answer incorrectly, you'll be tormented by the angels and sealed in cramped graves, stung and bitten by scorpions, viewing the horrors of Hell that await. On Judgement Day, the soul is reunited with a new body to stand in judgement before God. Males and females are judged equally, each person accountable for themselves. The right beliefs and the right actions are needed for Paradise. There is no doctrine of justification by faith alone or concept of original sin. Instead, there is a weighing. A balancing. Intentions are also judged. God will respond to genuine repentance. Then you will be sent to Heaven or Hell. Paradise is peace, bliss, refuge. A garden with flowing water and meadows, food and drink in abundance. It is a sensory delight. The spiritual reward is spending eternity in the presence of God. Husbands and wives remain together, which is different to Christian belief that there is no marriage in Heaven. Hell is a place of fire, with no escape from pain or regret, with boiling water to drink and food that chokes, so bad that you will pray for annihilation. There is hope that this will not be eternal, because it is said that it is for as long as Heaven and earth endure, *unless your lord wills otherwise.*

Obviously there are varying beliefs within Islam, but all Muslims believe in the importance of the awareness of death in everyday life. You should reflect on your mortality each night as you lay in bed, sleeping on your right side as if in the grave. If you should die in your sleep, you must be in a condition of purity.

Do good deeds. Prepare. Your time is coming.

☠☠☠

Summerland

Modern Paganism embraces a wide variety of spiritual beliefs revolving around the sacredness of the natural world. Some believe that after death there will be reincarnation or a union of the spirit with nature or an otherworld of the spirits (sometimes called Summerland). Others believe there is no life after death; we should focus on living this life on earth and the interconnectedness of all life – an appropriate aspect of religion as we face a human-created climate emergency which could lead to mass extinction.

Recently, I walked up to the ancient standing stones of Mitchell's Fold in Shropshire. The biggest of these was encircled by offerings of some kind – small corn rings, posies, feathers. A ritual had taken place. I could feel that this was a sacred place for the person leaving the offering. Though Paganism is becoming more accepted and followed, there is still a 'countercultural' feel about it, associated as it has been with witchcraft, 'hippies' and environmental protests. But maybe for this reason, and because of its inclusivity, it appeals to women, young people and those from the LGBT+ community.

The green man on Charles III's coronation invitation

This Life

An atheist does not believe in any god. Death is an end, a full-stop. You cease to exist. There is no afterlife or reincarnation. A good life and good death are what count. Because life passes quickly, you should spend your time wisely. Your culture will play a part in this. While atheism is merely the absence of belief, humanism is a positive attitude to the world, centred on human history, personal experience, thought, and hopes. Humanists believe the world is a natural place with no supernatural beings. Science and reason are the best ways to answer questions about the world. This life is our only one. Make the most of it. Make it meaningful. Make it ethical. Humans have evolved to have moral capacities and, while you should be free to decide how to live, consider the consequences of your actions and do no harm to others. We are all responsible for making the world a better place. Live a fulfilling life and don't worry about what will happen after death.

Sheol, Hades, Gehenna and Hell

According to Mark Berkson, in keeping with the tradition of diversity of opinion and debate, there is no officially agreed view of the afterlife in Judaism. He says that, out of the three [9]Abrahamic faiths today, Jews are the least concerned with the afterlife. This is true, he argues, in both the USA and Israel (which combined have 83 per cent of the world's Jewish population). According to surveys in recent years, 38–46 per cent of American Jews claim to believe in an afterlife, with only 16 per cent being absolutely sure. In a 2012 survey, some 56 per cent of Israeli Jews said they believed in an afterlife. Compare this to 86–90 per cent of American evangelical Christians, 82 per cent of Catholics and 85 per cent of American Muslims. As for Muslims in Asia, the Middle East and North Africa, it is almost 90–99 per cent (depending on the country). It could be claimed that Judaism puts greater emphasis on people's actions in life than on contemplating what might happen after death.

In the Hebrew Bible, God's covenant with the people of Israel does not promise an afterlife, though many believe in *olam ha-ba* (the world to come) – a perfect world at the end of days, after the Messiah comes and God has judged the living and the dead. In Old Testament books, such as Isaiah and Psalms, *Sheol* is mentioned, though without a detailed description. It seems to refer to an underworld where people go after death – 'a land of thick darkness, of shadow, nethermost pit in the deeps' without reward or punishment. More a diminishment of life than an annihilation. When the Hebrew scriptures were translated into Greek around 200 BC, the word *Hades* substituted *Sheol*. According to Steve Chalke, the Apostle Paul would have known other Second Temple texts in which new ideas were developed. In some, *Sheol* was home to both the righteous and the wicked, separated into respective areas. In others, it was a place of punishment for the wicked dead alone.

Sometimes, the Talmud equates *Sheol* with *Gehenna* – the place Jesus talked about, a cursed place beyond the walls of Jerusalem, notorious for child sacrifices during the reigns of the kings of Judah. In Jesus's time, the valley of Gehenna was a stinking, burning rubbish dump where wild animals fought over rotting food, with snarling and gnashing of teeth. Because the prophets had spoken of Gehenna, Jesus's Jewish audience would have understood this as a metaphor in a way that people may not today.[10] Perhaps Jesus is even the burning fire, purging our badness through the heat of his love.[11] Most English translations have replaced the word *Gehenna* with *Hell*,[12] and so a rubbish tip has evolved into the modern concept of Hell. Quite a leap.

The Valley of the Shadow of Death

> For I am convinced that neither death nor life, neither angels nor demons, neither the present nor the future, nor any powers, neither height nor depth,

nor anything else in all creation, will be able to separate us from the love of God that is in Christ Jesus our Lord.
Paul's letter to the Romans

In his controversial book, *Love Wins*, American writer and theologian, Rob Bell, questions post-Reformation views of Hell and salvation: 'Will only a few select people make it to Heaven and will billions and billions of people burn forever in hell and if that's the case how do you become one of the few?' Is it through 'what you believe or what you say or what you do or who you know or something that happens in your heart? ... Do you have to be baptised or converted or born again?' He believes that, to answer this, you have to understand who God is: 'What we believe about heaven and hell is incredibly important because it exposes what we believe about who God is and what God is like... the good news is that love wins.'

In his book *The Lost Message of Paul*,[13] Steve Chalke continues the conversation about Paul the Apostle 'that has been running since he first burst on to the stage of history, into the market squares of the Roman Empire, and put his pen to paper'. Like other theologians, he believes that Paul's message should be read in context, from first-century Pauline eyes, not from twenty-first-century Western eyes, because, in the intervening centuries, Paul's writing has been weaponised by medieval Catholicism and Reformist Protestants:

> His words have been used to justify cruelty towards and exclusion of black people, people of colour, women, people of other religions, the wrong sort of Christian people (Catholic, Orthodox or Protestant, depending on your point of view), non-believers and of LGBT people, to name but a few... For too many he is the author of structural social exclusion.

In 1215, the bishops of the Latin-speaking Church gathered in Rome for the fourth Lateran Council, where they committed to the doctrine of 'perpetual punishment with the devil' for those unworthy of Christ. Chalke makes a disturbing connection:

> Just as the Church's coffers were beginning to run dry and the Pope found himself searching for new ways to generate much-needed revenue, along comes a doctrine which scares the living daylights out of people by dangling them over an everlasting pit of living death, but then offers them a way out through penance and payment. The creation of fear through the threat of exclusion is a time-tested way of maintaining control.

Blimey.
Perhaps the Western half of the Church has got it wrong. The Orthodox

Church has never focused on Hell but on Christ and the salvation he has brought through the 'Harrowing of Hell' – His triumphant descent into the world of the dead for the three days between crucifixion and resurrection, where he closed Hell, saving those trapped inside. The Harrowing is described in the Bible (1 Peter 3:19–20) and in the Apostles' Creed (the earliest creed recognised by the whole Church, East and West). Chalke is clear here:

> This stunning Eastern picture of the emptying of hell by Christ as an expression of the extraordinary love of God for every single one of us stands in stark contrast to the condemnatory Western medieval Roman Catholic picture of God as a torturing tyrant.

Luther wanted to end the Church's encouragement of good works, which had become a money-making con. Instead, he preached that, to get to Heaven, you had to have your own personal faith in Christ. Chalke argues that Western Christian thought was influenced not only by such Lutheran theology but also by literature and art such as Dante's *Divine Comedy* and the vivid paintings of Bosch and Michelangelo. (Of the *Last Judgement* in the Sistine chapel, Chalke says it is 'sixteenth century social media used to its greatest impact'.) By now, in the west, damnation is seen as everlasting in a physical and spiritual hell.

Terrifying.

And not what Paul preached at all. He never even used the word 'hell'.[14]

Perhaps we should listen again to this man, 'the first-century thinker … shaped by the story of Judaism, influenced by his Hellenized upbringing and revolutionized by his encounter with Jesus'. In particular, we should re-examine Paul's phrase *pistis Christou*. Chalke contends this was intended to refer to the 'faithfulness *of* Christ', but it has been turned into 'faithfulness *to* Christ'. Now this is important. The translation of 'faith *in* Christ' was introduced by the sixteenth-century European reformers. The 'faithfulness of Christ' has been talked about through history by the Eastern Church. A sacrificial, loving faithfulness that led to Jesus's execution by the occupying Romans – a liberation that 'puts the emphasis firmly on Christ's faithfulness to his father's plan as the source of our acceptance by God, rather than on the ups and downs of our faltering faith.' Therefore, Chalke concludes, there should be no more 'salvation angst'.[15]

☠☠☠

Gotta Catch 'Em All

Salvation angst.

Hmm.

V IS FOR VALHALLA

This I understand.

Here I need to tell you something of my Christian faith over the years, which begins in 1972 in a small old-fashioned school in Paignton, where the girls wore boaters and white gloves, and where, every week, the local vicar led assembly. A lovely man, he made a big impact on my brother, Rhys, who heard the Gospel for the first time and which eventually, by a circuitous route, led to him becoming a Baptist minister (now in Atlanta, Georgia).

After assembly, Father C would take tea with the headmistress (a lady who reminded me of Enid Blyton). Father C always admired her silver teapot, unusual in that it had two spouts. One day, when the headmistress was in town, she spotted a teapot in the window of an antique shop. She stopped. It was most definitely hers. She went inside to enquire where it had come from. A vicar brought it in, the dealer said.

Well, this was just the start of it. Events unravelled with Father C ending up in a high-security Dartmoor prison. His crimes had gone much further than the teapot. It turns out that he was a kleptomaniac. Not only had he stolen the bishop's golden chalice and vestments (in which he used to dress up at home), but he also staged a bank robbery, his housekeeper as accomplice, armed with a Mars bar inside a paper bag.

Shock, horror, twist.

One evening, Rhys and I were watching the local news, when there he was, Father C, his crimes laid out for the whole of the West Country. We rushed into the kitchen, at the back of the shop where we were living at the time.

Father C's on the telly!!

Mum's heart sank. She'd been trying to keep the news from us, knowing we'd be upset, but there it was, all over *Spotlight*.

And yes, we were upset, but also quite impressed by his audacity, this quiet, gentle man. This might not seem like an auspicious start on our faith journey but, despite his sins, Father C had always been kind to us. Our family has never forgotten him. It's hard to judge him, as he was clearly suffering with his mental health.

In the following years, while he is in prison, his words stay with us. They resonate at the convent, where the nuns only say nice things about Jesus. And then, at the time of Dad's death, Rhys becomes really involved in the local Baptist church. He has a dramatic conversion and is baptised, becoming immersed in the Bible and church life. Mum and I go along to services on a Sunday evening. Long gone are the days of watching *The Muppets* or visiting Auntie Fay for high tea. Instead, I hear time and time again that I must confess my sins. I must ask God into my heart. But I can't even find my heart. It has been frozen. Every week I hear the good news, which rarely sounds much good coming from the booming voices of shouty preachers, all middle-aged men nothing like my quiet, loving dad.

And then Mum drags me to see the preacher Billy Graham at Ashton Gate in

Bristol. When he urges the crowd to confess their sins and walk to the front, I am terrified. Too terrified to do the walk. Too terrified to stay on my seat. I am frozen.

But why this fear? I believe in God. I always have, for as long as I can remember. But this God is different to the one the nuns told me about. He is vengeful and angry, and if I don't say 'the prayer' I'll be in Hell for ever. Presumably alongside my dad, who never talked about God or went to church. I lay awake in bed at night, terrified that I'll die in the night. That God, who loves me, will turn his back while I end up in the fiery furnace with the Devil, alongside Hitler and Genghis Khan and Jack the Ripper.

Why would God create me for this?

I pray all the time.

I love Jesus.

But my faith isn't real, because I haven't been 'born again' or had an epiphany, which seems impossible when my faith has been there all along.

(Bear with. We will get back to *pistis Christou* and the afterlife.)

This fear has me trapped for years. In London, Niall and I go to the local Baptist church. They are sweet kind people. The minister is gentle and thoughtful. So, we stay. When we have Johnny, they open a crèche just for him. But, when a new minister comes, he is another shouty one and my salvation angst returns. Meanwhile, I am befriended by an old lady who preaches from time to time. There have been women preachers in the Baptist church for decades, but I have never heard a woman preach until now. She is a bit shouty too but, even so, she is kind, and one day I say 'the prayer' with her and apparently I'm born again but I don't feel any different. By now we have three children; on top of my own salvation, I have theirs to worry about. I drag them to Sunday school – in London and then in Worthing – with an unwilling husband who has his own Catholic angst. The message is the same. We are going to Hell in a handcart.

When we move back to Teignmouth, I go to the old Baptist church. A new era. A new minster. Young, thoughtful, engaging, inclusive. I become a member. I join a house group with other women – young, thoughtful, faithful, questioning women – and I find a peace. God is love. Not a wishy-washy hippy love but a love that is strong, powerful, transforming, all-encompassing. This is relevant to me, here and now. Of course women can be preachers! Didn't Jesus first appear to a woman after his resurrection? Mary Magdalene believed straight away that this was her rabbi, her friend, the man she loved and now the God she loved. He told her to spread the good news. He trusted her, a woman at a time when women were not allowed to testify in court, who could be stoned for adultery, who were second-class citizens, to be the first evangelist.

And, while Mary utterly trusted him, the men she told were less faithful. One of them, Thomas, even had to put his hands in the wounds of Jesus before he could believe. So now, two millennia later, in Devon, I know with conviction that women can be preachers. And who are we to crush their God-given vocation?

And what about gay people? Why is homosexuality still seen as a sin? Johnny is gay. He was born gay. As his mother, I know that. Seventeen months apart in age, we brought up our sons the same, but they couldn't be more different. They are both our sons, and we love them equally. We want the same for them. For them to reach their potential. To meet a partner to share their life with. To be happy. To be good people. And yes, I hope they will find a faith that accepts them for who they are, created in God's image, but I also know that God loves them and will not turn His back on them. Ever. Why would God create Johnny and not let him have the same experiences in His creation? How dare we, mere mortals, say what is and what isn't right? But, sadly, people did and people still do. When our church agreed that gay people in a relationship could come into membership, many left. They said they weren't homophobic, but that this wasn't biblical. They dismissed the fact that Jesus said diddly squat about homosexuals. He had far bigger fish to fry, such as power and greed and… and yes, that old chestnut, love. Instead, they (mis)quoted Paul.

Pistos Christou.

We live with the legacy of Luther and Calvin, reformists who believed that salvation was by the grace of God and by our faith. And so our faith must be a gift of God's love. And so God's love must, logically, just be for those people God chooses.

Some of us are chosen and saved. Some of us are on the naughty list, born just to be eternally damned.

> Is salvation little more than a giant geographical lottery? … Would a God of love really create a world where only the Christian minority of the human race are treated with love? Would such a God really be content to consign the vast majority of the population of earth to judgement and then to some kind of hell.[16]

But once you get that *pistis Christou* is about *Christ's* faithfulness, then how good you are at faith is less important. Paul knew that the Jewish people's salvation was built on God's covenant with them; he had redeemed them before and they trusted him to do it again. After his transforming experience on the road to Damascus he saw that, through *Jesus's* faithfulness to his Father's plan, he was the Messiah for the whole world, Jews and Gentiles alike.[17]

☠☠☠

Wrath versus Anguish and Original Sin

Chalke writes of the time he asked Rabbi Jonathan Sacks about God's 'anger'. His answer: 'It is perhaps better, and far more accurate to understand

God's anger as his anguish – a dimension of his love, but never an emotion in opposition to it.' (When Chalke shared this with another rabbi friend, he smiled. 'Well, if you are going to take the Hebrew Bible and build it into your Christian understanding of life, it probably makes sense to ask a Hebrew what the words you are reading might actually mean.') So, Chalke concludes, if God is love, then the way he deals with us comes from love. So why do we put his love alongside wrath? 'But to speak of God's love in the same breath as God's anguish, as an expression of love, makes all the sense in the world.'[18]

As for 'original sin', the Eastern Church has never accepted this idea. Instead, it was developed by Augustine in the fifth century, in the Western Church, and refined at the Reformation. Chalke argues that this is 'a deeply pessimistic view of humanity and a deeply flawed theory' and that the Bible 'starts with original goodness rather than original sin'.[19] 'Sin' is not even mentioned in the story of Adam and Eve. Nor is the devil.

Most theologians now see the creation story as a fable rather than historical narrative, like those from other ancient civilisations. A myth, nonetheless, full of wisdom. Jewish theology interprets the story as the loss of innocence, of growing up, not about the fall of humanity. Why would the God of love give up on us? Aren't we told that God's love is unconditional? That he is a father who loves us? Would you wish this eternity on your children? Yes, we get frustrated and anguished by some of their decisions, but we never stop loving them or wanting the best for them. How much bigger is God than us? Aren't the consequences of wrongdoing punishment enough in the here and now?

And, so, we come to it: if God loves us, will he really throw us into the burning pit of Hell for ever and ever if we don't toe the line? As Chalke says, 'That's not love – it's megalomania.'[20] When Paul says 'love never fails', is this true or not? Does 'never' actually mean 'never'? Will we all get put in the Green Shield stamp book to be exchanged for the prize of everlasting life?

Some might accuse me of being flippant. Some of being a heretic. But this has been part of my daily thoughts for pretty much all of my remembered life. And, for me – post-loss, post-cancer, post-pandemic, post-fifty-five years of life – what it boils down to is something quite simple.

Love.

Steve Chalke has grasped this love and he has lived it through his work with disadvantaged young people. He believes Paul to be 'a revolutionary who saw a new inclusive world dawning and gave his life to help bring it in'. And it was Jesus who started this revolution. (Meek, mild. As if.)[21] He died to absorb sin so that everyone can have eternal life. He took the burden. But this burden wasn't sin in the abstract; it was the heavy weight of 'human pride, sin, folly and shame which, at that moment in history, concentrated themselves in the arrogance of Rome, the self-seeking of the Jewish leaders, and the distorted dreams of the Jewish revolutionaries, and the failures of Jesus' own followers'.[22]

Let's not filter Paul's words through fifth-century, sixteenth-century and twenty-first-century eyes. Let's remember his cultural heritage, immersed in universal redemption, a sense that God would bring judgement and justice and put the whole world right.[23]

And let's remember we are more than our individual self. We are all connected:

> The evils of consumerism, racism, sexism, class, power, inequality, wealth distribution, empire, privilege and entitlement implicate us all. None are free from complicity and a measure of responsibility – despite our best self-justifying stories. Sin and its effects are corporate, communal and complex, not merely personal.[24]

And if we can believe Paul as he spoke two thousand years ago, if we believe Jesus, who spoke to Paul, maybe some of that fear of death and eternal damnation and salvation angst will disappear, enabling us to live a full life here and now.

Here endeth the sermon.

Whatever our beliefs, we can look for comfort to our religion and culture to answer some of the questions facing our own death or grieving the loss of others. And now, as we look to the next chapter, we remember the increase in the popularity of Spiritualism following WW1. A generation in grief, the broken bodies of their sons, brothers, partners lying in 'some corner of a foreign field', keeping a connection with the dead was all that many had to grasp onto.

But, for now, in the words of the late Dave Allen, *Goodnight, thank you, and may your God go with you.*

W

IS FOR WELLINGTON

War

Wellington *noun*
1. meaning 'from the wealthy estate', originally a surname and place name famously borne by Arthur Wellesley as the Duke of Wellington (1769–1852) after his triumph over Napoleon Bonaparte at the Battle of Waterloo.
2. a knee-length waterproof rubber or plastic boot, named after the Iron Duke from 1817 (who also in his lifetime had a style of coat, hat, and trousers named for him as well as a variety of apple and pine tree).
3. beef rolled in pastry named Beef Wellington to celebrate his victory at Waterloo.

Woe, destruction, ruin, and decay;
the worst is death and death will have his day.
RICHARD II

In memory of Phoebe Hessel,
who was born at Stepney in the year 1713.
She served for many years,
as a private soldier in the 5th Regiment of Foot
in different parts of Europe
and in the year 1745 fought under the command
of the Duke of Cumberland
at the Battle of Fontenoy
where she received a bayonet wound in her arm.

Her long life, which commenced in the reign of
Queen Anne, extended to the reign of
George IV
by whose munificence she received comfort
and support in her latter years.
She died at Brighton, where she had long resided
December 12, 1821, aged 108 years.
St Nicholas Churchyard, Brighton
(Phoebe survived two husbands and all nine of her children.)

Lichen on Phoebe Hessel's headstone

Well might the Dead who struggled in the slime
Rise and deride this sepulchre of crime.
Siegfried Sassoon

Battlefield

Clatterbridge Cancer Centre, the Wirral, 2023

Battlefields had a significant role to play in the making of memory and in the construction of narratives relating to national character and identity – and nowhere was more important in this regard than Waterloo.[1]

According to the Battlefields Trust,[2] nearly everyone in the UK lives within half an hour's drive of a battlefield. I live just a few miles from Bromborough, the alleged site of the Battle of Brunanburh in AD 937, where the Saxon king Athelstan ended the threat of Viking control and defined the country of what we now know as England. Today, I am less than a mile away, at the site of my own battle – though I don't like that word. I didn't fight, I just followed orders. (Thank you, NHS.) It is the last of my six-monthly infusions of zoledronic acid. And, unless the cancer returns, I am done.

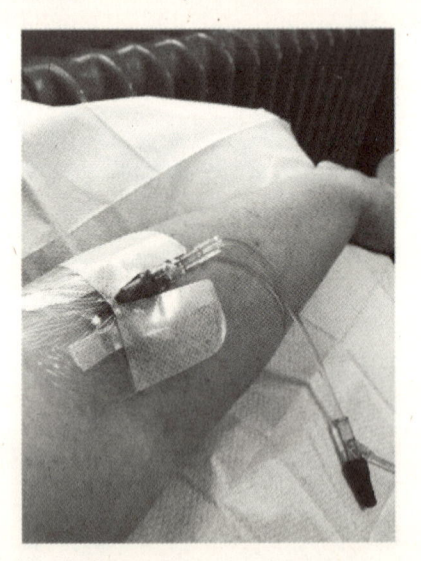

Infusion of zoledronic acid

Battlefields all over our isles have witnessed the deaths of many thousands, fighting for a cause, a place, a king. Not only are those battlefields sites of archaeological significance, but they are also burial grounds, sacred spaces where blood was spilled in the name of religion and land and honour. There might not be grave markers, but there will be memorials or monuments close by. Or even churches such as St Mary Magdalene[3] in Battlefield, the site of the Battle of Shrewsbury, where Henry IV defeated Hotspur in 1403 and 1,600 people are said to be buried.

Overseas, the Crimean War (1853–56) is said to be a war of many firsts: the first account of war written by a black woman, the first war to be extensively photographed with frontline war reporting. The first where rifles replaced muskets. The first to use trench siege warfare. The first with efficient army kitchens. The first where women were properly organised as nurses on campaign and the last in which wives could follow their husbands.[4] The Crimean War was also the first to inspire (what has become known as) 'battlefield tourism', with package tours for the upper classes who 'got up before dawn, settled themselves comfortably with their cushions, telescopes and picnic baskets, dodged the stray bullets from the Russians, and allowed themselves to be diverted by the ensuing slaughter'. A large crowd are said to have watched 6,000 slaughtered at Sebastopol.[5]

But it is Waterloo that made this idea of an elite jolly more nuanced.

☠☠☠

Waterloo

> You die twice: once when you take your last breath and later when someone says your name for the last time.
> Attributed to the Ancient Egyptians.
> Or Hemingway.
> Or Banksy.
> Take your pick.

High on the Blackdown Hills, in clear view of the M5, stands an icon of the West Country which commemorates the Duke of Wellington's victory at the Battle of Waterloo in 1815, which ended the Napoleonic Wars. In 1817, the winning competition design for the monument proposed a triangular pillar on a plinth topped by a cast-iron statue of the Iron Duke (whom we last saw shaking hands with Huskisson, the first railway death). Funds soon ran out and building work stopped. With public interest dwindling, the original design was moderated considerably, without the statue, before it was unveiled in the 1820s. In the 1840s, lightning badly damaged it and, to coincide with Wellington's death in 1852, it was repaired and completed, becoming the world's largest three-sided obelisk. Now, under the care of the National Trust, the Wellington Monument is renovated every decade or so and, following a recent overhaul, you can once again climb to the top.[6]

After peace had returned to the Continent, the Belgian site of the Battle of Waterloo became part of the Grand Tour of upper-class young men, but there were varying motives for visiting. For some, it was a patriotic duty, an act of commemoration, for others it was more personal, a pilgrimage to the place a loved one had died. Others were scavenging for souvenirs or were simply voyeuristic. Dark tourism comes in a spectrum of shades.

I haven't sought out battlefields, though, because we don't have to travel far, I have visited several. When they were small, we took the boys to Battle, site of the Battle of Hastings, where they played in the surrounding ancient woodland. The story of 1066 is captured in the Bayeux tapestry, and, whereas I've only seen a bowdlerised replica in Reading Museum, Izzy, my daughter, saw the original during a school trip to the battlefields of France. As a family, we visited Juno Beach in Normandy en route to the ferry home from a camping holiday. We stood on the sand where those landing craft beached and wandered round the impressive visitor centre which memorialises the thousands of Canadians who died on D-Day.[7]

I've driven my Canadian cousin to Scotland to seek out his Armstrong roots – to Stirling and the Wallace monument, from where you have a view of the bridge where the English were cut down in 1297, not far from where Robert Bruce was victorious in the Battle of Bannockburn in 1314. We went to Prestonpans, where the first battle of the Jacobite Rising of 1745 took place. Here we had a tour from a local historian and storyteller who brought to life Bonnie Prince Charlie's spectacular victory over the government forces. We took a train up to Inverness to visit Culloden, site of the tragic end of the Rising and the last pitched battle on British soil. Atmospheric and gloomy, you can feel the tragedy of the highlanders in your bones. In less than an hour, around 1,500 men were slain, most of them Jacobites. This is their burial ground, marked by a memorial cairn in the middle of the battlefield. Flags and clan markers show the scale of the bloodbath (with tokens left by *Outlander* fans).

I took him to the WW2 Air Forces Memorial at Runnymede, down the road from where the Magna Carta was signed, to remember the 20,265 men and women who were lost during operations from bases in the UK and Europe with no known graves. They came from all over the Commonwealth including a twenty-one-year-old from the small town of Westport, Ontario, uncle to my cousin, who was named after him. On 8 September 1943, Wesley's Hampden aircraft P1265 failed to return from a meteorological flight. Lost at sea, with no known grave, we found his name written in stone: Warrant Officer Class 1, Wesley Percival Coleman.

The importance of a name.

This wasn't dark tourism. It was personal. Sacred. Deeply moving to watch my cousin in tears for a young man he never knew but whom he has always revered.[8]

Wesley Coleman

World War I

The First World War marks a watershed between the death acceptance of the Victorian and twentieth-century death denial. Nineteenth-century religious doubt was compounded by events at the front. After the war, God receded in the world picture and death became a new form of trauma and taboo.
Kate Berridge[9]

They shall not grow old, as we that are left grow old.
Laurence Binyon

At the time, the Boer War was described as a Big Adventure – later reflected by Peter Pan, the lost boy who never grew up, who said that to die would be 'an awfully big adventure'. Following the humiliation at the close of the war in 1902, there was a push to indoctrinate young boys' minds with patriotic thoughts. Veterans visited schools, peddling this idea of adventure. Special attention was paid to public schools in these recruitment drives; privileged boys should set an example to those less fortunate. In time, the Great War would ravish the establishment with the death rate of Cambridge University as high as 26.5 per cent, compared to a general (still horrific) death rate of 11 per cent.[10] Overall, 880,000 British forces died, 6 per cent of the adult male population and 12.5 per cent of those serving.[11]

It has been said that, on the front, there was one dead body for every eighteen inches of ground.

Never before had death been known on such a scale.

Hard to comprehend, so we must turn to the poets for a glimpse of what it must have been like to be caught in this carnage. A Shropshire lad captured the annihilation in his 'Anthem for Doomed Youth'.

> What passing-bells for these who die as cattle?
> Only the monstrous anger of the guns.
> Only the stuttering rifles' rapid rattle
> Can patter out their hasty orisons.
> No mockeries now for them; no prayers nor bells,
> Nor any voice of mourning save the choirs, –
> The shrill, demented choirs of wailing shells;
> And bugles calling for them from sad shires.

Wilfred Owen died a week before Armistice was declared, almost to the hour, aged twenty-five.

The Box Boys

> As the stars that shall be bright when we are dust,
> Moving in marches upon the heavenly plain,
> As the stars that are starry in the time of our darkness,
> To the end, to the end, they remain.
> Laurence Binyon

Due to renewed interest in family genealogy, cheaper travel and the recent centenary of WW1, the memory boom[12] has contributed to an increase in battlefield tourism in France and Belgium. But you need go no further than your closest village or town to find a war memorial in a prominent place – village green, parish church, school, sports club. You will see name upon name, alphabetical order, sometimes the surname repeated. Each a living breathing man struck down in their prime. Cannon fodder. Their bodies never repatriated.

Growing up, every year we would switch on the telly for the Remembrance Service at the Royal Albert Hall and watch those red poppies fluttering down, each one representing a life. A death. The two-minute silence. The national anthem. The Queen in black, sombre and still. At school, I studied the war for History A level. My children studied the war poets as part of their syllabus. Now, as the Greatest Generation have passed away and so many of the Silent Generation are no longer with us, the world wars can seem as far off as the Battle of Hastings, but they are still just a few steps removed.

You just have to reach out your hand.

On 11 November 1918, Percy Box was in France, heading towards the front in a taxi, when Armistice was declared. A 2nd Lieutenant in the 1st Battalion, Somerset Light Infantry, Percy – my great-grandfather, who died when I was a toddler, around the same time as poor Miss Bowles – was already father to baby Barbara Box, who weighed in at three-and-a-bit pounds. As the Armistice bells tolled, Percy had already lost two brothers.

On 5 January 1915, Percy's younger brother Henry (Harry) Edward Box, a private in the 6th Battalion, Gloucestershire Regiment, caught meningitis at training camp and died shortly after at home, aged nineteen. He is buried in Greenbank Cemetery, Bristol. On 31 May 1917, Percy's older brother Gunner Robert Valentine Box of the 113th Heavy Battery, Royal Garrison Artillery, was killed in action during a British offensive at the Battle of Arras, aged twenty-eight.[13] Eventually Robert's headstone was placed in Mindel Trench British Cemetery, St Laurent-Blangy, Pas de Calais. The inscription reads: 'To live in hearts we leave behind is not to die.' It was chosen and paid for by his parents, Robert and Mary, my great-great-grandparents. Mary, the great-granddaughter of Mary who was enslaved on St Helena. Two sons gone in a flash. Such sadness. Such trauma passed down.

You just have to reach out your hand.

Mindel Trench British Cemetery

Greenbank Cemetery, Bristol

My great-grandfather, Percy Box

Pro Patria Mori

[T]he poppy is about both forgetting and remembering, ironic flower in its strange marriage of associations between opiates that induce oblivion and

a stimulus to remember bloody battlefields ... For it is hard to be conscientious about remembering the ever more abstract versions of other people's experience, things that happened not to you but 'for you'.
Kate Berridge[14]

Every soldier had a service record, with information about their military career, their all-important family, age, birthplace and trade and sometimes their private correspondence. Only a third survive. In the 1930s, many documents were disposed of before the records went into storage, but the majority were destroyed in an air raid at the Army Records Office in Walworth in 1940.[15]

A sun-faded photographic postcard used to be propped on Auntie Ruth's Welsh dresser that now stands in our back room. One day, on a pre-Christmas visit – 20 December 2015, to be exact – I studied the sepia faces of the men staring back at me. A dedicated *Blackadder* fan, I knew they were Tommies. I read the message on the back dated 20 December 1915. A century ago, to the day. A Christmas postcard sent from Lionel to one of his sisters, a nurse in Kent. I asked Ruth about him. He was her uncle, through her mother, Elsie, who had married George Gillespy twenty years after my great-grandmother, Mabel, died in childbirth. Not a blood relative of mine but someone Auntie Ruth talked about though he had died before she was born in 1926.

Lionel, sitting far left

I found Lionel's records online. Captain Lionel Tudor Wild of 'B' Company, 7th Battalion, Prince Albert's Somerset Light Infantry. Killed in action on 30 November 1917, aged 29. Mentioned in despatches.[16] Commemorated on Cambrai Memorial, Louverval.
We will remember them.

☠☠☠

Some Corner of a Foreign Field

> The tropes and traditions of nineteenth-century mourning were inappropriate to a loss of such magnitude. It fell to the architects to put into tangible and symbolic form the sense of tragedy felt by survivors.[17]
> Gavin Stamp

In previous wars, such as Waterloo and Crimea, only officers had their bodies repatriated; the rest were interred in mass graves. In 1915, when the scale of death became clear, the government decided, controversially, that there would be no repatriation and remains were not allowed to be disinterred for reburial back home. Not only would the numbers have made this impossible, but it would have been bad for morale. Equal in death, they would be buried where they fell alongside their comrades. To bring order to the chaos, the Imperial War Graves Commission, later the Commonwealth War Graves Commission (CWGC), was set up by Fabian Ware (aka Lord Wargraves) to inter the remains of the dead and record their graves. He later illustrated the sheer number of war deaths in a chilling way: 'Imagine the dead moving in one continuous column, four abreast. As the head of that column reaches the Cenotaph in London, the last four men would be in Durham.'

Edwin Lutyens, principal architect for France for the War Graves Commission, advised on the monuments which would transform the temporary graveyards into permanent, dignified cemeteries. After the war, whilst on a scouting mission to France,[18] he was moved deeply by the little wooden crosses, some of which were later sent home for the family to bury. He described them as 'a ribbon of isolated graves like a Milky Way across miles of country, where men were tucked in where they fell.'.[19] But something permanent was needed.

In time, Lutyens would oversee the creation of 126 cemeteries. He would design the Stone of Remembrance, which stands altar-like in the larger CWGC cemeteries and some of the vast monuments such as the Thiepval Memorial to the Missing of the Somme, which commemorates more than 72,000 British and South African men with no known grave. For each Stone of Remembrance, 'Their name liveth forevermore' was chosen for the inscription by the Commission's literary adviser, Rudyard Kipling. Each individual grave would be marked by the same rectangular headstone made from white Portland stone, the regimented rows like a parading battalion. For the unknown soldiers, Kipling chose 'Known unto God' to be inscribed on their gravestone. This was personal: he and his wife spent years of heartbreak searching the military hospitals of France for news of their son, John, reported missing after the Battle of Loos in 1915.[20]

The importance of a name.

Almost half the British dead were posted 'missing', leaving you wondering whether your son might walk through the door at any moment, or if his remains were forever lost in the mud of Flanders. In France alone, there are still about 100,000 British and Commonwealth soldiers missing. Farmers, construction workers and road builders frequently turn up their bones and get in contact with the CWGC, who are responsible for war remains found in France. They respond quickly. In the past, workers might well have discreetly buried back over the bodies, saying nothing, but now, knowing work will not be held up for longer than is necessary, they are happy to notify the CWGC, which means there are steadily more bodies being recovered, along with more artefacts which just might identify them.

During exhumation, the site is secured because of scavengers fuelling the black market with battlefield memorabilia. 'Rifles, belt buckles, bullets.' Worse still, 'the removal of army-issue and personal artefacts makes it much less likely that the soldier will ever be reunited with the most valuable item of all: his name'. Once exhumed, the remains are taken to a mortuary to await identification while, back in Maidenhead, 'war detectives' compile a list of possible missing men who fought in the area, the right age, from the correct regiment, etc. Sometimes a living descendant can be traced; DNA might confirm a match.[21] A surprisingly moving process for the family:

> A telephone rings in Australia and they are told that a man whom they have never met, who may not be a direct relation, who died long ago on the other side of the world, has been found in the field where he fell. Despite these several steps of remove, it is common for people to become personally invested and tearful. They have a great desire for a DNA match. It is as if war, in all its electric sadness, has reached a jolting hand out of the past.[22]

More than a century after their death, the soldier will be buried with full military honours in a nearby military cemetery – hopefully with a name, so that, in time, their name can be removed from the monuments to the missing. Otherwise, he will be buried as a soldier of the Great War known only to God.[23]

Westminster Abbey

> The elaborate Victorian death rituals were questioned after the beginning of the twentieth century and fully overturned by the first world war, the emphasis shifting from the body to memory... It separated funerary ritual from commemoration, mourning from remembrance, private grief from public acts of remembering.
> Kate Berridge[24]

In 1945, Armistice Day fell on a Sunday and, every year since then, the two-minute silence has been held on the nearest Sunday to 11 November, known as Remembrance Sunday. Since 1995, the silence is also held on 11 November, observed wherever you are, be it a supermarket or workplace or school. (A silence has also been held on the first Sunday after the death of Diana, and after the deaths at Hillsborough and Dunblane.)[25]

When hostilities finally ceased with the Armistice of 11 November 1918, just as my great-grandfather was in that taxi on the way to the front, the government knew they had to do something for the dead. And, when the Treaty of Versailles was signed on 28 June 1919, it planned a day of celebration. As a focus for this, the prime minister, Lloyd George, asked our man Lutyens to design a temporary structure. Constructed from wood, plaster and canvas, the memorial was unveiled on 18 July 1919, outside the Foreign Office in Whitehall, ready for the Victory Parade the following day. The Cenotaph ('empty tomb') deeply impacted the public who visited in droves, over a million people within two days, many of them laying wreaths. Classical rather than Christian, Lutyens's design spoke to everyone, encapsulating individual grief and communal loss, and very soon it was decided that a permanent Cenotaph would be made from Portland stone. A national memorial. Dedicated to 'The Glorious Dead', with no inscribed names, the Cenotaph – as we know it from years of watching the late Queen lay a wreath on Remembrance Sunday – was unveiled by George V at 11 a.m. on Armistice Day 1920, just as the Unknown Warrior was carried by on his way to Westminster Abbey for interment among the tombs of royalty, poets and inventors.

The decision not to repatriate had been difficult for the bereaved, no body to bury, no local graveside to visit. The idea of the Unknown Warrior was that an unidentified body from the front would be brought back to Britain for a public funeral, 'one body as a surrogate for all the bodies that had not come home, one funeral for all the funerals that had been prevented'.[26] The remains were placed in a coffin made from a Hampton Court oak and transported across the Channel on HMS *Verdun*, escorted by six destroyers and welcomed by a nineteen-gun salute at Dover. The coffin was then taken in a special white railway carriage to London, along with six barrels of Ypres soil so the soldier could lie on the earth where his comrades had died. On 11 November 1920, Coldstream guards escorted the gun carriage drawn by six black horses down the Mall to Whitehall, where George V was unveiling the Cenotaph. Then, alongside his three sons, the King walked behind the coffin to the Abbey, with Field Marshall Haig one of the pallbearers and the guard of honour made up of one hundred recipients of the VC. Most of the congregation were women who had lost both husband and sons, or their only son.[27] The tomb remained open for the next week, allowing thousands of mourners to pay their respects.[28]

Berridge suggests that these two ceremonies 'signified the psychological transfer from the body as the focus of the death ritual and the grave as a site of mourning, to the memorials, monuments and rituals of remembrance'.[29] She goes on to say:

> Names increasingly stood in for bodies and graves, on rolls of honour, inscriptions on memorials, and in books of remembrance. The lists and lines, ink and inscriptions were an effort to return to each individual his identity, and to tease out of the trauma of mass death something personal, human and emotive... the names were proof of the existence of the missing.

The importance of a name.

☠☠☠

The Interwar 'Pall of Death'

> Exhausted by war and pestilence, the English were losing their faith. The certainties which had governed High Victorian mourning were gone. An entire generation had been swept away. Death was as random, and terrifying, as it had been in medieval London, but with none of the consolations of piety.[30]

After the Great War, supposed to end all wars, Britain was devasted by loss. Every family grieved, but there were no meaningful funerals, and mourning dress was replaced with black armbands.[31] The men who returned were forever changed by trauma, by the carnage they had witnessed. Death was not the great adventure. It was brutal. And possibly meaningless. Moreover, when bodies had been blown to pieces, how could they be resurrected? Where was God in all this suffering? And as for Hell, Hell was back there in the mud and slime of those foreign fields. And so began a shift away from religion to a more secular society, highlighted by those war memorials and the two-minute silence which was introduced to mark Armistice Day, not in church, but in the civic sphere.

Women were more than passive mourners. 17,000 had worked in harrowing, dangerous conditions close to the trenches and in field hospitals on the Front.

Ambulance drivers. Nurses. Translators. Some, like the Red Cross nurse Edith Cavell, had made the ultimate sacrifice. At home, women were employed in hazardous occupations. By 1918, almost a million women worked in munitions, with many made ill from the poisonous chemicals; those who handled TNT were known as 'canaries', as their skin turned yellow from the toxic jaundice, with as many as 400 dying from exposure. There were also horrific explosions in these factories.

And then there was contagion, the visitation of the Spanish flu pandemic from 1919 to 1920, which killed more people than the war had. Hardly surprising then that the bereaved and traumatised looked beyond God for comfort. Spiritualism once again took off, as mothers and wives searched for ways to continue their bonds with the dead. There was a raft of books written from the viewpoint of soldiers from the afterlife, their bodies whole again, enabling the bereaved to hold a better image of their lost boys. Why would they contemplate Jesus's mutilated body when it could only remind them of the sacrifice their men had made?[32]

Added to this, over the next two decades, Britain would struggle with unemployment and poverty as another war loomed. But there was change on the home front. So many dead men meant a surplus of women. But some women, those who had worked during the war, chose to remain single; professions such as teaching and medicine offered opportunities for the unmarried.[33]

In 1918, women over thirty were given the vote, but many were pushed out of paid employment after the men returned to their old jobs. By the time WW2 broke out, women were more readily brought into the workforce and war effort.

The People's War

I am outside our Victorian terraced house, putting oil in my car, when an elderly man approaches me, accompanied by his middle-aged son. I used to live in your house, he says. I was a boy here during the war. I ask him if he wants to come in, have a nose. He is very keen, though I am a little worried at him climbing the very steep stairs to the attic room where he used to sleep. From the window up there, you can see the war memorial on the hill. We pause a moment. Safely back in the kitchen, he describes the old layout, clearly visualising family meals, huddled round the wireless in the small front room and back kitchen, where someone has since knocked through. Then he points to where our tumble dryer sits under the stairs. This is where my sister and I used to sleep during a raid, he says. We never had any bombs here, he adds. When you think of the devastation of the docks just a few miles away in Birkenhead, we were lucky.

As are we, I think. The latest census tells us that life expectancy for a male in West Kirby is eighty-two years of age, compared to seventy in Birkenhead (eighty-five to seventy-five for women).[34]

The postcode lottery.

WW2 brought random, violent death to our shores. London had endured Zeppelin raids in WW1, but nothing prepared its inhabitants for the relentless bombing campaign which claimed the lives of 40,000 civilians during the Blitz from September 1940 to May 1941, almost half of them Londoners. Hitler believed that destroying the capital would demoralise the whole population and force surrender but he also focused on industrial cities, ports, smaller towns and iconic cathedral cities identified from the German Baedeker guidebooks – all were bombed by the Luftwaffe.[35] In all there were around 70,000 fatalities, 52,000 injured and 2.25 million made homeless.[36]

While Grandpa was at training camp, Mum and Nan moved in with her parents, Percy and Minnie, in Bristol. During a raid they would come downstairs and go under the table rather than head to a shelter, as my great-grandmother was worried about a direct hit. When the bombing was heavy, Nan took my little mother to Carmarthen to stay with her sisters-in-law. For Mum it was an exciting time. Lots of aunties to make a fuss of her, friends to play with and a sailor billeted on her street with a pet monkey.

The legacy of war lingered in Devon in my 1970s childhood. Exeter and Plymouth had their hearts blitzed out of them, and you could still see the scars. Even my small hometown had played its part, sending out small fishing boats across the treacherous Channel as part of the rescue mission of Dunkirk. And the town was targeted for its mainline railway, port and boat builder's yard. In fact, Teignmouth suffered more air-raid deaths per capita than any other town, enduring twenty-one raids with seventy high explosives and 1,000 incendiaries.[37] Many families lost relatives. My sister-in-law is from an old Teignmouth family. Her dad's three-year-old cousin, Delphine, was killed in a raid along with her parents, Leslie and Dorcas. Up the road from where they lived, you can still see a crater, now a convenient passing place on the narrow back lane to Bishopsteignton. This was the village where the family of my stepfather Ralph's first wife, Joy, had their home. One day, while Joy's mother, Rosa, went with her oldest sister, Alice, to visit their cousins for tea in Teignmouth, teenage Joy stayed home nursing a headache. Her mother, aunt and their cousins all died in a direct hit.

All in all, during the war, seventy-nine people lost their lives in raids, with many injured. Even now, unexploded bombs are occasionally found in local waters.

You just have to reach out your hand.

On the other side of the country, my stepfather, Don,[38] was a young lad living with his family on their market garden in Essex. They were twice bombed at home. The first time the glass houses were all shattered, destroying their business. The second time a V-2 took out their neighbour's house, killing its occupants. Don woke up in the bedroom he shared with one of his brothers to see the stars. His mother sustained a head injury after which she was never quite the same again.

Death was here, shared in the public arena.

The Underground Front

By the summer of 1943, 36,000 miners had either signed up or taken higher paid work in heavy industry, leaving only three weeks of coal stock. Churchill put Ernest Bevin in charge of increasing production, which meant more men. Every month, ten numbers were placed in a hat and two numbers drawn out. Those whose National Service registration number ended with those numbers were sent to the collieries. So, irrespective of ability or background, one in ten eighteen-to-twenty-four-year-old men conscripted to serve in the armed forces now had to work in the pits – refusal meant imprisonment. About 48,000 Bevin boys took on the unskilled manual jobs while the experienced miners worked at the coal face. Contrary to popular belief at the time, only forty-one were conscientious objectors, but, because they were not in uniform, these men faced discrimination and hostility from locals who believed their own boys had been sent to the front in their place.

As we know from Gresford, mining is dangerous. Around 5,000 miners were killed in British mines during the war, and those who were disabled by an accident did not get a pension, nor were their dependants provided for. The programme did not end until 1948 and, with all records destroyed, it was hard to prove their service. They had no right to return to their previous jobs, no medals, no demob suit, not even a letter of thanks. It wasn't until 1995 that the government officially recognised their service and, finally in 2004, the Bevin boys took part in Whitehall's Remembrance Day service. Though largely forgotten, there are some memorials across the UK, including one in the little church at Rattlinghope (whose graveyard contains the tomb of the last sin-eater) and one in the National Memorial Arboretum.[39]

The Final Solution

More than any other atrocities in wartime before or since, the Holocaust defined the imagery of death in the twentieth century. An event in the past,

it retains great power to put us in touch with our own mortality and humanity in the present.[40]
Kate Berridge

Death in those foreign fields during the Great War had reduced the significance of the body in funerary rites. This in turn contributed to the popularity of cremation. In the next war, air raids on home soil had blown bodies to bits, making them unidentifiable, and, because of this, cremation became more common. For some time, Germany had been further ahead with this method of disposal than any other European country. And this technical knowledge, according to Berridge, enabled the manufacture of gas chambers and ovens for 'the express purpose of mass murder'.[41]

Towards the end of the War, as Britain faced the V-1 and V-2 rockets, there was a hint of the destruction to come in Japan. If Alan Turing et al. had not worked on Enigma, maybe the war would have dragged on another two years and Hitler would have developed the bombs that the Allies dropped on Hiroshima and Nagasaki that killed an estimated 200,000 people.

The aftermath of war was as devastating as it had been after the First World War. Rationing continued until the early 1950s. Austerity was tough. But there was hope. A new welfare state and National Health Service. Though with this new NHS, people were deprived the old way of death, at home surrounded by family, and were whisked away to die behind screens in hospital. Death was the great unmentionable, marked by a brief twenty-minute funeral in a local authority crem. The stoicism and stiff upper lips of the war years left a mark on the nation's attitude to death, which would last for decades. *You must not lose control.* For example, in the 60s and 70s, doctors would prescribe tranquillisers to bereaved widows to see them through the funeral without breaking down. I clearly remember Mum's GP offering her Valium, but Mum, being Mum, declined. (She hesitates when considering a paracetamol for a headache, whereas I would have bitten the doctor's hand off.)

Mum says that when Grandpa came back from Germany in 1945, he never talked to her about the war. None of them talked about the war. It was over. Why hark back? Leave the trauma behind. Look forward. And in time they would be told they never had it so good. And in time we Gen-Xers would ask our grandparents what they did in the war. And, because enough years had gone by, and because they were retired and had more time, and because they had a different, easier relationship with their grandchildren, sometimes they would respond. Sometimes they told stories. Grandpa, a gunner in the Royal Artillery, was going deaf from the big guns. My brother Peter asked him about his war, made him apply for the medals he had never wanted. Clearing German tanks of their occupiers, he had seen bad stuff. Dead men.

My partner's grandfather was in the merchant navy. Hailing from Birkenhead, he survived his ship being torpedoed, twice, during the North Atlantic convoys. The family joke that he was like Uncle Arthur from *Only Fools and Horses* but they are only too proud of his bravery. After WW1, there was a memorial to the merchant sailors and fishing fleets in Tower Hill with the names of 11,919 with 'no grave but the sea'. After WW2, this was extended, adding a further 24,000 names.

The importance of a name.

In the dawn of the new millennium, veterans and war children saw the past more clearly and worried for the future. Probed by their children and grandchildren, by social media, by big anniversaries, they realised the importance of remembering, of telling the subsequent generations about their past. And this included the full horrors of the genocide of six million Jewish people and all those othered by Hitler's despotic regime. Though it wouldn't be the end. More carnage was to follow in the killing fields of Cambodia, in Rwanda, Kosovo, Darfur, Afghanistan, Iraq. Even now, as war rages in Ukraine, Israelis and Palestinians are killing each other.

We know now that grief doesn't end. We can't block it out. So we must talk to our loved ones, to our enemies. We must find a way to end the trauma that has passed down the generations.

☠☠☠

Cold War

> Now I am become death, the destroyer of worlds.
> J. Robert Oppenheimer, quoting from the *Bhagavad Gita*

I am in the NAAFI canteen of Hack Green Secret Nuclear Bunker beneath the rolling countryside of Cheshire. Initially, Hack Green was used as a bombing decoy site for Crewe railway station (once the railway capital of the world) but, in 1941, it became RAF Hack Green to defend the land between Birmingham and Liverpool. Following WW2, it became a Cold War bunker with its own generating plant, air conditioning, nuclear fallout rooms and emergency water supply. In the event of a nuclear attack, Hack Green would be responsible for the territory stretching from Cheshire in the south to Cumbria in the north, headed by a regional commissioner to get the area back on its feet and to prepare for the re-establishment of national government.

No longer secret, Hack Green is now open to the public, for fans of dark tourism. We have just watched a film loop playing the full version of the public information film *Protect and Survive*.[42] (It's *The Finishing Line* all over again but for the whole of humankind.) We have been told in the calm reassuring voice of Patrick Allen how to wrap up your dead loved ones in polythene, tag them and bury them. I am with my partner, Neil, and his twelve-year-old daughter, Ella, eating 'wartime tomato soup and bread' and drinking tea from tin cups. (Ella has got used to going to odd places with her stepmother. Thankfully, she is a stoic child.) Neil, who grew up on the Wirral, says they were told at school not to worry, because the second the bomb hit the chemical plants of Ellesmere Port and Runcorn, the explosion would take out the whole of the Wirral and they'd be eviscerated in a moment. I think about Devon and suppose we would have suffered a hideous slow death. I remember the psychological existential threat of annihilation which hung over the childhoods and teenage years of Gen-Xers, seeping into pop culture. *The Young Ones* episode entitled 'Bomb'. 'Two Tribes' by Frankie Goes to Hollywood, with Patrick Allen parodying himself: 'Mine is the last voice you will ever hear. Do not be alarmed.' (Hard to relax after watching Reagan and Chernenko wrestling in the music video.) Murakami's film of Raymond Briggs's graphic novel *Where the Wind Blows*. (Not exactly *The Snowman*.) None of this helped my salvation angst.

Whilst tucking into a piece of carrot cake, now, underground in Hack Green, I am thankful for Ella's stoicism as she tells me dismissively about one of her friends, who is terrified at the possibility of nuclear attack with Putin pushing the button. I wish I had her presence of mind. *Why fret about tomorrow?*

Before we leave, we browse the selection of souvenirs. She chooses a fridge magnet. On the journey home, in the back of the car, Ella holds the magnet like a talisman. At some point, as we head onto the Wirral, the chemical plants in our view, she asks a question: do you reckon my magnet could survive a nuclear blast?

We swap a look, her dad and me. Is she actually worried? What should we say? Ella answers her own question. 'No point worrying. We'll all be dead.'

X

IS FOR X-FILES

The Unknown

X-Files *noun*
an unsolvable case.

There are more things in heaven and earth, Horatio,
Than are dreamt of in our philosophy.
HAMLET

Here lyes Bessy Bell,
But whereabouts I cannot tell.
THE NECROPOLIS, GLASGOW

From algebra to science, astronomy and spirituality, X stands for many things. X represents danger, the unknown, secrets, rejection, cancellation, love, an error or the end of something. It can also mean the crossing of a threshold, a change, a transition, a crossroads. And, of course, death.

In linguistics, X is a 'phonetic chameleon', making different sounds including silent ones. In her book, *Inventing the Alphabet*, Johanna Drucker says that X is 'the most intentional mark a human can leave', appearing in cave paintings long before the invention of writing systems. 'It registers within a natural landscape as a human-made mark.'[1] Born Malcolm Little, Malcolm X, an American human rights activist, adopted the letter X to symbolise the loss of his family's African name during their enslavement. If you cannot write your name, you can sign a legal document on the dotted line with an X, though this must be witnessed so it can be verified. X is also a symbol of crossing things out, so redacted information in reports or letters will be a series of XXXXXX.

χ is the Greek letter 'chi' and became shorthand for Christ (*Christos*, meaning 'anointed', written *χριστοσ*). Early Christians used X as a secret sign to indicate their faith as it symbolises the cross, a reminder of Christ's death by crucifixion. Ichthys, or IXNYy, or <>< is Greek for fish, and Christians could draw it in the sand to secretly profess their faith without persecution. X is still used as an abbreviation for Christ (Happy Xmas!). And check out those Ordnance Survey maps to see where a rotated X marks a place of worship. X can also signify a wind turbine or crossed swords, which indicate a battle site where many will have died. And we already know about Crossbones cemetery in Southwark, final resting place for the dispossessed. To show you are deadly serious about something, people say 'Cross my heart and hope to die' ('stick a needle in my eye' – ouch). Crossing your heart is the Christian practice of making the sign of the cross as a blessing or protection. Crossing your fingers also means you are hoping for good luck.

It is not only in Xianity where X is special. In the ancient mystic Jewish spiritual practice of Kabala, which attempts to uncover the secrets of the universe, X means both birth and death. In Hebrew, the letter X represents the sound 'kh' or 'ch' (as in 'Bach'), a guttural sound made at the back of the throat, often used for emphasis at the end of a word. Originally signifying peace, faith and wellbeing, the swastika, a kind of rotated X, was important in many religions, but sadly (and horrifically) misused by the Nazi Party and other far-right groups.

The letter X, as illustrated by the skull and crossbones (i.e., crossed bones in an X shape), portrays danger, first associated with pirates. By the end of the nineteenth century, it became a generalised hazard warning of death by poison. Both skull-and-crossbones and the X symbol on an orange background is the standard label for harmful and toxic substances throughout Europe. Xs are all over the pharmaceutical world. Vitamin X is one of the many names for the potentially deadly drug ecstasy or MDMA. One for the ravers, but I'll stick to vit C, in recommended daily amounts. Otherwise, there is always the benzodiazepine Xanax, a prescription drug used to treat anxiety, though this can also be dangerous if used incorrectly. X is also used to indicate the relative strength of booze – for example, the number of Xs on a bottle of moonshine marked how many times the batch had been through the still during distillation.

In maths and science, X denotes the unknown or a mysterious situation to be solved. Think algebra, where you must find the value known only as x. Or X can be multiplication. And there's the X axis. (All pretty much a mystery to me.) In the 1890s, Wilhelm Röntgen accidentally discovered a new form of radiation while experimenting with cathode rays and glass. He didn't fully understand them, so he named them X-rays. Early geneticists named the X chromosome because of its unique properties. Humans have an X chromosome or a Y chromosome. XX and XY are the chromosome pairs that most individuals possess, combining an X from the mother and either an X or Y from the father. The X is a somatic chromosome, not a sex chromosome. Most of its genes are not sex specific, but many are essential for life. Without an X chromosome, male embryos will die in utero. In most cases, XX stands for biologically female and XY for biologically male.

In astronomy, X is used for the name of a hypothetical planet or a comet of unknown orbit etc. In aerospace, the X symbol stands for experimental or special research. Several X-planes have accomplished aviation firsts, such as breaking altitude or speed barriers. According to X, formerly known as Twitter, Elon Musk's company SpaceX 'designs, manufactures and launches the world's most advanced rockets and spacecraft'. Musk is somewhat obsessed with the letter X. His first company, which was to become PayPal, was known as X.com. His Tesla Model X is an electric SUV, though Musk tends to drive his Model S. He named his youngest child X Æ A-12 – or X for short. (What the X?)

As we can see from this, X is much used in branding: X-Type Jag, Xbox, Product X (a protein powder for bodybuilders) and X, the Californian roller coaster with swivelling seats, to name a few. X is also used in censorship, as in X-rated films, which are violent or pornographic. Moreover, X marks the spot on a treasure map (those pirates loved an X), the ballot box, the scene of the crime, the crosshairs of a scope in a gun for fixing your target. And, randomly, *Xestobium rufovillosum* is the Latin name of the death watch beetle, the larvae of which bore through wood. The adult makes a tapping sound which used to be an omen of death.

Camp X was a top-secret WW2 training school on Lake Ontario in Canada, where over 500 allied secret agents were trained to go behind enemy lines. This included learning silent killing, sabotage, demolition, map reading, weaponry and Morse code. In fiction, *Secret Agent X* was the title of an American pulp magazine which ran from 1934 to 1939. A crime fighter working undercover for the government, his identity is never revealed. Agent X is also a mercenary who evolved from the Marvel comics Deadpool series, associated with the X-Men. (So many Xs in this franchise.) Agent X was a sort of American 007 in the short-lived drama series of the same name. A dead person in cartoons can be portrayed with an X over each eye. This could be because of the Christian last rites of anointing the dying with oil, in the shape of the cross on the eyes. Or because they were sewn shut to stop them opening.

Staying in popular culture, *Xanadu* (forget Kubla Khan and Coleridge) was 'an unconventional, campy story that blended the golden age of 1940s MGM musicals and 1980s New Wave augmented by mythological muses and roller skating'.[2] An unlikely mash-up of Gene Kelly, Olivia Newton-John and ELO, it flopped with the critics on release but has since become a cult classic. 'A place where nobody dared to go.' (Not a lot to do with death, but I had to mention it here.)

And, of course, there is *The X-Files*, an American television drama which ran from 1993 to 2002 with a tenth season in 2016 and an eleventh in 2018. Special agents Mulder and Scully investigate unsolved cases involving the paranormal including extra-terrestrial life. This cult series was embraced by the mainstream, who fell in love with its conspiracy theories and scepticism of governmental institutions.

Cue Greta Thunberg, the environmental campaigner whose distrust of governments the world over has been shown by her putting her words into actions, telling us we should all be a little more autistic. She repeatedly warns us of the existential crisis we are facing, calling us to action, now, urgently, because our house is on fire. Her deeds chime with Extinction Rebellion (XR), an international movement that uses non-violent civil disobedience to try to halt mass extinction and minimise the risk of social collapse. X (the shorter version of 'ex') signifies the end of something. Let's hope it's not the end of the earth.

And so, to Generation X: the tenth (X) generation of Americans since 1776 (when, on 4 July, thirteen American colonies severed their political connections to Great Britain). Gen-Xers, such as myself, are the middle-child, stuck between the Boomers and the Millennials, 'a low-slung, straight-line bridge between two noisy behemoths'.[3] The name was first coined by WW2 photographer Robert Capa about the young adults of the 1950s and was revived thirty years later by Douglas Coupland in his coming-of-age novel *Generation X: Tales for an Accelerated Culture* about three twenty-something dropouts in Southern California. We were self-reliant and independent. Latch-key children of divorces with two working parents. We had to get ourselves to and from school, get the dinner started, do our homework and hope we didn't get too many Xs when it was marked by our corduroy-clad teachers. We had to create our own entertainment, which invariably meant sex and booze, cool music and big hair. As we've grown up, we're the glue that holds it all together. But we have turned into helicopter parents, doing our children's school projects and constantly telling them how great they are and how much we love them (kiss, kiss, kiss, xxx). We might not have lived through a world war, but we lived through Thatcher and Cabbage Patch Kids. And it wasn't us who started the climate crisis. But we could do more. (Sorry, Greta.)

Y

IS FOR YEW

How a Yew Tree Saved My Life. What We Can Learn from this Ancient Tree

yew *noun*
taxus baccata
common yew, English yew

Ancient, poisonous, regenerative, the yew tree is one of the longest-lived native species in Britain. A symbol of both death and immortality, it provides food and shelter for woodland animals, protection and nesting for birds, chemotherapy drugs and carbon storage.

Rust-red bark. Evergreen needle-like leaves. Dioecious. 'Male flowers are insignificant white-yellow globe-like structures. Female flowers are bud-like and scaly, and green when young but becoming brown and acorn-like with age.' Unlike other conifers, the common yew does not bear its seeds in a cone, but in a red, fleshy, berry-like structure known as an *aril* which is open at the tip.[1]

Common in churchyards, usually on the south or south-west side of the church.

...slips of yew, silvered in the moon's eclipse.
MACBETH

In stiff unwieldy arms against thy crown:
The very beadsmen learn to bend their bows
Of double-fatal yew against thy state.
RICHARD II

David Williams, ob. 1760
Under this Yew-Tree
Buried would he be,
Because his father – he,
Planted this Yew-Tree.
FROM GUILSFIELD CHURCHYARD

☠☠☠

Teignmouth, 2006

We are having an extension built on the back of our house. To do this, some of our trees have to be lopped or crowned and a yew tree has to be cut down. This is not a conservation area, nor a site of special scientific interest and the tree itself isn't old, has no bats or dormice sheltering within and there is no tree preservation order (TPO). The day arrives and I am talking to the tree surgeon about the yew. A Devonian in his sixties, with a thick accent that even I struggle to understand, he has spent the morning up a beech. It's not a job for old men, he says. (I think.) Then we talk about the yew. I feel bad about it, but the extension needs to be done as the house is too small for five people. He says he'll leave the stump. As he puts on his heavy-duty gloves, he tells me about one of his old workmates who got sick when yew sap entered his bloodstream.

What happened? I ask, feeling worse than ever.

He died.

Oh.

By the end of the afternoon, his work is done. A sad stump remains. Our cat, Buzz, sits on it, surveying his patch.

In time, the house project is a disaster. We have a terrible builder chosen by a terrible architect and we lose a lot of money and spend a lot more having the cowboy's work redone.

My depression blooms.

The yew starts sprouting shoots.

Y IS FOR YEW

Hollowed-out Yew at St Bueno's, Berriew

☠☠☠

Life and Death

> Very old yew trees are rarely found outside of church grounds and this relationship between places of worship and a single tree species is unique in the Western world.[2]

The yew tree, an evergreen, is famed for its longevity, with no known upper age limit. There are various reasons for this: The wood is strong, as is the cylindrical shape of the tree. It is disease-resistant and has clever ways of adapting. It grows like a 'normal' tree for about 600 years, before hollowing out and thickening around the base, where new shoots form buttresses that stabilise and protect the tree. When the main trunk eventually dies, these shoots form a new tree. They often have internal roots, put down by the branches into its dying centre. These can also take root or fuse with the main trunk to support the crown. When boughs droop and touch the ground, they can take root and form new trunks or connect underground to the old one. These older, hollow trees can withstand storms that might topple younger ones.

It is hard to age a yew tree. You can examine old maps, look up tree records, measure its girth and study growth form. But never assume a yew is dying; it might have dead wood or discoloured needles, but it will still recover. They are considered ancient when they reach 900 years old, veteran at 500, notable at 300. Across England, there are at least 500 churchyards with yew trees older than the churches. There are about 800 ancient and veteran yews in the churchyards of England and Wales, three quarters of the British population, making churchyard yews globally important.

Perhaps because of its ability to regenerate, the yew has long been associated with immortality. The Druids held the yew tree sacred, believing it kept away evil forces and purified their worship space, erecting their temples close by and using their branches and foliage in ceremonies. Established in this country by the Celts, its funereal significance would have developed during the Roman occupation. There are still yew trees living from this time. Conversely, since Egyptian times, the yew has also been closely connected to death. The Romans used its wood to burn funeral pyres and believed it grew in Hell.

When St Augustine brought Christianity to these shores in AD 597, the old pagan beliefs chimed with the Gospels' concepts of the resurrection and eternal life. In a sensitive move, Pope Gregory suggested that places of pagan worship be converted into churches and, rather than replacing the established yews with a church, they built next to them. In time, as Christianity spread throughout the land, new yews were planted in churchyards and pagan rituals were incorporated into Christian traditions. Yews were central to this. When Easter replaced the spring festival of Eostre, yew boughs were used as palms. The red heartwood and white sapwood of the yew were symbolic of the blood and body of Christ, and its wood was burned for Ash Wednesday rituals. Priests waved yew twigs to sprinkle holy water and corpses were rubbed with an infusion of yew leaves before being buried along with yew shoots. This was done as a means of preservation and, also, to guarantee the deceased immortality. Perhaps this is why yew trees were planted on the graves of plague victims. Perhaps the yews would purify the diseased bodies and protect both the living and the dead.

From the Middle Ages, through a connection to the Virgin Mary, yews became associated with both virginity and fertility. Because its bark and roots can develop hair-like fibres, these were likened to a virgin's hair. William Camden, a Tudor antiquary, records how a Yorkshire priest beheaded a virgin for refusing his sexual advances. He hid her head in a yew. In time, this tree became a sacred site of pilgrimage. The name of the village was derived from 'holy hair' and, in time, thanks to the income from pilgrims, Houton was renamed Halifax. In churches dedicated to St Mary the Virgin, an honoured place was reserved for yew trees in many of the churchyards. St Mary's in Painswick, Gloucestershire, has the highest number of individually listed monuments in its churchyard in England, as well as ninety-nine yews (a mystical number). They used to be clipped annually on 8 September, the feast of the Nativity of Our Lady.

Y IS FOR YEW

St Mary's, Painswick

According to Robert Turner's *Botanologia* (1664), the yew is 'hot and dry' and 'will attract poysonous vapours and imbibe them'. He believed these gases or 'will o' the wisps' were released from decaying corpses at the south and west sides of the church. Because this is the location where yews were traditionally planted, the gases would gather under their branches before being absorbed by the trees. This, Turner believed, is what made a yew tree poisonous.

Yews are also found in other places of the churchyard, such as beside the path leading from the lychgate to the main doorway, and by the path leading to the lesser doorway. The priest and mourners would gather under the first yew to await the corpse-bearers. In some Anglo-Saxon churchyards, you can see where the yews were planted in a circle around the church, which tended to be built upon a central mound. The Ancient Yew Group believes that churchyard yews should be treated as artefacts of historic significance, in common with other parts of the church and churchyard. Often a churchyard yew is the oldest feature in an area, certainly the oldest living thing.

Once Upon a Time

Much folklore associates the yew with witches, ghosts and demons, who hide amongst the leaves and branches. Sometimes the tree is known as the guardian of the dead, with many seeing the tree as a symbol of mourning. Some believed its roots interfered with the corpses in graves or that the roots held each dead body in place by spreading a new root into each mouth. And there was an old saying that, if yew is brought into a house, or cut down and damaged, within a year someone will die (yikes). More positively, the yew was also said to have powers of love divination, so that if a young woman picked

D IS FOR DEATH

a yew sprig from a graveyard in which she had never been before, and then slept with it under her pillow, she would dream of her love.

The relationship between the yew tree and death are often referenced in early and modern literature such as in *Twelfth Night*, where Shakespeare uses imagery to illuminate the contemporary association with funerals: *Shroud of white stuck all with yew*.

Some other examples:

> Old Yew, which graspest at the stones
> That name the under-lying dead,
> Thy fibres net the dreamless head,
> Thy roots are wrapt about the bones.
> Tennyson, In Memoriam

> Never did tombs look so ghastly white. Never did cypress, or yew, or juniper so seem the embodiment of funeral gloom.
> Bram Stoker in the graveyard scene in *Dracula*.

The poem 'Yew Trees' by William Wordsworth combines not only the yew's links to death but also its longevity and hope.

> The message of the yew tree is 'blackness and silence'.
> Sylvia Plath. Enough said.

(Spoiler alert:) The supernatural powers of the yew led to its being used to make magician's wands. In *Harry Potter*, Voldemort's wand is made from yew and has the power of life and death. Because the yew remains poisonous after death, Voldemort's horcruxes and Death Eaters live beyond his death at Godric's Hollow.[3]

St Mary the Virgin, Mold

All Over the Isles

Three lifetimes of the yew for the world from its beginning to its end.[4]

The yew is important all over the British Isles. The early Irish regarded the yew as one of the most ancient beings on earth and staves made from its wood were kept in pagan burial sites, used for measuring corpses and graves. My children's Irish grandfather came from County Mayo. *Maigh Eo* translates to *Plains of Yew Trees* and was said to be the largest yew tree forest in the known world, there since before the Ice Age.[5] Known for its water-resistant qualities, wine barrels were made from staves of yew and the tree was known as 'the coffin of the vine'. Yew carvers had the highest status among early medieval Irish woodworkers, and, despite its toxicity, it was the most used wood found among surviving buckets from Ireland. It was also common in Anglo-Saxon settlements. Decorated yew buckets were used in high-status graves, with several examples from the sixth and seventh centuries, including the ship burial at Sutton Hoo.[6] The hollows of ancient yews were even used as homes by some early monks in Ireland and Wales.

In tenth-century Wales, the penalty for cutting down a consecrated yew was one pound – more than most earned in a lifetime. At Ystradgynlais, the groundsmen keep the yews pruned in the churchyard as a precaution; local legend has it that the world will end when the smallest yew grows as high as the belfry. In Pembrokeshire, the Bleeding Yews of Nevern have blood-red sap dripping down the trunks, which some believe is the trees bleeding in sympathy with Jesus on the cross. The Pulpit Yew in North Wales is so named because there are steps leading through its hollow up to a seat and podium from where John Wesley is said to have once preached.

In Scotland, just as churchyard yews protected churchyards, a yew outside a house would protect the home (this I can believe). An old Scottish tradition also held that yews would guide the deceased on their journey to the afterlife. Although yews were rare in the Highlands for a long time, Clan Fraser adopted a sprig of yew as their badge.[7] It is also said that, as a child, Pontius Pilate sat under a yew tree planted by St Ninian at Fortingall in Perthshire, believed to be the oldest on these isles and so large that funeral processions used to process through its split trunk.[8] According to Scotland's Yew Tree Heritage Initiative, all yews of any age are scientifically classified as living fossils, with the family roots dating back 200 million years. From the end of the last Ice Age, around 12,000 years ago, which devastated humankind, in all the areas where the yew recolonised the earth, it is referred to as the Tree of God, Divine Tree, World Tree, Tree of Life. 'The yew is in the 0.1% of species which are still here.'[9]

D IS FOR DEATH

All Saint's, Gresford

☠☠☠

Doctor, Doctor

The yew has always held a special place in medicine. Caesar records possibly the first case of yew poisoning when Cativolcus, chief of Eburones (Gaulish for yew tree), poisoned himself with yew rather than submit to Rome. Knowing of the yew's powers, in *Macbeth*, Shakespeare writes of the yew through the words of the third witch as she (literally) stirs the pot: 'Slips of the yew, cut at the eclipse of the moon.' The murder of Hamlet's father is described by his ghost to his son:

> Upon my secure hour thy uncle stole
> With juice of cursed hebenon in a vial
> And in the porches of mine ears did pour
> The leperous distilment; whose effect
> Holds such an enmity with the blood of man,
> That, swift as quicksilver, it courses through
> The natural gates and alleys of the body.

Scholars largely agree that 'hebenon' is yew.

With its known toxicity, it is no surprise that the yew has deathly links. Almost every part of the yew is poisonous to wildlife, which may contribute to its longevity. Counterintuitively, the only part that isn't toxic is the red flesh ('aril') of the berry, which, provided the seed inside is not crushed, can be eaten and pass through some animals without harm. Some birds, such as blackbirds, waxwings, thrushes and fieldfares, eat the berries and disgorge the seeds. But some can eat them with no ill effect, though it can be fatal if chewed or swallowed by humans. Yew leaves can kill cattle and horses; sheep and goats are not as badly affected. Deer can eat foliage freely. Insects use the leaves and bark for shelter, but few feed on them. Compared to other old trees, neither lichen nor fungi are particularly associated with the yew.

A homoeopathic tincture can be made from the young shoots of a yew and the berry flesh has been used by herbalists to treat a variety of ailments including cystitis, headache and neuralgia. (Don't try this at home.) But what is exciting and has saved many lives is the yew's anti-cancer compounds – highly poisonous taxane alkaloids. Though the cancer drugs now used are mostly synthetic, the clippings can still be used in the process and drug companies and research laboratories still buy it in bulk. The taxels have a broad spectrum of anti-cancer activity and treat cancers such as breast, colon and ovarian. Paclitaxel stops cancer cells from separating into new cells thereby blocking the growth of the cancer. This is the drug of which I had twelve weekly rounds. The drug that potentially saved my life.[10]

Coffin stone in the lychgate at Hope Bowdler, Shropshire, with yews behind

Shoot That Poison Arrow

> For the sun which at that time was bright and clear then lost its brightness so thick were the arrows.
> *Jehan Waurin, c.1450, on the Battle of Shrewsbury*

D IS FOR DEATH

The very hard, close-grained wood of the yew has long been used in furniture-making and for tool handles. One of the world's oldest surviving wooden artefacts is a yew spear head supposed to be from the Hoxnian inter-glacial period (between 424,000 to 374,000 years ago). But yew wood is perhaps best known as the material from which the medieval English longbows were made.[11]

Archers used these longbows with devastating effect during the Hundred Years War and were key to English victories at Crécy (1346), Neville's Cross (1346), Poitiers (1356) and Agincourt (1415). Archers were professional soldiers, hired in wartime by contract of 'indenture', earning 'equivalent to the income of a lesser knight', though from 1285 all able-bodied men between fifteen and sixty had to own a bow and arrows. In 1363 and 1388, it was proclaimed that all 'labourers and servants shall have bow and arrows and use the same on Sundays and Holy days, and leave all playing of tennis and or football'. Quite.

An unstrung longbow was the same height as a man. Drawing a war bow took great strength, with a draw weight of 100–120 lbs, so archers had to be trained from boyhood. A good bowman could shoot ten to twelve arrows per minute, as far as 220 metres.[12] Worked from a single trunk of wood, the bow combined heartwood and sapwood for maximum elasticity and strength. (Hence the saying 'a post of yew will outlast a post of iron'.) European yew was superior for bow-making but, by the sixteenth century, demand for yew across Europe was so high that the population was decimated, and old yew trees are rare on the Continent.

Some say Robert the Bruce (Robert I of Scotland) ordered bows to be made from the sacred yews at Ardchattan Priory in Argyll, which were then used during his victorious battle at Bannockburn in 1314.[13] Others say he cultivated yew trees on Inchlonaig, a tiny isle on Loch Lomond, to replace the yews he used for making the bows his archers used at Bannockburn. These yews can still be seen today on Inchlonaig ('island of yew trees').[14] He's also said to have hidden in a yew tree when on the run a few years earlier. His son's nemesis, Edward I, Hammer of the Scots, decreed in 1307 that yew trees should be planted in all churchyards to protect the church from storms. When Henry IV ordered his royal bowyer 'to cut down yew or any other wood for the public service', he exempted the estates of religious orders, and so churchyard yews survived his reign. (Though he did execute the Archbishop of York, so he wasn't all about the Church.)

Y IS FOR YEW

The versatility of yews at Powis Castle

☠☠☠

'We see the seasons alter.'

A Midsummer Night's Dream

> Trees are the ultimate multi-taskers in the fight against climate change… The UK's precious semi-natural ancient woodlands store a huge quantity of carbon and can continue to accumulate more despite being centuries old. Woods are our allies in the fight against a changing climate, yet just 13% of the UK's land area is covered by trees (compared with an EU average of 37%).[15]

The ancient yew tree, with its hollow trunk and dense evergreen foliage, is a distinctive feature of the British landscape and a sanctuary for wildlife. Pure yew woods (rare in Europe) can be found in dry, shallow soils of steep slopes where other tree species struggle. These hardy yews tolerate a wide range of soils and harsh conditions. There are around 20,000 hectares in the UK.[16]

Ancient woodland is home to more wildlife than any other UK habitat. Its trees have twisted bark, hollows, dead wood and gnarled roots, which provide protection and shelter for wild honeybees, nesting birds, roosting bats and mammals such as hibernating hedgehogs and dormice. These woods are also important in the fight against climate change. Not only do they prevent flooding and reduce the temperature in cities, but they also capture and store carbon. But, because 85 per cent of ancient woodlands are unprotected by government legislation, they are constantly under threat from development. The route of HS2 is another threat, held off for now. But if our ancient woods and trees are destroyed to make way for its path, then this transport system cannot be described as green. Instead of destroying these trees, we must plant more and look after the ones we already have.[17]

Paul Powlesland, founding barrister of Lawyers for Nature, believes the TPO system does not offer enough protection for ancient trees, as they are usually only granted if a tree is threatened. Too little, too late. However, Powlesland believes that protecting ancient trees can cross the political divide, uniting 'environmental lefties and political conservatives'.

> It speaks to who we are as a country. What is this land? What does it mean to be British? It's a chance for politicians to make themselves part of history. These yews have existed for thousands of years. Hopefully, if we protect them they will still exist when this entire civilisation is consigned to the history books. That's a magical thing.[18]

The ring of yews in the churchyard of St Mary the Virgin, Overton on Dee, Wrexham

Brampton Bryan, 2023

I'm church-crawling today and take in St Barnabas, the Grade I listed church in the small, sleepy village of Brampton Bryan situated in Herefordshire near the Welsh border, deep in the Marches. Destroyed during the Civil War, the church is believed to be one of only six English churches built or rebuilt during the Commonwealth Period (1649–60). But I am here to see the half-mile lumpy hedge that runs through the village, surrounding the church, hall and castle, reputed to be the 'longest free-form, or cloud, yew hedge in England'.

Before WW1, the hedge was trimmed and clipped every summer using ladders, hand shears and red cotton flags to stop the traffic. A massive endeavour. While the men were away at war, the hedge was left untended and got somewhat out of hand, which is how it became this cloud-like shape. For such a small village, they suffered a huge loss, with ten of those men not returning, memorialised inside the church: Frederick Charles Jones, Geoffrey Richard Jones, George Lucas, George Hughes, William Henry Fishwick, Adrian Goodall, Harry Lewis, William Edwards, Richard Jones, Frank Jukes. In the following war, Robert John Mortier Harley lost his life.

The hedge lives on.

Further into the century, the clippings were collected for use in developing the cancer drug Taxol, though now it is synthesised and the clippings are composted and applied a year later to the base of the hedge to keep it healthy. And healthy it is. On this hot day in July, as I drive into the village, I admire it while the temporary traffic lights are on red, allowing me to watch the men using cherry pickers and battery-operated hedge clippers.

In the churchyard, I find four yew trees, the smallest planted by village children. As part of the project Yews for the Millennium,[19] this was a cutting from an ancient yew of some 2,000 years. This happened all over England and Wales, in thousands of churchyards, parishioners raising money for the Conservation Foundation to protect and record the country's ancient yew trees. Almost 8,000 young yews were propagated from ancient ones and presented to local communities to celebrate the new millennium.[20]

In the wake of the destruction of the Sycamore Gap Tree, I hope this massive hedge stands far more of a chance at survival. And I hope to come back one snowy winter afternoon and see the yew cloud with a low sun casting its shadows on what apparently looks like a Christmas cake. And I'll check on that sapling.

D IS FOR DEATH

Yew Hedge at Brampton Bryan

Websites

Ancient Yew Group
The world's leading information portal and database on yew trees, containing information on 1,500 ancient and veteran yews and how to find them.
https://www.ancient-yew.org/

AB Welfare and Wildlife Trust
Charity providing advice for people who are dying or recently bereaved. Provides UK-wide advice on funeral law and can help with funeral arrangements, particularly burials in nature reserves. Call: 01423 530 900
https://www.ataloss.org/FAQs/ab-welfare-and-wildlife-trust

Caring for God's Acre
A charity that supports groups and individuals to care for and enjoy churchyards and burial grounds. With over 25,000 burial grounds across the UK, from small country medieval churchyards to large urban Victorian cemeteries, they reflect different cultures and religions, appealing local history and environmental lovers. For many, they may be the only local green space, but they are threatened from development and closure. Often managed by volunteers driven to preserve both the monuments and the ecology for whom the charity offers expert guidance on preservation of rare species of plants and wildflowers, on grassland management, on lichen on gravestones and on collapsing monuments. From botanical recording to conservation work, you can play our part. Love Your Burial Ground Week is held every June with awareness-raising ecological events accessible to everyone.

https://www.caringforgodsacre.org.uk/
The yew is a flagship species of the charity, which works with the Ancient Yew Group to protect and promote them.
https://www.caringforgodsacre.org.uk/resources/veteran-trees/
Churchyards are rich in biodiversity having escaped centuries of agriculture and pollution.
https://www.caringforgodsacre.org.uk/resources/biodiversity/
Recording memorials.
https://www.caringforgodsacre.org.uk/resources/recording-memorials/

Church of England
Churchyards are important for wildlife habitats and as refuges for plant life. Most churches have some green space and in some urban areas they are the only green 'breathing' space available for both wildlife and people. About 10,000 out of 16,000 churches have churchyards, which is the same area as a small national park. A precious resource which makes a huge difference to the biodiversity of the UK.
https://www.churchofengland.org/resources/churchcare/advice-and-guidance-church-buildings/biodiversity

National Memorial Arboretum
Part of the Royal British Legion, a UK charity with a 150-acre visitor site on the edge of the National Forest in Staffordshire. With memorials and trees to remember those who served and sacrificed and to pass on the baton of Remembrance through the generations. To 'celebrate lives lived and commemorate lives lost'.
https://www.thenma.org.uk/

Woodland Trust
The UK's largest woodland conservation charity.
https://www.woodlandtrust.org.uk/blog/2018/01/ancient-yew-trees/

Z
IS FOR ZADUSZKI

Celebrating Death around the World

Zaduszki *noun, Pol.*
1. *trans.*, the day of prayers for the souls.
2. commemoration of All the Faithful Departed.
3. All Souls' Day (2 November).
4. Day of the Dead.

Live a little; Comfort a little;
Cheer thyself a little.
As You Like It

'It is better to go to a home where there is mourning than to one where there is a party, because the living should always remind themselves that death is waiting for us all.'
Ecclesiastes 7:2

Z IS FOR ZADUSZKI

Wittgenstein claimed that death was not part of life. According to most of the world, Wittgenstein was wrong about that – or at least only correct in the most material sense. In most cultures death is always part of a more general vision of life. The opposite is less often true. What is supposed to be a window on eternity becomes a looking glass in which we see ourselves.[1]
Nigel Barley

☠☠☠

Remember Me

I am in B&M in Huddersfield, grabbing some snacks to sustain me throughout my day at the university. There is a section devoted to Halloween with quite an extensive selection of goods aimed at kids and probably students. Ceramic LED-lit pumpkins, monster sweets and marshmallows, giant spider webs, polyresin skeletons, ghost candles, eyeball lollipops, vampire costumes for two- to four-year-olds, tombstone bath fizzers, Halloween pet poop bags. A toddler is playing with a plastic skull, displayed at the perfect height for her. She is giggling, excited, happy, chatting away to her mum and nan and possibly poor old Yorick. It all seems very normal.

31 October: Halloween, All Hallows' Eve, All Saints' Eve. As a child, we did apple bobbing and lit candles. We even had a couple of family parties. I remember one dark Halloween, my nan dressing up in a white sheet and wafting past the window outside, making this small child wide-eyed in wonder. There was no trick-or-treating; that came much later, which is perhaps why I never let my kids go out and terrorise the neighbourhood, because it was never a family tradition. (Sorry, kids. I know how much you wanted to.) Coming from a Baptist background, it was not encouraged, and I felt uncomfortable.

That was then. Now, I wish I'd thought more deeply about it and had used it as an opportunity to talk about death and the afterlife and folk traditions. Festivals change in nature but, if you look, you can see the connections. Take harvest. This year, my old church collected for the local food bank. Not a marrow in sight. But harvest is still connected to the rhythms of church life. Long ago, there were Celtic harvest festivals such as Samhain ('summer's end'), which marked the end of the growing season and the beginning of winter, halfway point between autumn equinox and winter solstice. It was a time to honour the ancestors, leaving a place for them at the table to share in the feast. A time when the living and the dead made connections. Samhain has made a comeback and is celebrated at the same time as Halloween, a Christian feast day for two millennia.

All Hallows' Day or All Saints' Day or Hallowmas is celebrated on 1 November, the day after Halloween, a Christian feast day honouring not just canonised saints but all dead believers in Heaven. And then, on 2 November, comes All Souls' Day or the Commemoration of all the Faithful Departed, the third consecutive feast day of Hallowtide, where Christians, with variations between denominations, pray for and remember the souls of the departed. There might be church services, prayers for the dead and cemetery visits. In previous centuries, bells tolled to purify the dead in Purgatory; candles were lit to guide them through the darkness. There was also a custom in England to make and distribute soul cakes to children and paupers ('soulers') in return for their songs and prayers for the cake givers' dead family members, a sort of precursor to trick-or-treating.

> *A soul-cake, a soul-cake, please.*
> *Good missus, a soul-cake.*
> *One for Peter, two for Paul,*
> *Three for Him who saved us all.*

The tradition waned after the 1870 education reforms, as more children were in school and not able to roam as freely, but it persisted in Shropshire and Staffordshire until the 1950s and, even more recently, in Sheffield and Cheshire.

Despite the banishment of Purgatory at the Reformation, All Saints' Day is a principal feast in the Church of England calendar and All Souls' Day is commemorated or sometimes celebrated as a lesser festival, perhaps by prayers of intercession or the reading out of names of the parish dead. For Roman Catholics, who still believe in Purgatory, this is a feast day, with the opportunity to reflect on our own mortality, on our loved ones who are preparing for death, and on those who have gone before. It is also a time to meditate on grief, an experience common to all. The prophet Isaiah said the Messiah would be 'a man of sorrows and acquainted with grief'.[2] Christians believe this prophecy was fulfilled when Jesus wept in public over the death of his friend, Lazarus, and over the city of Jerusalem. Jesus, God in human form and body, showed how he understood grief when he said, 'blessed are those who mourn'.[3]

Continuing in this vein, the Eastern Orthodox Church celebrates Sunday of the Myrrh Bearers, recognising the women who carried myrrh to the tomb of Jesus on the third morning after the crucifixion, only to find it empty. These women had stayed faithful to Christ throughout his arrest and execution, standing by the cross and then accompanying him to his burial so that they would know where his tomb was. As the Sabbath was approaching and according to Jewish law, the burial preparations were brief, but, as soon as it had passed, the women returned at dawn, bringing expensive, preserving myrrh to anoint his body, an echo of one of the gifts bestowed on the infant Jesus by the Magi. The women, in particular Mary Magdalene, were the first witnesses to see and speak with the resurrected Jesus, who told them to tell the Apostles the good news. They were the apostles to the Apostles. The first evangelists. During the service on this second Sunday after Easter, the Bible readings are chosen to reflect the role of these women in Christ's death and resurrection.

Blood of the Lamb

Passover (*Pesach*) is the Jewish festival commemorating the liberation of the Children of Israel who were led out of Egypt by Moses. In the book of Exodus, during the tenth and final plague, the firstborn of every household was to be killed. At midnight every Egyptian firstborn – from the firstborn of Pharaoh to the firstborn of the lowest, even of livestock – would be struck down by the Angel of Death. God told Moses to tell the Israelites to mark their doors with the blood of a sacrificed lamb as a sign that death had already taken place, so that the Angel would pass over. In the Hebrew scriptures and Old Testament, when the Egyptians demanded that Pharoah banish the Israelites, they brought sacrificial lambs to the Temple, and the blood was offered to God for the forgiveness of sins. The lamb would take the place of the child. (Christians believe that Jesus took on this role through his crucifixion.) Celebrated in spring, in ancient times Passover marked the beginning of the agricultural cycle, so, as well as being the festival of freedom, Passover is also a symbol of hope and starting afresh.

All these connections.

Back to the autumn, in Eastern Europe, both All Saints' Day and All Souls' Day are celebrated by Catholics. In Poland, since the first centuries of Christianity, All Saints' Day (*Dzień Wszystkich Świętych*) was the time to pray for all the saints in Heaven and All Souls' Day (*Zaduszki* or *Dzień Zaduszny*) for the faithful dead whose souls were in Purgatory. On Zaduszki, it was believed that, for that one day of the year, these souls roamed the earth. A feast was held to feed the dead and, because these souls often took on the form of a vagabond (a *dziad*), the poorest would be invited. People cleaned their houses to be ready for the dead to visit. They covered the floor with sand, left the door or window open, and moved a bench up to the hearth on which they placed a bowl of water, a towel and a comb for the souls to freshen up. As with soul cakes, women traditionally baked special bread, giving some to the poor, to children, to the priests, and leaving the rest on the graves in the cemetery. This would please the dead or bring good fortune to the living. They would retire to bed early so as not to distract the dead from their celebrations, leaving the remnants of dinner until morning and the dogs chained up, as it was important not to disturb or anger their ancestors. If they did take out the waste, they would say a word of warning to the souls. To keep the peace, no music was played and inns were closed. As were churches – it was dangerous to witness the dead priests performing mass for the roaming souls.

Many of these Polish customs can be traced back to old Slavic traditions, but they are fading away. However, Zaduszki is still an important family holiday, a time for relatives to visit cemeteries together, taking flowers (usually chrysanths) and candles (*znicze*) to place at the graves of loved ones or the forgotten. Practising Catholics go to church, where a list of the dead will be read out during mass. The priest will also bless the graves. It is still important for the older generation to visit the graves of their lost family and friends, to clean them up and leave a candle. A Polish friend of mine, approaching her thirties and living in London, tells me that her grandmother still takes this holiday very seriously – though these days her duties are more time-consuming because, in her old age, she has so many more graves to look after, as so many have gone before her. It is said to be a beautiful time to visit Poland, seeing all the lit candles and to witness such a positive attitude to death, and while the young might not feel quite the same way, they certainly appreciate the family reunions, with 1 November a state holiday (even in Communist times).[4]

Feliz día de los Muertos

Coco, the 2017 Pixar film set in Mexico and featuring an all-Latino cast, is a reminder that family is for ever. Inspired by *el Día de los Muertos* (the Day of the Dead, celebrated on 1 and 2 November), the story follows twelve-year-old Miguel as he accidentally ends up in the Land of the Dead, a truly vibrant place. With the help of his deceased great-great-grandfather, a musician, he returns to the Land of the Living and reverses the family's ban on music. The film also acknowledges a more permanent but unknown afterlife, where souls go when no one from the living world remembers them. When we stop talking about our ancestors, their stories, they go to their 'final death'.

Veneration of the dead plays an important part across many cultures and religions. Just as Samhain can be seen as connected to the harvest, so this festival can be related to the Mayan corn harvest. It certainly combines the Aztec custom of celebrating ancestors with All Souls' Day, brought by Catholic Spanish colonisers in the early 1500s. In the old country, they had left wine and *pan de ánimas* (spirit bread) on the graves of deceased family members, covering them with flowers and lighting candles to illuminate their once-a-year journey to their former homes. The conquistadores brought these traditions to the New World (along with smallpox).

As in Poland, this is a joyful time in Mexico, a time for family reunions. Dead ancestors are the guests of honour and the living can continue bonds with them through food, drink and music. Tradition has it that the gates of Heaven are opened at midnight on 31 October to allow the souls of children to join their families on 1 November. The same happens for the souls of adults on 2 November. To welcome them, people build home altars (*ofrendas*) and decorate them with the favourite food and drink of their departed loved ones such as spicy hot chocolate and *pan de muerto* (bread of the dead), an eggy sweet round bread, or smaller round rolls, decorated with bone-shaped dough strips. They will display their photographs and multi-coloured clay or sugar skulls (*calaveras*) and skeletons (*calacas*). People also decorate their ancestors' graves with bright-orange marigolds (*cempasuchil*), candles and gifts of food.

It is a multi-sensory festival, and one of its most contemporary iconic symbols is La Calavera Catrina, made famous by Mexican artist Frida Kahlo (and Daniel Craig as 007 dressed up as a skeleton in the opening sequence of *Spectre*). *Día de los Muertos* is full of colour, tastes, and the sound of the wind blowing through the intricate cut-out designs of the colourful *papel picado* banners, again dating back to the Aztecs, who used mulberry and fig bark to make a rough paper for banners to decorate homes and temples. When the Spaniards brought tissue paper, this was used instead, its delicateness signifying the fragility of life and, because it is so lightweight, when it moves, families believe their loved ones have arrived. Even the colours of the paper have significance – black for death, purple for mourning, pink for celebration.

The festival is spreading around the world, and, while there could be accusations of cultural appropriation, a festival that connects the living and the dead, that takes away our fear, is one I want to celebrate.

In both Northern Ireland and the Republic of Ireland, Cemetery Sunday is a day when people gather in the local cemetery for the blessing of the graves mass. A time to remember family and forge connections with their community. It takes place in May or June when the weather is more conducive to outdoor gatherings (seeing as Ireland is renowned for its soft rain). In the weeks leading up to Cemetery Sunday, the community will tidy the graves and replace dead flowers in preparation.

People trying to trace their Irish roots via web forums and late-night emails to parochial offices might do well to attend the Cemetery Sunday service in their original family townland, and strike up some conversations with the other people present. Everyone congregates around their family plots, so it would be easy to find others with the same name, and identify common ancestors – after all, gravestones are essentially a three-dimensional family tree.[5]

☠☠☠

Ancestors

Sometimes DNA can show up surprises. I was listening to a podcast about two American couples who had conceived through IVF. Years later, when one of the families decided it would be fun for them all to do a DNA test, it turned out that one of the boys was not the biological son of the father. After some really good detective work, they found out that sperm had been mixed up and he was the biological son of another father whose wife had been treated at the same hospital. It was a massive shock, but actually, in the end, the families have become friends.

But it's the dead that ancestry – or genealogy – is concerned with. Ancestry is the line of descent of your family, and ancestors are anyone from whom you are descendants. Since TV programmes such as *Who Do You Think You Are?* and websites such as ancestry.co.uk and myheritage.com, many of us want to find out who we are and where we come from. (Not always good; I've told you about my discoveries in 'T Is for Terror'.)

The past is full of dead people and, somehow, we are all connected.

Part of Ghost Month, the seventh month of the lunar calendar, the Hungry Ghost Festival is an important festival in China, a time to remember ancestors. The spirits of the ancestors – the hungry ghosts – roam the earth, appeased by their descendants who offer food and burn incense and joss paper and release paper lanterns into rivers to guide the spirits home. Although it could be likened to Halloween, Hungry Ghosts shares a closer affinity to *Día de los Muertos*, *Pchum Ben* in Cambodia, *Sat Thai* in Thailand, *Awuru Odo* in Nigeria or the Festival of Cows in Nepal. Although the living worry about meeting the mischievous ancestors, it is a time to honour them, to continue bonds, and to reflect on mortality.

During the Torajan festival of *Ma'Nene* in South Sulawesi, Indonesia, the bodies of the dead are taken down from their cliffside tombs and removed from their coffins. The family then wash and dress them in fresh clothes and repair the coffin to last until the next *Ma'Nene*. Some families take photographs with their ancestor before carrying them around the village, then placing them back in their coffin to return to their tomb for another year.

These rituals are similar to those carried out by the Malagasy people of Madagascar, who believe that the spirit does not immediately depart after death, that it can only travel to the afterlife when the body has fully rejoined the earth, bones to dust. So, the families must look after their ancestors until their body is completely decomposed. While their soul remains in this world, they act as mediums between God and the living family. Every five to seven years, usually during the dry winter months, families visit their ancestors' crypt, sometimes after a long journey on foot. Here they conduct a sacred rite called *Famadihana* – the Turning of the Bones – an act of caring for their ancestors until they can continue their journey. During the ceremony, loved ones' graves are exhumed, the bodies wrapped in special straw mats, and the families carry the remains back to the village, where they are laid gently side by side, and cleaned and dressed in fresh silk shrouds. In return for sharing stories with them, the ancestors will bless and protect the living. After a feast and a good party with music and dancing, the ancestors are taken back to the family tomb, where money, gifts and alcohol will be left to keep them going until the next *Famadihana*. Then the tomb is closed. The costly practice is now in decline, but we can learn a lesson from the Malagasy about death and grief: our loved ones will always be part of our lives.

We know from grief therapy that it is healthy for us to continue bonds with the dead. Chinese Buddhists burn messages for the deceased, and this ritual has been embraced by grief therapists across the world; writing a letter to a loved one with all the things you never said, before ritually burning it, can be a healing process. In Japan, there is a wind phone that allows you to speak to the dead. You pick up the phone, and you speak to your loved one. You put your words out there to be carried by the wind in the hope they will reach listening ears.

The dead are always with us.

☠☠☠

David Jarrett, who, we met in 'H Is for Health; I Is for Illness', spent some time in Ghana with the Wessex-Ghana stroke partnership,[6] where he was impressed by the artisan tradition of coffin-making. 'These are figurative coffins, made by specialized carpenters to reflect the jobs, lives or passions of the departed. A pilot might be buried in an aeroplane-shaped coffin, a shoe manufacturer in a giant shoe, and so on. Much of the socialising in Ghana centres on weddings and funerals. It is worth typing "Ghanaian coffins" into Google Images.'[7] But Jarrett learned much more. He believes that all large hospitals in developed countries should forge similar connections with institutions in the developing world, because 'We have stolen a lot of their precious resources and we should give something back.' He adds: 'The developed world has always taken the talented educated people from the developing world – the very people who could make the most difference in their own countries.'[8]

From a long career in medicine, Jarrett knows that transcultural beliefs about death 'are complex and poorly taught'. He says, 'There are books on transcultural medicine but they tend to focus on the different religious beliefs and rituals surrounding death for Muslims, Hindus, Jews, Christians and those of other religions. The different cultural attitudes to disease, medicine and death are harder to define ... I learned the hard way that a rectal examination is a gross violation for some First Nations Canadians.'[9]

Live and Let Die

> It is also a celebration of rebirth. Slow dirges give way to joyous uptempo numbers and cathartic dancing as the body is 'cut loose', and the soul ascends to heaven.[10]
> Richard Fausset

Built by the French on reclaimed land at the turn of the seventeenth century, New Orleans is bordered on three sides by swamp and the Mississippi on the other. Levees were built to protect the city from flooding but, with much of it being below ground level, it was impossible to bury the dead in the European way. So tombs were raised above ground level and, because of the heat, bodies decomposed quickly, so that, within a year, only the bones would remain. They would then be moved to a pit at the back of the tomb, making room for more bodies.

New Orleans funerals as we know them gained popularity in the nineteenth century, and in the early 1900s jazz was incorporated. Mourners take part in the funeral procession, the 'second line', following a brass band playing sombre music from home to the church or cemetery. When the deceased is laid to rest, their body is 'cut loose'. Then the mourners can also cut loose, with the band playing upbeat music to celebrate the life of the deceased as they dance away from the burial ground, twirling umbrellas, showing that you can grieve the loss while celebrating the life lived.

These traditional funerals have survived Katrina and the pandemic, but will they survive gentrification and the disappearance of traditionally black neighbourhoods?

Cool Runnings

In Manitou Springs in Colorado, there are coffin races held in honour of Emma Crawford, a local musician who was buried on her beloved mountain in the late 1800s, only to be shoddily reinterred in a shallow grave to make room for a station and saloon. After heavy rain, Emma's coffin was washed down the mountain and into the town, where she was found by children. Imagine. Once relatives had claimed her, Emma was properly reburied. Since 1995, Emma has been celebrated with the annual coffin race, where teams of four dress up and race down the mountain with a home-made coffin – in a macabre *Cool Runnings* kind of way.[11]

☠☠☠

Döstädning

Marie Kondo writes about the Japanese art of tidying, focusing on what you want to keep, rather than what you want to chuck out. If an object sparks joy, then it can stay. This perhaps echoes William Morris's philosophy: 'Have nothing in your houses that you do not know to be useful or believe to be beautiful.' But Margareta Magnusson takes this further. Aged 'somewhere between eighty and one hundred years old', she practises *döstädning*, the art of Swedish death cleaning.[12] 'We must all talk about death,' she says. 'If it's too hard to address, then death cleaning can be a way to start the conversation.' Psycho-therapist Amy Morin agrees: 'Going through all of your things can serve as a reminder of who you are, how you see yourself and how you want others to see you after your death – your legacy.'[13]

It's much more than having a spring clean, damp-dusting the skirting boards and casting off some clothes to the charity shop. It's about taking a long, hard look at your life in the context of your death and what you will leave behind.

(I did not buy the book as it would take up too much room in my over-cluttered house. But I have it on Kindle.)

☠☠☠

Till We'm All Down Arnos Vale

> The facts of death, as important as the facts of life, warrant a more enlightened approach.[14]
> Kate Berridge

Back to the UK now, to Arnos Vale, a large Victorian garden cemetery in the heart of Bristol, forty-five acres which hold the history of the city. In 1998, the owner struggled to keep it open and tried to lock the gates, but locals prevented him. The Arnos Vale Army camped outside for several years, making sure the cemetery was opened in the mornings for families to visit graves, and closed at night to keep out intruders. In 2003, the Council made a compulsory purchase and handed over its management to the Arnos Vale

Cemetery Trust, which now incorporates Arnos Vale Natural Burial Woodland. Wander through a woodland trail amongst the splendid tombs, native wildflowers, birdsong and hidden roosting bats. Sit in a café or browse the gift shop, where I bought my stepdaughter a suffragist model turned from yew. (So cool. There are a few of these women buried here.) As well as theatre productions, comedy nights and concerts, you can watch a film in the Anglican chapel (last Halloween Johnny saw *Twilight*). Family events include woodland story walks, creating a miniature coffin or headstone inspired by different nations and times, teenage spooky tours, learning how to read a grave. In the past, there has been a festival called Life, Death (and the Rest) to bust taboos around death. (Please come back!) In the meantime, go to the Remembrance Service at Soldiers' Corner, the Christmas market or a death café. (Or you can even get married here.)

Sunrays through the trees at Arnos Vale

Oh, so Bristol

Z IS FOR ZADUSZKI

All these festivals and events held countrywide help us do better, do as the rest of the world does with death, where children grow up in companionship with their ancestors, honouring them, continuing bonds with them, partying with them. These traditions and celebrations help take away the fear of death, especially for children. Which brings us back to where we started, at Hallowtide, with the toddler in Huddersfield's B&M. Somehow, the mum and nan were including the little girl in death talk. This is a start. If only children were allowed to discuss death more openly. If only it were part of the National Curriculum. As Lyons and Winter say: 'Rather than worrying that our children won't be able to cope with it, let's give them the opportunity to ask questions and decide for themselves. We might find these death-aware children are the more open-minded, resilient and emotionally switched-on adults of the future.'[15]

Yes.

Back in the late 90s when our kids were little, three of them under five, we took them a couple of times to a local cemetery in Nunhead, another of the Magnificent Seven. One May, while Mum and Ralph were staying with us, we thought it would make a nice trip to go to the annual open day. Mum looked somewhat perturbed when I suggested it. To her, an open day suggested gaping tombs and the walking dead. Don't worry, I said. It'll be nice. It's an old Victorian place with lots of trees. You just have to be careful where you walk. What about the children, she asked. She had a point; they weren't known for their calmness. But Izzy would be in a pushchair and the boys could be shared between the remaining three adults, so we shouldn't lose any of them to the underworld. (We didn't.)

The Nunhead Cemetery open day is a big deal nearly three decades on, but back then we were all pleasantly surprised when we turned up. There were stalls and plant sales and some craft activities. Tea and cakes. Woodturning displays. Charities. But our kids were happy skipping amongst the (more stable) headstones. I watched them. Even though they didn't understand the purpose that this place once had, they were at ease. Their normal wild selves. And I remembered the boneyard up the road from our sweetshop in Torquay. I remembered the little girl skipping around the graves with her bothers, eating Spangles and listening to Slade on the transistor radio.

Endings

Our little lives are rounded with a sleep.
THE TEMPEST

There are only two days with fewer than twenty-four hours in each lifetime, sitting like bookends astride our lives: one is celebrated every year, yet it is the other that makes us see living as precious.[1]
KATHRYN MANNIX

And so we come to the end of this book. But I hope there will be life beyond it. Let's keep on talking. Keep on listening. Keep on reading other writers far more knowledgeable than me. (I've included some in the bibliography.)

If you take nothing else way from reading *D Is for Death*, then it is to face your fears. Writing this book has enabled me to understand and to come to terms with my mortality. It has shown me that how we live is so important. Every moment of every day. And I ask this of you: tell the important people in your lives that you love them. Give them a hug. Talk to them about their death and funeral plans. Laugh with them. Cry with them. Walk with them. Be present. Take your dog out even on those dark, dreary days and feel the soft rain on your skin.

We are all going to die, that much is true. But there is still a long way for us to travel in order to achieve equality in healthcare, in death and in memorialisation. In the words of William Gladstone: 'Show me the manner in which a nation cares for its dead, and I will measure with mathematical exactness, the tender mercies of its people, their loyalty to high ideals, and their regard for the laws of the land.' But even a statement from the Liberal prime minister is riddled with complexity, as we know his career was financed by his family's profiteering from the sugar plantations of Guyana and by the huge compensation they received at abolition. This summer, six of Gladstone's descendants travelled to the island as the country commemorated the 200th anniversary of a revolt at Demerara, a rising by enslaved people which helped pave the way for abolition. They went to apologise for their ancestors' wrongs, pledging reparations to fund research into the impact of slavery.

ENDINGS

Every story in this book is complex and, if I have been flippant at times, I don't mean to detract from any of that complexity. There are many rabbit holes to go down. Life-and-death is indeed a huge, interconnected warren. I hope this book will light your way a little as you delve into it.

Acknowledgements

Writing this book has taken a long time, during which I have read a lot and chatted loads with many people. Only a handful have looked at me in horror when I answer the question 'what is your book about?' with the D word: death. By far the majority have been very open and willing to talk about death, generous in their sharing of stories. I mention just a few of these people here but I am grateful to everyone, even those who struggle with talking about the subject that has been at the centre of my thought process throughout this project.

I am very grateful to the Society of Authors, which awarded me an Authors' Foundation grant to help with the writing of this book, and to the Royal Literary Fund, which helped me financially through the dark days of my cancer treatment and which has given me work as a writing fellow at the Universities of Manchester and Huddersfield, where I have learned so much from the students about writing non-fiction.

Thank you to the wonderful people I met at the Death Café in Frodsham, including Iris Keating and Lucy Biggs. Thank you to Rachel Kemp, medical director and consultant in palliative medicine at Marie Curie, for talking to me about palliative care. Thank you to Elaine White for her memories of the Flixborough disaster. Thank you to all the key holders who keep the churches open in Shropshire, Herefordshire and Devon, where I like to go church-crawling. Thank you to my writing tribe who meet on Exmoor every year, especially Rina Vergano, who continues to inspire me. And to Gus, for keening. Thank you to my family, near and far, for bearing with me; all the stories I have included are shared in love and gratitude. You have made me the person I am today. Thank you to Legend for believing in this book, in particular my editor, Christian Müller. Finally big thanks to my partner and best friend, Neil, for indulging me in my pursuit of knowledge of all things deathly. For spending hours with me in graveyards. For keeping me positive. After all, what can be regarded as a morbid subject is, in reality, life-affirming. Let's keep the conversation going.

Endnotes

A IS FOR ACCIDENTS

1. https://darwinawards.com/darwin/ accessed 5/7/22.
2. Some say that twirly jolly red-and-white striped pole outside your local barber's dates to the Middle Ages, the red symbolic of blood, and the white, bandages.
3. https://greatdisasterspodcast.files.wordpress.com/2017/12/prologue.pdf, p. 3.
4. Williamson, S., *Gresford: The Anatomy of a Disaster*, Liverpool University Press, 1999 pp. 34-35.
5. Returning to work after just eight hours' absence.
6. Williamson, p. 23.
7. Quoted in Williamson, p. 198.
8. Ibid., p. 182.
9. Williams, H.M.R., 'The Gresford Mining Disaster Memorial', 8/6/20 https://howardwilliamsblog.wordpress.com/2020/06/08/the-gresford-mining-disaster-memorial/ accessed 13/7/23.
10. *The Sunday Times*, 23/9/34 quoted in Williamson, p. 47.
11. Quoted by Traynor, L., *Mirror*, 26/11/14. (I haven't been able to find out what the situation is now.).
12. https://www.fishermensmission.org.uk/our-work-1/sea-safety/.
13. At the time of writing, dark tourism has been much on the news with the death of passengers inside OceanGate's *Titan* submersible en route to the graveyard of the *Titanic*. There was controversy over the attention this had on the news while hundreds are dying weekly on small boats in Europe.
14. Easthope, L., *When the Dust Settles*, Hodder and Stoughton, 2022, pp. 67-68 (A wonderful book about 'catastrophic events and frail bodies and loss and bereavement. A book about 'hope and revival and laughter. Friendship, resilience and love'. I urge you to read it.).
15. Carter et al., 25/3/06, https://www.theguardian.com/uk/2006/mar/25/immigration.ukcrime1 accessed 13/7/23.
16. Anson, J., 15/11/17, https://www.lancashiretelegraph.co.uk/leisure/15662222.the-tide-comes-faster-galloping-horse-meet-queens-guide-sands-cedric-robinson/ accessed 13/7/23.
17. https://www.lancashiretelegraph.co.uk/news/6224074.told-not-go/ 3/10/05 accessed 13/7/23.
18. BBC, 3/2/14, https://www.bbc.co.uk/news/uk-england-lancashire-25986388 accessed 13/7/23.
19. Easthope, p. 65.
20. https://www.bbc.co.uk/news/uk-england-lancashire-25986388.
21. From the *Morecambe Visitor*, cited at http://www.greatdisasters.co.uk/morecambe-bay-cocklepicking-disaster/.
22. https://www.bbc.co.uk/news/uk-england-lancashire-25986388.
23. Siddle, J., *Liverpool Echo*, 5/2/14, https://www.liverpoolecho.co.uk/news/liverpool-news/liverpool-gangmaster-who-left-23-6672655 accessed 13/7/23.
24. https://www.bbc.co.uk/news/uk-england-lancashire-25986388.
25. https://www.gla.gov.uk/whats-new/press-release-archive/05022019-glaa-remembers-morecambe-bay-cockling-disaster-15-years-on/ 5/2/19 accessed 13/7/23.
26. Sandercock, H., 27/2/20 https://www.thegrocer.co.uk/brexit-and-the-workforce/gs-warns-of-slavery-risk-amid-new-immigration-laws-and-glaa-funding-cuts/602383.article accessed 13/7/23.
27. Cited in *The Times*, 19 March 2022.
28. According to the TUC, deaths per year from pneumoconiosis peaked at over 1,600 per year from the early 1950s to the late 1960s.
29. Jenson, M., Lawford, C., Norman, A., Ogden, E., 'Safety Under Scrutiny – Flixborough 1974', *Loss Prevention Bulletin 269*, Oct 2019, p. 14.
30. Jenson et al., p. 15.

D IS FOR DEATH

31 https://staysafeapp.com/blog/history-workplace-health-safety/.
32 https://www.football-stadiums.co.uk/articles/the-burnden-park-stadium-disaster/.
33 You still can't buy a copy of *The Sun* in Merseyside because of the lies printed about the fans.
34 Conn, D., 26/4/16. https://www.theguardian.com/uk-news/2016/apr/26/hillsborough-inquests-jury-says-96-victims-were-unlawfully-killed accessed 13/7/23.
35 Burnham, A, 'The Collapse of the Last Hillsborough Trial Shows our Legal System is Broken', *The Guardian*, 30/5/21.
36 Easthope, pp. 67–68.
37 https://wp.sunderland.ac.uk/seagullcity/victoria-hall-disaster/ accessed 13/7/23.
38 A charred rocking horse was one of the prizes and is part of the British Museum's 'Teaching History with 100 Objects': 'The horse offers the opportunity to explore 19th century childhood, philanthropy and social reform.' http://teachinghistory100.org/objects/a_victorian_disaster accessed 13/7/23.
39 As if the families hadn't suffered enough, William McGonagall of Dundee, often regarded as the worst poet in the history of the English language, who specialised in disaster poems, commemorated the tragedy in 'The Sunderland Calamity'.
40 https://www.paisley.org.uk/paisley-history/glen-cinema/ accessed 13/7/23.
41 https://www.summerlandfiredisaster.co.uk/ accessed 13/7/23.
42 RIP, Bernard.
43 It can be viewed for free on the BFI website (if you dare).
44 The duke was now PM and they'd had a falling-out in Parliament.
45 https://www.newportonayhistory.org.uk/transport/tay-bridge-disaster-public-inquiry accessed 13/7/23.
46 Dalton, A., 1/2/13, https://www.scotsman.com/news/transport/memorial-sparks-tay-bridge-deaths-row-1551617 accessed 13/7/23.
47 https://www.ice.org.uk/what-is-civil-engineering/what-do-civil-engineers-do/tay-bridges/ accessed 13/7/23.
48 Amongst the survivors was Robin Gibb of the Bee Gees.
49 https://www.londonremembers.com/subjects/colin-j-townsley-g-m-station-officer accessed 13/7/23.
50 'Signal Passed at Danger' or 'SPAD'.
51 Chaired by Lord Cullen who had also presided over inquiries into Piper Alpha and Dunblane.
52 An automatic warning system would have prevented this.
53 https://www.theguardian.com/uk-news/2019/oct/17/ladbroke-grove-paddington-train-crash-inquiry. Treverton-Jones, Greg, 17/10/19, accessed 8/1/24. A personal and graphic account of the crash and its aftermath.
54 https://www.rac.co.uk/drive/advice/legal/seat-belt-law/ accessed 13/7/23.
55 https://www.brake.org.uk/get-involved/take-action/mybrake/knowledge-centre/uk-road-safety accessed 13/7/23.
56 https://www.roadpeace.org/working-for-change/improved-investigations/ accessed 13/7/23.
57 https://www.roadpeace.org/remembering-lives-lost/roadside-memorials/ accessed 13/7/23.
58 Mann, C., quoted by Campbell, D., 12/12/14 https://www.theguardian.com/society/2014/dec/12/home-accident-risk-nhs-doctor accessed 13/7/23.
59 https://england.shelter.org.uk/media/press_release/45_of_private_renters_have_been_victims_of_illegal_acts_by_their_landlord_or_letting_agent_ 14/9/21 accessed 13/7/23.
60 Taylor, R., 25/5/19 https://news.sky.com/story/disgraceful-theresa-may-criticised-for-citing-her-grenfell-response-as-a-success-11727859 accessed 13/7/23.
61 www.grenfelltowerinquiry.org.uk accessed 13/7/23.
62 Easthope, p. 185.
63 Symonds, T., 14/6/22 https://www.bbc.co.uk/news/uk-61724373 accessed 13/7/23.
64 Townsend, M., 16/5/21 https://www.theguardian.com/uk-news/2021/may/16/grenfell-relatives-say-they-will-fight-attempts-to-demolish-tower accessed 13/7/23.
65 Easthope, p. 197.
66 Kernick, G., 29/7/20, https://www.bennettinstitute.cam.ac.uk/blog/danger-narratives-we-use-silence-grenfell-and-rebe/ accessed 13/7/23.
67 Ward, L., 25/1/18 https://www.britsafe.org/publications/safety-management-magazine/safety-management-magazine/2017/the-duty-of-learning-from-errors/ accessed 13/7/23.
68 Easthope, p. 123.

ENDNOTES

B IS FOR BONES

1. The Bible, John 20:13–14.
2. Roach, M., *Stiff: The Curious Lives of Human Cadavers*, Penguin, 2004, p. 84.
3. 'Mothers and Babies: Reducing Risk through Audits and Confidential Enquiries across the UK'.
4. https://www.npeu.ox.ac.uk/assets/downloads/mbrrace-uk/reports/maternal-report-2021/MBRRACE-UK_Maternal_Report_2021_-_Lay_Summary_v10.pdf, p. 1, accessed, 13/7/23.
5. Ibid., p. 3.
6. Medial Intercostal Artery Perforator Flap Reconstruction.
7. John Reynes, cited in Horrox, R., 'Purgatory, Prayer and Plague: 1150–1380 in Jupp, P. and Gittings, C. (ed.) *Death in England*, Manchester University Press, 1999, p. 92.
8. https://www.history.co.uk/history-of-death/death-in-the-dark-ages accessed 23/7/23.
9. Horrox, p. 97.
10. Horrox, p. 93.
11. Bynum, Caroline Walker. 'Death and Resurrection in the Middle Ages: Some Modern Implications.' *Proceedings of the American Philosophical Society*, vol. 142, no. 4, 1998, p. 591. JSTOR, http://www.jstor.org/stable/3152283 accessed 26/9/22.
12. Rugg, J., 'From Reason to Regulation', *Death in England*, p. 204.
13. Powner DJ, Ackerman BM, Grenvik A. 'Medical diagnosis of death in adults: historical contributions to current controversies.' Lancet 1996; 348: 1219–23 cited in 'Diagnosing Death', Jacobe, S. 'Journal of Paediatrics and Child Health', 2016, p. 574 https://onlinelibrary.wiley.com/doi/pdf/10.1111/jpc.12889 accessed 13/7/23.
14. Jacobe, S. https://onlinelibrary.wiley.com/doi/pdf/10.1111/jpc.12889 p. 573.
15. Ibid., p. 576.
16. Roach, p. 39.
17. Roach, p. 42.
18. Ibid., p. 40.
19. I won't call it 'moonlighting' as body snatchers couldn't work under a full moon for risk of discovery.
20. At least some good came of bodysnatching in the name of science and medical progress. But the Dredgermen of the Thames were a different kettle of fish, dredging the river for victims of murder or suicide and looting their bodies.
21. Rugg, J., *Death in England*, p. 226.
22. Hammond, C., *Should You Bash a Bible Bump?* https://www.bbc.com/future/article/20130205-should-you-bash-a-bible-bump 5/2/13 accessed 13/7/23.
23. Interestingly, it was opened by Professor Susan Standring, editor in chief of *Gray's Anatomy*.
24. Roach, p. 56.
25. Ibid., p. 61.
26. Ibid., p. 62.
27. Osteoarchaeologists work on the historical past.
28. Black, S., *Written in Bone: Hidden Stories in What We Leave Behind*, Penguin, 2022, p. 11.
29. https://bodyworlds.com/ accessed 13/7/23.
30. The Human Tissue Act 2004 has made this more tricky in the UK.
31. Doughty, L., *Will My Cat Eat My Eatballs?* W&N, 2020, p. 20.
32. Ibid., p. 163.
33. Roach, p. 71.
34. Black, p. 3.
35. https://richardiii.net/finding-reburying-richard/updates/ accessed 13/7/23.
36. https://richardiii.net/finding-reburying-richard/a-message-from-philippa/ accessed 13/7/23.
37. https://richardiii.net/finding-reburying-richard/updates/ accessed 13/7/23.
38. Horrox, R., in *Death in England*, p. 131.
39. Roach, p. 170.
40. Ibid., p. 173.
41. There's even a Hollywood film called *21 Grams*. I've not watched it.
42. Roach, p. 176–79.
43. Roach, p. 186.
44. Ibid., p. 195.
45. Bynum, C.W, p. 596.

D IS FOR DEATH

C IS FOR CONTAGION

1. By Gift Republic.
2. Furtado, P., *Plague, Pestilence and Pandemic*, Thames and Hudson, UK, 2022, p. 7.
3. Furtado, p. 11.
4. https://www.who.int/health-topics/plague#tab=tab_1 accessed 13/7/23.
5. Arnold, C., *Necropolis: London and Its Dead*, Pocket Books, 2007, p. 26.
6. *Deadly Diseases*, Horrible Science, Scholastic Children's Books, 2000, p. 79.
7. I recently spent a weekend there, staying at a Wetherspoons hotel. Our room overlooked the kebab shop and I'm pretty sure there were at least nine hundred poor souls queuing outside at one in the morning.
8. Furtado, p. 75.
9. You can see the place where his 'heart' (internal organs) was buried in nearby St Lawrence's, the 'Cathedral of the Marches'. After he was embalmed, Arthur's body processed to Worcester Cathedral where it was interred.
10. Cardinal Wolsey survived several encounters with the Sweat only to lose his head over the whole Catherine of Aragon divorce saga. Double bummer. https://www.hevercastle.co.uk/news/sweating-sickness/ 15/4/20 accessed 13/7/23.
11. https://theconversation.com/what-was-sweating-sickness-the-mysterious-tudor-plague-of-wolf-hall-37194 6/2/15 accessed 13/7/23.
12. For reimagined events of this time, do read Maggie O'Farrell's *Hamnet*.
13. Ward, J.P. and Bucholz, R.O., 25/4/12, http://www.cambridgeblog.org/2012/04/shakespeares-globe-theatre-would-a-theater-by-any-other-name-smell-as-sweet/ accessed 13/7/23.
14. Ainley, O, 23/4/20, https://www.whatsonstage.com/ballymena-theatre/news/shakespeare-plague-disease-influence_51308.html, accessed 13/7/23.
15. Tichenor, A., 27/8/21, https://www.folger.edu/blogs/shakespeare-and-beyond/speaking-what-we-feel-shakespeares-plague-plays/ accessed 13/7/23.
16. Greenblatt, S., 7/5/20, https://www.newyorker.com/culture/cultural-comment/what-shakespeare-actually-wrote-about-the-plague accessed 13/7/23.
17. Shapiro, J., quoted in Young, R., and Hagan, A., '"He Didn't Flee": Shakespeare and the Plague', 6/4/20 https://www.wbur.org/hereandnow/2020/04/06/shakespeare-plague-coronavirus accessed 13/7/23.
18. Shapiro, J., *The Year of Lear*, Simon and Schuster, 2015, p. 277.
19. Covid's equivalent of colloidal silver? He later mentions a debate in the coffee-house about remedies, 'some saying one thing, some another.'.
20. Doig, A. *This Mortal Coil*, Bloomsbury, 2023, pp. 15–16.
21. Wall, C. *Introduction to A Journal of the Plague Year*, Penguin Classics, 2003, p. xx.
22. It only takes one. Think Typhoid Mary (we will come to her in a bit).
23. https://www.passionsspiele-oberammergau.de/en/home accessed 13/7/23.
24. https://www.who.int/news-room/fact-sheets/detail/cholera asccessed 13/7/23.
25. Furtado, p. 143.
26. James Newland, 1856, cited in Furtado, p. 151.
27. Furtado, p. 152.
28. https://www.who.int/news-room/fact-sheets/detail/typhoid accessed 13/7/23.
29. https://www.who.int/health-topics/tuberculosis#tab=tab_1.
30. Clarke, I., 'Tuberculosis: A Fashionable Disease?', 24/3/19, https://blog.sciencemuseum.org.uk/tuberculosis-a-fashionable-disease/ accessed 13/7/23.
31. https://blog.sciencemuseum.org.uk/tuberculosis-a-fashionable-disease/ accessed 13/7/23.
32. For a nuanced look at the campaign's success, have a read of this blog post from the London School of Hygiene and Tropical Medicine: https://www.who.int/health-topics/hiv-aids#tab=tab_1.
33. Kershaw, H., 'Remembering the "Don't Die of Ignorance Campaign"', *Placing the Public in Public Health: Public Health in Britain, 1948-2010*, LSHTM, 20/5/18, https://placingthepublic.lshtm.ac.uk/2018/05/20/remembering-the-dont-die-of-ignorance-campaign/ accessed 13/7/23.
34. https://www.tht.org.uk/our-work/about-our-charity/our-history/how-it-all-began.
35. DeCapua, J., 'AIDS: The Lazarus Effect', 8/12/10, https://www.voanews.com/a/decapua-aids-lazarus-effect-9dec10-111605079/157017.html accessed 13/7/23.
36. https://covid19.who.int accessed 13/7/23.

ENDNOTES

37. Rudd, J., 'Lady Mary Wortley Montague: "Mother of Inoculation"', 29/4/21 https://www.around-townmagazine.co.uk/lady-mary-wortley-montagu-mother-of-inoculation/ accessed 13/7/23.
38. Foussianes, C., 'Catherine the Great, Vaccine Queen', 2/1/21 https://www.townandcountrymag.com/society/tradition/a35091190/catherine-the-great-vaccine-queen/ accessed 1/5/23.

D IS FOR DISPOSAL

1. Paul Pettitt cited in https://www.nationalgeographic.com/culture/article/131216-la-chapelle-neanderthal-burials-graves accessed 13/7/23.
2. https://www.northcornwallclusterofchurches.org.uk/our-churches/st-enodoc/ accessed 13/7/23.
3. A big shoutout to church members and volunteers everywhere who hold the keys (and clean, change the flowers, protect from bat droppings, cut the grass, and look after the tombs and ecology).
4. Check out #tinylions on Twitter.
5. 'Empty tomb' in Greek, when bodily remains are elsewhere.
6. Where the Queen lay in state.
7. Dare I mention *The Da Vinci Code*?.
8. From the French *charnier* (flesh).
9. Pepys diary entry for 7 September 1666.
10. Or barrows, burial mounds or *kurgens*.
11. A single chamber megalithic tomb, two standing stones topped with a capstone (*cromlech* in Welsh).
12. https://www.historicenvironment.scot/visit-a-place/places/maeshowe-chambered-cairn/history/ accessed 9/01/23.
13. The custom of setting aside an acre of ground around the church for burials. Today the term is used to draw attention to the ecology of a churchyard and its importance as a wildlife haven.
14. Also here is the Bowdler family gravestone; Mrs Bowdler was the mother of the editor of the *Family Shakespeare* (remember the Harvey sisters of Bristol, ancestors of my mother?).
15. See 'W is for War'.
16. Ross, P., *Tomb with a View*, Headline, 2020, p.
17. Arnold, C., *Necropolis: London and its Dead*, pp. 1–8.
18. Bowdler, p. 8.
19. Migrants from northern Europe who settled in England in the fifth and sixth centuries, the dominant political force until the Norman conquest of 1066.
20. Arnold, pp. 68–71.
21. https://www.museumoflondon.org.uk/collections/other-collection-databases-and-libraries/centre-human-bioarchaeology/osteological-database/medieval-cemeteries/east-smithfield-black-death-medieval accessed 13/7/23.
22. Horrox, R., 'Purgatory, Prayer and Plague: 1110–1380' in Jupp, P.C. and Gittings, C. (eds), *Death in England*, MUP, 1999, p. 105.
23. Arnold, p. 37.
24. Ibid., p. 94.
25. Ross, p. 43.
26. Arnold, p. 122.
27. https://www.glasgownecropolis.org/history accessed 13/7/23.
28. Arnold, p. 24.
29. Ibid., pp. 44–45.
30. Hurrah for IKB!.
31. Ross, p. 34.
32. Ibid., p. 45.
33. Arnold, p. 162.
34. Though we know from the ongoing controversy of who owns the Elgin Marbles that the past is still very much with us.
35. Update: in Jan 2023, the ash tree finally succumbed to a fungal disease and has toppled over, dead.
36. Inspired by the monument to King Mausolus of Halicarnassus, one of the Seven Wonders of the World, a mausoleum is a large above-ground structure for burials with shelves on which to lay coffins.
37. To commemorate the death of his wife, Eleanor, Edward I not only commissioned three tombs but also twelve stone crosses to mark each place her body rested overnight on her final journey

from Nottinghamshire to London. https://www.english-heritage.org.uk/visit/places/eleanor-cross-geddington/history/ accessed 13/7/23.
38   Quoted in Arnold, p. 179.
39   Ibid., p. 226.
40   Arnold, p. 224.
41   Ross, p. 115.
42   Ibid., p. 116.
43   Lane. P., Price, J., and Spencer, S., 'The Last Journey: The Funeral Rites and Cultural Needs of Gypsies and Travellers', 2022, p. 24.
44   https://www.mariecurie.org.uk/talkabout/articles/how-to-have-an-environmentally-responsible-death/284416.
45   https://cremationink.com/aquamation.
46   https://cremationink.com/aquamation/resomation.
47   https://recompose.life/.
48   Built by Sir Thomas Acland for the old and infirm of his estate, similar to Blaise Hamlet in Bristol, where my maternal grandmother used to take me for walks. Chocolate box pretty.
49   The company Sacred Stones opened a barrow in 2016, the first of its kind in 3,500 years. There are several in the UK now. https://www.sacredstones.co.uk/.

E IS FOR ELEGY

1   https://www.artofdyingwell.org/ accessed 13/7/23.
2   Over 100 writers are buried here or have memorials. The deans decide who gets a place based on merit.
3   There is some fine examples of memento mori here, the church that Elizabeth I described as the 'fairest, goodliest and most famous parish church in England'.
4   Now holiday accommodation so you too can visit, hopefully less painfully.
5   'A still life artwork which includes various symbolic objects designed to remind the viewer of their mortality and of the worthlessness of worldly goods and pleasures' https://www.tate.org.uk/art/art-terms/v/vanitas accessed 13/7/23.
6   Or like Joel Goodman's photo taken for the *Manchester Evening News*, a street scene of the city on New Year's Eve, 2015.
7   Remember Eyam, the village in Derbyshire which sacrificed itself during the plague? Seward's father was rector of the parish church there in Anna's early years.
8   Seward, A., *Llangollen Vale, with Other Poems*. Printed for G. Sael, No. 192, Strand, 1796, pp. 37–40.
9   Christie, A., *The Murder on the Links*.
10 Quine is Scots for queen.
11 Berridge, p. 21.
12 Lawson, M., 17/10/17, https://www.theguardian.com/tv-and-radio/shortcuts/2017/oct/17/axed-who-killed-crimewatch-and-why accessed 14/7/23.
13 I've taken up ballet again after a break of forty years!.

F IS FOR FUNERAL

1   Lyons and Winter, *We All Know How This Ends*, Green Tree, 2021, p. 8.
2   Arnold, p. 74.
3   If you've ever watched *Amadeus*, you will see that Mozart is conveyed to the graveyard in a parish coffin (and tipped unceremoniously into a pauper's mass grave – though in reality it was simply an unmarked grave).
4   'Lych' is old Eng. for corpse or body. Many lychgates are now war memorials.
5   Some lychgate stone coffin rests still remain such as at St Andrew's, Hope Bowdler, Shropshire, and St Pancras, Widecombe-in-the-Moor, Devon. You can still see coffin stones on some surviving corpse roads.
6   *The Works of Charles Lamb*.
7   From the French word for 'harrow', a frame with metal teeth for breaking up the earth.
8   https://www.parliament.uk/about/living-heritage/transformingsociety/private-lives/death-dying/dying-and-death/burying/.

ENDNOTES

9. This update was written in the 90s, not long before her own death.
10. Mitford, p. 51.
11. Ibid., p. 43.
12. A casket is an American coffin with four sides, as opposed to a British one, which traditionally had six.
13. Mitford pp. 45–50.
14. Mitford, p. 25.
15. Iserson, K.V., *Death to Dust: What Happens to Dead Bodies?*, Galen Press, 1994, cited in Mitford, p. 63.
16. Mitford, p. 212.
17. Boseley, S. and Godwin, P., 'Have a Nice Death: The Americans pioneered a fast-food, hard-sell approach to death. It is not the British Way', *The Guardian*, 27/2/96, cited in Mitford, p. 224.
18. Berridge, K., *Vigor Mortis*, p. 21.
19. Mitford, p. 141.
20. Arnold, p. 29.
21. https://squaremilehealthwalks.wordpress.com/2022/05/04/pardon-chapel/ 4/5/22 accessed 14/7/23.
22. https://www.parliament.uk/about/living-heritage/transformingsociety/private-lives/death-dying/dying-and-death/burying/ 1/5/14 accessed 14/7/23.
23. Doughty, S., 12/2/15, https://www.dailymail.co.uk/news/article-2951586/Church-England-allow-funerals-suicides-General-Synod-votes-sweep-away-ban-signal-compassion-vulnerable.html accessed 14/7/23.
24. Frisby, H., *Traditions of Death and Burial*, Shire Publications, 2019, p. 87.
25. https://www.coop.co.uk/funeralcare/funeral-services/religious-funerals/jewish-funeral accessed 14/7/23.
26. Challenger, G., Friends, Families and Travellers Report https://www.gypsy-traveller.org/wp-content/uploads/2017/03/Cemetery-Culture-and-Traditions_v2.pdf accessed 14/7/23.
27. https://www.travellerstimes.org.uk/features/my-grandfathers-coffin-came-home-our-house-gypsy-and-traveller-funerals 30/3/21 accessed 14/7/23.
28. Astley, O., 14/10/22 https://www.derbytelegraph.co.uk/news/derby-news/funeral-director-opens-up-traveller-7698933 accessed 14/7/23.
29. Lane. P., Price, J., and Spencer, S., 'The Last Journey: The Funeral Rites and Cultural Needs of Gypsies and Travellers', 2022, p. 4.
30. ONS, 2011, cited in Lane et al., p. 4.
31. House of Commons 2019b; Shelter Scotland, 2015, cited in Lane et al., p. 5.
32. Millan and Smith, 2019; House of Commons, 2019a, cited in Lane et al., p. 5.
33. Lane et al., p. 7.
34. Smithers, R., 3/5/18 https://www.theguardian.com/lifeandstyle/2018/may/03/co-op-offers-no-frills-cremation-service accessed 14/7/23.
35. https://www.churchofengland.org/life-events/funerals/arranging-funeral/funeral-locations.
36. https://www.history.co.uk/history-of-death/death-rituals-and-superstitions.
37. The Apostles' Creed is a statement of Christian faith often recited at funerals. All the former presidents and first ladies of the USA said it at the funeral of President George Bush Senior, except for Donald and Melania Trump. As the Americans say: 'Go figure.'.
38. https://greenundertakings.co.uk/funeral-wishes/.
39. Chapman, S., *Funeral Arranging and End of life Decisions*, p. 24.
40. https://www.somersetwillowcoffins.co.uk/.
41. https://reviewspot.co.uk/reviews/cancer-blog/road-runner-cartoon-socks-selecting-a-coffin-and-mind-the-death-gap.
42. Frisby, p. 86.
43. Cardboard, banana leaf, willow, bamboo.

G IS FOR GHOSTS

1. Owens, S., *The Ghost: A Cultural History*, Tate Publishing, 2017, p. 7.
2. Ibid., pp. 8–10.
3. Owens, pp. 17–18.

4   https://www.english-heritage.org.uk/visit/places/berry-pomeroy-castle/history/ accessed 16/7/23.
5   You can read them here and their English translation. http://www.anselm-classics.com/byland/about.html accessed 16/7/23.
6   Jackson, E., https://blogs.bl.uk/digitisedmanuscripts/2020/10/byland-abbey-ghost-stories.html accessed 16/7/23.
7   Owens, p. 33.
8   https://churchmonumentssociety.org/monument-of-the-month/the-john-donne-monument-d-1631-by-nicholas-stone-st-pauls-cathedral-london.
9   John Wesley, 'An Account of the Disturbances in my Father's House', The Arminian Magazine, Vol.7, 1784, pp. 654–56 https://archive.org/details/arminian-magazine-entirebook/page/653/mode/2up.
10 Owens, p. 113.
11 https://www.realmarykingsclose.com/the-story-of-annies-doll/ accessed 16/7/23.

H IS FOR HEALTH; I IS FOR ILLNESS

1   Doig, A., *This Mortal Coil: A History of Death*. Bloomsbury, 2023, pp. 42-43.
2   Schneider, E. C., 'Health Care as an Ongoing Policy Project', *New England Journal of Medicine*, 383, 2020, pp. 405–8, cited in Doig, p. 48.
3   Schoenman, J.A., 'The Concentration of Healthcare Spending', *NIHCM Foundation Brief* [Online], 2012. Both cited in Doig, pp. 48–49.
4   Doig, pp. 293–96.
5   Ibid., pp. 298–99.
6   Thank you, Cameron, for prising that off me when even Thatcher, who snatched the milk off school children, believed child benefit sacrosanct.
7   https://merl.reading.ac.uk/explore/online-exhibitions/colonial-failure/#growing_potential accessed 17/7/23.
8   http://filestore.nationalarchives.gov.uk/pdfs/small/cab-128-18-cm-50-83-43.pdf accessed 17/7/23.
9   Tweddell, L., 8/1/08 https://www.nursingtimes.net/archive/the-birth-of-the-nhs-july-5th-1948-08-01-2008/accessed 17/7/23.
10 Ibid.
11 Mannix, K., *With the End in Mind*, William Collins, 2017, p. 2.
12 Jarrett, D., *33 Meditations on Death: Notes from the Wrong End of Medicine*, Transworld Digital, 2020, p. 184.
13 15/9/09 https://web.archive.org/web/20091017060802/http://www.thisisbristol.co.uk/homepage/TV-chef-Keith-Floyd-dies-heart-attack/article-1339257-detail/article.html accessed 17/7/23.
14 Jarrett, pp. 256–57.
15 Ibid., p. 146.
16 Ibid., pp. 186-7.
17 Ibid., p. 56.
18 Ibid., pp. 252–53.
19 Gawande, A., *Being Mortal*, Profile Books, 2015, pp. 55, 76.
20 Ibid., p. 213.
21 Lyons, A., and Winter, L., *We All Know How this Ends*, Green Tree, 2021, p. 17.
22 Philip Gould, *When I Die: Lessons from the Death Zone*, https://www.youtube.com/watch?v=S2eUw0CUuMc accessed 17/7/23.
23 Mannix, pp. 9–10.
24 Ibid., p. 123, 153.
25 In the UK, you can also choose to receive hospice care at home.
26 Lyons and Winter, p. 15 (Read their manifesto on pp. 18–19. It's good. In fact, read the whole book.).
27 Mannix, p. 113.
28 Ibid., p. 131.
29 Ibid., pp. 177–78, 219.
30 Gawande, p. 186.
31 Ibid., p. 182.
32 Gawande, p. 243.
33 Mannix, p. 293.

ENDNOTES

34 Ibid., p. 158.
35 Ibid., p. 161.
36 Mannix, p. 22.
37 Jarrett, pp. 135–36.
38 Ibid., p. 109–10.
39 Ibid., p. 21.
40 Jarrett, pp. 126–27.
41 Mannix, p. 96.
42 Gawande, pp. 21–23.
43 Ibid., pp. 101-6.
44 Mannix.
45 Jarrett, p. 29.
46 Gawande, p. 127.
47 Lyons, A. (2021), p. 26.
48 Jarrett, pp. 191–93.
49 Mannix, p. 125.
50 https://www.alzheimersresearchuk.org/ accessed 17/7/23.
51 https://www.dementiauk.org/ accessed 17/7/23.
52 Doig, p. 310.
53 Ibid.

J IS FOR JET; K IS FOR KEENING; L IS FOR LAMENT

1 Frisby, H., *Traditions of Death and Burial*, Shire Publications, 2019, p. 42.
2 This is how the Duke of Portsmouth referred to funerals.
3 Arnold, p. 189.
4 Jalland, p. 243.
5 Frisby, p. 46.
6 Berridge, K., *Vigor Mortis*, Profile Books, 2001, p. 139.
7 Scholz, D, https://lilacandbombazine.wordpress.com/2018/07/30/layers-of-sorrow-the-fabrics-of-mourning/ accessed 16/7/23.
8 Berridge, p. 24.
9 The name comes from the city of Parramatta in Australia, where prison inmates made this high-quality cloth.
10 Arnold, pp. 207–8.
11 Arnold, pp. 208–9.
12 *Cassells*.
13 Frisby, p. 53.
14 Arnold, p. 211.
15 Berridge, p. 138.
16 Scholz, D., https://lilacandbombazine.wordpress.com/2018/07/30/layers-of-sorrow-the-fabrics-of-mourning/ accessed 16/7/23.
17 Arnold, p. 212.
18 Cherrell, K., https://burialsandbeyond.com/2019/11/05/jays-mourning-warehouse/ accessed 16/7/23.
19 Ibid.
20 Frisby, p. 47.
21 *Cassells*.
22 https://www.english-heritage.org.uk/visit/inspire-me/history-of-jet-jewellery/ accessed 16/7/23.
23 Ibid.
24 https://burialsandbeyond.com/2019/10/26/whitby-jet-what-why-and-when/#more-723 accessed 16/7/23.
25 https://www.english-heritage.org.uk/visit/inspire-me/history-of-jet-jewellery/ accessed 16/7/23.
26 Scholz, D., https://lilacandbombazine.wordpress.com/2019/03/18/a-visit-to-whitby-part-2/ accessed 16/7/23.
27 Frisby, p. 53.
28 Darby, E., and Smith, N., 'In Mourning for Prince Albert' in https://www.historytoday.com/archive/feature/mourning-prince-albert accessed 8/6/23.

D IS FOR DEATH

29 Ibid.
30 Frisby, p. 46.
31 https://www.historytoday.com/archive/feature/mourning-death-prince-albert.
32 Darby and Smith.
33 Cited in Rugg, J., 'From Reason to Regulation: 1790–1850', *Death in England*, p. 216.
34 Jalland, P., 'Victorian Death and Its Decline: 1850–1918', *Death in England*, p. 236–68.
35 Berridge, pp. 12–15.
36 Ibid., p. 13.
37 Dickens, C., *The Old Curiosity Shop*. And what about Mr Mould in *Martin Chuzzlewit* or the undertaker that Oliver Twist is apprenticed to after being kicked out of the workhouse?.
38 Berridge, p. 17.
39 Ibid., p. 19.
40 Bown, N., Burdett, C., Thurschwell, P., eds. *The Victorian Supernatural*. Cambridge: Cambridge University Press, 2004 cited in Diniejko, A., https://victorianweb.org/victorian/religion/spirit.html.
41 http://www.spiritualistchurchkeighley.co.uk/principles.html accessed 16/7/23.
42 https://victorianweb.org/victorian/religion/spirit.html accessed 16/7/23.
43 Hill, C.B.T., 'A Study of Spiritualism in the Life and Work of Elizabeth Barrett Browning', University of Birmingham Research Archive, e-theses repository, p. 6.
44 Jalland, pp. 248, 293.
45 Gavin, M., http://www.keeningwake.com/about/ accessed 16/7/23.

M IS FOR MYTHS

1 Barley, N., *Dancing on the Grave*, John Murray, 1995, p. 63.
2 Addy, S.O., *Household Tales with Other Traditional Remains, Collected in the Counties of York, Lincoln, Derby and Nottingham*, 1895, p. 98.
3 Frisby, H., *Traditions of Death and Burial*, Shire Publications, 2019, p. 29.
4 Frisby, p. 45.
5 Frisby, p. 44.
6 https://beyondthename.weebly.com/old-welsh-customs.html#6 accessed 20/6/23.
7 Ibid.
8 One of Radio 4's *A History of the World in 1000 Objects*.
9 Berridge, p. 194.
10 Addy, p. 124.
11 Ibid., pp. 122–26.
12 https://beyondthename.weebly.com/old-welsh-customs.html#6 accessed 21/06/23.
13 Addy, p. 64.
14 Frisby, p. 16.
15 Frisby, H., 'Death, Dying, and Funerals in Victorian (and slightly later) Yorkshire', p. 18, http://centre-for-english-traditional-heritage.org/TraditionToday8/2_Frisby_Death_Dying.pdf accessed 17/7/23.
16 Addy, p. 101.
17 'Guidance Note: Operation London Bridge', the Central Council of Church Bell Ringers https://cccbr.org.uk/guidance-note-operation-london-bridge/ accessed 17/7/23.
18 Frisby, p. 22.
19 Addy, p. 116.
20 Addy, p. 105.
21 https://www.myblackdog.co/ accessed 17/7/23.
22 http://www.sane.org.uk/what_we_do/black_dog accessed 17/7/23.
23 https://www.mhinnovation.net/resources/living-black-dog-video accessed 17/7/23.
24 Cited in Frisby, p. 17.
25 Ibid.
26 *The Observer's Book of Birds*, 1972, p. 115.
27 Frisby, p. 17.
28 Addy, pp. 64–65.
29 Frisby, *Traditions of Death and Burial*, p. 59.
30 https://sheelanagig.org/theories/ accessed 17/7/23.

ENDNOTES

31. Also known as the 'Devil's door', it was left open during a baptism service so that the evil spirit, believed to be in a child, could escape.
32. Stevens, J., 8/3/21 https://www.theguardian.com/world/2021/mar/08/big-vagina-energy-the-return-of-the-sheela-na-gig accessed 17/7/23.
33. https://www.liverpoolmuseums.org.uk/stories/caul-object-of-sailors-supersitions accessed 17/7/23.
34. Prince George's log entry for 11 July 1881, Royal Navy archives.
35. He was knighted at Greenwich, his boat moored nearby, the Queen using the same sword that the first Queen Elizabeth had used to knight Sir Francis Drake. The *Gipsy Moth* is still at Greenwich, near the *Cutty Sark*. It's hard to believe such a tiny boat could sailed 29,000 miles.
36. McCrum, R., 5/4/09, https://www.theguardian.com/uk/2009/apr/05/donald-crowhurst-lone-sailor accessed 17/7/23.
37. https://www.yachtingworld.com/features/donald-crowhurst-fake-world-sailing-story-the-mercy-123426 2/10/19 accessed 17/7/23.
38. McCrum.
39. Ibid.
40. https://www.yachtingworld.com/features/donald-crowhurst-fake-world-sailing-story-the-mercy-123426.
41. Frisby, *Traditions* p. 11.
42. Ibid., p. 39.
43. Ibid., p. 59.
44. Frisby, p. 58.

N IS FOR NEXT OF KIN

1. https://www.missingpeople.org.uk/ accessed 17/7/23. The Presumption of Death Act 2013 simplifies this process. Lord Lucan, last seen in 1974, was finally presumed dead, with his death certificate issued in 2016.
2. Jarrett, pp. 114–15.
3. Ibid., p. 20.
4. Ibid., p. 19.
5. Jarrett, pp. 19–20.
6. Grubb et al. (2010) cited in Griffith, R., 9/4/20, https://www.britishjournalofnursing.com/content/legal/the-law-and-death/ accessed 25/6/23.
7. Griffith and Tengnah (2008) cited in Griffith, R., 9/4/20 https://www.britishjournalofnursing.com/content/legal/the-law-and-death/#B8 accessed 17/7/23.
8. https://www.nhs.uk/conditions/brain-death/ accessed 17/7/23.
9. Jarrett, p. 259.
10. https://www.gov.uk/government/publications/public-health-funerals-good-practice-guidance/public-health-funerals-good-practice-guidance 16/9/20 accessed 17/7/23.
11. https://www.publichealthfunerals.org/information-advice/what-is-a-public-health-funeral/#1523452929-1-31657805698352 accessed 17/7/23.
12. King, E., *Ashes to Admin: Tales from the Caseload of a Council Funeral Officer*, Mirror Books, 2023.
13. http://evansaboveonline.co.uk/after-death/collecting-the-body/ accessed 17/7/23.
14. https://www.organdonation.nhs.uk/uk-laws/ accessed 26/1/24.
15. https://www.britishjournalofnursing.com/content/legal/the-law-and-death/#B8.
16. Griffith, R., 9/4/20, https://www.britishjournalofnursing.com/content/legal/the-law-and-death/ accessed 17/7/23.
17. Assets are the personal property of the deceased, including jewellery, furniture, bank accounts, life insurance policies, investments, land, property – physical and intangible.
18. https://www.gov.uk/valuing-estate-of-someone-who-died/check-type-of-estate accessed 17/7/23.
19. https://www.dignityindying.org.uk/assisted-dying/our-position/ accessed 17/7/23.
20. Between 300 and 650 terminally ill people take their own lives in the UK each year. https://www.dignityindying.org.uk/why-we-need-change/suicides/ accessed 17/7/23.
21. Jarrett, pp. 248–49.
22. Gawande, pp. 244–45.
23. Lyons and Winter, pp. 69–70.
24. Ibid., p. 71.

D IS FOR DEATH
O IS FOR OPERATION LONDON BRIDGE

1. Rennell, T., *Last Days of Glory: The Death of Queen Victoria*, St Martin's Press, 2001 .
2. Knight, S., 17/3/17 https://www.theguardian.com/uk-news/2017/mar/16/what-happens-when-queen-elizabeth-dies-london-bridge accessed 25/7/23.
3. Ibid.
4. Ibid.
5. Tay Bridge for the Queen Mother on which Diana's ceremonial funeral was based, Forth Bridge for Prince Philip, Duke of Edinburgh, Menai Bridge for Charles III.
6. Ibid.
7. Ibid.
8. Cannadine, D., 'The Context, Performance and Meaning of Ritual: The British Monarchy and the "Invention of Tradition", c. 1820–1977' in Hobsbawm, E., and Ranger, T. (eds), *The Invention of Tradition*, Cambridge University Press, 1983, pp. 117–18.
9. https://www.stpauls.co.uk/nelson-wellington-and-churchill.
10. One of my dear friends, daughter of a vice-admiral, was married here and it was a delight to attend.
11. https://www.nationalarchives.gov.uk/nelson/gallery8/.
12. From the Greek, 'flesh-eating stone'.
13. https://www.nationalarchives.gov.uk/nelson/gallery8/legend.htm.
14. https://www.nmrn.org.uk/news/extraordinary-life-horatia-nelson 29/1/23 accessed 22/7/23.
15. My older brother, Peter, remembers one of her sons, Percy Box, our great-grandfather. More of him and his brothers in 'W Is for Wellington'.
16. My dear friend, Val, took me there for a day trip when I visited her in Pisa while on her third year abroad as part of her Italian degree at Lancaster. Stunning and memorable, not just because we narrowly missed the ferry.
17. Levy, M., 'Napoleon in Exile: The Houses and Furniture Supplied by the British Government for the Emperor and His Entourage on St Helena', *Furniture History*, vol. 34, 1998, pp. 57.
18. https://napoleonswillow.weebly.com/the-real-napoleons-willow.html accessed 10/8/23.
19. 'Lost Diary of Andrew Darling', *Kalgoorlie Western Argus*, Dec 14, 1915 https://trove.nla.gov.au/newspaper/article/33599543 accessed 24/7/23.
20. https://www.metmuseum.org/art/collection/search/823856 accessed 24/7/23.
21. Berridge, K., Vigor Mortis, Profile Books, 2002, p. 77.
22. Ibid., p. 73.
23. Ibid., p. 75.
24. Ibid., p. 78.
25. Ibid.
26. Ibid., p. 75–76.
27. Ibid., p. 77.
28. https://www.hellomagazine.com/royalty/20210521113646/prince-harry-haunting-memory-princess-diana-funeral/ accessed 26/7/23.
29. Berridge, p. 102.
30. Ibid., p. 100.
31. Ibid., pp. 84–91.
32. Ibid.
33. Shelley cited in Berridge, p. 98.
34. Berridge, pp. 95–97.
35. https://www.unicef.org/emergencies/yemen-crisis, https://www.bbc.co.uk/news/world-middle-east-29319423 both accessed 26/7/23.
36. The fallout of events on 7 October 2023 (what would have been my dad's 90th birthday) will further devastate children all over the Middle East.
37. Allsopp, J., 27/6/23 https://www.birmingham.ac.uk/news/2023/how-coverage-of-the-titan-submersible-refugee-boats-reflects-the-dehumanisation-of-refugees accessed 26/7/23.
38. Reider, D., 23/6/23 https://thelead.uk/ugliest-contrast-between-titanic-sub-and-refugee-boat-accountability accessed 26/7/23.
39. Craig, D.J., 2022 https://magazine.columbia.edu/article/war-atrocities-yemen-linked-us-weapons accessed 26/7/23.

ENDNOTES

40   Small Arms Survey (an independent research project at the Graduate Institute of International and Development Studies in Geneva). https://www.smallarmssurvey.org/sites/default/files/resources/SAS-BP-Civilian-held-firearms-annexe.pdf accessed 17/7/23.
41   https://www.gunviolencearchive.org/ GVA is an independent data collection and research group with no affiliation with any advocacy organisation. See also https://abcnews.go.com/US/countries-show-us-americas-gun-violence-epidemic/story?id=80495637 which includes a gun violence tracker. Frightening. And https://www.usnews.com/news/best-countries/articles/2023-01-30/how-the-u-s-compares-to-the-world-on-guns all accessed 28/7/23.
42   https://www.theguardian.com/us-news/2017/nov/15/the-gun-numbers-just-3-of-american-adults-own-a-collective-133m-firearms accessed 28/7/23.
43   'A well-regulated Militia, being necessary to the security of a free State, the right of the people to keep and bear Arms, shall not be infringed.'
44   https://www.sandyhookpromise.org/blog/stories/president-obama-reflects-on-gun-violence-in-america/.

P IS FOR POTTER'S FIELD

1   Samuel, p. 133.
2   https://www.samaritans.org/about-samaritans/media-guidelines/ accessed 26/7/23.
3   I have been transcribing some of her letters written from 'Ceylon' in the late 1800s/early 1900s. Her husband George, my great-grandfather, later remarried and had another child, Ruth, the little bridesmaid at my grandparents' wedding and later teenage Wren, activist and champion composter (for whom I delivered the eulogy). More on the Gillespys in 'T Is for Terror'.
4   Samuel, J., *Grief Works*, Penguin Life, 2018, pp. 137–38.
5   Ibid., p. 139.
6   Ken Doka first coined the phrase 'disenfranchised grief' in 1989 to refer to 'losses in the mourner's life of relationships that are not socially sanctioned'. So for me it was a double disenfranchisement: of me being a powerless child and of Dad's unspeakable suicide.
7   Lloyd, C., *You Are Not Alone*, Bloomsbury Tonic (2013).
8   https://www.samaritans.org/about-samaritans/our-history/ accessed 26/7/23.
9   The National Suicide Prevention Alliance is a cross-sector, England-wide coalition working to reduce suicide, https://www.samaritans.org/about-samaritans/our-organisation/national-suicide-prevention-alliance/ accessed 26/7/23.
10 https://www.who.int/news-room/fact-sheets/detail/suicide accessed 10/8/23.
11 https://www.samaritans.org/about-samaritans/research-policy/suicide-facts-and-figures/understanding-suicide-statistics/ accessed 10/8/23.
12 https://commonslibrary.parliament.uk/research-briefings/cbp-7749/ accessed 10/8/23.
13 Also, the title of Cariad Lloyd's wonderful book on grief.
14 https://www.spuk.org.uk/world-suicide-prevention-day-2022/.
15 More of this in 'U Is for Unfinished'.
16 https://media.samaritans.org/documents/Ethnicity_and_suicide_July_2022.pdf accessed 10/08/23.See also https://www.ons.gov.uk/peoplepopulationandcommunity/healthandsocialcare/healthinequalities/bulletins/sociodemographicinequalitiesinsuicidesinenglandandwales/2011to2021, https://nspa.org.uk/wp-content/uploads/2022/02/Equality-and-diversity-in-suicide-prevention-Dr-Duleeka-Knipe.pdf, https://www.ethnicity-facts-figures.service.gov.uk/health/mental-health/adults-reporting-suicidal-thoughts-attempts-and-self-harm/latest all accessed 10/8/23.

Q IS FOR QUILT; R IS FOR RAINBOW; S IS FOR SCARVES AND SHOES

1   Frisby, H., *Traditions of Death and Burial*, p. 73.
2   Doka K.J. (ed.). *Disenfranchised Grief: New Directions, Challenges, and Strategies for Practice.* Champaign, IL: Research Press; (2002), cited in Albuquerque, S., Teixeira, A.M., and Rocha, J.C., 'COVID-19 and Disenfranchised Grief', *Front Psychiatry*, 12, 2021, 638874, published online 12/2/21 https://www.ncbi.nlm.nih.gov/pmc/articles/PMC7907151/#B6 accessed 12/8/23.
3   A reflection of the size of a grave.
4   https://www.aidsmemorial.org/quilt-history.
5   https://www.aidsmemorial.org/interactive-aids-quilt.

6. https://whatsyourgrief.com/creating-memorial-quilt-lori-mason/.
7. https://www.zakfoster.com/about.
8. Berridge, p. 26.
9. Frisby, p. 23.
10. Mitford, p. 67.
11. Berridge, p. 104.
12. Abernethy, L. 16/2/19 https://metro.co.uk/2019/02/16/queerly-departed-meet-cemetery-tour-guides-retelling-forgotten-lgbtq-stories-100-years-ago-8628146/ accessed 26/8/23.
13. https://outstoriesbristol.org.uk/people/biographies/amelia-edwards/ accessed 26/8/23.
14. https://queerfuneralguide.co.uk/wp-content/uploads/2020/11/queer-funeral-guide-2019.pdf.
15. Arnold, p. 97.
16. Ross, p. 139.
17. Ibid.
18. Ibid., p. 137.
19. Ibid., p. 140.
20. Ibid.
21. Ibid., p. 159.
22. https://www.smartcremation.com/articles/tattooing-cremation-ashes/.
23. https://www.star-registration.com/en-gb/collections/stars.
24. Jarrett, p. 172.
25. Mannix, pp. 270–71.
26. My nan was less than four pounds when she was born in 1918 and the doctor baptised her in her first bathwater as she was not expected to live through the night.
27. Frisby, p. 144.
28. Ross, p. 149.
29. Ibid., p. 153.
30. Water is symbolic as the *mizuko* leaves the waters of the womb to return to its former liquid state to prepare for rebirth.
31. You can see these statues at Crossbones. Some of them wear red balaclavas.
32. https://www.miscarriageassociation.org.uk/story/water-baby/.
33. https://www.stillbornproject.org.uk/ accessed 12/8/23.
34. Heazell, A. in Klooster, A., *Still Born*, Affect Formations Publishing, 2021, p. 4.
35. Ibid., p. 43.
36. Biggs, L., *The Guardian*, 17/8/19 https://www.theguardian.com/lifeandstyle/2019/aug/17/the-words-that-helped-after-the-stillbirth-of-our-son accessed 24/8/23.
37. https://www.presentascent.co.uk/about.
38. https://www.tommys.org/baby-loss-support/rainbow-baby.
39. Liddiard, K. 22/8/21 https://www.sheffield.ac.uk/ihuman/news/rethinking-rainbow-baby accessed 24/8/21.
40. Walter, T., cited in Berridge, p. 94.
41. https://liverpoolfcfans.forumcommunity.net/?t=26438638 and https://bleacherreport.com/articles/2431915-how-everton-stood-by-liverpool-in-the-26-years-since-hillsborough-disaster.
42. https://www.thisisanfield.com/2014/07/lfc-donate-hillsborough-scarves-charities/ all accessed 26/8/23.
43. Attributed to Ernest Hemingway.
44. A People's Festival of Storytelling and Remembrance to revive lost traditions and create new ones. Held across Scotland annually from 1–7 November https://www.toabsentfriends.org.uk/ accessed 28/8/23.
45. https://www.toabsentfriends.org.uk/news/festival-events-2019/remembering-the-invisible/ accessed 28/8/23.
46. https://encyclopedia.ushmm.org/tags/en/tag/shoes.
47. https://www.yadvashem.org/articles/general/shoes-on-the-danube-promenade.html.

T IS FOR TERROR

1. https://www.gov.uk/government/publications/prevent-duty-guidance.
2. https://www.gov.uk/government/history/past-prime-ministers/tony-blair.

ENDNOTES

3. https://www.iwm.org.uk/history/the-blitz-around-britain.
4. Arnold, p. 34.
5. In 'E Is for Elegy'.
6. His physician was William Harvey ('B Is for Bones') who stayed with him throughout the war. His manuscripts were looted by rioters, which is a shame as they would have been a great insight into his thinking.
7. Brewer, C., *The Death of Kings*, Abson Books (2005) pp. 172–74.
8. Duncan Campbell, 12/3/18 https://www.theguardian.com/uk-news/2018/mar/12/ruth-ellis-files-bbc-documentary-murder-case-cant-let-go.
9. https://www.theguardian.com/lifeandstyle/2010/sep/18/albert-pierrepoint-ian-sansom tt.
10. Her naked, bald ghost is said to haunt Holyrood Palace.
11. https://www.lancs.live/news/lancashire-news/pendle-witches-story-lancashire-trial-16318258.
12. Marchant, L., https://www.raws.scot/post/launch-of-the-accused-witches-trail.
13. Ibid.
14. Thomas Potts (clerk of the court), from *The Wonderful Discovery of Witches in the County of Lancaster*, 1613.
15. Thomas Baines, *History of Lancashire*, 1867 cited in https://www.pendlewitches.co.uk/.
16. Castelow, E., 31/7/19 https://www.historic-uk.com/CultureUK/The-Pendle-Witches/ accessed 29/8/23.
17. https://www.thehistorypress.co.uk/articles/the-pendle-witches/.
18. https://www.daysofhorror.com/episode/meg-shelton-last-of-the-lancashire-witches-1705/.
19. From *Still I Rise* by Maya Angelou.
20. https://visitlancaster.org.uk/museums/maritime-museum/the-transatlantic-slave-trade/.
21. Ibid.
22. Stone, P. *111 Dark Places in England That You Shouldn't Miss*, Emons, 2021, p. 100.
23. https://sugarhouse.lancastersu.co.uk/name.
24. https://www.museumoflondon.org.uk/discover/mapping-londons-legacy-slavery-docklands.
25. https://www.london.gov.uk/programmes-strategies/arts-and-culture/commission-diversity-public-realm/new-memorial-victims-transatlantic-slave-trade.
26. https://www.liverpoolmuseums.org.uk/transcript-of-age-of-slave-apologies-case-of-liverpool-england.
27. https://liverpoolexpress.co.uk/slavery-historian-awarded-citizen-of-honour/.
28. https://www.manchester.ac.uk/discover/news/diversity-in-statues-and-public-memorials.
29. https://www.theguardian.com/world/2020/sep/01/david-olusoga-i-wanted-to-join-protesters-who-tore-down-colston-statue.
30. https://www.theguardian.com/commentisfree/2020/jun/08/edward-colston-statue-history-slave-trader-bristol-protest.
31. https://www.bbc.co.uk/news/uk-england-bristol-59727161.
32. Olusoga, D., cited 5/1/22 in https://www.independent.co.uk/news/uk/crime/david-olusoga-edward-colstonblack-lives-matter-britain-george-floyd-b1987625.html.
33. https://exhibitions.bristolmuseums.org.uk/the-colston-statue/.
34. Imogen Tyler (2020) 'Facing the Past, Transforming the Future: Doing Reparative History with Communities in Lancaster' (Blog). Online at: https://www.lancasterslaveryfamilytrees.com/.
35. https://www.ucl.ac.uk/lbs/.
36. https://www.theguardian.com/world/2023/mar/16/laura-trevelyan-quits-bbc-to-campaign-reparative-justice-slavery-caribbean.
37. https://www.bbc.co.uk/news/uk-politics-65125332.
38. https://www.bbc.co.uk/news/world-latin-america-61315877.
39. Ibid.
40. Ibid.

U IS FOR UNFINISHED

1. Lyons and Winter, *We All Know How This Ends*, Green Tree (2021) p. 183.
2. Dr Richard Wilson cited in Lyons and Winter, p. 186.
3. Samuel, J., *Grief Works: Stories of Life, Death, and Surviving*, Penguin Life (2018) p. xi-xiii.
4. Lloyd, p. 207.
5. Lyons et al. describe this secondary loss: 'Suddenly the grass needs mowing and the bins need emptying because the person who once did those things is no longer here'. p. 190.

D IS FOR DEATH

6. https://royalpinner.org.uk/.
7. Lloyd, p. 130.
8. Stroebe, M. and Schut, H. 'The dual process model of coping with bereavement: rationale and description', *Death Studies*, Vol. 23, issue 3, 1999, pp. 197-224.
9. Tonkin, L. 'Growing around grief – another way of looking at grief and recovery', *Bereavement Care*, Vol. 15, issue 1, 1996.
10. Samuel, p. xii.
11. Ibid.
12. Ibid., p. xiii.
13. Lyons and Winter, p. 190.
14. Ibid p. 190.
15. Ibid.
16. Cariad Lloyd refers to your individual experience of grief as your 'grief-mess'.
17. https://www.lifedeathwhatever.com/unsaid.
18. Lewis, C.S., *A Grief Observed*.
19. 'Anticipatory grief', first coined by Lindemann in 1944, refers to grieving that takes place before the actual loss. Cited in Worden, J.W., *Grief Counselling and Grief Therapy*, Springer Publishing (2018). A balance between holding on and letting go, for either the person dying or for those preparing for their death.
20. https://www.cruse.org.uk/understanding-grief/effects-of-grief/complicated-grief/.
21. https://www.cruse.org.uk/understanding-grief/effects-of-grief/complicated-grief/, https://www.betterup.com/blog/complicated-grief.
22. Samuel, p. xiii.
23. Ibid., p. 137.
24. https://www.theguardian.com/uk-news/2022/oct/07/search-ends-saddleworth-moor-keith-bennett-no-remains-found.
25. Samuel, p. 135.
26. Samuel, pp. 135–37.
27. Lyons et al., p. 191.
28. Connecting through rituals prompt by National Hospice Cooperative, from *The Grief Deck: Rituals, Meditations, and Tools for Moving through Loss*, Princeton Architectural Press, 2022.
29. Pinter, H., *Various Voices: Sixty Years of Prose, Poetry, Politics, 1948–2008*, Faber (2009).
30. Pinter, H., *No Man's Land*. In 2016, Patrick Stewart played Hirst to Ian McKellen's Spooner at the Wyndham, conveying 'the exuberance of memory and the imminence of extinction', according to Michael Billington, 20/9/16 https://www.theguardian.com/stage/2016/sep/20/no-mans-land-review-ian-mckellen-and-patrick-stewart-capture-the-contrasts-of-pinters-masterwork.
31. Lloyd, p. 167.
32. Samuel, p. 259.
33. Lyons and Winter, p. 191.
34. Lloyd, p. 164.

V IS FOR VALHALLA

1. https://www.historyextra.com/period/ancient-history/history-afterlife-meaning-what-happens-when-we-die/.
2. cited in Almond, P., *Afterlife: A History of Life after Death*, I.B. Tauris (2016) in,https://www.historyextra.com/period/ancient-history/history-afterlife-meaning-what-happens-when-we-die/ accessed 12/9/23.
3. Ibid.
4. Berridge, p. 7.
5. A stupa (heap) is a place of burial or shrine or a receptacle for religious objects. Bell-shaped.
6. Meaning 'interval, intermediate state, transitional process, in between', referring to the gap between lives.
7. https://www.bbc.co.uk/bitesize/guides/zddbqp3/revision/6.
8. https://www.theguardian.com/cities/2015/jan/26/death-city-lack-vultures-threatens-mumbai-towers-of-silence.

ENDNOTES

9. Berkson, M., *Death, Dying and the Afterlife: Lessons from World Cultures*, from Lecture 9, The Great Courses, 2016.
10. Chalke, *The Lost Message of Paul*, SPCK (2019) pp. 218–19.
11. Ibid., p. 250.
12. Ibid., p. 217.
13. Chalke, S., *The Lost Message of Paul* SPCK. Kindle Edition.
14. Chalke, p. 176.
15. Ibid., p. 98.
16. Chalke, p. 175.
17. Chalke, pp. 103–4.
18. Ibid., pp. 114–15.
19. Ibid., pp. 118–19.
20. Ibid., p. 127.
21. From the 1999 Easter campaign by the Churches' Advertising Network.
22. Ibid., p. 14.
23. Ibid., pp. 212–13.
24. Ibid., p. 209.

W IS FOR WELLINGTON

1. https://www.futurelearn.com/info/courses/wellington-and-waterloo/0/steps/24872.
2. The Battlefields Trust is a volunteer-run charity dedicated to the protection, research, and interpretation of Britain's battlefields. https://www.battlefieldstrust.com/.
3. A 'closed church', now looked after by the Churches Conservation Trust. https://www.visitchurches.org.uk/visit/church-listing/st-mary-magdalene-battlefield.html.
4. https://media.nationalarchives.gov.uk/index.php/no-place-for-ladies-the-untold-.
5. https://robertgravesoratorio.co.uk/tourist-wars/.
6. https://www.nationaltrust.org.uk/visit/somerset/wellington-monument.
7. https://www.junobeach.org/.
8. The name of First Offr. ATA Amy Johnson is also recorded on the memorial.
9. Berridge, p. 36.
10. Berridge, p. 34–8.
11. https://www.parliament.uk/business/publications/research/olympic-britain/crime-and-defence/the-fallen/ accessed 26/1/24.
12. 'Memory boom' is a term first used by Pierre Nora. It refers to the significance of memory arising from academia and society over the last few decades.
13. For British soldiers the average daily loss rate at Arras was the highest of the war at 4,076. Total casualties numbered 158,000, with the Germans losing around the same. The Vimy Memorial contains the names of over 11,000 Canadian soldiers with no known graves in France, many of whom died in the fight for Vimy Ridge, Arras.
14. Berridge, p. 29.
15. https://www.longlongtrail.co.uk/soldiers/how-to-research-a-soldier/how-to-find-a-soldiers-service-record/.
16. Lionel would have done something that warranted his name to be included in an official account written by a superior officer and sent to the War Office. The name, rank, number and regiment/unit would be published in *The Gazette*, but not the reason for the MID. An oak leaf emblem could be worn with the Victory Medal ribbon.
17. Stamp, G., *Silent* Cities, RIBA, 1977, p. 3 cited in Arnold, p. 246.
18. Lutyens was accompanied by his friend J.M. Barrie, who wanted to visit the grave of George Llewelyn Davies, son of family friends. (In another connection, Lutyens designed the stage set for *Peter Pan*.) When Barrie's thirteen-year-old brother died in a skating accident, his mother's bereavement profoundly affected him. She said she found comfort knowing her dead son would be a boy forever. Barrie said, 'When I became a man, he was still a boy of 13.' (Like the ten-year-old girl inside me and Cariad Lloyd's 'eternal adolescent'.).
19. Berridge, p. 248.
20. Arnold, p. 46.

D IS FOR DEATH

21. Ibid., p. 189.
22. Ibid., p. 190.
23. Ross, p. 185.
24. Berridge, p. 9.
25. Berridge, p. 277.
26. Berridge, p. 55.
27. Ibid.
28. Arnold, p. 251.
29. Berridge, p. 56.
30. Arnold, p. 256–57.
31. Just as with the banishing of the tolling bell during the plague, too much black would have been bad for morale. Not only that, but women were needed in war work which made restrictive, expensive mourning wear out of the question, driving sales of Courtaulds' black crape into irreversible decline. Arnold, p. 255.
32. Berridge, p. 51.
33. https://www.iwm.org.uk/history/12-things-you-didnt-know-about-women-in-the-first-world-war.
34. https://www.wirralintelligenceservice.org/state-of-the-borough/wirral-population/life-expectancy/ accessed 14/10/23.
35. Revenge for the Allied bomber Harris's raid on the city of Lübeck.
36. https://www.parliament.uk/business/publications/research/olympic-britain/crime-and-defence/the-fallen/.
37. https://www.teignmouthshaldonww2.co.uk/index.php/teignmouth-bombings.
38. Both widowed twice, Mum married Don, an old friend, in 2012. He is one of the loveliest people I know.
39. https://www.iwm.org.uk/memorials/item/memorial/64364.
40. Berridge, p. 59.
41. Ibid., p. 60.
42. Produced by Richard Taylor Cartoons of *Charley Says* fame. A descendant of the wartime *The Protection of Your Home Against Air Raids*, *Protect and Survive* was first published as a booklet in 1980 – intended to be distributed to households if the situation became dire but actually you could only ever buy it.

X IS FOR X-FILES

1. Cited by Brandon, E.M., 28/7/23 https://www.fastcompany.com/90929636/how-the-letter-x-became-historys-most-mysterious-symbol.
2. https://www.forbes.com/sites/davidchiu/2020/08/12/xanadu-remembering-the-cult-movie-musicals-amazing-soundtrack-album-40-years-later/?sh=498e43d15fc4.
3. https://www.pewresearch.org/short-reads/2014/06/05/generation-x-americas-neglected-middle-child/.

Y IS FOR YEW

1. https://www.woodlandtrust.org.uk/trees-woods-and-wildlife/british-trees/a-z-of-british-trees/yew/.
2. https://treesforlife.org.uk/into-the-forest/trees-plants-animals/trees/yew/.
3. https://www.wizardingworld.com/features/whats-in-a-wand-tree-symbolism-and-wandlore-in-harry-potter.
4. From the fourteenth century *Book of Lismore* https://druidry.org/druid-way/teaching-and-practice/druid-tree-lore/yew.
5. https://treesforlife.org.uk/into-the-forest/trees-plants-animals/trees/yew/.
6. https://blog.nms.ac.uk/2019/08/09/holy-buckets-insular-identities-in-the-viking-age/.
7. https://scotlands-yew-trees.org/yew-trees.
8. Down south in Runnymede, the Magna Carta was signed under the same yew that would later be a meeting place for Henry VIII and Anne Boleyn.
9. https://scotlands-yew-trees.org/.
10. https://www.rcpe.ac.uk/sites/default/files/vol28_4.1_12.pdf.
11. The earliest known example of a yew longbow was found in the Alps alongside 'the iceman Otzi', 1.82m long, dated to around 3300 BC.
12. People with the surname Archer, Bowman, Bowyer or Fletcher are probably descendants of English

ENDNOTES

medieval bowman, of bowyers who made bows, or fletchers who made arrows (*fleche* is French for arrows).

13 https://treesforlife.org.uk/into-the-forest/trees-plants-animals/trees/yew/.
14 https://scotlands-yew-trees.org/yewtree/robert-bruces-yew/.
15 https://www.woodlandtrust.org.uk/trees-woods-and-wildlife/british-trees/how-trees-fight-climate-change/.
16 https://www.wildlifetrusts.org/habitats/woodland/beech-and-yew-wood.
17 https://www.woodlandtrust.org.uk/blog/2018/01/ancient-yew-trees/.
18 https://www.theguardian.com/environment/2019/sep/28/britain-ancient-yews-mystical-magnificent-and-unprotected 28/9/19 Patrick Barkham.
19 https://conservationfoundation.co.uk/projects/we-love-yew/.
20 https://www.bramptonbryan.org.uk/hedge/.

Z IS FOR ZADUSZKI

1 Barley, N. *Dancing on the Grave*, Abacus, 1997, p. 11.
2 Isaiah 53:3.
3 One of the beatitudes that Jesus preached during the Sermon on the Mount.
4 It is the most travelled day in the country with, sadly, road accidents at their peak.
5 http://atriptoireland.com/2013/06/02/cemetery-sunday-in-ireland/ 2/6/13.
6 www.wgstroke.org.
7 Jarrett, p. 238.
8 Ibid., pp. 244-5.
9 Jarrett, pp. 224-3.
10 Fausset, R., New Yorker, 13/6/19.
11 https://manitousprings.org/emma-crawford-coffin-races/.
12 Magnusson, M., *The Gentle Art of Swedish Death Cleaning: How to Free Yourself and Your Family from a Lifetime of Clutter*, Canongate, 2020.
13 https://www.nbcnews.com/better/health/what-swedish-death-cleaning-should-you-be-doing-it-ncna816511.
14 Berridge, p. 7.
15 Lyons and Winter, p. 16

ENDINGS

1 Mannix, p. 17, https://www.mariecurie.org.uk/talkabout/articles/how-to-have-an-environmentally-responsible-death/284416

Bibliography and Useful Books

S.O. Addy *Household Tales with other Traditional Remains, Collected in the Counties of York, Lincoln, Derby and Nottingham*, 1895
Catharine Arnold *Necropolis: London and Its Dead* Pocket Books, 2007
Nick Arnold *Deadly Diseases* Horrible Science, Scholastic Children's Books, 2000
Julian Barnes *Nothing to be Frightened of* Vintage, 2009
Nigel Barley *Dancing on the Grave: Encounters with Death* John Murray, 1995
Mark Berkson *Death, Dying and the Afterlife: Lessons from World Cultures* The Great Courses, 2016
Kate Berridge *Vigor Mortis* Profile Books, 2001
Sue Black *Written in Bone: Hidden Stories in What we Leave Behind* Transworld Digital, 2020
Roger Bowdler *Churchyards* Britain's Heritage, Amberley Publishing, 2019
Clifford Brewer *The Death of Kings* Abson Books, 2000 ed.
Steve Chalke *The Lost Message of Paul: Has the Church Misunderstood the Apostle Paul* SPCK, 2019 Kindle ed.
Sarah Chapman *Funeral Arranging and End-of-Life Decisions* The Book Guild, 2022
Agatha Christie *The Murder on the Links*
Daniel Defoe *A Journal of the Plague Year* Penguin Classics, 2003 ed.
Joan Didion *The Year of Magical Thinking* Fourth Estate, 2012 ed.
Andrew Doig *This Mortal Coil: A History of Death* Bloomsbury, 2022
John Dougherty *The Hare Shaped Hole* Frances Lincoln, 2023
Caitlin Doughty, *Will My Cat Eat My Eyeballs: Big Questions from Tiny Mortals about Death* W&N, 2019
Lucy Easthope *When the Dust Settles: Stories of Love, Loss and Hope from an Expert in Disaster* Hodder and Stoughton, 2022 Kindle ed.
Helen Frisby *Traditions of Death and Burial* Shire Publications, 2019
Peter Furtado *Plague, Pestilence and Pandemic: Voices from History* Thames and Hudson, 2021
Atol Gawande *Being Mortal* Wellcome Collection, 2015
Kathryn Harkup *A Is for Arsenic: The Poisons of Agatha Christie* Bloomsbury Sigma, 2016

Isabella Holmes *The London Burial Grounds: Notes on Their History from the Earliest Times to the Present Day* Originally published by TF Unwin, 1896, now available online at https://wellcomecollection.org/works/g47ypqnp

W.H. Howe *Everybody's Book of Epitaphs* Pryor Publications, 1995

M.R. James *The Collected Ghost Stories* Delphi Classics, 2013 Kindle ed.

David Jarrett *33 Meditations on Death: Notes from the Wrong End of Medicine* Transworld Digital, 2020,

Peter C. Jupp and Clare Gittings (ed) *Death in England: An Illustrated History* Manchester University Press, 1999

Evie King *Ashes to Admin: Tales from the Caseload of a Council Funeral Officer* Mirror Books, 2023

Rabbi Steve Leder *For You When I Am Gone* Bantam Press, 2022

C.S. Lewis *A Grief Observed* Faber and Faber, 1966

Julian Litten *The English Way of Death* Robert Hale, 2002 ed.

Cariad Lloyd *You Are Not Alone* Bloomsbury Tonic, 2023

Beth Lovejoy *Rest in Pieces* Duckworth, 2021

Anna Lyons and Louise Winter *We All Know How This Ends* Green Tree, 2021

Margareta Magnusson *The Gentle Art of Swedish Death Cleaning* Canongate, 2020

Kathryn Mannix *With the End in Mind: How to Live and Die Well* William Collins, 2018

Jessica Mitford *The American Way of Death* Virago, 1998 ed.

Terry Nation *Survivors* Orion, 2020 Kindle ed.

Julia Neuberger and John A. White (eds) *A Necessary End* Papermac, 1991

Susan Owens *The Ghost: A Cultural History* Tate Publishing, 2019

Samuel Pepys *Diary of Samuel Pepys – Complete* A Public Domain Book, 1893, Kindle ed.

Harold Pinter *Various Voices: Sixty Years of Prose, Poetry, Politics, 1948-2008*, Faber, 2009

Edgar Allan Poe *Terrifying Tales* Simon and Schuster, 2014 Kindle ed.

Max Porter *Grief Is the Thing with Feathers* Faber and Faber, 2016

Rennell, T. *Last Days of Glory: The Death of Queen Victoria* St Martin's Press, 2001

Mary Roach *Stiff: The Curious Lives of Human Cadavers* Penguin, 2004

Peter Ross *A Tomb with a View: The Stories and Glories of Graveyards* Headline, 2020

Julia Samuel *Grief Works* Penguin Life, 2018

James Shapiro *The Year of Lear: Shakespeare in 1606* Simon and Schuster, 2016

Philip R. Stone *111 Dark Places in England That You Shouldn't Miss* Emons, 2021

Adinda van 't Klooster, *Still Born* Affect Formations, 2018 ed.

Evelyn Waugh *The Loved One* Penguin, 2012 Kindle ed.

Stanley Williamson *Gresford: The Anatomy of a Disaster* Liverpool University Press, 1999

Patricia Wiltshire *Traces: The memoir of a Forensic Scientist and Criminal Investigator* Blink Publishing, 2020

J. William Worden *Grief Counselling and Grief Therapy* Springer, 2018 ed.

About the Author

Photo: Kristy Garland

A child of the 70s, Sophie Duffy grew up on a diet of *Blue Peter* and *The Wombles*. But it's not all been fun and games. Over the years she has curated a catalogue of loss but her sense of the world being a good place shines through the heartache. Duffy finds humour and pathos in the mundane and the tragic and is particularly fond of dysfunctional, unconventional families and the complexities of everyday modern life. As part of Creative Writing Matters, Sophie appraises manuscripts, mentors novelists and helps run the Exeter Novel Prize. She lives on the Wirral and also writes under the pseudonym Lizzie Lovell.